D0202872

DECOLONIZING SOCIAL WORK

Contemporary Social Work Studies

Series Editors:
Lucy Jordan, The University of Hong Kong, China and
Patrick O'Leary, Griffith University, Australia

Series Advisory Board:
Lena Dominelli, University of Durham, UK
Jan Fook, University of Southampton, UK
Peter Ford, University of Southampton, UK
Lorraine Gutiérrez, University of Michigan, USA
Lucy Jordan, University of Southampton, UK
Walter Lorenz, Free University of Bozen-Bolzano, Italy
Patrick O'Leary, University of Southampton, UK
Joan Orme, University of Glasgow, UK
Jackie Powell, University of Southampton, UK
Gillian Ruch, University of Southampton, UK
Sue White, University of Birmingham, UK

Contemporary Social Work Studies is a series disseminating high quality new research and scholarship in the discipline and profession of social work. The series promotes critical engagement with contemporary issues relevant across the social work community and captures the diversity of interests currently evident at national, international and local levels.

CSWS is located in the School of Social Sciences (Social Work Studies Division) at the University of Southampton, UK and is a development from the successful series of books published by Ashgate in association with CEDR (the Centre for Evaluative and Developmental Research) from 1991.

Other titles in this series:

Intercountry Adoption
Edited by Judith L. Gibbons and Karen Smith Rotabi
978-1-4094-1054-6

Practice and Research
Ian F. Shaw
978-1-4094-3917-2

For information about other titles in this series, visit www.ashgate.com

Decolonizing Social Work

Edited by

MEL GRAY
University of Newcastle, Australia

JOHN COATES
St. Thomas University, Canada

MICHAEL YELLOW BIRD
Humboldt State University in Arcata, USA

TIANI HETHERINGTON
Griffith University, Australia

ASHGATE

© Mel Gray, John Coates, Michael Yellow Bird and Tiani Hetherington 2013

All rights reserved. No part of this publication may be reproduced, stored in a retrieval system or transmitted in any form or by any means, electronic, mechanical, photocopying, recording or otherwise without the prior permission of the publisher.

Mel Gray, John Coates, Michael Yellow Bird and Tiani Hetherington have asserted their right under the Copyright, Designs and Patents Act, 1988, to be identified as the editors of this work.

Published by
Ashgate Publishing Limited
Wey Court East
Union Road
Farnham
Surrey, GU9 7PT
England

Ashgate Publishing Company
110 Cherry Street
Suite 3-1
Burlington, VT 05401-3818
USA

www.ashgate.com

British Library Cataloguing in Publication Data
Decolonizing social work. -- (Contemporary social work
  studies)
  1. Social work with indigenous peoples. 2. Social work with
  indigenous peoples--Study and teaching.
  I. Series II. Gray, Mel, 1951-
  362.8'4-dc23

The Library of Congress has cataloged the printed edition as follows:
Decolonizing social work / by Mel Gray, John Coates, Michael Yellow Bird and Tiani
Hetherington.
     pages cm. -- (Contemporary social work studies)
  Includes bibliographical references and index.
  ISBN 978-1-4094-2631-8 (hardback) -- ISBN 978-1-4094-2632-5 (ebk) -- ISBN 978-
1-4094-7278-0 (ePUB) 1. Social work with indigenous peoples. I. Gray, Mel, 1951- II.
Coates, John, 1948- III. Yellow Bird, Michael.
  HV3176.D43 2013
  362.84--dc23

2012041827

ISBN 9781409426318 (hbk)
ISBN 9781409426325 (ebk – PDF)
ISBN 9781409472780 (ebk – ePUB)

Printed and bound in Great Britain
by MPG PRINTGROUP

Contents

Acknowledgements

Many people have been instrumental in helping to bring this book to fruition and to them we wish to express our deepest gratitude. First, we wish to thank our chapter authors from around the world who have so willingly shared their knowledge, insight, experience and understanding on the destructive aftermath of colonization, and its ongoing manifestations. We thank you, especially, for your patience as you responded, sometimes repeatedly, to our many editorial comments, queries and suggestions.

We also wish to thank Claire Jarvis for her unwavering belief in us and this project and her ongoing and willing support every step of the way. Thanks to all the folk at Ashgate Publishing who recognized value in broadening the scholarly attention of social workers to the many aspects of decolonization. We thank you for welcoming our idea and encouraging us to write this book as a follow-up to the success of *Indigenous Social Work around the World* (2008). Your support was invaluable and much appreciated.

Thirdly, and most importantly, we wish to recognize the sterling efforts of Indigenous Peoples and their allies on every continent as they struggle to overcome the pervasive and ongoing pernicious effects of colonization. The challenges are great, and we hope that our book will, in some small way, further your cause. We hope our book is informative and useful for everyone who wishes to learn more about, and support the cause of, those who fight unstintingly for justice for all.

This book is written in recognition of the many efforts of Indigenous Peoples and their scholars, who have persevered to overcome and write about the negative impacts of colonization, to contribute to our expanded understanding of oppression and the advancement of social work theory and practice.

List of Contributors

Editors

Mel Gray, PhD, is Professor of Social Work in the School of Humanities in Social Science at the University of Newcastle in New South Wales, the highest ranked social work research program in Australia. She has published extensively on international social work and social development. Recent books include *Indigenous Social Work around the World* (with Coates and Yellow Bird, Ashgate 2008), *Social Work Theories and Methods* (with Webb, Sage 2008), *Evidence-based Social Work* (with Plath and Webb, Routledge 2009), *Ethics and Value Perspectives in Social Work* (with Webb, Palgrave 2010), *International: Social Work* – 4 vols (with Webb, Sage 2010), *Sage Handbook of Social Work* (with Midgley and Webb, 2012), *Environmental Social Work* (with Coates and Hetherington, Routledge 2013), *Social Work Theories and Methods* (2nd edn with Webb, Sage 2013), and *The New Politics of Social Work* (with Webb, 2013 Palgrave).

John Coates, PhD, retired from his position as Professor and Director, School of Social Work at St Thomas University in Fredericton, New Brunswick, Canada in July 2012. He is Chair and founding member of the Canadian Society for Spirituality and Social Work. His recent publications include *Ecology and Social Work* (Fernwood Press 2003); *Spirituality and Social Work: Selected Canadian Readings* (with Graham, Swartzentruber and Ouellette, Canadian Scholars Press, 2007); *Indigenous Social Work around the World* (with Gray and Yellow Bird, Ashgate 2008); and *Environmental Social Work* (with Gray and Hetherington, Routledge 2013). He has published numerous journal articles and co-edited several journal issues in the area of spirituality and social work, and environmental social work, most recently *Critical Social Work*, 11(3), 2010 (with Fred Besthorn) and *International Journal of Social Welfare*, 21(3), 2012 (with Mel Gray).

Michael Yellow Bird, PhD, is an enrolled member of the Three Affiliated Tribes (Arikara and Hidatsa). He is a Professor and the Director of Graduate Education in the Department of Social Work at Humboldt State University, Arcata, California. He has held faculty at the University of Kansas, the University of British Columbia, Arizona State University and the University of Kansas. He is the former Director of the Global Indigenous Nations Studies Program at the University of Kansas. He has published widely, co-editing *For Indigenous Eyes Only: The Decolonization Handbook* (with Wilson, School of American Research, 2005), *Indigenous Social Work around the World: Towards Culturally Relevant Education and Practice* (with Gray and Coates, Ashgate, 2008), and *For Indigenous Minds Only* (with Waziyatawin (Wilson), School of American Research, forthcoming). His teaching, writing, research and community work focus on social work with Indigenous peoples, decolonizing social work, neurodecolonization, neuroscience and social work, and employing mainstream and traditional Indigenous mindfulness practices in tribal communities to promote health and well-being.

Tiani Hetherington, PhD, is a Lecturer in Social Work at Griffith University, Queensland, Australia. She is a graduate of the University of Newcastle where she completed her PhD on a 'Comparative Study of Social Work Practice with Indigenous Communities in New Brunswick, Canada and Alice Springs, Australia'. She worked closely with Mel Gray and John Coates as a research assistant on *Indigenous Social Work around the World* (Ashgate, 2008) and attended the Writer's Workshop in New Brunswick which preceded that publication. Tiani has published with Gray and Coates, 'An "ecospiritual" perspective: Finally a place for Indigenous approaches' (2006), *British Journal of Social Work*, 36, 1–19 and (2007), 'Hearing Indigenous voices in mainstream social work', *Families in Society*, 88(1), 53–64.

Contributors (Alphabetical by First Name)

Anaru Eketone is from the Ngati Maniapoto and Waikato tribes of the North Island of *Aotearoa* New Zealand. He has taught at the University of Otago since 2000 and is a Senior Lecturer in the Department of Sociology, Gender and Social Work. Prior to that, he worked for ten years as a youth worker in South Auckland and six years as a health promotion adviser in Dunedin. He is married to Margaret and together they have two adult children.

Ann Joselynn Baltra-Ulloa 'Jos' , is a Chilean Mapuche woman, social work lecturer and PhD candidate at the University of Tasmania, School of Social Sciences, Department of Social Work in Australia where she teaches intercultural social work in the BSW and MSW programmes. She has worked with migrant and refugee communities in Australia for many years. Her research interests are in refugee resettlement, decolonized social work practice and whiteness in social work and her PhD is dedicated to exploring social work encounters with people of refugee background. Her dream is to forge connections with Latin American scholars and contribute to international dialogue, action and change on issues of forced migration, the treatment of refugees in re-settlement countries and the rights of First Nation peoples across the globe.

Carol Malina Kaulukukui, MSW, is a Native Hawaiian cultural practitioner who integrates Indigenous perspectives in her work as a mental health clinician. She is on faculty of the University of Hawai`i Myron B. Thompson School of

Social Work, where she coordinates the Hawaiian Learning Program, a workforce development initiative providing enhanced cultural training to Native Hawaiian MSW students, as well as at the University's John A. Burns School of Medicine, where she helps to implement a cultural immersion programme for medical students. She also develops culture-based interventions at a residential treatment facility for substance abusing women.

David Strug is Professor Emeritus in the Wurzweiler School of Social Work at Yeshiva University in New York City. He has travelled to Cuba frequently in recent years, where he has conducted research and published on the development of social work, the elderly and community healthcare. He co-authored *Love, Loss and Longing: The Impact of U.S. Travel Restrictions on Cuban-American Families* (with Jeanne Parr Lemkau, Latin America Working Group Education Fund, 2007) and co-edited *Community Health Care in Cuba* (with Susan Mason and Joan Beder, Lyceum, 2010). He received his PhD in anthropology from Columbia University, his MSW from the Hunter College School of Social Work in New York City and his Masters in Public Health from the University of California at Berkeley.

Flavio F. Marsiglia, PhD, is the Distinguished Foundation Professor of Cultural Diversity and Health at the Arizona State University School of Social Work and Director of the Southwest Interdisciplinary Research Center (SIRC). SIRC is an exploratory centre of excellence on minority health and health disparities research funded by the National Institute on Minority Health and Health Disparities of the National Institutes of Health (NIH). He developed *Keepin' it REAL*, a culturally specific substance abuse prevention intervention for pre-adolescents. Flavio leads a global health initiative with colleagues in several countries, has authored numerous journal articles, and co-authored *Diversity, Oppression and Change: Culturally Grounded Social Work* (with Stephen Kulis, Lyceum, 2009).

Hamilton McCubbin, PhD, 'Ham' is of Native Hawaiian ancestry, born and raised in the Hawaiian Islands and attended a school for Indigenous youth named in honour of King Kamehameha I. Ham served as the institution's first Chancellor and CEO of its three-campus, state-wide extension, and early childhood education programmes. His higher education took place on the continental United States and included the universities of Wisconsin, Minnesota, Yale and Stanford. With Indigenous roots, Ham's scholarly work has focused on theory, research and practice in pursuit of understanding the plight, transformation and resilience of Indigenous people and their families.

Jon K. Matsuoka is the President and CEO of the Consuelo Foundation. Prior to joining the Foundation, he was Dean of the University of Hawai`i, Myron B. Thompson School of Social Work for 10 years and on the faculty for 25 years. As dean, he led efforts to indigenize the school's programmes and curriculum by forming a Kupuna (Elder) Council, establishing relationships with Native

Hawaiian organizations and communities, and promoting Indigenous matters throughout social work education. At the Foundation, Dr Matsuoka advances sustainability and the socioeconomic development of marginalized communities in the Philippines and Hawai`i.

Linda Kreitzer, PhD, Associate Professor at the University of Calgary, Central and Northern Alberta region, began her social work career in the United States in 1978. She immigrated to Great Britain in 1981 where she worked in British Social Services. Between 1994 and 1996 she taught social work at the University of Ghana in Legon, Ghana. In 1996 she completed her Masters in Social Work degree at the University of Calgary in international social work, specifically examining refugee issues. After working in Armenia for a year, she began her PhD at the University of Calgary in 2000 exploring a culturally appropriate social work curriculum at the Department of Social Work, University of Ghana, Legon. She completed her PhD in 2004 and her book *Social Work in Africa: Exploring Culturally Relevant Social Work Education and Practice in Ghana* was published in April 2012.

Lourdes de Urrutia Barroso is Professor of the Department of Sociology at the University of Havana in Cuba. She began her career in social work in 1998, with the introduction of the specialization in social work in the sociology degree, being involved in the development of the programme and director of the social work elective. Later, she was Director of the School of Social Workers annexed to the University of Havana. She has published numerous teaching texts and scholarly articles in Brazil and Sweden. She has participated in teaching exchanges with schools of social work, including the Universidad Pública de Navarra y Alicante in Spain, and Gothenburg and Malmo in Sweden.

Mary Pat Sullivan, PhD, has been a Senior Lecturer on the MA Social Work Programme at Brunel University in London since 2004. She is also Programme Director of the Gerontological Social Work Research Programme for the Brunel Institute for Ageing Studies. Dr Sullivan obtained an Honours Bachelor of Social Work and Masters of Social Work in Canada, and worked in the area of healthcare and older people for over 15 years. In 2003 she was awarded a PhD in Gerontology from King's College London. Dr Sullivan's research includes evidence-informed gerontological social work, social work with diverse populations, medical and practical ethics, and evidence-informed health promotion initiatives for older people. From 2007-2010 she was part of a Jordan–UK collaboration funded by the British Council to support the development of social work education in Jordan.

Michael Thaweiakenrat Loft lives and resides in the Mohawk community at Kahnawake. His father attended Indian residential school for 11 continuous years and, as such, he has a particular interest in the needs of this population group. At the undergraduate level, Loft teaches First Nations issues and social work and the Aboriginal field course. He is also a founding member of Indigenous Access

McGill, a support and mentoring programme for Indigenous students. He has two decades of practice experience in child protection, and with individuals and families who attended Indian residential school.

Nicole G. Ives, PhD, is Associate Professor at McGill University School of Social Work and Coordinator and founding member of Indigenous Access McGill, a programme that supports Indigenous students in the School of Social Work and the broader university. Her areas of research include refugee and immigrant studies, Indigenous social work education and Indigenous social and educational policies. Dr Ives has taught the history and philosophy of social work, Aboriginal field studies, policy and practice with refugees, qualitative research methods, and migration and social work. She has published articles focused on Indigenous social work education, Indigenous social policy and refugee resettlement.

Noreen Mokuau, DSW, is a Native Hawaiian woman born and raised in Hawai`i. She is Professor and Dean at the Myron B. Thompson School of Social Work at the University of Hawai`i at Mānoa. She provides leadership in advancing the School's mission of social justice in the context of a local to global perspective. Her scholarship and service focuses on health and wellness for Native Hawaiian, Asian and other Pacific Islander populations. She has received the university's highest awards in teaching and community service. Her work is inspired by her faith in Ke Akua, her deep aloha for her husband, family and friends, and her unwavering commitment to helping others.

Paula Toki Araullo Tanemura Morelli, PhD, is of Filipino and Japanese ancestry raised on Molokai and Oahu, Hawai`i. Her research facilitates the development of community-based, Indigenous programmes in Hawai`i through application of strengths-enhancing methods. She is an Associate Professor at the University of Hawai`i, Myron B. Thompson School of Social Work, chair of the PhD Program and behavioural mental health concentration, and Editor-in-Chief of *Le`a Publications' Journal of Indigenous Social Development* in electronic format.

Peter John Mataira, PhD, is a Māori of the Ngatiporou Tribe in Ruatoria, Aotearoa (New Zealand). His research with community-based Indigenous programmes in Hawai`i aided in development of the Strengths Enhancing Evaluation Research (SEER) framework. He is an Assistant Professor at the University of Hawai`i, Myron B. Thompson School of Social Work, Director of Indigenous Affairs, MSW foundation curriculum chair and co-editor of the *Journal of Indigenous Social Development*.

Sahar Sulieman Al-Makhamreh, PhD, has been a lecturer on the BA social work programme at Al-Balqa' Applied University in Jordan since 2005. She has also been a head of department and Dean Assistant for Developing and Planning at Princess Rahma University College Al-Balqa' Applied University. She is one of the cofounders of the Jordanian Association of Social Workers. Dr Sahar is also a research Fellow at the School of Health and Social Studies at the University of Warwick in the UK where she obtained her PhD on health and medical social work as an emerging profession in Jordan. She was awarded UNHCR scholarship for developing research in the area of Bedouin and refugees populations. Her research is in the area of inter-professional relationships, health inequality, developing and professionalizing social work, cultural and gender sensitivity in Middle Eastern social work practice.

Samantha Wehbi has an interest in international social work and activism; her work has included community practice on queer issues, disability rights and feminist organizing. She has worked as a social development consultant, as a programme manager, as a director of services as well as other positions within community organizations. She is currently Associate Professor at Ryerson University School of Social Work in Canada and is principal investigator on a research project exploring the experiences of disability rights activists in Lebanon, her country of origin.

Shawn Wilson, PhD, is an Opaskwayak Cree from northern Manitoba, Canada, who now makes his home in Bundjalung territory in Australia. His main area of interest lies in discussing the ways of knowing, being and conducting research used by Indigenous Peoples. His book *Research is Ceremony: Indigenous Research Methods* (Fernwood Press, 2008) examines some of the similarities in philosophy underlying Indigenous Peoples' research methodologies in Canada and Australia. In addition to further articulating Indigenous philosophies and research paradigms, his research focuses on the interrelated concepts of identity, health and healing, culture and well-being.

Shayne Walker is of Kai Tahu and Ngati Kahungunu descent. His interest in Kaupapa Māori research had its genesis in a strong practice background of working with Māori whanau in community organizations, youth work and foster care. He has been a Senior Lecturer in the Department of Sociology, Gender and Social Work at the University of Otago since 1996. His research seeks to be emancipatory in nature and rejects cultural deficit models that do not deconstruct the structural causes of so-called Māori inequalities. His research interests are Māori social services development, alternative care, resiliency, indigeneity and care and protection.

Vidya Rao, PhD, is Head of the Department of Social Work at the Jain Vishva Bharati Institute, a university located in the interior areas of the state of Rajasthan, a western state bordering Pakistan. Prior to that she was Professor in the Centre for Social Justice and Governance, School of Social Work, Tata Institute of Social Sciences in Mumbai, India, where she taught for many years. Professor Rao has held faculty positions in the Asian Institute of Technology, Bangkok, Thailand;

School of Social Work at the University of Michigan; and Madras School of Social Work, Chennai, India. She has published widely on social security, governance, politics, welfare rights, and the growth of philanthropic charities. She is currently writing a book on *Social Welfare in Post Reform India.* In addition to her academic work, she has organized management training programmes for senior civil servants, government officials and NGO functionaries.

Preface:
United Nations Declaration on the Rights of Indigenous Peoples through Indigenous Eyes

Michael Yellow Bird

After a long, 20-year struggle, the landmark United Nations Declaration on the Rights of Indigenous Peoples was adopted during the 62nd session of the United Nations General Assembly at its headquarters in New York City on 14 September 2007 (United Nations, 2008). This was a milestone for Indigenous Peoples for several reasons not the least of which being that they were involved in, and co-wrote, the Declaration; it explicitly recognizes that nation states have colonized Indigenous lands and, to this day, have colonizing powers such that disputes with Indigenous Peoples over issues of sovereignty, territories and cultural and human rights continue unabated. Mere recognition of the history of dispossession and trauma for Indigenous Peoples was a major milestone given that throughout the world, they have been consistently, repeatedly and brutally marginalized and denied human, political, economic, social, cultural and territorial rights by occupying settler, nation state governments. Secondly, the Declaration provides a twofold strategy that 'aims at empowering indigenous groups by according them control over the issues which are internal to their communities' and 'it refers to procedures of participation and consultation in order to ensure that these Peoples are involved in the life of the larger society of a State' (Errico, 2007: 755). Thirdly, under the continuing colonial policies of many settler governments and agencies, Indigenous Peoples face numerous oppressions, including *genocide* (deliberate destruction of the people), *ethnocide* (deliberate destruction of the culture rather than the people themselves), *ecocide* (destruction of their natural environments) and *linguicide* (destruction of Indigenous languages) (Maybury-Lewis, 2002). Thus, critiques of human rights charters and debates about definitions of social justice notwithstanding, the importance of the adoption of this Declaration on the Rights of Indigenous Peoples by the United Nations cannot be overstated (Johnson and Yellow Bird, 2012). It acknowledges 'that indigenous peoples have suffered from historic injustices as a result of inter alia their colonization and dispossession of their lands, territories, and resources, thus preventing them from exercising, in particular, their right to development in accordance with their own needs and interests' (United Nations, 2008: 2). Secondly, it recognizes the urgent need to respect and promote the inherent rights of Indigenous Peoples 'which derive from their political, economic and social structures and from their cultures, spiritual traditions, histories and philosophies, especially their rights to their lands, territories and resources … affirmed in treaties, agreements and other constructive arrangements with [nation states]' (p. 2). Most importantly, however, it is the first time that an international organization of some standing has recognized, promoted and vowed to protect the rights and freedoms of Indigenous Peoples (United Nations, 2008). To this end, the Declaration contains 46 articles that address individual and collective rights, cultural rights and identity, rights to education, health, employment, language and others (United Nations Permanent Forum on Indigenous Issues, 2007). Most important for Indigenous Peoples are the articles recognizing their collective rights and sovereignty:

- *Article 1* states that Indigenous Peoples, as a collective or as individuals, have the right to full enjoyment of all the human rights and fundamental freedoms recognized in the Universal Declaration of Human Rights and international human rights law (United Nations, 2008: 2).
- *Article 2* states that Indigenous Peoples have the right to be free from any kind of discrimination, in the exercise of their rights, in particular that based on their Indigenous origin or cultural identity.
- *Article 3* states that Indigenous Peoples have the right to self-determination, which means they can freely determine their political status and pursue their economic, social and cultural development.
- *Article 4* says they have the right to maintain and strengthen their distinct political, legal, economic, social and cultural institutions, while retaining their rights to participate fully, if they so choose, in the political, economic, social and cultural life of nation states.

While these key articles recognize Indigenous rights that have not been uniformly embraced by the nation states in which they reside, they also create the potential for controversy if participation as full citizens in nation states is a matter of individual choice. In Australia, for example, by law all citizens are required to participate in government elections and the choice 'not to do so' would constitute an infringement of the law of Australia as a nation state. As with all human rights charters, nation states do not uniformly recognize all their provisions and there are great variations of their application, which leads to constant human rights abuse and claims of this nature lodged in the international court in The Hague. Nevertheless, the endorsement of the UN Declaration on the Rights of Indigenous Peoples by a majority of the members of the UN General Assembly is a significant step toward dealing with the continued oppression and marginalization of Indigenous populations around the globe, who have consistently been regarded as an impediment to progress and development (Burger 1990). This misconception has contributed to a settler political discourse that has classified and cast Indigenous populations as 'backward', 'wild', 'savage' and 'barbarian' (Keal, 2003: 67).

The timing of the charter is also significant given neo-liberal economic policies fuelling globalization that have served to put the poorest populations, frequently

Indigenous Peoples, in economic peril as wealth and resources are concentrated in the hands of a handful of multinational corporations owned and controlled by the world's wealthiest citizens. To counter this, several national Indigenous rights movements have emerged to defend their natural resources and fragile economies against further incursion. For example, the Zapatista movement in the Chiapas state of Mexico was born out of the struggle against the North American Free Trade Agreement (Yashar, 2005) and the Bolivian movement which brought Indigenous farmer Evo Morales into power was primarily a struggle against the increasing control of multinational corporations over the natural resources of the state (Albó, 2007). Mostly recently, the Peruvian Congress acceded to the demands of Indigenous protestors to revoke a free-trade agreement with the USA, which would have opened Amazonian lands to gas and oil exploration (*Cultural Survival*, 2009).

The pivotal question, then, relates to the extent to which the Declaration will support Indigenous Peoples, who are not free to exercise full autonomy and pursue political, economic and social development on their own terms, consistent with their cultural values and beliefs, in the nation states in which they reside. How will it help their struggle against unwanted mining and hydroelectric projects that contaminate their lands and waters? How will it help oppressed Indigenous Peoples in post-colonial contexts at the 'bottom of the heap' (Burger, 1990: 82), that is, those living far below the poverty line with low life expectancy, high rates of illiteracy and unemployment, the least schooling, medical care and welfare, the worst housing, the lowest salaries, and high rates of disease, violence and loss of homes and lands?

While there is some optimism that the Declaration marks a new era for protecting and acknowledging the sovereignty of Indigenous Peoples, it is only one, albeit imperfect step, in the evolving international legal standards concerning Indigenous Peoples. While the UN General Assembly has passed the Declaration as a resolution, it has yet to be acknowledged as a binding convention under international law. Only Bolivia has so far incorporated the articles of the Declaration into its national legal framework.

Social workers have the opportunity to become engaged in Indigenous politics, as the chapters in this book show, but before they can become effective advocates for Indigenous Peoples' rights, they must confront the continuing effects of colonialism and the ways in which the profession has been, and continues to, participate in colonizing projects. This requires reflection on social work's complicity in these projects and, in this age of state apologies to Indigenous Peoples – perhaps national and international social work organizations should consider official apologies for their participation in stealing Indigenous children from their families, as well as standing aside when Indigenous Peoples' territories, sovereignty and rights were seized by colonizing settler states. The decolonization of social work requires that the profession acknowledges its complicity in these unjust practices, ceases its participation in processes that disadvantage Indigenous Peoples, condemns the past and continuing effects of colonialism, and collaborates with Indigenous Peoples to engage in decolonizing actions against multinational companies, professional organizations, public agencies and private not-for-profit projects.

The decolonization of social work first and foremost means acknowledging and harnessing the strengths of Indigenous communities rather than engaging in blaming games that compounding deleterious effects of several hundred years of colonization. Indigenous Peoples have exhibited remarkable resilience in resisting colonial incursions and attempts to eliminate them completely have failed. Indigenous people have and will continue to survive and resist further incursions into their territories, natural resources, sacred sites, languages, beliefs, values, networks and systems of governance, intellectual property rights and sovereignty. Social workers have the opportunity either to support Indigenous Peoples' rights or continue with practices that further erode them. In post-colonial struggles for Indigenous Peoples' rights it is important to remember that charters such as the UN Declaration of the Rights of Indigenous Peoples (United Nations, 2008) help to shift the balance of power and go some way to ensure the solidarity of Indigenous Peoples around the world.

References

Albó, X. (2007). The history of a Bolivia in search of change. *Indigenous Affairs*, 7–21 [Online]. Available at: http://www.iwgia.org/iwgia_files_publications_files/IA_1-2-07.pdf [accessed: 7 July 2009].

Burger, J. (1990). *The Gaia Atlas of First Peoples: A Future for the Indigenous World* (1st US edn). New York: Doubleday.

Cultural Survival. (2009). A victory for Indigenous peoples: Controversial free trade laws revoked by Peru's congress [Online]. Available at: http://www.culturalsurvival.org/ourpublications/news/article/victory-indigenous-peoples-controversial-free-trade-laws-revoked-perus- [accessed: 30 June 2009].

Errico, S. (2007). The draft UN Declaration on the Rights of Indigenous Peoples: An overview. *Human Rights Law Review*, 7(4), 741–55.

Johnson, J. and Yellow Bird. (2012). Indigenous Peoples and Cultural Survival. In M. Lynne and Link, R.J. (eds), *Handbook of International Social Work: Human Rights, Development, and the Global Profession*. New York: Oxford University Press, 208–213.

Keal, P. (2003). *European Conquest and the Rights of Indigenous Peoples: The Moral Backwardness of International Society*. New York: Cambridge University Press.

Maybury-Lewis, D. (2002). Genocide against Indigenous Peoples. In A.L. Hinton (ed.), *Annihilating Difference: The Anthropology of Genocide*. Berkeley, CA: University of California Press, 43–92.

United Nations. (2008). *United Nations Declaration on the Rights of Indigenous Peoples* [Online]. Available at: http://www.un.org/esa/socdev/unpfii/documents/DRIPS_en.pdf [accessed: 11 November 2011].

United Nations Permanent Forum on Indigenous Issues. (2007). *Indigenous Peoples, Indigenous Voices*. New York: United Nations.

Yashar, D.J. (2005). *Contesting Citizenship in Latin America: The Rise of Indigenous Movements and the Postliberal Challenge*. New York: Cambridge University Press.

PART I
Theory: Thinking about Indigenous Social Work

Introduction
Scoping the Terrain of Decolonization

Mel Gray, John Coates, Michael Yellow Bird and Tiani Hetherington

In this opening chapter, we introduce the notion of decolonizing social work and outline the structure of the book and the chapters that follow. As we saw in the Preface, recognition of the rights of Indigenous Peoples worldwide reached a new level following the UN General Assembly's adoption of the *United Nations Declaration on the Rights of Indigenous Peoples* on 13 September 2007 (United Nations General Assembly, 2008). The Declaration is a major step toward recognizing the need to improve the situation of impoverished and marginalized Indigenous Peoples throughout the world and represents a strong political statement that acknowledges their rights to self-determination, to own and control their territories and resources, and to preserve their cultures. Most importantly, it affirms that 'all doctrines, policies and practices based on or advocating superiority of Peoples or individuals on the basis of national origin or racial, religious, ethnic or cultural differences are racist, scientifically false, legally invalid, morally condemnable, and social unjust' (United Nations General Assembly, 2008: 2).

Similarly, the emergence of Indigenous social work must be seen in light of the profession's struggle to deal with many of these trends, circumstances and issues. Decolonization can be seen as a continuation of social work's advocacy on social justice and of progressive elements within the profession that challenge hegemonic forms of practice. In *Indigenous Social Work around the World*, Gray, Coates and Yellow Bird (2008) raised awareness of Indigenous social work and explored various practice and educational approaches in working with Indigenous Peoples. Given that there are a number of important themes and ideas in social work that affect Indigenous Peoples: colonialism, oppression, sovereignty, self-determination, cultural rights and the relevance of Western social work approaches, to name a few, Indigenous social work, especially at the international level, represents an important and necessary shift that is bringing new and fresh perspectives into the ambit of social work theory, research, education and practice. Increasing interest in international social work has also had a flow-on effect of enhancing the desire of the profession to develop culturally relevant practice approaches. Moreover, the number of social work education programmes that include international content in their curriculum continues to grow. These various developments can be brought together as diverse attempts to decolonize social work. Hence, following on the success of *Indigenous Social Work around the World*, this edited collection seeks to showcase further case studies of diverse attempts to decolonize social work and further the work of those seeking to make social work relevant to a wider audience.

Various terms and concepts have been used to elucidate the terrain of Indigenous social work and related processes of indigenization and internationalization, all of which are pertinent to the project of decolonizing social work. This chapter begins by noting the tensions and difficulties in clarifying terminology relating to Indigenous Peoples given the vast diversity in the way in which different terms are used in various locations. This is an area vociferously resistant to Western social work's penchant for certainty and logic. Prior writing in social work has viewed indigenization narrowly as a process of importation – and adaptation – of Western, mainly US, models of social work into developing non-Western contexts but, beyond this limited view, lies the broader realm of a truly culturally relevant practice and scholarship (see Chapter 1).

Clarifying Terminology

We begin by clarifying that we see *Decolonizing Social Work* as essentially, though not exclusively, concerned with the rights of Indigenous Peoples and, at the outset, we wish to make some tentative points on terminology and capitalization of the interrelated terms Indigenous, Indigenous Peoples, indigenization and decolonization. These are complex and somewhat controversial topics and in no way is there an even consensus on appropriate definitions and terms. For example, according to Lotte Hughes' (2003) *No Nonsense Guide to Indigenous Peoples*, there is no unambiguous definition of Indigenous Peoples: 'The topic of Indigenous identity opens a Pandora's box of possibilities, and to try and to address them all would mean doing justice to none' (Weaver, 2001: 240). Despite this, we argue that there is always variation around definitions regarding 'identity' throughout even the 'Western European' world. It is primarily Western theorizing that would like to assume that Indigenous Peoples should be described (that is, ascribed with) uniformity. However, there is and always will be variation in the world regarding the question of 'identity'. This is the 'essentializing' that many post-colonial scholars (including the editorial team in this book) wish to avoid. Thus we want to acknowledge here that there is a 'double standard' in the sense that the diversity of labels for 'Anglos', whites, Europeans, Westerners, settlers and so on also needs to be acknowledged and unpacked.

Indigenous Peoples themselves claim the right to define who they are and reject the notion that outsiders do that for them (Smith, 1999; Weaver, 2001; Yellow Bird, 1999a, 1999b). Indigenous people have the individual and group rights to self-identify as Indigenous. Indigenous Peoples are usually referred to in the plural to reflect the global tapestry and diversity of Indigenous people. Anthropologists use the term 'indigenous' to refer to non-dominant or minority groups in particular territories. For example, Indigenous Peoples in Australia are referred to as 'aboriginal' – a word now capitalized as 'Aboriginal' to reflect the national identity of Australia's Indigenous Peoples in the same way that Europeans, for example, lay claim to a common heritage. In its broadest sense, Aboriginal means original inhabitants of the land; by way of contrast, 'indigenous' means born or produced naturally in a land or region or native to that region. However, the people who were there first may also call themselves First Peoples or First Nations – a term used in relation to the Indigenous Peoples of North America just as Aboriginal is used to refer to the Indigenous Peoples of Australia – Aboriginal and Torres Strait Islander Peoples, sometimes abbreviated as ATSI (Bennett, Green, Gilbert and Bessarab, 2013). Indigenous Peoples may also prefer to refer to themselves from their specific tribe or region of origin (see for example Chapters 4 and 14). It is not always easy to determine who the first peoples were given the world history of migration. Hence it may be safer to say that Indigenous Peoples arrived in a territory before nation states were formed, that is, prior to colonization, and some have chosen to resist being part of a nation state (Scott, 2009). In any way, some Indigenous Peoples, such as Native Americans, were organized into nations long before European colonists arrived, hence the term 'First Nations' who claim to be descendants from the original inhabitants of a territory or, in Australia, original owners of the land.

Hughes (2003) estimated that there were more than 7,000 Indigenous societies around the globe with an estimated world population of 300–500 million Indigenous people who self-identified as Indigenous – as descendants of the original inhabitants – and had distinct social, political and cultural identities embodied in languages, traditions, political and legal institutions distinct from those of the national society. The International Work Group for Indigenous Affairs (IWGIA) (2009) estimated the global Indigenous population to be at least 350 million, including approximately 5,000 different cultural groups. Notwithstanding these numerical differences, to distinguish this distinct identity of Indigenous Peoples, this term is hence forward capitalized in the same way that English, Asian, Indian, African and so on are capitalized whether or not English, Asian, Indian and African people live in England, Asia, India and Africa respectively.

In countries, such as Africa, where all Africans are indigenous, indigenous might be used as a lower-case word. However, when referring to a minority indigenous people in Africa, such as the San, Indigenous would be capitalized. In the same way, Indians are indigenous to India, Chinese indigenous to China and Europeans indigenous to Europe.

When the term 'indigenization' is used, it refers mainly to attempts of Africans in Africa and Asians in southeast Asia, and now more recently Chinese in China, to preserve their cultural heritage and identity in the face of outside influences (see below). The term was first used in the social work discourse in relation to Africa to denote the effects of colonization in reducing the importance of local and indigenous cultures, while promoting Western cultures and ways of life – seen as part of the modernization process (see Osei-Hwedie, 1993). In China, however, indigenization refers to attempts to develop a uniquely Chinese form of social work to ward off the effects of globalization. It is mainly from Africa and China that the contemporary indigenization discourse in social work stems. While first used in relation to Africa, the development of social work in China since the early 1990s has reignited the indigenization discourse in social work (see Cheung and Liu, 2004; Tsang, Yan and Shera, 2000; Tsang and Yan, 2001; Yan and Cheung, 2006; Yan and Tsang, 2008; Yang, 2005; Yuen-Tsang and Wang, 2002). Here it has taken an interesting turn due to its links with modernization (see Yan and Tsui, 2008; Yunong and Xiong, 2008). Chinese social work scholars, therefore, express some ambiguity about whether or not to embrace Western models of social work because they do not wish to be seen as 'backward' in any way. They want to modernize but not necessarily to indigenize, according to Yunong and Xiong (2008).

Indigenous people express unease with the term 'indigenization' because of its tendency to promote a blanket or generic approach to working with Indigenous people, as 'Other', and miss the fact that there are many Indigenous Peoples and cultures, all of whom are custodians of the lands in which they live. For this reason, Gray et al. (2008) described indigenization as 'an outmoded concept' though, as shown below, there are many contexts where the notion still has currency. As noted by Yellow Bird (2008: 286), for Indigenous people, indigenization is the personal and collective process of decolonizing Indigenous life and restoring true self-determination based on traditional Indigenous values (see also Porter, 2005). Hence, here, indigenization 'portrays centre-periphery relationships in more cultural-political terms' (Giulianotti and Robertson, 2009: 41). According to Friedman (1999: 391), for developed societies in particular, it registers 'an increasing fragmentation of identities, the break-up of larger identity units, the emergence of cultural politics among indigenous, regional, immigrant, and even national populations'. Indigenous people may want to reclaim their status as a distinct political and cultural grouping and, at the same time, may want the diversity of their cultures and languages acknowledged and maintained. Indigenization counters a collective identity because it emphasizes the 'local' and hence identifies cultures in terms of their unique characteristics. This is the sense in which the term is used in social work where indigenization often refers to the adaptation of Western social work theory and methods to local contexts (see for example, Barise, 2005; Gray and Coates, 2008; Shawky, 1972; Yellow Bird, 2008).

Indigenous people appear equally uncomfortable with the notion of hybridity or heterogenization as this too denies their right to retain a unique, collective cultural identity (Giulianotti and Robertson, 2009). While they prefer an essentialist approach that recognizes and acknowledges the uniqueness of their cultural and Indigenous identity and right to retain it (see Chapter 1), they will quickly assert their collective rights when threatened by settler societies and governments (United Nations General Assembly, 2008, see Preface).

Our position is that debates concerning 'authentic' Indigenous identity only serve as distractions and, moreover, this standpointism is problematic because it typically succumbs to Western discourses, such as culturalism, that reify so-called 'traditional' Indigenous 'culture'. Furthermore, the intent to carve out a separate 'Indigenous only' domain, in some ways, is contradictory to Indigenous ways of being and knowing that recognize the interrelationship of all things (see also Agrawal, 1995; Nakata, 2006, 2007). Furthermore, as Weaver (2001) aptly notes:

> the self-appointed 'identity police,' those who divide communities and accuse others of not being 'Indian' enough because they practice the wrong religion, have the wrong politics, use the wrong label for themselves, or do not have the right skin color, should also be an issue of concern. Some indigenous people ask, 'Are you Indian, or are you Christian?' as if these are mutually exclusive categories. I have seen caring indigenous people driven to tears at their jobs at a Native community center when they were berated for having some white ancestry. People have been publicly humiliated because someone decided that their tribal affiliations were inappropriate. This harassment and badgering is conducted by indigenous people, against indigenous people. The roots for this type of behavior probably lie deep in the accusers' own insecurities about identity and racism learned as part of the colonization process. (Weaver, 2001: 251)

'Indigenous Peoples' is a modern term used by international organizations to describe culturally and geographically dispersed groups with diverse histories but, despite often considerable cultural divergence, Indigenous Peoples share significant symmetries that have evolved from the common experiences of European colonialism. These similarities are founded in an ancestral birthright in the land, a common core of collective interests concerning the protection of human, territorial and cultural rights, and the shared experience of dispossession, discrimination, exploitation and marginalization precipitated through the colonial projects perpetrated against indigenous communities by colonial and neocolonial state administrations.

In addition to this international designation, Indigenous Peoples have been referred to in terms of several different labels: Aboriginal, Indian, native, ethnic minority, First Peoples and occasionally as the 'Fourth World' (Corntassel and Primeau, 1995; Manuel and Posluns, 1974). Indigenous Peoples is the designation used by the United Nations to recognize these, and other groups, collectively. The cultural survival of Indigenous Peoples concerns the protection and restoration of Indigenous Peoples' territories, natural resources, sacred sites, languages, beliefs, values, relationships, systems of governance, sovereignty, self-determination, human rights and intellectual property. Getting settler populations to understand and accept these rights is an important issue in cultural survival and essential role for decolonizing social work.

Indigenous Peoples reside on all of the inhabited continents of Earth – in Africa, the Americas, Asia, Europe and Oceania – and in all geographical regions: deserts, arctic and subarctic areas, islands, mountains, grasslands, woodlands, rainforests, wetlands and coastal areas. Most identify themselves according to the reciprocal relationships they hold with their physical environments and territories, along with their affiliation in an extended family, clan, band, village, tribe, confederacy or nation. There is no typical Indigenous group. Each has its own unique history, worldview, culture, language, dress, food, sacred and secular ceremonies, and social and political organizations. Indigenous Peoples may or may not have a stable political, economic or social relationship with mainstream society (Scott 2009).

The issue of defining which groups of peoples can and cannot be considered Indigenous has been, and in some ways continues to be, a significant challenge for international fora. Former chairperson of the United Nations Permanent Forum on Indigenous Issues, Elsa Stamatopulou (1994) described these groups as diverse populations who reside on ancestral lands, share a lineage with the original inhabitants of these lands, have distinct cultures and languages, and regard themselves as different from those who have colonized and now control their territories. While the definitions created by a range of organizations and authors have varied, sometimes significantly over the past 50 years, recently a broad consensus has formed within the international community. Four core principles have been agreed upon in defining Indigenous Peoples:

1. Indigenous Peoples generally live within, or maintain attachments to, geographically distinct territories.
2. Indigenous Peoples tend to maintain distinct social, economic, and political institutions within their territories.
3. Indigenous Peoples typically aspire to remain distinct culturally, geographically and institutionally rather than assimilate fully into national society.
4. Indigenous Peoples self-identify as Indigenous or tribal. Many Indigenous groups believe that defining who is Indigenous 'is best answered by indigenous communities themselves'. (Corntassel, 2003: 75)

Perhaps more than anything *Decolonizing Social Work* recognizes the limitations and imperialist frameworks (Midgley, 1981, 2008) inherent in Western social work that must be contested on behalf of populations that have been victimized rather than helped by these approaches. It is part of the long-standing struggle in social work against hegemonic forms of practice seen in its critical focus (see for example, structural social work (Mullaly, 2009); feminist social work (Bricker-Jenkins, Hooyman and Gottlieb (1991); anti-racist social work (Dominelli, 1997) and critical theory (see Gray and Webb, 2013; Pozzuto, Angell and Dezendorf, 2005). Decolonization continues this critical focus as it seeks locally and culturally relevant forms of scholarship, research, education and practice that create a space for open dialogue and debate for the constant – and inherent – tensions emanating from the paradoxical processes of internationalization, globalization, universalization and localization (Gray, 2005). It also seeks to strike a balance in acknowledging 'the diversity of [Indigenous] cultures, traditions, and differing, yet related, ways of seeing, knowing and doing of Indigenous People worldwide' (Ormiston, 2010: 50).

Decolonizing Social Work requires that the profession acknowledge its complicity and ceases its participation in colonizing projects, openly condemns the past and continuing effects of colonialism, collaborates with Indigenous Peoples to engage in decolonizing activities against public and private colonizing projects, and seeks to remove the often subtle vestiges of colonization from theory and practice.

Decolonizing Social Work allows for the acknowledgement and incorporation of the strengths of Indigenous communities rather than a perpetuation of blaming-the-victim approaches compounding the adverse effects of several hundred years of colonial projects. From a strengths perspective, Indigenous Peoples' resistance to, and continued existence in spite of, colonialism demonstrates a strong will to social justice – to protect and restore Indigenous territories, natural resources, sacred sites, languages, cultures, beliefs, values, relationships, systems of governance, intellectual property and self-determination. Hence, ultimately, *Decolonizing Social Work* recognizes and credits the strengths and contributions of Indigenous knowledges, traditions and practices, and supports Indigenous Peoples' cultural survival and Indigenous rights. It means recognizing that the cultural knowledges and practices of Indigenous Peoples serve as an important counterweight to Western ways of thinking and behaving. Healthy Indigenous communities require more than struggle against and recovery from the adverse effects of colonization (see Crichlow, 2002). Decolonization supports, as Wilson (Chapter 16) points out, creating a place for the re-emergence of, and the strengths within, the unique cultural heritage of Indigenous groups. Decolonization means accepting Indigenous Peoples' lived experience as a starting point when searching for solutions to the problems and issues they face, which, in many instances, are also relevant to non-Indigenous Peoples and global problems, such as climate change, pollution, war, poverty and hunger, to name a few. It means putting people's needs, uniqueness and knowledge first and seeing all the activities in which we engage from here on in as honest attempts to discern the nature of decolonized social work.

The purpose of this book is to pave the way for contemplative review and paradigmatic shifts in social work theorizing, education, research and practice. In this way, this book intends to provide an opening for social workers to consider specific theoretical, practice, education and research issues in working with Indigenous Peoples, immigrants and refugees, and people of all cultures. To this end, the book is divided into four parts as follows:

1. Theory: Thinking about Indigenous social work.
2. Practice: From the bottom up.
3. Education: Facilitating local relevance.
4. Research: Decolonizing methodologies.

Part I: Theory

Thinking about Social Work as a Decolonizing Profession

Part I reflects upon the effects of Western colonization on social work and the consequences for Indigenous and local peoples. It recognizes that social work has been seen to be part of colonization (Collier, 1993; Crichlow, 2002; Hodge, Limb and Cross, 2009; Margolin, 1997; Yellow Bird and Gray, 2008). Gray et al. (2008) referred to Indigenous social work as straddling two vastly different worlds, namely, the Indigenous and the Western worlds. This made it extremely difficult for social work practitioners working with Indigenous Peoples or in non-Western contexts, or even with cultures other than their own in Western contexts, to make mainstream social work practice models fit these contexts. This difficulty reflects the tension within social work concerning what constitutes professional social work practice and what can be appropriately transported to other cultures. While social work has contributed internationally and has much to offer, there is a lengthy debate in the professional literature about the problems associated with the uncritical transfer of Western social work (see for example, Gray, 2005; Gray et al., 2008). Numerous studies report that local Indigenous helpers without any formal social work training could better relate to, identify the problems of, and negotiate appropriate solutions for Indigenous communities than their 'professional' counterparts (for example, Hetherington, 2009; How Kee, 2003, 2008; Waller and Patterson, 2002). Indigenous forms of healing and helping are more likely to be compatible with Indigenous Peoples' values and worldviews because they are culturally grounded or situated within Indigenous Peoples' own cultural traditions (Hurdle, 2002; Voss, Douville, Little Soldier and Twiss, 1999). Nevertheless, professional social work remains a presence in Indigenous communities and has to find ways to overcome its historically strained relationship with Indigenous Peoples arising from their overwhelmingly negative experiences with child removal and image as agents of colonization (Baldry, Green and Thorpe, 2006; Gray and Valentine, 2005; Hudson and McKenzie, 1991; Valentine and Gray, 2006; Waterfall, 2002; Yellow Bird and Chenault, 1999).

Adding to this complexity, most social workers, including Indigenous practitioners, are educated at mainstream modern universities where programmes are delivered by Western experts in the English language (Ives, Aitken, Loft and Phillips, 2007; Sinclair, 2004). In other words, the dominant social work model of education largely socializes students into Western norms, values and ways of thinking (Gair, 2008; Hart, 2003; Lynn, 2001; Mafile'o, 2004, 2008; Weaver, 2000; Young, 2008). As a primarily Western caring science, social workers can alter their practice of social work to become more culturally grounded and locally relevant to have a positive impact on culturally diverse Indigenous and local peoples.

Hence Part I – and the book generally – attempts to find constructive ways to think about social work as a decolonizing profession, one that seeks to reconcile differences and deal with diversity by adjusting its interventions and approaches to reflect the needs of diverse communities beginning – in Chapter 1 – with an outline of the theoretical terrain. Mel Gray and Tiani Hetherington view indigenization, Indigenous social work and decolonization in light of the profession's struggle to deal with diversity, thus beginning this exploration of ways in which social workers might rethink their practice in light of the expressed needs and aspirations of Indigenous Peoples.

In Chapter 2, Vidya Rao examines the evolution of social work in India to highlight the way in which the profession there has been trying to decolonize its substantive theoretical content and concomitant methods. An effort is made to differentiate the idea of decolonization from indigenization by focusing on the methods required to deal with Indian social problems embedded in their cultural contexts. Like Kreitzer in Chapter 9, Rao shows social work's resistance to decolonizing practices.

In Chapter 3, John Coates examines spirituality, ecology and healing in Indigenous social work as a path to decolonizing social work. Spirituality is an important part of healing for Indigenous Peoples as they have experienced disconnection from the source of their traditional teachings through colonization and suffered spiritual disconnection due to displacement from their lands. Today, many Indigenous Peoples seek to reclaim the roots, values and ways of life that supported the development of their peoples. Since the 1990s, the topic of spirituality in social work has received growing attention, with various authors arguing for social work to incorporate spirituality as part of its knowledge and practice foundation. In contrast, the profession has been particularly slow to engage with the environmental movement. This has possibly been due, in part, to the narrow interpretation of the person-in-environment approach to be almost exclusively social. More recently, there has been a 'greening' of spirituality or connections made between ecology and spirituality in social work. This recent literature on spirituality and environmental or ecosocial work is creating a space where Indigenous voices are being heard. Indigenous social work and traditional healing begin with a spiritual sense of interconnectedness. Western social work has much to learn from these approaches in terms of expanding understanding of the person–environment relationship and the world around us. This chapter reviews the nature and emergence of holistic and inclusive ecospiritual approaches in social work that offer hope for the profession to be more effective in its pursuit of social justice and healing.

In Chapter 4, Jos Baltra-Ulloa examines why decolonized social work is more than cross-culturalism arguing that, despite the increasing literature on cross-cultural social work practice, the meaning of *crossing culture* remains elusive. As a mainstream social work model, cross-cultural practice is often discussed in the discourse relating to ethnic minorities and Indigenous cultures. However, cross-cultural perspectives are problematic to the extent that they are constructed from within the dominant culture. For the most part, cross-cultural approaches have been designed, developed, tested and promoted by Western practitioners as ways of helping the cultural other. There has been a lack of realization, however, that helping is in the eye of the one helped – the recipient of help must feel helped. A culturally relevant helping encounter for Indigenous people would be devoid of rigid formulae and discern a meaningful relationship between local cultural values and universal social work principles and standards. It requires a commitment to genuine connection and an ongoing process of interaction, wherein the helpee determines what works and what does not. This chapter offers a critique of cross-cultural social work, outlines its limitations in dealing with Indigenous Peoples, and suggests an approach that allows the worker and client to focus on learning about one another rather than the worker merely searching for culturally competent models.

Part II: Practice

From the Bottom up

Cross-cultural and cultural awareness training is often promoted in social work as a way to learn about 'other' cultures and increase the cultural competence of practitioners (Atkinson, Morten and Sue, 1989; Devore and Schlesinger, 1987; Green, 1982; Harper-Dorton and Lantz, 2007; Lum, 1999; Weaver, 2004). A well-established principle of cross-cultural practice is that language provides a window into another culture since it embodies the way a society thinks: 'Through learning and speaking a particular language, an individual absorbs the collective thought processes of a people' (Little Bear, 2000: 78). One learns best or most effectively about other cultures by spending time in and learning from community members through grassroots engagement. Thus Indigenous social work is not about cultural awareness, cultural sensitivity, cultural competence or cross-cultural practice: it is about community connection (see Blackstock, 2003; Hetherington, 2009; Nimmagadda and Martell, 2008; Thibodeau and Peigan, 2007). It is this way of relating – rather than a way of practice – that we seek to articulate in this second volume.

In Chapter 5, Lourdes de Urrutia Barroso and David Strug examine community-based social work in Cuba. They trace the development of a unique local approach that arose in response to social change in the 1990s when Cuba's economic crisis, emerging social problems and the need for social workers for community practice all shaped this community-oriented approach. The Cuban social work programme, which integrates social work practice skills with political sociology and political economy, is a strong model for social work training in other developing countries to address social problems related to national economic difficulties. Although this approach directly contrasts with the individually oriented models of other Western contexts, this chapter argues that social workers in Cuba and other countries have much to learn from one another, despite the differences that exist between them.

In Chapter 6, Flavio Franciso Marsiglia discusses social work practice with Mexican-Americans where social workers, in order to become culturally grounded practitioners, incorporate Indigenous ways of helping that may not match concepts learned in mainstream social work education. Lessons from social work practice with Mexican-Americans suggest that social workers need to act as cultural mediators, and in order to be able to mediate effectively between these two cultures (or worlds), they must be familiar with both cultures and, ideally, fluent in both languages. Social work practitioners' backgrounds and professional experience may not be sufficient to reconcile contradictions or gaps in their practice. If they cannot interpret or understand cultural value conflicts, practitioners would do well to seek the assistance of cultural experts already located in the community. By becoming familiar with community-based natural helping networks and belief systems, the social work profession may develop increased effectiveness at mediating between communal or family-oriented types of helping and the more individualistic types of interventions used by many of the agencies for which they work.

In Chapter 7, Noreen Mokuau and Peter Mataira examine the trajectory of historic trauma for Native Hawaiians and Māori, and explore the position that they are building on cultural strengths and resiliency to rise from the trauma despite continuing challenges and disparities. Factors indicative of historical trauma, such as physical, cultural, economic, sociopolitical and psychological dimensions, are also framed as elements of contemporary growth and change. For too long, Native Hawaiians and Māori have been viewed as a people with many problems, and the limitation of such a view is that it negates all the progress and good work of many people, including historical leaders who have left legacies that provided some protection from debilitating historical events. In order to foster the continued 'rise' for these native populations, a role for Indigenous social work is to foster a focus on cultural strengths and resiliency. Implications for Indigenous social work with Native Hawaiians and Māori are drawn.

In Chapter 8, Sahar Al-Makhamreh and Mary Pat Sullivan examine social work in Jordan which is in its infancy and the potential for decolonized practice. Up until the twentieth century, family members and highly respected tribal and religious leaders acted as counsellors, healers and advisers in times of crisis or personal need. During the twentieth century, however, the country began to face serious socioeconomic challenges, including poverty, unemployment, population growth and the effects of continued political instability in the Middle East. This has paved the way for more formal 'helping' contributions such as social work to support traditional 'natural' responses to social need. An increasing number of individuals has embarked on a career in social work despite the government's reluctance to recognize the profession though the development of formal social work education has lagged behind other Middle-Eastern countries such as Egypt where social work education can be traced back to 1935 (with the adoption of a primarily US model). In Jordan, resource issues seem to represent far more than finances. Here the complex sociocultural context, including gender and religious sensitivities, shapes practice in such a way that it is difficult to separate social norms from social work practice. This chapter argues for recognition of the value of localization or authentication in shaping culturally relevant social work in Jordan.

Part III: Education

Facilitating Local Relevance and Responsive Social Work Education
in Touch with Indigenous Ways

Social work education needs to attract and retain Indigenous students and graduates. To this end, steps need to be taken to overcome and remove the social and cultural barriers that prevent Indigenous students from entering the education system, including higher education programmes like social work. The chapters in Part III comprise case studies of attempts to develop responsive social work education programmes that are in touch with Indigenous ways. All attest there is a huge bridge to be built, as, from an Indigenous perspective, due to education and labelling, Westerners are seen as lacking in understanding of, and therefore judgmental towards, Indigenous cultures (Nakata, 2006, 2007). This has resulted in resistance to outside intervention or the foreign imposition of mainstream social work education and its individualistic helping approaches. Social work education needs to acknowledge Indigenous family and community values, childrearing practices and the cooperative nature of Indigenous cultures (Limb, Hodge and Panos, 2008; Lynn, 2001; Lynn et al., 1998; Marais and Marais, 2007).

In the first chapter of Part III (Chapter 9), Linda Kreitzer examines the indigenization of social work in Africa from an historical perspective, links it to colonization and outlines persistent struggles with developing Indigenous theories and practices. This chapter highlights the progress of social work education and practice in Africa from 1971 to 1990. It provides a synopsis of the forces that have influenced and challenged the profession in its struggles to decolonize social work education and make social work practice more Africentred. Based on historical research, particularly documentary analysis of the conference proceedings of the Association of Social Work Education for Africa (ASWEA) between 1973 and 1986, it describes the dissatisfaction of African social work practitioners and academics with Western social work models and curricula, as well as the challenges to developing African-centred approaches. These conference proceedings are important historical records of the evolution of social welfare, social work education and the social work profession in Africa.

In Chapter 10, Paula Tanemura Morelli, Peter Mataira and Malina Kaulukukui examine decolonizing social work education in Hawai`i, where social workers are working to implement initiatives to promote cultural coexistence, and economic and political equality. Here a focus on indigenization is a departure from Western multiculturalism as it involves defining an identity and mission relative to the local community to which the social work profession is accountable – Pacific constituencies that subscribe to divergent life philosophies. The primacy of family and genealogy, traditional practices, the wisdom of elders, intuitive intelligence, servant leadership, a sense of place, environmental kinship and spirituality, collectivism and restorative values over retribution are critical Indigenous elements that support the sustainability of human well-being. Hawai`ian approaches to thinking about social issues, research, ways of knowing and practice are not bound by 'universal' theoretical and methodological strictures that define human behaviour. Thus, in Hawai'i, social workers are in the process of decolonizing mainstream narratives through indigenizing their understanding of, and response to, social problems in the Pacific. This process of discovery has led to the realization that the notion of a multicultural 'melting pot' is a discourse of cultural and political hegemony used to justify Western cultural and political penetration into new domains. In reality, multiculturalism and social equity rarely coexist. These important themes have the potential to guide social work practice in Hawai'i down a path to greater cultural relevance both locally and globally.

In Chapter 11, Samantha Wehbi critically examines international student placements in light of increasing interest in the internationalization of social work. She argues that there is a need for social work educators to provide students with opportunities to reflect on their motivation to undertake international placements to avoid practices that inadvertently reinforce oppressive North–South relations. Wehbi's experience is that students undertake international placements due to their fascination with other cultures and liking for people of another country. Further, they want to make a difference and 'give something back' for the privilege they enjoy. However, there are problems associated with these motivations, not least their potential to perpetuate cultural imperialism and voyeurism, cultural homogeneity and ethnocentrism, outmoded charity perspectives and the exoticization of other cultures. Wehbi suggests that, at the very least, some practical benchmarks are required when non-Indigenous students – and scholars or supervisors – engage in international placements or research. These are important if Western social work students and academics are to avoid charges of disingenuity, opportunism and a lack of integrity. As a bare minimum, they should have either language translation facilities or a grasp of the local language so they can access and understand first-hand sources, including policy documents and legislation; preferably supervisors should have visited and spent time in the country in question in a research fieldwork capacity; and, most importantly, they should engage and closely consult with Indigenous stakeholders and researchers in preparation for student placements.

In Chapter 12, Nicole Ives and Michael Thaweiakenrat Loft seek to build bridges with Indigenous communities through social work education. They argue that lack of familiarity between Indigenous and non-Indigenous Peoples contributes to the serious deficiency of understanding of contemporary issues facing Indigenous communities by those outside these communities and to the difficulties in moving forward in finding relevant, equitable solutions to these issues. Ives and Loft explore approaches to community engagement and connection through the medium of social work education. They describe how social work education can be used to liberate and heal ruptures to our social fabric caused by human rights violations in Indigenous communities. They challenge social work instructors to engage Indigenous communities in the process of social work learning by facilitating community connections and engaging in mutual dialogue. They provide a rationale for the importance of facilitating relationship building among Indigenous communities, schools of social work and their wider universities, and students in a social work educational context. These connections can help students gain experience and insight into the cultural, social, economic and health contexts of Indigenous communities from the community's perspective as well as help students foster self-reflection to integrate cultural knowledge and experiences into future practice. To this end, Ives and Loft highlight – through use of case examples – teaching approaches that: (i) challenge students to critically connect course teachings to their own cultural identity, assumptions, ways of knowing and being, and ways of practising with diverse cultural groups and communities; and (ii) underscore the commitment to the learning of both students and teachers, Indigenous and non-Indigenous.

Part IV: Research

Decolonizing Methodologies and the Politics of Indigenous Social Work Research

As an emerging field within the discipline, Indigenous social work draws on a number of multiple, often conflicting and competing discourses, including indigenization; cross-cultural practice, culturally sensitive social work practice, cultural appropriateness, cultural competence and cultural safety; anti-oppressive, anti-discriminatory and anti-racist practice; international social work; decolonization theory; Indigenist research and Indigenous standpointism; social ecology or environmental (green or eco) social work; and spirituality in social work (see Hetherington, 2009; Gray et al., 2008). Overarching these competing positions are more fundamental ideological debates concerning Indigeneity and authenticity. Questions surrounding who has the right to speak for whom; whether there is a place for non-Indigenous social workers in Indigenous social work; and the ethics of conducting research with Indigenous communities strike at the heart of these oftentimes polarizing debates (Gilchrist, 1997; Paradies, 2006; Weaver, 2001).

A related consideration is that Indigenous Peoples impart knowledge through oral tradition (Baskin, 2002, 2003, 2006; Voss et al., 1999). Elders and traditional teachers are reluctant to have their teachings written down as Westerners have often exploited these in ways that were not intended by their originators. For example, Indigenous spirituality should not be confused with the New Age spirituality that permeates the social work literature (Gray, 2008; Smith, 1999). The New Age movement tends to emphasize personal transformation and healing and, in so doing, often misappropriates (or commodifies) sacred traditions, in particular those of American Indian and Aboriginal Australian Peoples (see Briskman, 2007; Weaver, 2001). There is great potential for local, Indigenous knowledge to be used politically to highlight the needs and interests of Indigenous Peoples (Agrawal, 1995) and structural barriers, such as poverty and the over-representation of Indigenous children in the child welfare system (Briskman, 2007; Weaver and

Congress, 2009). However, careful consideration regarding the safeguarding of Indigenous healing and helping practices is needed lest they be co-opted by Western agendas. In other words, great care should be taken in the dissemination of this knowledge so that it will not be generalized or romanticized by Western interests (Agrawal, 1995; Coates et al., 2006; Gray et al., 2007).

Indigenous social work involves a personal (and political) commitment to Indigenous Peoples that engages with their real-world concerns for continuing survival: the achievement of community, identity, nationalism and sovereignty. We believe that there is ample opportunity for Indigenous Nations Studies scholars to work with the social work profession to address the lack of political attention to advancing land and cultural rights and sovereignty in Indigenous social work. So what are the lessons to be learnt here for social workers who wish to, or find themselves by chance, working with Indigenous Peoples?

Professional social workers as outsiders to the community cannot compete with local helpers and their close and long-standing relationships with community members. For local helpers helping is a *way of life,* not outside of it like isolated social work interventions in response to narrowly defined needs. Thus, findings emerging in Indigenous research suggest that clients are best served when professional helpers collaborate with local helpers, validate cultural ways of framing problems and intervene in ways that complement traditional helping practices already in place within Indigenous communities (Hart, 2002; How Kee, 2003, 2008; Waller and Patterson, 2002). Social workers – as outsiders – must resist the tendency to privilege professional discourse above Indigenous ways of helping, healing and connecting (Sinclair, Hart and Bruyere, 2009; Ungar, 2004). Due to cultural incompatibilities between non-Indigenous social workers and Indigenous Peoples, the ability to work alongside Indigenous colleagues is vital. Non-Indigenous practitioners – or outsiders – have to learn from their Indigenous colleagues and co-workers, allowing them to take the lead in client interactions. Importance is thus placed on a position of not knowing for non-Indigenous social workers. In other words, while not denying that mainstream social work may have something of value, non-Indigenous social workers must challenge what have they have learnt in social work and relearn Indigenous ways from shadowing their Indigenous colleagues and being *in* the community.

Indigenous social work involves much more than simply visiting the community, doing the work and then leaving. Rather it means being a *culturally embedded practitioner* spending time in and becoming *part of the community*, learning through direct experience and sustained interaction with people in the community. Social workers have to look to grassroots people for information since there is no one who knows better than they what is needed. One has to be a presence in the community to gain trust. While social workers can learn objective facts about Indigenous history and culture, this intellectual knowledge cannot replace the subjective meanings and understandings that arise through *being in the community*, and first and foremost, listening to community members' stories. Essentially, then, there are ethical issues in Indigenous research that must be considered, not least questions of who owns the knowledge. How will the knowledge be used? Will it promote Indigenous Peoples' interests and political causes? It requires that the researcher takes a partisan stance that ensures positive outcomes for Indigenous Peoples. Given these concerns, participatory action research is often seen as a method of choice in which local people are engaged in community studies from problem definition through to the dissemination of research findings (Briskman, 2007; Gair, Thompson and Miles, 2005; Gilchrist, 1997; Sinclair, 2003; Young, 1999).

In Chapter 13, Anaru Eketone and Shayne Walker discuss Kaupapa Māori social work research and critically analyse Kaupapa Māori methodology, which developed as part of the broader Māori critique of Westernized notions of knowledge, culture and research. It offers a methodology conceived, developed and carried out by Māori, to benefit Māori and, as such, is a decolonizing methodology. It is localized, critical, emancipatory, transformative and empowering. It differs from other forms of research involving Māori people, such as culturally safe or culturally sensitive research in that it critiques dominant, racist, Westernized hegemonies and promotes Māori self-determination. Eketone and Walker outline the main principles of Kaupapa Māori research and demonstrate its core processes through a case study, ending with an examination of its wider implications for Indigenous research.

In Chapter 14, Jon Matsuoka, Paula Tanemura Morelli and Hamilton McCubbin examine the unique features of Indigenous and immigrant populations as a backdrop to culturally relevant research with Indigenous and immigrant communities, defined as populations endowed with Indigenous histories and cultures, and traumatic life experiences. Given their Indigenous origins and immigration experiences, Indigenous and immigrant communities present important challenges for present and future social work practice, including the profession's need to minimize its historic dependence on stereotypes and to proactively seek understanding of the historical and cultural roots of Indigenous and immigrant populations, their belief systems and values, cultural traditions and practices, and assimilation and adaptation to the host or majority culture. The profession has a compelling need to develop theories, research methodologies and intervention strategies based upon knowledge of the unique histories and cultures of Indigenous and immigrant populations, and their vulnerabilities, strengths and resilience. The social work profession has a commitment to serve these populations guided by competencies based on culturally relevant research and evidence-based practice and policies.

In Chapter 15, Michael Yellow Bird shows how the results of neuroscientific research can be applied to decolonizing social work interventions to enhance human well-being. He focuses on *neurodecolonization*, a conceptual framework, which he created, that uses mindfulness research to facilitate an examination of the ways in which the human brain is affected by the colonial situation and an exploration of mind-brain activities that change neural networks and enable individuals to overcome the myriad effects of trauma and oppression inherent in colonialism. Yellow Bird argues that understanding how the mind and brain are affected by colonialism is an important paradigm in decolonizing social work. While many Indigenous Peoples experience the direct, unrelenting, negative effects of colonialism, social workers who choose to confront it directly and vigorously, eschew its false privileges and promises, face secondary trauma as they encounter the tsunami of devastation it creates and realize they can do little about it. Yellow Bird maintains that neurodecolonization benefits both Indigenous Peoples and social workers and is critical to the overall enterprise of decolonization.

In the final chapter of Part IV (Chapter 16), Shawn Wilson discusses the necessity of developing and using an Indigenist research paradigm to create an Indigenous vision for the future. The chapter integrates Indigenous knowledge with wider scholarly literature and demonstrates the knowledge embedded in the cultural heritage of marginalized and disadvantaged groups (see also hooks 1990). If Indigenous social services were to progress beyond their constant reactionary crisis mode of functioning, Indigenist research would need to shift the focus away from how communities want *not* to be and instead create a vision for how communities and families want to be. Armed with this vision, Indigenist research might guide social work education and practice towards this desired future. Indigenist research works from a worldview in which knowledge is relational: Indigenous people are not *in* relationships, they *are* relationships. This is Indigenous truth and reality. Implementing this research paradigm requires Indigenist researchers to build theoretical frameworks and research methods congruent with Indigenous belief systems. Action based upon this knowledge may then lead to the gaining of wisdom. Only when wisdom flows from Indigenist knowledge-building processes can it meaningfully create the vision to guide social policy and service provision, thus completing the cycle of building social work interventions truly accountable to Indigenous communities.

In the final, concluding chapter, the editors draw together the arguments advanced regarding decolonizing social work and point to the future, continuing story of Indigenous Peoples' survival.

References

Agrawal, A. (1995). Indigenous and scientific knowledge: Some critical comments. *Indigenous Knowledge and Development Monitor*, 3(3) [Online]. Available at: http://www.iss.nl/ikdm/IKDM/IKDM/index.html [accessed: 29 February 2012].

Atkinson, D.R., Morten, G. and Sue, D.W. (1989). *Counselling American Minorities: A Crosscultural Perspective* (3rd edn). Dubuque, IA: William C. Brown Publishers.

Baldry, E., Green, S. and Thorpe, K. (2006). Urban Australian Aboriginal people's experience of human services. *International Social Work*, 49(3), 364–75.

Barise, A. (2005). Social work with Muslims: Insights from the teachings of Islam. *Critical Social Work*, 6(2) [Online]. Available at: http://www.criticalsocialwork. com/units/socialwork/critical.nsf/EditDoNotShowInTOC/554026006519AFC 38525700F004B57B6 [accessed: 24 January 2006].

Baskin, C. (2002). Circles of resistance: Spirituality in social work practice, education and transformative change. *Currents: New Scholarship in the Human Services*, 1(1) [Online]. Available at: http://www.ucalgary.ca/currents/ [accessed: 29 February 2012].

Baskin, C. (2003). Within the outsider: Challenges of an Indigenous pedagogue. *Native Social Work Journal*, 5, 172–84.

Baskin, C. (2006). Aboriginal worldviews as challenges and possibilities in social work education. *Critical Social Work*, 7(2) [Online]. Available at: http://www. criticalsocialwork.com/ [accessed: 29 February 2012].

Bennett, B. and Zubrzycki, J. (2003). Hearing the stories of Australian Aboriginal and Torres Strait Islander social workers: Challenging and educating the system. *Australian Social Work*, 56(1), 61–70.

Bennett, B., Green, S., Gilbert, S. and Bessarab, D. (eds). (2013). *Our Voices: Aboriginal and Torres Strait Islander Social Work*. South Yara: Palgrave Macmillan.

Blackstock, C. (2003). First Nations Child and Family Services: Restoring peace and harmony in First Nations communities. In L. Kufeldt and McKenzie, B. (eds), *Child Welfare: Connecting Research, Policy and Practice*. Waterloo, Canada: Wilfrid Laurier University Press, 331–42.

Bricker-Jenkins, M., Hooyman, N. and Gottlieb, N. (eds). (1991). *Feminist Social Work Practice in Clinical Settings*. Newbury Park: Sage.

Briskman, L. (2003). Indigenous Australians: Towards postcolonial social work. In J. Allan, Pease, B. and Briskman, L. (eds), *Critical Social Work: An Introduction to Theories and Practices*. Sydney, Australia: Allen & Unwin, 92–106.

Briskman, L. (2007). *Social Work with Indigenous Communities*. Sydney, Australia: The Federation Press.

Cheung, M. and Liu, M. (2004). The self concept of Chinese women and the indigenization of social work in China. *International Social Work*, 47(1), 109–27.

Coates, J., Gray, M. and Hetherington, T. (2006). An ecospiritual perspective: Finally a place for Indigenous approaches. *British Journal of Social Work*, 36(3), 381–99.

Collier, K. (1993). *Social Work with Rural People: Theory and Practice* (2nd edn). Vancouver, Canada: New Star Books.

Corntassel, J.J. (2003). Who is Indigenous? 'Peoplehood' and ethnonationalist approaches to rearticulating Indigenous identity. *Nationalism and Ethnic Politics*, 9(1), 75–100.

Corntassel, J.J. and Primeau, T.H. (1995). Indigenous 'sovereignty' and international law: Revised strategies for pursuing 'self-determination'. *Human Rights Quarterly*, 12(2), 343–65.

Crichlow, W. (2002). Western colonization as disease: Native adoption and cultural genocide. *Critical Social Work*, 3(1) [Online]. Available at: http://www.criticalsocialwork.com/# [accessed: 29 February 2012].

Devore, W. and Schlesinger, E.G. (1987). *Ethnic Sensitive Social Work Practice* (2nd edn). Columbus, OH: Merrill.

Dominelli, L. (1997). *Antiracist Social Work* (2nd edn). London: Macmillan.

Friedman, J. (1999). Indigenous struggles and the discreet charm of the bourgeoisie. *Journal of World-Systems Research*, 5(2), 391–411.

Gair, S. (2008). Missing the 'Flight from Responsibility': Tales from a non-Indigenous educator pursuing spaces for social work education relevant to Indigenous Australians. In M. Gray, Coates, J. and Yellow Bird, M. (eds), *Indigenous Social Work around the World: Towards Culturally Relevant Education and Practice*. Aldershot: Ashgate, 219–30.

Gair, S., Thomson, J. and Miles, D. (2005). Reconciling Indigenous and non-Indigenous knowledges in social work education: Action and legitimacy. *Journal of Social Work Education*, 41(2), 371–82 [Online]. Available at: http://www.cswe.org/CSWE/publications/journal/ [accessed: 29 February 2012].

Gilchrist, L. (1997). Aboriginal communities and social science research: Voyeurism in transition. *Native Social Work Journal*, 1(1), 69–85.

Gilbert, S. (2008). Review of *Social Work with Indigenous Communities*, by L. Briskman. *Australian Social Work*, 61(4), 436–8.

Giulianotti, R. and Robertson, R. (2009). *Globalization and Football*. London: Sage

Gray M. (2005). Dilemmas of international social work: Paradoxical processes in indigenization, imperialism and universalism. *International Journal of Social Welfare*, 14(2), 230–37.

Gray, M. and Coates, J. (2008). From Indigenization to Cultural Relevance. In M. Gray, Coates, J. and Yellow Bird, M. (eds), *Indigenous Social Work around the World: Towards Culturally Relevant Education and Practice*. Aldershot: Ashgate, 13–29.

Gray, M. and Webb, S.A. (eds). (2013). *The New Politics of Social Work*. Basingstoke: Palgrave.

Gray, M., Coates, J. and Hetherington, T. (2007). Hearing Indigenous voices in mainstream social work. *Families in Society*, 88(1), 55–66.

Gray, M., Coates, J. and Yellow Bird, M. (eds). (2008). *Indigenous Social Work around the World: Towards Culturally Relevant Education and Practice*. Aldershot: Ashgate.

Gray, M. and Fook, J. (2004). The quest for universal social work: Some issues and implications. *Social Work Education*, 23(5), 625–44.

Gray, M. and Valentine, B. (2005). Devising practice standards for Aboriginal out-of-home care. *Illinois Child Welfare*, 2(1–2), 116–23.

Green, J.W. (1982). *Cultural Awareness in the Human Services*. Englewood Cliffs, NJ: Prentice-Hall.

Hart, M.A. (2002). *Seeking Mino-Pimatisiwin: An Aboriginal Approach to Healing*. Halifax, Canada: Fernwood Publishing.

Hart, M.A. (2003). Am I a modern day missionary? Reflections of a Cree social worker. *Native Social Work Journal*, 5, 299–313.

Harper-Dorton, K.V. and Lantz, J.E. (2007). *Crosscultural Practice: Social Work with Diverse Populations*. Chicago, IL: Lyceum Books.

Hetherington, T. (2009). Indigenous social work: A comparative study of New Brunswick (Canada) and Alice Springs (Australia). Unpublished doctoral thesis, University of Newcastle, Newcastle, Australia.

Hodge, D., Limb, G. and Cross, T. (2009). Moving from colonization toward balance and harmony: A Native American perspective on wellness. *Social Work*, 54(3), 211–19.

hooks, b. (1990). *Yearning: Race, Gender and Cultural Politics*. Toronto, ON: Between the Lines.

How Kee, L. (2003). Drawing lessons from locally designated helpers to develop culturally appropriate social work practice. *Asia Pacific Journal of Social Work*, 13(2), 26–45.

How Kee, L. (2008). The Development of Culturally Appropriate Social Work Practice in Sarawak, Malaysia. In M. Gray, Coates, J. and Yellow Bird, M. (eds), *Indigenous Social Work around the World: Towards Culturally Relevant Education and Practice*. Aldershot: Ashgate, 97–106.

Hudson, P. and McKenzie, B. (2003). Extending Aboriginal control over child welfare services: The Manitoba child welfare initiative. *Canadian Review of Social Policy*, 51, 49–66.

Hughes, L. (2003). *The No-Nonsense Guide to Indigenous Peoples*. Oxford: New Internationalist Publications in association with Verso.

Hurdle, D.E. (2002). Native Hawaiian traditional healing: Culturally based interventions for social work practice. *Social Work*, 47(2), 183–92.

Ives, N., Aitken, O., Loft, M. and Phillips, M. (2007). Rethinking social work education for Indigenous students: Creating space for multiple ways of knowing and learning. *First Peoples Child and Family Review*, 3(4), 13–20.

International Work Group for Indigenous Affairs (IWGIA). (2009). *Indigenous Peoples: Who Are They?* [Online]. Available at: http://www.iwgia.org/sw641. asp [accessed: 23 March 2010].

Limb, G., Hodge, D. and Panos, P. (2008). Social work with Native people: Orienting child welfare workers to the beliefs, values and practices of Native American families and children. *Journal of Public Child Welfare*, 2(3), 383–97.

Little Bear, L. (2000). Jagged Worldviews Colliding. In M. Battiste (ed.), *Reclaiming Indigenous Voice and Vision*. Vancouver, Canada: University of British Columbia Press, 77–85.

Lum, D. (1999). *Culturally Competent Practice: A Framework for Growth and Action*. Pacific Grove, CA: Brooks/Cole.

Lynn, R. (2001). Learning from a Murri way. *British Journal of Social Work*, 31(6), 903–16.

Lynn, R., Pye, R., Atkinson, R. and Peyton-Smith, J. (1990). Anti-Racist Welfare Education: Pie in the sky? In J. Petruchenia and Thorpe, R. (eds), *Social Change and Welfare Practice*. Sydney, Australia: Hale & Iremonger, 83–5.

Lynn, R., Thorpe, R., Miles, D., Butcher, A., Cutts, C. and Ford, L. (1998). *Murri Way! Aborigines and Torres Strait Islanders Reconstruct Social Welfare Practice*. Townsville, Australia: Centre for Social Research, James Cook University.

Mafile'o, T. (2004). Exploring Tongan social work. *Qualitative Social Work*, 3(3), 239–57.

Malife'o, T. (2008). Tongan Social Work Practice. In M. Gray, Coates, J. and Yellow Bird, M. (eds), *Indigenous Social Work around the World: Towards Culturally Relevant Education and Practice*. Aldershot: Ashgate, 121–34.

Manuel, G. and Posluns, M. (1974). *The Fourth World: An Indian Reality*. New York: The Free Press.

Marais, L. and Marais, L.C. (2007). Walking between worlds: An exploration of the interface between Indigenous and first-world industrialized culture. *International Social Work*, 50(6), 809–20.

Margolin, L. (1997). *Under the Cover of Kindness: The Invention of Social Work*. Charlottesville, VA: University of Virginia Press.

McKenzie, B. and Morrissette, V. (2003). Social Work Practice with Canadians of Aboriginal background: Guidelines for respectful social work. In A. Al-Krenawi and Graham, J.R. (eds), *Multicultural Social Work in Canada: Working with Diverse Ethno-Racial Communities*. Toronto, Canada: Oxford University Press, 251–82.

Midgley, J. (1981). *Professional Imperialism: Social Work in the Third World*. London: Heinemann Educational Books.

Midgley, J. (2008). Promoting Reciprocal International Social Work Exchanges: Professional imperialism revisited. In M. Gray, Coates, J. and Yellow Bird, M. (eds), *Indigenous Social Work around the World: Towards Culturally Relevant Education and Practice*. Aldershot: Ashgate, 31–45.

Mullaly, B. (2009). *Challenging Oppression and Confronting Privilege*. Toronto, ON: Oxford.

Nakata, M. (2006). Australian Indigenous studies: A question of discipline. *The Australian Journal of Anthropology*, 17(3), 265–75.

Nakata, M. (2007). *Disciplining the Savages: Savaging the Disciplines*. Canberra, Australia: Aboriginal Studies Press.

Nimmagadda, J. and Martel, D.R. (2008). Home-Made Social Work: The two-way transfer of social work practice knowledge between India and the USA. In M. Gray, Coates, J. and Yellow Bird, M. (eds), *Indigenous Social Work around the World: Towards Culturally Relevant Education and Practice*. Aldershot: Ashgate, 141–52.

Ormiston, N.T. (2010). Re-conceptualizing research: An Indigenous perspective. *First Peoples Child and Family Review*, 5(1), 50–6.

Osei-Hwedie, K. (1993). The challenge of social work in Africa: Starting the indigenisation process. *Journal of Social Development in Africa*, 8(1), 19–30.

Paradies, Y.C. (2006). Beyond black and white: Essentialism, hybridity and Indigeneity. *Journal of Sociology*, 42(4), 355–67.

Poonwassie, A. and Charter, A. (2005). An Aboriginal Worldview of Healing: Inclusion, blending and bridging. In R. Moodley and West, W. (eds), *Integrating Traditional Healing Practices into Counseling and Psychotherapy*. Thousand Oaks, CA: Sage, 15–25.

Porter, R. (2005). The Decolonization of Indigenous Governance. In W.A. Wilson and Yellow Bird, M. (eds), *For Indigenous Eyes Only: A Decolonization Handbook*. Santa Fe, NM: School of American Research Press.

Pozzuto, R., Angell, B. and Dezendorf, P. (2005). Therapeutic Critique: Traditional versus critical perspectives. In S. Hick, Fook, J. and Pozzuto, R. (eds), *Social Work: A Critical Turn*. Toronto: Thomson, 25–38.

Scott, J.C. (2009). *The Art of Not Being Governed: An Anarchist History of Upland Southeast Asia*. New Haven, CT: Yale University Press.

Shawky, A. (1972). Social work education in Africa. *International Social Work*, 15(1), 3–16.

Sinclair, R. (2003). *Participatory Action Research: Aboriginal and Indigenous Social Work* [Online]. Available at: http://www.aboriginalsocialwork.ca/ [accessed: 29 February 2012].

Sinclair, R. (2004). Aboriginal social work education in Canada: Decolonizing pedagogy for the seventh generation. *First Peoples Child and Family Review*, 1(1), 49–61 [Online]. Available at: http://www.fncfcs.com/pubs/onlineJournal. html [accessed: 29 February 2012].

Sinclair, R., Hart, M.A. and Bruyere, G. (2009). *Wicihitowin: Aboriginal Social Work in Canada*. Halifax, Canada: Fernwood Press.

Smith, L.T. (1999). *Decolonizing Methodologies: Research and Indigenous Peoples*. New York, NY: St. Martin's Press.

Stamatopoulou, E. (1994). Indigenous Peoples and the United Nations: Human rights as a developing dynamic. *Human Rights Quarterly*, 16(1), 58–81.

Thibodeau, S. and Peigan, F.N. (2007). Loss of trust among First Nation people: Implications when implementing child protection initiatives. *First Peoples Child and Family Review*, 3(4), 50–8 [Online]. Available at: http://www. fncfcs.com/pubs/onlineJournal.html [accessed: 29 February 2012].

Tsang, A.K.T. and Yan, M-C. (2001). Chinese corpus, western application: The Chinese strategy of engagement with western social work discourse. *International Social Work*, 44(4), 433–54.

Tsang, A., Yan, M. and Shera, W. (2000). Negotiating multiple agendas in international social work: The case of the China–Canada collaborative project. In Social Work and Globalisation, *Canadian Social Work Special Issue*, 2(1), 147–61.

Ungar, M. (2004). Surviving as a postmodern social worker: Two Ps and three Rs of direct practice. *Social Work*, 49(3), 488–96.

United Nations General Assembly. (2008). *United Nations Declaration on the Rights of Indigenous Peoples* [Online]. Available at: http://www.un.org/esa/socdev/unpfii/documents/DRIPS_en.pdf [accessed: 29 February 2012].

Valentine, B. and Gray, M. (2006). Keeping them home: Aboriginal out-of-home care in Australia. *Families in Society*, 87(4), 537–45.

Voss, R.W., Douville, V., Little Soldier, A. and Twiss, G. (1999). Tribal and shamanic-based social work practice: A Lakota perspective. *Social Work*, 44(3), 228–41.

Waller, M. and Patterson, S. (2002). Natural helping and resilience in a Dine (Navajo) community. *Families in Society*, 83(1), 73–84.

Walmsley, C. (2004). Talking about the Aboriginal community: Child protection practitioners' views. *First Peoples Child and Family Review*, 1(1), 63–71.

Waterfall, B. (2002). Native people and the social work profession: A critical exploration of colonizing problematics and the development of decolonized thought. *Journal of Educational Thought*, 36(2), 149–66.

Weaver, H.N. (2000). Culture and professional education: The experiences of Native American social workers. *Journal of Social Work Education*, 36(3), 415–28.

Weaver, H.N. (2001). Indigenous identity: What is it, and who really has it? *American Indian Quarterly*, 25(2), 240–55.

Weaver, H.N. (2004). The elements of cultural competence: Applications with Native American clients. *Journal of Ethnic and Cultural Diversity in Social Work*, 13(1), 19–35.

Weaver, H.N. (2008). Indigenous Social Work in the United States: Reflections on Indian tacos, Trojan horses and canoes filled with Indigenous revolutionaries. In M. Gray, Coates, J. and Yellow Bird, M. (eds), *Indigenous Social Work around the World: Towards Culturally Relevant Education and Practice*. Aldershot: Ashgate, 71–82.

Weaver, H.N. and Congress, E. (2009). Indigenous People in a landscape of risk: Teaching social work students about socially just social work responses. *Journal of Ethnic and Cultural Diversity in Social Work*, 18(1), 166–79.

Yan, M.C. and Cheung, K.W. (2006). The politics of indigenization: A case study of development of Social Work in China. *Journal of Sociology and Social Welfare*, 33(2), 63–83.

Yan, M.C. and Tsang, A.K.T. (2008). Re-Envisioning Indigenization: When *bentuhuade* and *bentude* social work intersect in China. In Gray, M., Coates, J. and Yellow Bird, M. (eds), *Indigenous Social Work around the world: Towards Culturally Relevant Education and Practice*. Aldershot: Ashgate, 191–202.

Yan, M.C. and Tsui, M.S. (2007). The quest for Western social work knowledge: Literature in the USA and practice in China. *International Social Work*, 50(5), 641–53.

Yang, R. (2005). Internationalisation, indigenisation and educational research in China. *Australian Journal of Education*, 49(1), 66–88.

Yellow Bird, M. (1999a). What we want to be called: Indigenous Peoples' perspectives of racial and ethnic identity. *American Indian Quarterly*, 23(2), 1–21.

Yellow Bird, M. (1999b). Indian, American Indian and Native American: Counterfeit identities. *Winds of Change*, 14(1), 86.

Yellow Bird, M. (2008). Terms of Endearment: A brief dictionary for decolonizing social work with Indigenous Peoples. Postscript. In M. Gray, Coates, J. and Yellow Bird, M. (eds), *Indigenous Social Work around the World: Towards Culturally Relevant Education and Practice*. Aldershot: Ashgate, 271–91.

Yellow Bird, M. and Chenault, V. (1999). The Role of Social Work in Advancing the Practice of Indigenous Education: Obstacles and promises in empowerment orientated social work practice. In K.G. Swichser and Tippeconnic, J.W. (eds), *Next Steps: Research and Practice to Advance Indian Education* (3rd edn). Charleston, WV: ERIC Clearinghouse on Rural Education and Small Schools, 201–35.

Yellow Bird, M. and Gray, M. (2008). Indigenous People and the Language of Social Work. In M. Gray, Coates, J. and Yellow Bird, M. (eds), *Indigenous Social Work around the World: Towards Culturally Relevant Education and Practice*. Aldershot: Ashgate, 49–58.

Young, S. (2008). Indigenous child protection policy in Australia: Using whiteness theory for social work. *SITES*, 5(1), 102–23.

Young, W.D. (1999). Aboriginal students speak about acceptance, sharing, awareness and support: A participatory approach to change at a university and community college. *Native Social Work Journal*, 2(1), 21–58.

Yuen-Tsang, A.W.K. and Wang, S. (2002). Tensions confronting the development of social work education in China: Challenges and opportunities. *International Social Work*, 45(3), 375–88.

Yunong, H. and Xiong, Z. (2008). A reflection on the indigenization discourse in social work. *International Social Work*, 51(5), 611–22.

Chapter 1

Indigenization, Indigenous Social Work and Decolonization: Mapping the Theoretical Terrain

Mel Gray and Tiani Hetherington

This opening chapter attempts to map the complex theoretical terrain of Indigenous social work, a term used to describe First Nations (in North America) or Aboriginal (in Australia) social work and seen by people in North America and Australia and New Zealand as specific to a form of practice with minority Indigenous populations in mainly Western societies. Embracing Indigenous social work means being comfortable with uncertainty and diversity rather than attempting to condense complex histories and cultures into measureable units of analysis. Indigenous social work is far more comfortable with, and deals better with, uncertainty and complexity than Western social work (Gray, Coates and Yellow Bird, 2008).

This resistance can be seen in the history of the term 'indigenization', which has its origins in Africa. Its repeated use in relation to 'making Western approaches relevant' gives a clear message that Western approaches do not fit (see Chapter 2 and Gray and Coates, 2008 for a history of the use of this term in social work). The term 'making social work indigenous' has been used in Africa and Asia for decades to highlight the imperialism of Western social work (Midgley, 1981).

Not only do the discourses vary globally but there are also tensions between the global and the local – between internationalizing and localizing processes – and the way in which globalization is understood for this affects people's views about its effect on local processes and practices (Gray, 2005). This impact is often expressed as 'homogenization' – a process in which local cultures and practices are distilled with wider ones. Since these issues arise mainly in contexts where local cultures feel threatened – and where due to their history, concerted attempts are being made to recover, reclaim, or maintain traditional cultural practices and languages – they are considered problematic. This does not necessarily mean that heterogenization – or the coexistence of many cultures – is preferred, for, as is shown below, another dynamic comes into play that has been conceptualized as essentialism and hybridity. It is with this complex theoretical terrain as reflected in the challenges of terminology discussed in the Introduction, that this opening chapter maps the theoretical landscape of Indigenous social work for discussion in subsequent chapters.

Towards Cultural Relevance

While historically the literature on 'indigenization' developed mainly in relation to social work practice in developing countries in Africa, Asia and South America (see, for example, Asamoah and Beverley, 1988; Brigham, 1982; Campfen, 1988; Hammoud, 1988; Shawky, 1972; Walton and Abo El Nasr, 1988), China presents an interesting contemporary case study for those interested in international social work or, more specifically, in the transfer of Western social work to non-Western contexts (Gray, 2005, 2008). While not a central focus in this volume, the Chinese experience has spawned a growing literature on the emergence of culturally relevant social work education in China in the last 15 years (see, for example, Tsang, Yan and Shera, 2000; Tsang and Yan, 2001; Yan and Tsui, 2007; Yuen-Tsang and Wang, 2002) and has reignited debates on the 'indigenization' of social work (see, for example, Cheng, 2008; Hutchings and Taylor, 2007; Gray, 2008; Jia, 2008; Yunong and Xiong, 2008). It offers a good example of the way in which many of the terms and concepts relating to decolonizing social work are played out.

As a result, it might be argued that a new field of knowledge development, namely, 'indigenized social work' could be emerging which 'independent of its imported origins … stands on its own in addressing local problems and in providing its own local training and textbooks' (Adair, 1999: 415). 'Indigenization' requires sensitivity to local cultures and contexts but time has come to extend the debate beyond 'indigenization as making social work fit local contexts' (Gray et al., 2008). It is also necessary to critique the ethnocentric nature of the 'indigenization' discourse and the approaches used in knowledge development to discern what might be involved in extending Indigenous research. Rather than a mere strategically planned process of disciplinary development – as it is portrayed in the social work literature, 'indigenization' is also a naturally occurring process when foreign and local cultures come into contact with one another be that within Western contexts, between Western and non-Western contexts, or within non-Western contexts. It follows that *an exclusively ethnocentric form of Indigenous social work would be counterproductive to forms of practice that incorporate knowledge and interventions from other cultures*. In fact has this not been one of the major concerns within mainstream social work in regards to professional practice in multicultural contexts? It has spawned a variety of approaches to deal with diversity, such as culturally sensitive and culturally competent social work practice but these have more often addressed minority issues in Western contexts rather than the development of culturally relevant social work education and practice in non-Western contexts (see Gray et al., 2008 for a fuller discussion of this).

The existing social work literature on 'indigenization' questions the relevance of Western social work as a professional model of practice with universal application. It is part of the profession's continuing struggle with diversity, specifically its inability to work effectively with people from non-Western cultures. Calls for 'indigenization' originated – and continue to arise – from the growing realization of the limitations of Western research, education and practice models (Gray et al., 2008). They have spawned 'a deepening sensitivity to the rich potential that exists in local customs and behaviours peculiarly driven by indigenous traditions' (Adair, 1999: 405). *A current understanding of 'indigenization' holds that social work knowledge should arise from within the culture, reflect local behaviours and practices, be interpreted within a local frame of reference, and thus be locally relevant, that is, it should address culturally relevant and context-specific problems.* Indigenization calls for Indigenous research that emanates from, adequately represents and reflects back upon the cultural context in which problems arise. Thus the development of Indigenous knowledge is reflexive and requires that researchers – and social workers – integrate their reflections on local cultures, society and history into their work (see How Kee, 2008; Nimmagadda and Balgopal, 2000; Yang, 2005)

Indigenous social work insists upon cultural relevance and culturally specific knowledges and practices, *which may or may not be universal or even cross-Indigenous* (for example, Hart, 2002; Lynn, 2001). There are two streams of literature pertaining to Indigenous social work, and both relate to contexts where there is a history of colonization. One arises in developing nations in Africa, Asia and South America and another in developed Western contexts, like the USA, Canada and Australia, where it is associated primarily with professional education and practice relating to Aboriginal or First Nations Peoples. However, regardless of origin, an Indigenous social work that results from indigenized knowledge development processes is not necessarily only a social work of and for Aboriginal or First Nations people nor is it exclusive to developing countries (Gray et al., 2008). It refers to a form of social work which seeks effective culturally appropriate research, education and practice. *In this sense it is a decolonized form of social work.* It also refers to attempts to make dominant or mainstream models relevant to culturally diverse client populations. Although not without its critics, Family Group Conferencing, which originated in New Zealand, is an example of an Indigenous social work model that has enjoyed cross-cultural application (Shlonsky et al., 2009; Sundell and Vinnerljung, 2004).

Juxtaposed against processes of 'indigenization' are attempts by social work to internationalize, that is, to continue spreading the profession to as many countries as possible around the world in the belief that social work is useful in solving personal and social problems wherever it is practised. Unlike globalization of trade that relates to the spread of global capitalism, with which it is often confused, *internationalization refers to increased interaction among people and cultures that focuses on mutual understanding and respect* (Yang, 2005). But, as Gray (2005) noted, internationalization is not without its problems for it often leads to, or opens doors to, universalization and adaptation. This often makes it more difficult to develop Indigenous theory and practice, as Yang (2005: 66) says, 'free from the tyranny of massive and totalising ideologies'. Often, though, those who seek to internationalize, that is, universalize, social work, fail to question its transportability across cultures and languages or its relevance to the contexts in which it is being transplanted (Yunong and Xiong, 2008). There is too the paradoxical question of how something that is imported can be Indigenous – how a universal social work might simultaneously be culturally relevant (see Gray, 2005; Gray and Fook, 2004). Replicating social work – its theories, concepts, methods, standards of education and so on – does not chart new ground for the development of Indigenous social work. It merely repeats forms of education and practice in new contexts or extends the reach of international social work. Thus Indigenous social work is not just about making models of education and practice fit new contexts. It is also about the development of local, empirically based knowledge about culturally appropriate solutions to particular contexts (see Gray et al., 2008; Gray and Fook, 2004).

Indigenous social work thus seeks to highlight the unique culture and consequent plight of particular minority cultures and, in so doing, insists upon 'culturally sensitive' and culturally specific knowledges and practices. First Nations' Indigenous social work has in many contexts, but especially in Canada, Australia and the USA, emerged to meet the needs of Indigenous groups in an effort to overcome the aftermath and injustices of assimilation, isolation and cultural displacement perpetrated by colonizers with the firm belief that they were divinely guided to strip Indigenous Peoples of their children and culture, lands and rights, and many in the USA today still hold to these beliefs.

It is thus not just an effort to find effective local personal and family interventions, it is also a political process that incorporates history and cultural priorities, seeks to redress colonization and establish a mainstream model that is effective and relevant for particular populations. As a specific form of indigenized social work, its goal is to make the profession and discipline of social work relevant or applicable to the particular culture of the – Indigenous – client.

One can easily see tensions emerging here between models that are exclusive and singularly dedicated to a particular culture, and an approach that seeks effectiveness and cultural relevance. Merely increasing the number of Indigenous case studies or the number of Indigenous social workers or scholarly contributions by them, or research on what is unique and different in Indigenous cultures, does not necessarily lead to Indigenous social work (Weaver, 2000). A theorist or researcher who accepts the need for Indigenous social work in terms of one of these models may research culturally unique traits, concepts or practices without regard to how commonly they occur, how widely they are accepted, how they integrate conceptually, or how meaningful they are for contemporary research, education and practice (see Adair, 1999). This is compounded by urban-rural differences which are a major issue in Canada and Australia as the needs of Indigenous people living in urban communities are frequently overlooked in the social work discourse, with some exceptions (Baldry, Green and Thorpe, 2006; Levin and Herbert, 2004). The practical reality is that there are very large proportions of Indigenous people living in cities whose lives are urban and they are often physically, and sometimes socially, disconnected from their First Nations or Indigenous communities (which was, of course, one of the goals of colonization). For example, there is considerable public attention to the horrible conditions in many First Nations communities but very little attention to urban realities where about half the Indigenous population resides.

Rethinking the Interplay between the Local and the Global

Rethinking Globalization

Globalization is a highly contested concept (see Giulianotti and Robertson, 2009; Hopkins, 2002; Martell, 2010). Rather than merely a contemporary economic process that aims to remove barriers to international trade, Robertson interprets globalization as a 'long-term, complex and multi-phased historical process, underpinned by subtle and shifting interdependence between the local and the global, or the universal and the particular' (in Giulianotti and Robertson, 2009: xiv). Giulianotti and Robertson (2009: 1) distinguish between two models of globalization: 'world globalization' and 'global globalization'. They link the former to 'the historical emergence and international diffusion of Western modernization – notably capitalism, industrialism and bureaucratization – from the nineteenth century onwards'. The latter, however, might be more akin to our analysis of decolonizing social work for it includes 'an appreciation of how ancient civilizations, Islam, south and east Asia, and Africa, for example, have constructed distinctive forms of globality and have contributed to particular kinds of transcultural interdependence' (Giulianotti and Robertson, 2009: 1). Global globalization 'posits in part that non-Western societies modernize in distinctive and selective ways relative to the West' (Giulianotti and Robertson, 2009: 2). In this way, rather than 'a 'triumph of the West' over the rest', global globalization leads to 'increased concrete interdependencies of societies and to the greater consciousness of the world as a whole' (Giulianotti and Robertson, 2009: 2).

Giulianotti and Robertson (2009), drawing on Robertson's (1992) earlier work on the phases of globalization, examine several historical epochs over the past 500 years in the process of global globalization. The first phase of globalization that they call the *germinal* phase is crucial for Indigenous Peoples for it was the period of colonial subjugation as Europe spread its influence from the early fifteenth to the mid eighteenth century (the second phase). The third *take-off* phase saw 'a strong accentuation of principles of national self-determination and identification' (Giulianotti and Robertson, 2009: 4) and the fourth – *struggle-for-hegemony* – the creation of the Third World. In the fifth *uncertainty* phase – from the late-1960s to 2000 – notions of global 'civil society' and global citizenship come to the fore in the face of contemporary 'risks', such as the militant Islamism which emerged as the West's radical other. It is in this phase that Indigenous struggles for recognition began with the formation of the

International Work Group for Indigenous Affairs (IWGIA),[1] an international human rights organization created by human rights activists and anthropologists in 1968 to support Indigenous Peoples worldwide.

Giulianotti and Robertson (2009: xv) believe that globalization has entered a sixth, 'millennial' stage since 2000, distinguished in part by a climate of fear alongside the intensification of surveillance and security across social settings' (see also Scott, 2009). Following their analysis and interpretation, we might see social work as *the highly complex interplay between the global and the local, or between the particular and the universal* (see Gray, 2005). We might see Indigenous social work as similarly driven, given more recent attempts to develop an Indigenous Peoples' bill of rights, to organize international conferences on Indigenous social work and to foster a global identity for Indigenous social workers. At the same time, Indigenous social work takes on a particular hue – and varying degrees of saturation – to use a photographic metaphor, in local contexts, as the chapters in this book show (see also Gray et al., 2008).

Giulianotti and Robertson (2009) provide an interesting framework from which to view the history of Indigenous Peoples whose identity centres on the legacy of colonial subjugation during the *germinal* and *incipient* phases in their model. Disputes surround the determination of who the First Peoples were, and their rights to land claims, given the history of migration of the world's peoples. Generally, however, Indigenous people are those who were found living on the lands the colonists sought to conquer and appropriate during this period. The death and destruction and political and cultural subjugation of these peoples has left scars to the present day where Indigenous Peoples still constitute the poorest of the world's population and remain minority cultures. This is the legacy of colonial subjugation and the rise of modern Western culture following the Enlightenment of the *incipient* phase. During this period, the Aborigine's Protection Society (APS) was formed in London in 1837 by prominent abolitionists, who realized that emancipation from slavery had not diminished the problem of European exploitation of Aborigines. At this time, Aborigine referred to non-whites and not necessarily First Peoples. In New Zealand the Waitangi Treaty (see Chapters 7 and 13) was signed in 1840 and in Ghana – West Africa – the first African APS was launched in 1897 (see Chapter 9).

European colonization met with strong resistance from Indigenous Peoples during this period. Hughes (2003) marks 1876 as a historic moment when the Indians triumphed at the battle of Little Bighorn, recorded in European history as Custer's Last Stand. But retribution was exacted with intensified force – here, as in Africa and South America and other regions of the world, where colonists encountered strong resistance and won some victories.

Despite Indigenous resistance and the abolitionist movement, the loss of Indigenous cultures and languages was intensified by modernization projects

---

1   See http://www.iwgia.org/sw617.asp – note 'indigenous peoples' is not capitalized on this website.

in the *take-off* phase from the 1870s to the mid-1920s, most importantly the spread of Western Christianity. Indigenous Peoples were forced off their lands onto Christian mission stations and into residential boarding schools that sought to assimilate them into Western culture. This meant conversion to Christianity and forsaking traditional languages, values and practices. Overlooked was the existing structure of governance and social organization of Indigenous cultures, which closely identified with land, ancestors, tribe, kin and clan, a structure that long-preceded European colonization. Two key historic developments during this phase in Lotte Hughes' (2003) history is the formation in the early 1920s of the Alaskan Native Brotherhood and Society for American Indians and the unsuccessful challenge – mounted in 1923 – by Deskaheh, an Indigenous leader from the Iroquois Confederacy to seek help from the League of Nations in Geneva in their dispute with the Canadian Government.

Social work emerges during this period and is strongly identified with the colonial 'civilizing' mission, being part of the system of child removal that perpetuated into the *struggle-for-hegemony* phase of the mid-1920s to the late-1960s (such as the Stolen Generations in Australia, residential schools and the 60s scoop in Canada, see Human Rights and Equal Opportunity Commission (HREOC), 1997 and Sinclair, 2004). In the subsequent *uncertainty* phase up until the turn of the century, the Indigenous movement grew in strength in tandem with the independence struggles of colonized peoples, decolonization, the rise of Red Power in North America and Black Power in the USA, the flowering of the human rights movement, and the advent of the United Nations (Hughes, 2003). Two North American Councils formed in the USA and Canada in 1974 and 1977 respectively led to the first international non-government conference focusing on Indigenous issues in Geneva in 1977. From then on the international Indigenous movement gained in intensity and became increasingly politicized with the explosion of civil society organizations among the world's poor in the South across Africa, South America and Asia-Pacific region. In the sixth *millennial* phase, these protests became linked to the anti-globalization movement, and consciousness-raising projects grew through the Internet. Among the main projects is the move to have Indigenous remains returned to their ancestral lands (Hughes, 2003). As noted by Gray et al. (2008), for the Indigenous Peoples' struggle, globalization meant a new form of colonizing expansion but unlike imperialistic modernization, it could be harnessed to raise awareness of Indigenous rights and the plight of the world's Indigenous Peoples. At the same time, the focus on climate change and impending ecological disasters has rekindled interest in Indigenous knowledges and understandings of environmental sustainability (see Gray, Coates, and Hetherington, 2013).

Rethinking the Homogenization-Heterogenization Debate

In the social sciences, concepts like culture, identity, agency and self-determination are used to decipher the way in which local – and Indigenous – cultures engage with 'the global'. Giulianotti and Robertson (2009: 31) note how 'the arising arguments are often predicated upon conventional binary oppositions – notably between the local and the global, or the particular and the universal – and are flavoured by a critical preference for one perspective over the other'. In this regard, they draw attention to:

> an axial problem in the sociology of globalization … the homogenization-heterogenization debate. Homogenization arguments generally posit that globalization is marked by growing cultural convergence at the transnational level. Conversely, heterogenization arguments contend that global processes maintain or facilitate cultural diversity or divergence [although] … rival 'schools of thought' tend not to strike absolutist poses. (Giulianotti and Robertson, 2009: 38)

Thereafter, they examine these two conceptual or theoretical orientations in more detail:

> Homogenization theories posit that social actors and their local cultures are orchestrated into passively absorbing or otherwise reproducing the cultural products, practices, and predilections of the world's most powerful corporations and nations … [T]hese theories of global cultural convergence have produced a diversity of keywords and theories, such as cultural imperialism, synchronization, Americanization, Westernization, and globalization [sic]. (Giulianotti and Robertson, 2009: 38–9)

By way of contrast, theories of cultural heterogenization pivot on a variety of keywords, notably 'creolization', 'indigenization' and 'vernacularization' (Giulianotti and Robertson, 2009: 41). Perhaps of most immediate interest, particularly for developed societies, indigenization registers 'an increasing fragmentation of identities, the break-up of larger identity units, the emergence of cultural politics among Indigenous, regional, immigrant, and even national populations' (Friedman, 1999: 391, cited in Giulianotti and Robertson, 2009: 41–2). Giulianotti and Robertson (2009: 32), in proceeding to their substantive analysis of 'football's cultural globalisation', emphasize – and go on to exemplify consistently throughout – the *interdependencies* between the global and the local. It is these kinds of interdependencies that we are trying to discern in this book. Rather than perpetuate binary oppositions, we aim to create a space for dialogue on the ways in which forces of globalization and localization – homogenization and heterogenization – are playing out in particular contexts. Rankopo and Osei-Hwedie (2011), for example, provide an example of the difficulties of developing locally and culturally relevant social work education in a university environment pushing for internationalization, and there are a growing number of empirical case studies of the tensions between these processes in social work (see Gray et al., 2008).

In social work, as in football, there are 'trends towards both commonality or uniformity and divergence and differentiation' (Giulianotti and Robertson, 2009: xv) captured more fully by the broad homogenization-heterogenization opposition 'which registers trends towards *cultural* convergence and divergence' (Giulianotti and Robertson, 2009: xv, emphasis added). Conventional binary oppositions place cultural imperialism at one end of the continuum and compensatory resistance grounded in local identity and cultural reclamation at the other. Rather than perpetuate irresolvable differences, Giulianotti and Robertson (2009: 31) point to the 'need to 'account for the complexity of cultural globalization' by appreciating 'the intensive analytical and empirical *interdependencies* of the global and the local, or the universal and the particular' (original emphasis).

Bearing this in mind, we need to accept that social work varies greatly across diverse international contexts, mainly because it remains *nationally* rooted in specific social policies while seeking a common international professional identity. It has organs of internationalization – like the International Federation of Social Workers (IFSW) and International Association of Schools of Social Work (IASSW) – that seek a common international definition of social work and global education standards, despite the increasing variability and degrees of relevance of social work across diverse international contexts (Gray and Webb, 2008; Gray et al., 2008).

In the same way, Indigenous Peoples are seeking a common identity for Indigenous social work by harnessing the benefits of internationalizing processes. While social justice was a major factor in the emergence of social work, for much of the twentieth century, mainstream Western social work was strongly associated with the history of colonization and modernization, but the profession has started once again to embrace a strong social justice and human rights culture that has the potential to work in the interests of Indigenous Peoples and cultural minorities (see Finn and Jacobson, 2003). Rather than see social work as hemmed in by two historical influences: colonization and globalization, it might be more useful to recognize that we are living in a post-colonial global society where there is 'legitimacy of difference' and 'the development of transnational standards of citizenship and rights' (Yeatman, 2000: 95). However, the term 'post-colonial' is somewhat problematic for Indigenous Peoples as it implies that colonization is 'finished business.' Hence Smith (1999: 25) asks, 'Post-colonial? What? Have they left yet?'. Nevertheless, post-colonial scholars, such as Young (2003: 4), maintain that post-colonialism can be regarded as an activity of liberation since it 'names a politics and philosophy of activism that contests that disparity, and so continues in a new way the anti-colonial struggles of the past'.

Given that the 'politics of difference' is tied to the recognition of minority groups, it represents a challenge to the homogenizing effects of neo-liberal individualism and its implications for *national* health and welfare provision. It denotes a multiculturalism that respects cultural diversity in both the private and public spheres and requires structural pluralism, a system that is responsive to people's special needs, even if they constitute a minority group (see Husband, 2000). However, multiculturalism is also problematic for Indigenous Peoples. As Weaver (1998) and Voss, Douville, Little Soldier and Twiss (1999) assert, Indigenous Peoples are not just ethnic or cultural minorities within a larger society; they are more than a special client population or social problem group. As we have seen, however, movements that strive to foster a unique cultural identity, such as Indigenous in the First Nations' sense, seek a special kind of recognition and attention that calls for the highlighting of difference. Ways need to be found to do this without setting up an oppositional position whereby Indigenous identity is located in the fissures where mainstream social work does not fit. Rather than focus solely on how Indigenous social work differs from Western social work in laying claim to what is unique about Indigenous cultures, histories and politics, ways need to be found to harness Indigenous social work's inherently *critical* stance for the good of the profession as a whole and *vice versa*. Staying at the cultural imperialism end of the continuum merely locks us into a 'them and us' discourse. This is counterproductive because Indigenous Peoples are invariably minorities in the societies in which they are situated and, from the perspective of the politics of difference – or the theory of cultural recognition – they are always constructed – by themselves and others as 'Other' (Paradies, 2006; Sinclair, 2004). The recognition discourse creates a space for the creation of homogeneous categories that require some sort of 'special recognition' while respecting the cultures of others as well as an international professional identity. This more nuanced standpoint 'highlights the complex interdependencies between the global and the local' (Giulianotti and Robertson, 2009: 33).

Rethinking the Essentialism-Hybridization Debate

Essentialism

How culture is defined is pivotal to understanding the interdependencies of the local and global that we are seeking. It is important that we do not see societies – whether Indigenous or Western – as 'passive recipients of global cultural content … local cultures are not 'fixed' in time and space. Rather, we need to explore the routes and roots of any culture; its mobility and its senses of 'dwelling fixity'' (Giulianotti and Robertson, 2009: 33–4). We also need to be wary of simplistic defences of local cultures that imply unidirectional global flows from the West to the rest.

Culture might be seen as both a boundary of resistance and of imposition or domination. In fact these processes are interrelated: As *resistance*, it comes into play when external forces seek to subdue or *dominate*. Such events, according to Badiou (2001), herald a return to sameness or the *essential*, enduring features of cultural identity. Likewise, Kaya (2007) notes that 'the increase of people's demands for their ethnic, religious, and racial identities' – referred to as 'the cultural turn in the social sciences' – runs the danger of 'reducing social life to cultural elements ... [The] recent increase in identity politics has come with a shift from a general politics based on ideal universal progress to a politics of identity based on gender, local, religious, or ethnic identities' (Kaya, 2007: 707). However, in this discourse, identity politics revolves around *'resistance to imposed or fixed identities'* (Kaya, 2007: 708, emphasis added). Unlike multiculturalism, which calls for 'recognition of the other' based on the idea that all cultures have equal value and worth, identity politics is divisive and provokes conflict. Hence a perspective that celebrates 'difference', 'division' and 'incompatibility' needs to be problematized for it holds little promise 'of solving the problem of living together' (Kaya, 2007: 722). While post-structuralists and postmodernists criticize the modernist 'essentialized – fixed identity – approach' to cultural constructions, its opposite of fluidity and hybridity is not helpful to the Indigenous cause. More in their interests are post-colonialist and feminist privileging of 'lived experience' and 'local knowledges' in the reclamation and preservation of culture and ethnicity. But they walk a fine line in defending identity without resorting to simplistic 'essentializing discourses'. Once fixed categories are dissolved it becomes difficult to explain the experience of racism, sexism, discrimination, oppression, marginalization and so on.

Postmodern and post-structural 'multiplicity' overturn the very hierarchical systems which, feminists and post-colonialists argue, engender oppression and marginalization. So in seeking to ground identity in 'lived experience' and 'local embeddedness or situatedness', post-colonialist and feminist theorists enable 'explorations of embodiment, narrativity and social location' (Wuthnow, 2002: 185) as markers of a distinct identity. For them the fluid, mobile, disembodied nomad perpetuates colonialist discourse whereby the white settlers become the fluid shapeshifters while Indigenous Peoples are constructed as embodied, immobile, situated and objectified – exotic subjects for study: they were always there living close to the land grounded, embedded and wedded to location while the settlers assume a new identity, move on, progress and integrate into society. Feminists must cling to identity markers like gender, race and ethnicity in a world which renders whiteness and Western-ness as invisible norms and which marginalizes local knowledges such that 'knowledges produced in locale are denigrated as local, subaltern, and other' (see Wuthnow, 2002: 190). This does not allow for solid critique and support for Indigenous Peoples attempting 'to secure political rights, self-determination and cultural survival' (Wuthnow, 2002: 190). For feminists like Wuthnow (2002: 195):

> the 'local' need not be based on an essentialized notion of place ... the term 'local' refers ... not to geographical location, but rather to a status of marginalization within broader discursive realms ... For Hall the local [is] conceptualized variously as marginality, difference and diversity ... In marked contrast to Deleuze ... his notion of the local relies on a sense of place and of 'roots' ... yet

he is very careful to elaborate notions of these concepts that avoid essentialized
grounding … the 'local' acts as an important base for counterhegemonic politics.

The 'local' is not a fixed place – a fact waiting to ground identities – but lives in
memory and in history and is recounted or narrated through stories, reconstruction
and remembering (Hall, in Wuthnow, 2002). An 'essentialized approach' attempts
to construct fixed ahistorical ethnic or racial identities by articulating the 'salient
features' of a population group. It assumes that something is 'shared' by a
'group' of people – or a whole population of people – whatever their location. To
describe a certain group of people we inevitably highlight their salient features
but without a proper footnote or disclaimer, these salient features can easily be
taken as 'essentialized features' which reinforce stereotypes and do not allow for
individuality. They overlook the fact that there are many facets to the identities
people adopt or ascribe to others (Paradies, 2006). An empirical approach would
subject 'salient – so-called shared – features' to examination. Without some
factual grounding, discussions about the salient features of particular cultures
remain speculative.

Hybridity

Accoding to Wang and Yueh-yu Yeh (2005: 176), 'with the rise of postcolonialism,
the concept of hybridity … has become a new facet of the debate about global
culture in the social sciences'. It creates a 'third space' (Bhabha, 1994), where
different cultural elements encounter and transform one another. Through the
notion of hybridization which 'is not merely the mixing, blending and synthesizing
of different elements' to form a 'culturally faceless whole' but rather to generate
'new forms and … new connections' (Wang and Yueh-yu Yeh, 2005: 175), post-
colonialists challenge essentialism. They present another scenario for the outcome
of cultural globalization – other than 'hegemonic westernization and postmodern
diversity' (Wang and Yueh-yu Yeh, 2005: 176) – that seeks 'cultural convergence'
as a result of ongoing interaction within and between cultures (Giulianotti and
Robertson, 2009). Post-colonialists recognize the heterogeneous, contextual,
historically contingent nature of 'social experiences and cultural identities'
(Hall, 1995: 225). This non-essentialist approach 'transcends the compulsion to
unceasingly patrol identity borders that have been constructed around primitivist,
romantic and colonial discourses … and starts us on the long and difficult journey
of freeing ourselves from 'myth-making' and the internalized racism of identity
politics' (Paradies, 2006: 362). An essentialist approach requires that Indigenous
social workers articulate the particular Indigenous frameworks, philosophies
or worldviews that undergird Indigenous social work practices. However, non-
essentialists or hybridists argue against the possibility of delineating distinctive
cultures of this nature which have remained uncontaminated by the external
influences of colonization, globalization, indigenization and internationalization,
as the case may be. Notwithstanding the possibility of isolated communities that

have not encountered foreign cultures, in most communities where social work is found, there would be varying degrees of hybridization, even cultures able to retain a traditional heritage and traditional cultural practices while living in and adopting Western belief systems, such as Christianity (see How Kee, 2008; Nimmagadda and Martell, 2008). In this regard Weaver's (2001: 251) observation bears repeating:

> While we as indigenous people were busy guarding against cultural appropriation, we may have missed a much bigger threat to indigenous community… [by] the self-appointed 'identity police', those who divide communities and accuse others of not being 'Indian' enough because they practice the wrong religion, have the wrong politics, use the wrong label for themselves, or do not have the rights skin colour … Some Indigenous people ask, 'Are you Indian, or are you Christian?' as if these are mutually exclusive categories.

Conclusion

So, how might we then move forward to a more enlightened stance on Indigenous social work and attempt to deal with all of the debatable labels, arguments and categorizations presented in this chapter? How does the social work profession acknowledge and embrace the complexities, ambiguities and uncertainties involved in incorporating decolonizing practices into our work? The chapters in this book attest social workers' preparedness to work with discomfort and have the difficult conversations often necessary to progress theorizing and develop a deeper understanding as Indigenous and non-Indigenous social workers work together in facing the challenges of developing culturally relevant research, education and practice.

References

Adair, J.G. (1999). Indigenisation of psychology: The concept and its practical implementation. *Applied Psychology: An International Review*, 48(4), 403–18.

Agrawal, A. (1996). Indigenous and scientific knowledge: Some critical comments. *Indigenous Knowledge and Development Monitor*, 3(3).

Asamoah, Y.W. and Beverley, C.C. (1988). Collaboration between Western and African schools of social work. *International Social Work*, 31(3), 177–93.

Badiou, A. (2001). *Ethics*. Translated by Peter Hallward. New York: Verso.

Baldry, E., Green, S. and Thorpe, K. (2006). Urban Australian Aboriginal people's experience of human services. *International Social Work*, 49(3), 364–75.

Bhabha, H.K. (1994). *The Location of Culture*. London: Routledge.

Brigham, T.M. (1982). Social work education patterns in five developing countries: Relevance of US Microsystems model. *Journal of Education for Social Work*, 18(2), 68–75.

Campfen, H. (1988). Forces shaping the new social work in Latin America. *Canadian Social Work Review*, 5, 9–27.

Cheng, S-L. (2008). A response to the debates between Hutching and Taylor and Jia on the global standard and social work's development in China. *International Journal of Social Welfare*, 17(4), 396–9.

Finn, J. and Jacobson, M. (2003). *Just Practice: A Social Justice Approach to Social Work*. Peosta, IA: Eddie Bowers Publishing.

Friedman, J. (1999). Indigenous struggles and the discreet charm of the bourgeoisie. *Journal of World-Systems Research*, 52(2), 391–411.

Giulianotti, R. and Robertson, R. (2009). *Globalization and Football*. London: Sage.

Gray, M. (2005). Dilemmas of international social work: Paradoxical processes in indigenisation, imperialism and universalism. *International Journal of Social Welfare*, 14(2), 230–37.

Gray, M. (2008). Some considerations on the debate on social work in China: Who speaks for whom? *International Journal of Social Welfare*, 17(4), 400–6.

Gray, M. and Coates, J. (2008). From Indigenization to Cultural Relevance. In M. Gray, Coates, J. and Yellow Bird, M. (eds), *Indigenous Social Work around the World: Towards Culturally Relevant Education and Practice*. Aldershot: Ashgate, 13–29.

Gray, M. and Fook, J. (2004). The quest for universal social work: Some issues and implications. *Social Work Education*, 23(5), 625–44.

Gray, M. and Webb, S.A. (2008). The myth of global social work: Double standards and the local-global Divide. *Journal of Progressive Human Services*, 19(1), 61–6.

Gray, M., Coates, J. and Hetherington, T. (eds). (2013). *Environmental Social Work*. London: Routledge.

Gray, M., Coates, J. and Yellow Bird, M. (eds). (2008). *Indigenous Social Work around the World: Towards Culturally Relevant Education and Practice*. Aldershot: Ashgate.

Hall, S. (1995). New Ethnicities. In B. Ashcroft, Griffiths, G. and Tiffin, H. (eds), *The Postcolonial Studies Reader*. Routledge: London.

Hammoud, H.R. (1988). Social work education in developing countries: Issues and problems in undergraduate curricula. *International Social Work*, 31(3), 195–210.

Hart, M.A. (2002). *Seeking Mino-Pimatisiwin: An Aboriginal Approach to Helping*. Halifax, Nova Scotia: Fernwood Publishing.

Hopkins, A. (2002). *Globalization in World History*. London: Pimlico.

How Kee, L. (2008). The development of culturally appropriate social work practice in Sarawak, Malaysia. In M. Gray, Coates, J. and Yellow Bird, M.

(eds), *Indigenous Social Work around the World: Towards Culturally Relevant Education and Practice*. Aldershot: Ashgate, 97–106.

Human Rights and Equal Opportunity Commission (HREOC). (1997). *Bringing Them Home: National Inquiry into the Separation of Aboriginal and Torres Strait Islander Children from their Families*. Sydney: HREOC.

Husband, C. (2000). Recognising diversity and developing skills: The proper role of transcultural communication. *European Journal of Social Work*, 3(3), 225–34.

Hughes, L. (2003). *The No-Nonsense Guide to Indigenous Peoples*. Oxford: New Internationalist Publications in association with Verso.

Hutchings, A. and Taylor, I. (2007). Defining the profession? Exploring an international definition of social work in the China context. *International Journal of Social Welfare*, 16, 382–90.

International Work Group for Indigenous Affairs (IWGIA). (2009). *Indigenous Peoples: Who Are They?* [Online]. Available at: http://www.iwgia.org/sw641. asp [accessed: 23 March 2010].

Jia, C. (2008). Correcting misconceptions about the development of social work in China: A response to Hutchings and Taylor. *International Journal of Social Welfare*, 17(1), 98–101.

Kaya, I. (2007). Identity politics: The struggle for recognition or hegemony? *East European Politics and Societies*, 21(4), 704–25.

Levin, R. and Herbert, M. (2004). The experience of urban Aboriginals with health care services in Canada: Implications for social work practice. *Social Work Health Care*, 39(1–2), 165–79.

Lynn, R. (2001). Learning from a 'Murri Way'. *British Journal of Social Work*, 31, 903–16.

Martell, L. (2010). *The Sociology of Globalization*. Cambridge: Polity.

Midgley, J. (1981). *Professional Imperialism: Social Work in the Third World*. London: Heinemann Educational Books.

Nimmagadda, J. and Balgopal, P. (2000). Transfer of knowledge: An exercise of adaptation and indigenization. *Asia Pacific Journal of Social Work*, 10(2), 4–18.

Nimmagadda, J. and Martell, D. (2008). Home-Made Social Work: The two-way transfer of social work practice knowledge between India and the USA. In M. Gray, Coates, J. and Yellow Bird, M. (eds), (2008). *Indigenous Social Work around the World: Towards Culturally Relevant Education and Practice*. Aldershot: Ashgate, 141–152.

Paradies, Y.C. (2006). Beyond black and white: Essentialism, hybridity and Indigeneity. *Journal of Sociology*, 42(4), 355–67.

Rankopo, M.J. and Osei-Hwedie, K. (2011). Globalization and culturally relevant social work: African perspectives on indigenization. *International Social Work*, 54(1), 137–47.

Robertson, R. (1992). *Globalization: Social Theory and Global Culture*. London: Sage.

Scott, J.C. (2009). *The Art of Not Being Governed: An Anarchist History of Upland Southeast Asia*. New Haven, CT: Yale University Press.

Shawky, A. (1972). Social work education in Africa. *International Social Work*, 15(1), 3–16.

Shlonsky, A., Schumaker, K. et al. (2009). *Family Group Decision Making for Children at Risk of Abuse and Neglect: Systematic Review*. Campbell Collaboration Social Welfare Group.

Sinclair, R. (2004). Aboriginal social work education in Canada: Decolonising pedagogy for the seventh generation. *First Peoples Child and Family Review*, 1(1), 49–61.

Smith, L.T. (1999). *Decolonizing Methodologies: Research and Indigenous Peoples*. New York: St. Martin's Press.

Sundell, K. and Vinnerljung, B. (2004). Outcomes of family group conferencing in Sweden: A 3-year follow-up. *Child Abuse and Neglect*, 28(3), 267–87.

Tsang, A.K.T. and Yan, M-C. (2001). Chinese corpus, western application: The Chinese strategy of engagement with western social work discourse. *International Social Work*, 44(4), 433–54.

Tsang, A.K.T., Yan, M.C. and Shera, W. (2000). Negotiating multiple agendas in international social work: The case of China-Canada collaborative project. *Canadian Social Work Review*, 2(1), 147–61.

Voss, R., Douville, V, Little Soldier, A. and Twiss, G. (1999). Tribal and shamanic-based social work practice: A Lakota perspective. *Social Work*, 44(3), 228–41.

Walton, R.G. and Abo El Nasr, M.M. (1988). Indigenization and authentization in terms of social work in Egypt. *International Social Work*, 31(2), 135–44.

Wang, G. and Yueh-yu Yeh, E. (2005). Globalization and hybridization in cultural products: The cases of Mulan and Crouching Tiger, Hidden Dragon. *International Journal of Cultural Studies*, 8(2), 175–93.

Weaver, H.N. (1998). Indigenous people in a multicultural society: Unique issues for human services. *Social Work*, 43(3), 203–11.

Weaver, H.N. (2000). Culture and professional education: The experiences of Native American social workers. *Journal of Social Work Education*, 36(3), 415–28.

Weaver, H.N. (2001). Indigenous identity: What is it, and who really has it? *American Indian Quarterly*, 25(2), 240–55.

Wuthnow, J. (2002). Deleuze in the postcolonial: On nomads and indigenous politics. *Feminist Theory*, 3(2), 183–200.

Yan, M.C. and Tsui, M.S. (2007). The quest for Western social work knowledge: Literature in the USA and practice in China. *International Social Work*, 50(5), 641–53.

Yang, R. (2005). Internationalisation, indigenisation and educational research in China. *Australian Journal of Education*, 49(1), 66–88.

Yeatman, A. (2000). The Subject of Democratic Theory and the Challenge of Co-Existence. In A. Vandenberg (ed.), *Citizenship and Democracy in a Global Era*. London: Macmillan.

Young, R.J.C. (2003). *Postcolonialism: A Very Short Introduction*. New York: Oxford University Press.

Yuen-Tsang, A.W.K. and Wang, S. (2002). Tensions confronting the development of social work education in China: Challenges and opportunities. *International Social Work*, 45(3), 375–88.

Yunong, H. and Xiong, Z. (2008). A reflection on the indigenization discourse in social work. *International Social Work*, 51(5), 611–22.

Chapter 2
Decolonizing Social Work: An Indian Viewpoint

Vidya Rao

This chapter provides an overview of the evolution of social work in India to highlight the profession's attempts to decolonize its substantive theoretical content and concomitant practice methods. An effort is made to differentiate the idea of decolonization from indigenization by focusing on the methods required to deal with Indian social problems embedded in their cultural contexts. It claims that indigenization goes beyond the mere adaptation of Western concepts and theories, and refers to the idea that social work theories and methods can be derived from the histories and cultures of non-Western Indian civilization.

Professional social work in India has seen several shifts in professional discourse – written texts and the language spoken among specialists inside social work – professionals and clients – and outside – the state, the market and civil society. Social work is understood as a form of social practice operating according to conventions and generally accepted rules, even if these are not explicitly stated or formalized or consciously complied with (Bombay Association of Trained Social Workers, 2002; Joseph and Fernandes, 2006).

The social work profession in India is an interesting case for the study of paradigm shifts and decolonization processes, through an analysis of the discourses about the status of social work practice, the structuring of social care and protection, the role played by professional social workers in representing the interests and rights of marginalized people and efforts to decolonize the minds of the ruling elite from the neo-liberal mindset (Levien, 2007). Analysis of the professional discourse of social work reveals declared and tacit attitudes regarding the ways in which poverty, poverty alleviation, need, problem, marginalization, helping, intervention, equality, social justice, human rights, fundamental rights and so on are constructed on the basis of interdisciplinary scholarly work (see, for example, Banerjee, 2005; Datt and Ravallian 2011; Deaton and Drèze, 2009; Kumaran, Bina and Parasuraman 2003; Nair, 1981; Nayak and Siddiqui, 1989; Singh, 1980; Wadia, 1961, 1968).

The journey from the colonial social service administration in 1936 to post-independence social work with specializations in medical and psychiatric social work (1948), criminology and correctional administration (1950s), family and child welfare (1950s), urban and rural community development (1960s), social welfare administration (1972) and rural social work (1980s and 1990s) mark the first phase in which social work expanded into specialist fields of practice. The next phase – beginning in the 1980s, albeit allowing for some overlap between the phases, was the gradual inclusion of social advocacy, equal access to education, policies of positive discrimination, constitutional provisions for the development of disadvantaged classes and human rights violations in the curriculum of some elite social work educational institutions like the Tata Institute of Social Sciences and the Delhi School of Social Work. The inclination to intervene to reduce inequality at the societal level was the first sign that professional social work had become aware of the necessity to address social disparities as structural issues rather than confining itself to apolitical casework and community development. Prior to this realization, the clinical approach that dominated practice appeared ineffective, inadequate, ill-prepared, hypocritical, irrelevant and stuck in a piecemeal approach to resolving deep-seated structural social problems (Rao, 1995).

The political nature of social work implicit in a rights-based pro-poor approach was acknowledged first by a few left-oriented professional social workers beginning in 1985, and grudgingly by conservative traditionalist social work educators much later. Left-oriented professional social workers insisted that the causes of the problems faced by excluded individuals and groups were structural in nature and that structural change was needed if equality were to be achieved and poverty eradicated (Patkar, n.d.). This political strand has evolved only recently into structural social work – the current phase – which is beginning to engage with critical theoretical knowledge to resist neo-liberal anti-people state forces and work towards equality and social justice (Banerjee, 2005; Bhargava and Reifeld, 2005; Jodhka, 2001; Oommen, 2005). This new phase arises from the work of social work educators, such as Bodhi (2010, 2011a, 2011b) and Ramaiah (2004, 2006, 2007, 2010, 2011), who raised questions about the extent to which social work in India has been able to confront or challenge the oppression, subjugation, exclusion and exploitation of the *Dalits* and tribes through its empowerment rhetoric. Such examinations are especially pertinent given the profession's uncertain history regarding its identity, mandate, methods and status in Indian society (Dasgupta, 1967; Desai, 2002; Gore, 1973; Kumar, 2002; Kumarappa, 1941; Nayak and Siddiqui, 1989; Ranade, 1954; Rao, 1993). A similar frame of inquiry known as Aboriginal social work had emerged across the world a decade earlier. Canadians Morrisette, McKenzie and Morrissette (1993) had contended that Aboriginal (social work) practice rests on four key principles: the recognition of a distinct Aboriginal worldview, the development of Aboriginal consciousness about the impact of colonialism, cultural knowledge and traditions as an active component of retaining Aboriginal identity and collective consciousness and empowerment as a method of practice (Center for Community Organization and Development Practice, 2012).

Unlike education, law and medicine in India, professional social work discourse has been the subject of surprisingly little empirical research. Writing about sociology and social policy, Dhanagare (2004) asks whether Indian sociology, as a body of knowledge, has proved its utility for and justified its role in society. The questions he raises for sociology are just as pertinent for social work: what is the relationship between social work and social policy? Is the generation of knowledge about social reality a sufficient goal for social work, or does its relevance have to be independently endorsed by administrative and political elites who usually author statements of social policy? In other words, a discussion on the relevance of social work to social policy involves self-questioning as to whether or not the profession ought to seek approval from the state and its functionaries. Engagement with the decolonizing discourse and efforts to indigenize social work is the first step in such self-examination (Alatas, 1993).

Decolonization and Indigenization

More than 30 years ago, Gunnar Myrdal (1953) warned against the uncritical adoption of Western theories and methodologies by scholars in developing countries and emphasized the need to remould social science theories to reflect the problems faced by developing countries. Indian scholar J.E. Singh Uberoi (1968: 119) claimed, 'The aim and method of science are no doubt uniform throughout the world but the problem of science in relation to society is not'.

The institutional and theoretical dependence of Indian scholars on Western social science has resulted in what has been referred to as the 'captive mind' (Alatas, 1972, 1974). Mental captivity – or the phenomenon of the captive mind – refers to a way of thinking that is dominated by Western thought and its application in an imitative and uncritical manner to the study of Indian society. The captive mind is trained almost entirely in the Western sciences, reads the works of Western authors and is taught predominantly by Western teachers, either directly or through their works. This is manifested at a metatheoretical and epistemological level as well as in the areas of problem selection, choice of research methods, theoretical interpretation and suggested policies and solutions. Mental captivity exists within a context of dependency, where adaptation of Western theory is perceived as the only option. Among the characteristics of the captive mind is the inability to raise original problems or devise novel analytical methods as well as alienation from the pressing issues of indigenous society (Alatas, 2000).

Indigenization

The call to indigenization means more than approaching indigenous problems in a social scientific manner with a view to modifying and adapting concepts, theories and methods developed in Western settings. Yet, for most of its existence, social work in India has relied primarily on received Western models which take no account of a sociopolitical and economic context dominated by ethnocentric factors, such as caste, tribe, culture, religion and ethnicity that have a direct impact on government policies and programmes for the development of poor and marginalized sectors of the population (Center for Community Organization and Development Practice, 2012).

Given that indigenization goes beyond mere adaptation of Western concepts and theories (see Gray, Coates and Yellow Bird, 2008), *Dalit* and tribal social work in India comes closest to a decolonized social work that seeks to derive its theories and methods from the histories and cultures of Indian civilization. The need for indigenization exists not only because of the inappropriateness of Western theories, but also because of the need to mould our own ideas about equality and inequality, inclusion and exclusion, social justice and injustice, rights and fairness, democracy and anarchy, modernity and tradition, normal and abnormal, and other dichotomies that are not embedded in Indian history and culture (Alatas, 1993; Nimmagadda and Balgopal, 2000; Nimmagadda and Chakradhar, 2006; Nimmagadda and Cowger, 1999; Wilson and Yellow Bird, 2005). Portraying these ideas as dichotomous as Western social science theories do goes against the Indian ethos. Ironically, conventional social work in India was so captive that a form of native colonialism within a free society that had rid itself of foreign colonial rule was perpetrating marginalization processes to retain the status quo (Sainath, 1996). The work of critical social work activists serves as a constant reminder that social work needs to reflect constantly on the usefulness of its received knowledge and practice theories.

To place the problems of imitation and indigenization in a structural perspective, it is useful to draw on Foucault's enormous and wide-ranging influence on Indian scholarship (Menon, 2009; Sainath, 1996). Specifically, Foucault (1974) draws a connection between power and social scientific knowledge. To Foucault (1977) the designative philosophy of language is simply one procedure that serves to control, limit and elide (omit in pronunciation or articulation) the reality of discourse. Foucault's (1974, 1977) understanding of how truth is imposed and power wielded through the various procedures of control and the delimitations of discourses are particularly relevant to the paradigm shifts in social work in India, where the deployment of Western social work knowledge operates through three major strategies:

1. The incorporation of problems into the domain of social work practice.
2. The professionalization of social work.
3. The institutionalization of professional social work.

The Incorporation of Problems into the Domain of Social Work Practice

This requires the creation of abnormalities and the power to intervene. Once a domain subject to pathological processes is discovered, various techniques designed to normalize can be and are applied. This is brought out very well by Sainath (1996). To Sainath (1996), seeing the problem of poverty as a process rather than an event in the form of outbreaks of epidemics or the sale of children in Orissa forms the bigger challenge. The process of poverty, it turns out, is a ruthless, grinding one, and one that is full of amazing contradictions. Sainath (1996) has captured the actual state of affairs in which the poorest in India survive. These are tales of poignant misery and, at the same time, of admirable courage. At another level, it is about the needs and aspirations of the 'insulted and the humiliated', to borrow a phrase from Dostoyevsky. It is about policies, government programmes launched with great fanfare and soon left to take their own wayward course, making a mockery of their intended aims. At another level, these are about the idiocy of what has been termed 'development'. There are dams that have displaced people who will never benefit from the dams anyway. There are dams that are under perpetual construction, with the contractors assured of a guaranteed ongoing income. There are missile ranges which displace village after village, with the villagers and the tribals losing not only their land but also the very world they belong to. They form the multitudes migrating to big cities, ending up as virtual slaves of contractors in an alien world. No debates on the pros and cons of liberalization or Nehruism – centralization – can substitute for the reasons for such gruelling poverty. These tales are chillingly macabre because the Indian elite, especially the middle class, which has been reared on this very 'development', on the heads and shoulders of the poor in India, is not aware of the sufferings of its victims (Sainath, 1996).

The Professionalization of Social Work

The professionalization process occurs by way of the burgeoning fields and subfields of social work studies and action. The goal here is creating a specialized type of knowledge that seeks to identify the nature of developing societies, with a view to formulating policies and steering them in the right direction to produce a regime of truth and norms about mainstreaming, modernization and development.

Until about the 1950s, public opinion held that a strong commitment to a cause and passion for humanitarian work was sufficient for anyone to engage in social work. At the time, the idea of professional social work – and the necessity for professional education for 'doing social work' – was unfamiliar to Indian people, especially when many social reformers were engaged in the abolition of superstitious practices, such as *sati*, the now illegal practice of immolation of a widow on her husband's funeral pyre, running orphanages, promoting women's education and the freedom movement *without a professional social work education*. The introduction of professional social work education was seen as a process of modernizing and secularizing traditional 'social work'. Accepting professional social work education as necessary for 'doing social work' was the second strategy that marked a shift from parochial charity to systematic secular social service administration.

In the 1980s, however, there was a concerted initiative, mainly from social work academia, to introduce a law to license professional social work practitioners as is the practice in some Western countries. However, there was little support for the idea that one has to undergo formal higher education and be licensed to be able to practise social work, especially from untrained social workers already in permanent employment. In fact, this initiative split professional social workers right down the middle. Those who opposed this initiative believed that it was not possible to license social workers as they were employed in a variety of sectors which were not amenable to being brought under uniform norms and criteria for licensing.

The Institutionalization of Professional Social Work

Social work becomes institutionalized through the establishment of national – and international – organizations, local agencies, higher education programmes and professional alumni associations. Historically, these have served as agents for embedding Western social work structures in India as social work academics, primarily from Delhi, Mumbai (Bombay) and Chennai (Madras) – the three metropolitan cities of India – took the initiative to form the Indian Association of Trained Social Workers, the Bombay Association of Trained Social Workers and the Association of Schools of Social Work in India. Along with other local and national professional bodies, these structures enabled them to participate in international conferences, where they learnt about the latest Western theories and practice models, which they used to professionalize – Westernize – social work education and practice at home. Many of these academics were also founding members of international organizations like the International Council of Social Welfare and the International Federation of Social Workers.

Indian membership in these associations mainly comprised social work academics and a few local elite social work practitioners. Most were active until the mid-1980s when they degenerated into a state of suspended animation, coming to life only when national or international conferences were held. This was the period when activists leading local social movements questioned the relevance of social work education and urged academia to adopt indigenous knowledge and teaching-learning material from outside the social work discipline.

Simultaneously, during the 1980s, the academics who were active in the international associations also tried their best to get a law enacted to accredit social work educational institutions but without success. Despite several attempts, professional social work has not been able to gain statutory legitimacy mainly due to a lack of consensus among professional social work academics and practitioners.

A core process for institutionalizing social work – and entrenching the dominance of Western social work in the discourse – was the organization of academic disciplines. Those among the indigenous social work academics that aspired to attain the level of disciplines for their areas of study faced numerous obstacles. For example, academics, who had attended several international conferences on women in different parts of the world, introduced women's studies as a discipline in higher education in the early 1980s. Despite consistently working on violence against women over several decades, academics at the Tata Institute of Social Sciences – a premier Indian school of social work where the author taught for many years – took

25 years to get women-centred social work introduced into the MA social work programme because patriarchy was and still is deeply entrenched in the minds of fellow academics. Still domestic violence is seen as a result of individual pathology – alcoholism and personality disorder – by some social workers who, due to their mental captivity, cannot comprehend the link between poverty, patriarchy and the trajectory of economic development India has chosen.

A set of propositions that is presented as constituting Indian social work needs to fulfil complex requirements to be able to belong to the *discipline* of professional social work. Typically, these include clinical social work methods in which Western social work theorists have gained a comparative advantage. Works that seek to indigenize social work in their respective societal contexts and emphasize critical, innovative social work methods are not generally accepted as part of the social work discipline. For Indian indigenous social work to qualify for membership, it must not question the status quo, social structures of caste, class, religion, patriarchy, age, sexual orientation and the state or economic institutions. Statements about cultural contexts, identities, ethnicity and social work methods are true only if they correspond to objectively verifiable evidence. In a world in which positivist social science dominates, Indian social work, whose epistemological validity is being denied, cannot hope to have its voice heard.

Decolonization

Social workers' inability to see problems experienced by individuals as embedded in structural factors, such as casteism, patriarchy and the hegemony of Hindu religious and cultural traditions, despite clarion calls raised by Gandhi, Ambedkar and other intellectual leaders and reformers, mirrors the failure of 'captive minds' to be creative in identifying the real sources of problems and in developing appropriate interventions. Instead, underdevelopment and poverty are perpetuated by the policies and actions of Western social work knowledge brokers and their allies in India.

This state of affairs brought forth various reactions from Indian intellectuals, one of which was the call from academics and practitioners to indigenize social work theory and methods of practice (Agoramoorthy and Hsu, 2009; Alphonse, George and Moffatt, 2008; Dasgupta, 1967; Gore, 1973; Mohan, 1970; Mukundarao, 1969, 1972; Narayan, 2000; Nagpaul, 1972, 1993). However, as a legacy of colonialism, there was no indigenous material on social work theory and methods published in the vernacular languages, like Bengali, Tamil and Hindi. Even though English was accepted as an official language post-independence in the 1950s, there was also little published material on social work in India – in English or the vernacular languages.

The call to indigenization does not simply mean modifying and adapting concepts, theories and methods developed in Western settings. It means developing knowledge on the Indian sociopolitical and economic context, written in local languages, which takes account of ethnocentric factors, such as caste, tribe, religion and culture. These factors directly impact on government policies, and programmes for the development of poor and marginalized sectors of the population. What then might decolonized social work look like in India? It would certainly differ in fundamental ways from Western social work as the following examples show.

The separation of religion and state is an important principle of governance in Western society but not in India. The word secularism is used differently in India than in Western countries, where it is taken to mean atheism or a purely worldly non-theistic approach, which rejects other-worldly beliefs. India is a country where religion is central. The reason behind India's unique model of secularism lies in the fact that India has never been a mono-religious country. In terms of the age-old philosophy, as expounded in Indian religious scriptures, secularism in India has always meant respect for all religions and cultures, and non-interference of religion in government affairs, even though, to an outsider, the hegemony of Hinduism may appear to permeate public life and state affairs. Thus decolonized social work in India cannot distance itself from religion: in working with individuals, groups and communities, social workers are ever mindful of related religious, caste, ethnic and cultural differences.

Whereas Western social work emphasizes that individuals are autonomous self-determining actors, able to make independent decisions, individuals in India are never in a position to make decisions free of caste, ethnic or religious norms governing individual and community behaviour. Social work's traditional response to the issues faced by tribal people was rooted in a statist discourse which cast *tribes* as backward, isolated and in need of assimilation into mainstream Indian society. As a reaction against statist practice, *Dalit* and tribal social work began to develop at the Tata Institute of Social Sciences (TISS) in 2005. Its aim is to liberate people from the inhumane, discriminatory system, where inequality is based on purity and pollution closely linked to caste and descent. *Dalit* and tribal social work laid the ground for decolonization through teaching anti-caste practices aimed at promoting a casteless egalitarian society (Bodhi, 2010, 2011a, 2011b; Ramaiah, 2004, 2006, 2007, 2010, 2011). It drew on Western reflexive social work, particularly anti-racist, black, feminist and Aboriginal, Indigenous or First Nations social work practice. Within the *Dalit* and tribal practice framework, casework is seen as unuseful, while family and group counselling and community development is favoured.

The concept of community, often romanticized in Western social work literature, presumes that communities of shared interests or location are relatively homogeneous. However, community in the decolonizing *Dalit* and tribal framework refers to the diversity of people fragmented in terms of caste, religious or ethnic differences in India. Organized communities along caste, ethnic or religious lines in India would surely result in social fragmentation and amount to a divide-and-rule policy.

Further, decolonized social work questions neo-liberal government policies by aligning with new social movements. It questions notions of modernity and development that perpetuate selfishness, greed, consumerism and materialist ways of living. It asks whether restrained consumption, the conservation of natural resources and the environment, hard work, self-reliance and concern for others is antithetical to modernity.

The critical social work perspectives and methods introduced in *Dalit* and tribal social work, disability studies and mental health at TISS in 2005, albeit grudgingly, represents India's variants of anti-racist and anti-oppressive practice. However, students continue to do their field placements in urban NGOs, where they do not experience the oppressive and discriminatory practices taking place in rural life. These contexts tend to reinforce Western social work practice providing little opportunity for students to learn indigenous decolonizing transformative methods.

Thus one can see how Western discourse continues to be perpetuated within a closed professional community with strict rules of practice. In Foucauldian (1977) terms, Western-influenced social work exercises power through the privileging of its discourse in the scheme of things. This takes place in conferences, workshops and classrooms wherein Indian points of view become indistinguishable from Western points of view. The danger of imitating theories based on unrealistic assumptions such as that of 'economic man' (*sic*), is quite clear (Alatas 1993). Uncritical imitation perpetuates factorgenic and redundant theories, based on erroneous assumptions about the nature of the culturally innocent Indian human person. In development studies, for example, factorgenic analyses serve to reduce the problems of underdevelopment to general, anonymous forces, such as market size, terms of trade, direct foreign investment penetration and so forth, thereby making them out to be less complex than they really are. The result is normalization in the form of dehumanizing policies that seek to redress material problems while neglecting or even obstructing expressions of cultural and spiritual experience. Universal social work, for its part, supports this lack of critical thinking by contributing to a common understanding of the diverse dimensions of humankind (Gray and Fook, 2004).

Decolonized social work changes the criteria by which Indian social work academics' and practitioners' interpretation and analyses of social problems are judged. Indianness refers to the search for the essences of native cultures *vis-à-vis* the culture of the 'Other' and highlighting the differences between the two. The call to indigenize social work is simultaneously the call for a liberating discourse that is able to break through the regimes of power and techniques of control and normalization. Whereas evidence-based social work contributes to the normalization of developing societies, its interpretive methods are not necessarily able to uncover the same processes of normalization that are propagated by indigenous actors – the problem of indigenization. The situation of academic dependency in which Indian social work finds itself leaves it susceptible to the wholesale adoption of Western ideas and techniques, which, in turn, perpetuates this process of normalization. The idea, then, is to break out of this cycle with a liberating decolonizing discourse. The quest for indigenous forms of discourse is simultaneously the quest for a liberating discourse because of the specific historical circumstances in which India finds itself.

The Real Challenge for Decolonizing Social Work in India

The real challenge for social work is the uncertainty surrounding its role and status in Indian society, especially its relationship to the state, which has failed to legitimize the profession as a sanctioned provider of social services. As a consequence, social work has remained largely apolitical despite the increased social mobilization and political contestation that has left the state facing a crisis of governability. There is a vast difference between India of the 1950s and India today. Analysis of the changes in the party and federal system shows that there has been an erosion of the Nehruvian centralized state that sought to bring about mass economic development. Under Nehru, the state was in a commanding position, directing the development of industries and educational reforms, and managing the economy. A multiparty electoral system, strong regional parties and free market ideas and practices have displaced centralized planning and a controlled economy with states (provinces) increasingly becoming centres of power (Bagchi, 2007; Khilnani, 2004). The interventionist national state has increasingly given way to the decentralized regulatory state. The balance of power has shifted from Parliament, the Prime Minister, the Cabinet and elected representatives to the Supreme Court, the Election Commission and the President. For the most part, social workers work in the non-government sector and only interact with various levels of government when government action or inaction affects the people with whom they work. By and large, professional social work in India is apolitical and has yet to engage in the changing political landscape or to articulate what kind of state is acceptable.

For the most part, professional social work has continued to treat mental health, domestic violence, atrocities against scheduled castes and tribes (Indigenous Peoples recognized in the Indian Constitution) variously as a crime, deviance, a law and order issue, an aberration, or as personal pathology rather than view these as structural problems – constructed by relations of domination, power and exclusion. This has also created an impression in the minds of the marginalized that professional social work's disengagement with this reality has been strategic as its main goal is to gain approval from the capitalist ruling classes. Without critical social science knowledge and decolonizing social work strategies mere engagement in the delivery of social welfare services implies that social work practice is essentially remedial. This has raised questions as to the purpose of social work.

Looking back, the political developments over the last few decades *inter alia* the consensus on national unity, the move to a secular democracy, and more recently a decentralized state, have had a visible impact on the development of social work which, today, stands coopted by forces that reinforce capitalist, neo-liberal tendencies. Professional social work itself has become an object for, rather than an agent of, change striving for equality and justice. There are a few exceptions, however. Critical social work activist Medha Patkar (n.d.) has written on these issues in the newsletters of the National Alliance of People's Movement (http://napm-india.org/). Economists like Prabhat Patnaik have written extensively on the nature of the Indian state in various media outlets, including NAPM's website and Macroscan, an alternative economics web centre managed by the Economic Research Foundation in New Delhi (http://www.macroscan.org/default.htm).

Sociologists Desai (1977) and Joshi (1996) unfailingly exposed the class interests being served by state development policies and the hiatus between lofty policy and its actual implementation in the 1980s. Joshi (1996) warned of the inherent danger of statism in the social sciences and social scientists becoming mere tools of the government. Practically every decision taken by the government has had implications for the common person in terms of the degree of equality and liberty available to her or him and in terms of what and how much she or he gets. Policy questions such as whether to subsidize the big farmers or the small, whether to set prices of public corporations at the levels that tax or subsidize rich consumers, whether to build roads for private motor vehicles or for mass transportation, to improve infrastructure in rural or urban areas and so on affect the common person. In such a context, professional social work is in a position to analyse the nature, role and function of the state because it functions in the interstitial spaces between the people and the government. But the near absence of social work theory and research addressing immediate practical problems has prevented social work in India from raising fundamental questions about the nature, role and function of the state. Though theoretically social work cannot avoid the politics of development, with few exceptions, neither social work academics nor practitioners have articulated their assessment of the changed nature of the Indian state because of the blinkers that professional social work wears. This then raises questions as to the continuing relevance of professional social work in India

Continuing Relevance of Professional Social Work?

In the contemporary context, relevant social work would be politically active and involved in, among other concerns, democratic decision-making, social action for social change, rural development and community work, development and environment, disaster management and income management and employment generation programmes. Though these areas have only recently been incorporated into the curriculum of professional social work education, there is a lack of clarity about the theoretical framework or ideological perspective on the nature of the relationship between civil society and the Indian state that professional social work education and these new subjects ought to have.

State-led development strategies have made all kinds of demands on professional social workers in the NGO sector. Concepts like urbanization, industrialization, tribalization, criminalization, empowerment, peoples' participation, democratization, governance and family first entered the parlance of professional social work academia after 2000. By and large, the profession was overwhelmed by these concepts and processes, and the task of bringing about structural change, given it did not have appropriate sociological, political or economic evidence-based knowledge to comprehend these forces and their implications for the oppressed and exploited, let alone intervene to make a difference. Interrogation of the relationship between social work and social policy offered an opportunity to assess the social utility of the discipline. It was expected that professional social work would critique state policies as an act of representing the perspectives and voices of the marginalized. Yet social workers have not been called upon by policy makers to formulate development policies, or to advise on appropriate means for direct intervention. Nevertheless, despite its lack of political engagement, in the last 70 years of its existence in Indian academia, professional social work has managed to carve out a niche for itself. Its influence permeates social policy issues more indirectly than directly because of its avowed commitment to equality, social justice, secularism, diversity, inclusive development and democracy. Grudging acknowledgement of social work's political nature only began in the mid-1980s. Though not widespread, this realization was significant for a paradigmatic change from the remedial and residual orientation of social work to a rights-based approach.

There is also grudging acknowledgement that professional social work has played a role, along with legal professionals and feminists, in converting private personal problems into public social issues and in putting them on the political agenda. For example, while the Protection of Women From Domestic Violence Act, 2005, primarily meant to provide protection to the wife or female live-in partner from domestic violence at the hands of the husband or male live-in partner or his relatives, the law also extends its protection to women who are sisters, widows or mothers. Domestic violence under the act includes actual abuse or the threat of abuse whether physical, sexual, verbal, emotional or economic. Harassment by way of unlawful dowry demands to the woman or her relatives would also be covered under this definition. All these issues that were under wraps in deference to family honour were politicized and put on the political agenda by social workers, lawyers and feminists. Finally, the issue of domestic violence was made into a law. However, the police at the village level and the protection officers at the district level are not aware of this law. Social workers are engaged in awareness-building exercises for those who are expected to protect women from domestic violence at the grassroots level.

Discussions about the relevance of professional social work continue to take place among social workers. These discussions have streaks of introspection that prompt questions as to whether professional social work in India has its own body of knowledge and, if so, whether it has proved its utility for meeting the aspirations of the marginalized sections of the population. Has the profession proved itself equal to the task of generating relevant knowledge responsive to the Indian social reality? Does the profession require the endorsement of administrative and political elites, who author social policy statements and design poverty reduction and social welfare programmes? Does Indian social work require endorsement from the international professional community?

These are difficult questions to answer, especially since scholarly writing on the impact of social and political change on professional social work education and practice remains scarce. Some of the elite sections of professional social work, who were part of women's movements and succeeded in getting women's policy adopted by state and national governments, also have contributed little to professional social work literature. Even among the few who have contributed, to some extent, there continues to be a hiatus between the writing of those activists who have taken up issues pertaining to poor, *Dalit* and Muslim women's rights and those who have taken up issues about the status and rights of women in general (Ramaiah, 2004, 2007, 2010, 2011). As such, evidence of decolonized social work is scarce and scattered in the social work literature.

It is not as though the small number of academically oriented professional social workers with a social science and law background are insensitive to the issues concerning *Dalits*, tribes, Muslims, migrant labourers, displaced persons, mentally ill vagrants, homeless destitute persons, persons with disability, single women, domestic violence, human rights violations, victims of mass violence, victims of natural or human-made disasters and issues pertaining to victimization, exploitation, oppression and marginalization. But they appear to have been totally engrossed in activism and their writing has mainly presented a particular argument to the public, policy makers and the courts. Rather than any concern with the professional development of social work, their sole objective is to canvas public opinion and influence political decisions in favour of the marginalized. Hence their contribution to indigenous social work knowledge has not been visible in the mainstream social work literature. As a result, many social work students continue to refer to imported literature and find a disconnection between Western theory and Indian reality. Most student social workers are left on their own to integrate and indigenize their theoretical knowledge in supervised field training (Nanavatty, 2007).

In earlier decades, educational institutions were the main centres of knowledge production in professional social work. Since the 1980s there has been a gradual emergence of research and knowledge production outside these professional enclaves. Non-social workers in NGOs have contributed a great deal to the production of theoretical knowledge for the profession. A large proportion of this indigenous social work theoretical knowledge is now available on the Internet, a major source of information for today's students of social work. The emergence of new modes of knowledge production, for example, various tools used for assessing social impact, vulnerability, deprivation, empowerment, rating organizational strength of self-help groups, measuring NGO performance, indices for measuring protection of human rights, gender justice, and participatory micro-planning by non-social workers, is expected to alter the discourse about the perspectives, substantive content and methods of professional social work not just in India but the world over.

Where does this leave Indian professional social work? There is a need for professional social work in India to learn from experience to experiment and evaluate, to stand firm and engage in the politics of development along with marginalized people. These are some of the ongoing challenges confronting professional social work in India but the future is likely to prove even more daunting.

Conclusion: Decolonization Social Work in India?

Under pressure from critical political social work activists, professional social work slowly realized the contradictions between the country's Constitutional amendments of 1993 giving extensive powers to local self-governing bodies for managing common natural resources and the neo-liberal policies, such as the Special Economic Zone, which were enacted without much public debate in the initial years of the twenty-first century (Prabhu, 1992, 2005; Patkar, n.d.). On the one hand, the government appeared to give more powers to local governments and, on the other, it was taking the powers of local governments away by enacting anti-people, anti-poor laws denying citizenship rights so as to accelerate economic growth and reap the benefits of demographic dividends in a globalizing context. The hollowness of these public policy decisions did not go unnoticed. The adverse impact of these policies on the poor and the marginalized gave impetus to professional social work to start looking anew at theories of democracy, state formation, the links between ideology and governance, theories of people's participation, interest group theories, theories on marginalization processes, people's loss of control over shared natural resources and so on. New foci on *inter alia Dalit* and tribal social work, women-centred social work and disability rehabilitation introduced in the curriculum in the past five years are evidence of the efforts to look at the theories from an indigenous perspective. And renewed interest in Indian thinkers like Gandhi, Ambedkar and others has inspired anti-oppressive, liberatory and critical – political – social work. These have proved helpful for engaging in a meaningful intra-professional dialogue on decolonizing professional social work.

Professional social work in India has taken the opportunity presented by state-sponsored development projects that involved involuntary displacement and deprivation of livelihood security, and began to reimagine its role *vis-à-vis* the state, economic institutions and civil society, in the politics of development and democracy. For instance, social workers are increasingly engaged in the rehabilitation and resettlement of displaced people, and in claiming land, water and forestry rights for indigenous people. The Indian government's development projects have a history of not delivering on promises for adequate resettlement and rehabilitation packages to displaced people and their families. To respond to this history, starting from the 1980s, critical political social work activists, who were only a small section of the professional social work community, educated the people about their rights, the state's obligation to protect citizenship rights and how to get the government to deliver on its promises. Extending relief to the victims of (hu)man-made or natural disasters like the Bhopal Union Carbide tragedy and the tsunamis during the 1980s, 1990s and 2000s facilitated the learning process to reflect on the nature, roles and relationship between state, civil society and market *vis-à-vis* social work's role. There was realization that as long as professional social work continued to consider politics as dirty because it is seen to compromise social work values and principles, not only will the relevance of professional social work be questioned, but there is every likelihood its work will die a natural death in India (Mohan, 1999).

Partly as a result of this reflection and praxis, the profession has begun its journey of decolonizing social work and is hoping to regain some of its past legitimacy. It has at long last realized that emphasis on service delivery or mobilizational work alone would amount to work half done. Today professional social work's brief is to contribute to nation-building, development and democratization efforts from a pro-poor standpoint. This implies that professional social work in India has to redefine itself in professional literature, journals and other publications, locally and internationally. Professional social work in India can learn to engage more effectively in the political processes of development via democratic politics and become an agent of social change – learn to do what is known as structural critical social work. Underdevelopment and poverty are perpetuated by colonized social work education and practice by Western social work knowledge brokers and their allies in India. The inability to see problems experienced by individuals as embedded in casteism, patriarchy and the hegemony of Hindu religious cultural traditions, can be seen as the perpetuation of 'captive minds' incapable of seeing the real sources of problems and developing appropriate interventions. Although social workers are active in more than 450 small and big people's movements in different parts of the country, there is almost no evidence of this paradigm shift in the formal scholarly professional social work literature of the past 25 years. Few professional social work activists have written about their work, hence the difficulty finding evidence of decolonized professional social work literature in India. This points to the need for social work scholars to complement and support decolonizing practices with relevant scholarship.

References

Agoramoorthy, G. and Hsu, M.J. (2009). Lighting the lives of the impoverished in India's rural and tribal drylands. *Human Ecology*, 37(4), 513–17.

Alatas, S.F. (1972). The captive mind in development studies. *International Social Science Journal*, 34(1), 9–25.

Alatas, S.H. (1974). The captive mind and creative development. *International Social Science Journal*, 36, 691–9.

Alatas, S.F. (1993). On the indigenization of academic discourse. *Alternatives: Global, Local, Political*, 18(3), 307–38.

Alatas, S.F. (2000). Academic dependency in the social sciences: Reflections on India and Malaysia. *American Studies International*, 38(2), 80–96.

Alphonse, M., George, P. and Moffatt, K. (2008). Redefining social work standards in the context of globalization: Lessons from India. *International Social Work*, 51, 145–58.

Bagchi, A. (2007). Role of planning and planning commission in the new Indian economy: Case for a review. *Economic and Political Weekly*, 42(44), 92–9.

Banerjee, M.M. (2005). Social work, Rawlsian social justice, and social development. *Social Development Issues*, 27(1), 6–24.

Bhargava, R. and Reifeld, H. (2005). *Civil Society, Public Sphere, and Citizenship: Dialogues and Perceptions*. New Delhi: Sage.

Bodhi, S.R. (2010). The history of dalit and tribal social work: Interview with Sruthi Herbert. *Marian Journal of Social Work*, 3, 14–27.

Bodhi, S.R. (2011a). Rural, rurality, caste and tribes: The dalit and tribe centered social work rural practicum. *Indian Journal of Social Work*, 72(1), 149–62.

Bodhi, S.R. (2011b). Professional social work education in India: A critical view from the periphery. *Indian Journal of Social Work*, 72(2), 289–300.

Bombay Association of Trained Social Workers (BATWA). (2002). *Declaration of Ethics for Professional Social Workers*. Mumbai: BATWA.

Center for Community Organization and Development Practice. (2012). *Curriculum for the MA in Social Work*. Presented to the Meeting of the Board of Studies, School of Social Work, Tata Institute of Social Sciences (TISS), 27 February 2012.

Dasgupta, S. (ed.). (1967). *Towards a Philosophy of Social Work in India*. New Delhi: Popular Book Services.

Datt, G. and Ravallion, M. (2011). Has India's economic growth become more pro-poor in the wake of economic reforms? *World Bank Economic Review*, 25(2), 157–89.

Deaton, A. and Drèze, J. (2009). Nutrition in India: Facts and interpretations. *Economic and Political Weekly*, 14 February [Online]. Available at: www.econdese.org [accessed: 10 March 2012].

Desai, A.R. (1977). *Rural Sociology in India*. Bombay: Popular Prakashan.

Desai, M. (2002). *Ideologies and Social Work: Historical and Contemporary Analyses*. Jaipur: Rawat Publishers.

Dhanagare, D.N. (2004). Social policy concerns in Indian sociology. *Sociological Bulletin*, 53(1), 4–30.

Foucault, M. (1974). *The Archaeology of Knowledge*. Translated by A. Smith. London: Tavistock.

Foucault, M. (1977). *Discipline and Punish: The Birth of the Prison*. London: Allen Lane.

Gore, M.S. (1973). *Social Work and Social Work Education*. Bombay: Asia Publishing House.

Gray, M., Coates, J. and Yellow Bird, M. (eds). (2008). *Indigenous Social Work around the World: Towards Culturally Relevant Education and Practice.* Aldershot: Ashgate.

Gray, M. and Fook, J. (2004). The quest for a universal social work: Some issues and implications. *Social Work Education*, 23(5), 625–44.

Jodhka, S.S. (ed.). (2001). *Community and Identities: Contemporary Discourses on Culture and Politics in India.* New Delhi: Sage.

Joseph, J. and Fernandes, G. (ed.). (2006). *An Enquiry into Ethical Dilemmas in Social Work.* Mumbai: College of Social Work.

Joshi, P.C. (1996). *Culture, Communication and Social Change.* New Delhi: Vikas Publishing House.

Khilnani, S. (2004). *The Idea of India.* London: Penguin.

Kumar, A. (2002). Social work in India: A bright future? *Indian Journal of Social Work*, 63(1), 80–90.

Kumaran, G., Bina, R. and Parasuraman, F.S. (2003). *Listening to People Living in Poverty.* New Delhi: Books for Change.

Kumarappa, J.M. (1941). Social work: Its nature scope and status. *Indian Journal of Social Work*, 2(1), 12–22.

Levien, M. (2007). India's double-movement: Polanyi and the National Alliance of People's Movements. *Berkeley Journal of Sociology*, 51

Menon, N. (2009). Foucault and Indian scholarship. *Critical Encounters: A Forum of Critical Thought from the Global South* [Online]. Available at: http://criticalencounters.wordpress.com/2009/02/25/foucault-and-indian-scholarship/ [accessed: 10 March 2012].

Mohan, B. (1970). The need for psychiatric social work in India. *International Social Work*, 13, 12–17.

Mohan, B. (1999). Social work in the next millennium: The end or a new beginning. *Indian Journal of Social Work*, 60(1), 168–86.

Morrisette, V., McKenzie, B. and Morrissette, L. (1993). Towards an Aboriginal model of social work practice: Cultural knowledge and traditional practices. *Canadian Social Work Review*, 10(1), 91–108.

Mukundarao, K. (1969). Social work in India: Indigenous cultural bases and the processes of modernization. *International Social Work*, 12, 29–39.

Mukundarao, K. (1972). Letter to the Editor. *International Social Work*, 15, 4.

Myrdal, G. (1953). The relation between social theory and social policy. *British Journal of Sociology*, 4(3), 210–42.

Nagpaul, H. (1972). The diffusion of American social work education to India: Problems and issues. *International Social Work*, 15, 3–17.

Nagpaul, H. (1993). Analysis of social work teaching material in India: The need for indigenous foundations. *International Social Work*, 36, 207–20.

Nair, T.K. (1981). *Social Work Education and Social Work Practice in India.* Madras: Association of School of Social Work in India.

Nanavatty, M (2007). Social work education and professional development. *Jharkhand Journal of Development and Management Studies*, 5(3), 2483–96.

Narayan, L. (2000). Freire and Gandhi: Their relevance for social work education. *International Social Work*, 43(2), 193–204.

Nayak, R.K. and Siddiqui, H.Y. (eds). (1989). *Social Work and Social Development*. New Delhi: Gitanjali Publishing House.

Nimmagadda, J. and Balgopal, P. (2000). Transfer of knowledge: An exercise of adaptation and indigenization. *Asia Pacific Journal of Social Work*, 10(2), 4–18.

Nimmagadda, J. and Chakradhar, K. (2006). Indigenization of AA in South India. *Asian Pacific Journal of Social Work*, 16(1), 7–20.

Nimmagadda, J. and Cowger, C.D. (1999). Cross-cultural practice: Social worker ingenuity in the indigenization of practice knowledge. *International Social Work*, 42(3), 261–76.

Oommen, T.K. (2005). *Crisis and Contention in Indian Society*. New Delhi: Sage.

Patkar, M. (n.d.) *Medha Patkar* [Online]. Available at: http://en.wikipedia. org/wiki/Medha_Patkar [accessed: 10 March 2012].Also see Articles by Medha Patkar. http://www.citizen-news.org/search/label/Articles%20of%20 Medha%20Patkar.

Prabhu, P. (1992). Tribal deaths in Thane district: The other side. *Economic and Political Weekly*, 27(47), 2527–30 [Online]. Available at: http://www.jstor.org/ discover/10.2307/4399148?uid=3737536&uid=2129&uid=2&uid=70&uid=4 &sid=47698740855737 [accessed: 10 March 2012].

Prabhu, P. (2005). The Right to live with dignity. *Environmental Portal: Knowledge for Change* [Online]. Available at: http://www.indiaenvironmentportal.org.in/ feature-article/right-live-dignity [accessed: 10 March 2012].

Ramaiah A. (2004). Dalits to accept globalization: Lessons from the past and present. Available at Social Science Research Network (SSRN) [Online]. Available at: http://ssrn.com/abstract=568582 [accessed: 10 March 2012].

Ramaiah A. (2006). Cultural diversity acclaimed but social and economic diversity ignored: The case of Dalits in India. *International Journal of Diversity in Organizations, Communities and Nations*, 5(5), 173–90.

Ramaiah, A. (2007). *Laws for Dalit Rights and Dignity: Experiences and Responses from Tamil Nadu*. Jaipur: Rawat Publication.

Ramaiah A. (2010). Social Democracy in Indian Villages: The experience of Dalits in Southern Tamil Nadu. In I. Ahmad and Upadhyay, S.B. (eds), *Dalit Assertion in Society: Literature and History*. Hyderabad: Orient Blackswan.

Ramaiah A. (2011). Relevance of Dr Ambedkars demand for separate settlement: Ever increasing violence against Dalit human rights. *Mainstream*, 49(17) [Online]. Available at: http://www.mainstreamweekly.net/article2700.html [accessed: 10 March 2012].

Ranade, S.N. (1954). Social work as a profession. *Indian Journal of Social Work*, 15(3), 184–8.

Rao, M. (1993). Social work education: Some questions on relevance, direction and emphasis. *Indian Journal of Social Work*, 54(4), 609–12.

Rao, V. (1995). Political context of social work. Unpublished pre-doctoral paper. Mumbai, India: Tata Institute of Social Sciences.

Sainath, S. (1996). *Everybody Loves a Good Drought: Stories from India's Poorest Districts*. London: Penguin.

Singh, P. (2007). *Naxal Threat and State Response* [Online]. Available at: http://hrm.iimb.ernet.in/cpp/pdf/NAXAL_THREAT_AND_STATE_RESPONSE(IIM).pdf [accessed: 10 March 2012].

Singh, R.R. (ed.). (1980). *Social Work Perspectives on Poverty*. New Delhi: Concept Publications.

Singh Uberoi, J.P. (1968). Science and Swaraj. *Contributions to Indian Sociology*, 2, 119.

Wadia, A.R. (1961). Philosophy of social work. *Indian Journal of Social Work*, 22(1), 61–4.

Wadia, A.R. (1968). *History and Philosophy of Social Work in India*. University of Michigan: Allied Publishers.

Wilson, W.A. and Yellow Bird, M. (2005). *For Indigenous Eyes Only: A Decolonization Handbook*. Santa Fe, NM: School of American Research.

Chapter 3

Ecospiritual Approaches: A Path to Decolonizing Social Work

John Coates

This chapter reviews decolonization as developed within three discourses – Indigenous, spirituality and environment. Decolonization involves the recognition of colonization, and the efforts of Indigenous Peoples and other marginalized groups to break free – to decolonize – from the hegemony of modernist Western thinking that has supported political, economic, cultural and ideological imperialism (Coates, 2003; Yellow Bird, 2012). The chapter reviews the developments and objectives of these three discourses as each critiques the Western colonizing worldview and its negative consequences. While differences exist, the commonalities among these interweaving discourses support the emergence of holistic and inclusive ecospiritual approaches that enable the social work profession to be part of the decolonization project and, in so doing, become more effective than is currently the case in the pursuit of social and ecological justice.

Decolonization

Decolonization initially referred to the return of political control to conquered peoples. However, as Smith (1999: 98) points out, decolonization 'is now recognized as a long-term process involving the bureaucratic, cultural, linguistic and psychological divesting of colonial power' in which the ideologies and mechanisms of control created through colonization continue to oppress and manipulate how people perceive the world and their place in it (Dempsey and O, 2003). The need for decolonization persists not only to reclaim political rights, but also to overcome one of the more insidious practices of colonization – the 'ideological infiltration of our internal lives' (Dempsey and O, 2003: para. 2) which impacts on self-worth and self-understanding as well as collective cultural identity. Hence the decolonization discourse for Indigenous Peoples concerns attempts to overcome the dehumanizing effects of colonialism – 'collective traumas' (Dempsey and O, 2003: para. 4) – brought about through deliberate and systematic practices of: cultural and geographical dislocation, forced assimilation programmes such as mission and residential schools, social and cultural marginalization and eradication that resulted in considerable personal distress (see also Miller, 2001). Strategies for decolonizing are foremost in the minds of many

Indigenous scholars (see, for example, Baskin, 2011; Sinclair, Hart, and Bruyere, 2009; Wilson and Yellow Bird, 2005) who argue not only for the reclaiming of language, culture and land but also for resistance to ongoing oppression in areas such as educational practices (Iseke-Barnes, 2008) and forms of helping (Sinclair et al., 2009).

In *Decolonizing Methodologies*, Smith (1999) builds on the work of Edward Said to show how colonization shapes systems of belief as formal and informal representations become accepted as universal 'regimes of truth', to use a Foucauldian term, that serve to marginalize 'the Other'. As social work emerged in the twentieth century to support the modernization, industrialization and urbanization of Western societies, it absorbed these 'regimes of truth' into its assumptions, conceptualizations and practices and involved itself in the colonization of Indigenous Peoples, such as the 1960s scoop in Canada, and continues to do so through its ongoing struggle with cross-cultural practice (see Chapter 4). It is important that social workers become better able to identify and critique their colonizing values and 'regimes of truth' so as not to inadvertently continue to oppress through ill-informed efforts under the guise of 'good intentions' (Baskin, 2006; Duran and Duran, 2000; Sinclair, 2004). Understanding the 'complexity of colonial oppression and how it is systematically exercised' (Iseke-Barnes, 2008: 124) is essential for decolonizing social work practice for the 'legacies of devastating colonial histories are a constant part of the contemporary reality of groups of colour' (Weaver, 1999: 218). It is these regimes of truth – situated within particular cultural and social systems – that need to be decolonized (Wilson, 2001).

While the language of decolonization is not common in social work's environmental and spiritual literature, ecological language on the connectedness and interdependence of all things, holism, inclusion and the sacredness of place has begun to permeate the social work discourse on spirituality and the environment (see, for example, Besthorn, 2002; Coates, 2003; Gray, 2008; Mary, 2008; Zapf, 2009). This ecospiritual discourse celebrates cultural diversity and 'many ways of knowing', thus opening the door for decolonizing practices relevant not only to Indigenous Peoples but also to mainstream social work.

Indigenous Knowledge and Social Work

Over recent decades, a growing cohort of Indigenous social work scholars has drawn attention to the longstanding and persistent negative consequences of colonization, the relevance and importance of traditional Indigenous beliefs and practices in healing and recovery, and their application to Indigenous and mainstream social work education and practice (Baskin, 2002, 2006, 2011; Bruyere, 2007; Hart 2002, 2008, 2009; Sinclair, 2009; Weaver, 1999, 2004; Wilson and Yellow Bird, 2005; Yellow Bird, 2004). The first Indigenous social work education programmes in Saskatchewan and Alberta came into existence in 1974, initiating a 'respect for Indigenous traditions and culture' (Sinclair,

2009: 21). Other dedicated programmes followed and contributed to Indigenous helping traditions being increasingly recognized and discussed in social work education in Canada. Indigenous approaches were deliberately anti-colonial and educational and practice efforts sought to enable Indigenous Peoples to address the historic and enduring negative consequences of government policies (Hart, 2008; Sinclair, 2009).

For Indigenous Peoples, colonization is associated with the exploitation of land, confinement on isolated reserves and the coercion of residential schools, which sought to destroy their cultures and served to deny generations of Indigenous People the privileges of citizenship – access to education and employment, as well as adequate housing, fresh water and healthcare (Calma and Priday 2011; Carniol, 2005; Royal Commission on Aboriginal Peoples, 1996). Indigenous people on reserves lived in fourth world conditions (Manuel and Posluns, 1974) and such deprivation continues today (Adelson, 2005; Houpt, 2011; Keevil, 2011). The pervasive, severe and lasting impacts of colonization continued when professional services, including social work, devalued and degraded traditional Indigenous knowledge and practices, and forced irrelevant and frequently destructive Western practices upon Indigenous Peoples. The imperialism inherent in the international dominance of Anglo-American knowledge has continued to expand the colonization process through the globalization of education and practice (see Gray et al., 2008).

Indigenous scholarship has been discouraged and constrained for many reasons, including the small number of Indigenous academics and lack of awareness of Indigenous knowledge and practices by mainstream academics. Of importance is the fact that many First Nations social workers and academics are called to practise in their communities to confront urgent challenges arising from pervasive poverty and the psychological distress of colonization (Sinclair, 2009). Through their perseverance and tenacity, Indigenous Peoples are reclaiming their voice and regaining the right to define their futures through decolonizing efforts toward self-government and the restoration of traditional practices and ways of knowing. As the number of Indigenous academics has grown in North America so too has the breadth of Indigenous social work scholarship (see, for example, Baskin, 2009, 2011; Graveline, 1998; Hart, 2002, 2008; Henderson-Youngblood, 2000; Lynn, 2001; Morrisette, McKenzie and Morrissette, 1993; Sinclair et al., 2009; Weaver, 1999, 2004; Wilson, 2009).

Indigenous helping methods are rooted in collective and holistic philosophies informed by Indigenous spiritualities (Bruyere, 2007; Hart, 2009). Spirituality influences all interactions and promotes 'inner exploration' as well as responsibility for 'the collective wellbeing of the people and the life around them' (Hart, 2009: 35). For Hart (2009), this anti-colonial Indigenous perspective emphasizes the importance of respect and sharing, wholeness, balance, relationships, harmony, growth, healing and *mino-pimatisiwin* which he translates as 'the good life'. The integrity of these value-based approaches is reflected in Hart's (2009: 36) description of the interdependence among their key concepts. Balance and wholeness result in attending to all 'aspects of the whole' and 'nurturing the connections' thereby contributing to harmony, which involves 'all entities fulfilling their obligations to each other and to themselves'. Growth is seen to involve the balanced development of the whole person – body, heart, mind and spirit. Healing focuses on restoring the qualities of balance, harmony and responsibility of the individual in relationship. All of these elements promote the good life: 'life in the fullest, healthiest sense ... is the goal of growth and healing and includes efforts by individuals, families, communities, people in general and all life entities' (Hart, 2009: 36).

Indigenous perspectives recognize that all creatures are mutually interdependent. In this understanding, human beings often hold a lesser status than other species and have responsibility to past and future generations (see Johnston, 2003). There are many Indigenous Peoples, and their cultures and worldviews are diverse, but they share a respect for the individual (in the context of the collective), holistic thinking, a close relationship between the physical and spiritual, the sacredness of the Earth and the wisdom of living within its self-regulatory and self-healing capacities.

Sinclair (2009: 19) notes the importance of personal and community histories and cultures and how colonization has affected First Nations' individuals, families and communities. She argues that it is essential to have an 'understanding of the historical impact of colonialism in the contemporary social, political and economic contexts and to assess how these dynamics have influenced and are currently manifesting in the social work milieu'. Hart (2009: 169) argues for the value of asserting Aboriginal values and worldviews so that research and knowledge development can be 'for Indigenous People, by Indigenous People, with Indigenous People'. Sinclair (2009: 24) points to the necessity of engagement with the Eurocentric writing of 'dead White guys' 'to provide new perspectives and foundations from which to approach [Indigenous] social work theory, pedagogy and practice'.

Despite these efforts to seek a broader foundation, colonization – and its pernicious effects – persists in these contemporary neo-liberal times. As anti-colonialism – through the 'beliefs, teachings and practices' of Indigenous Peoples – is brought into the classroom, so might social work education open itself to critiques of the profession's modernist foundations and unquestioning acceptance of what Hart (2009: 26–7) describes as 'dominion, self-righteousness, and greed'. Inherently, such a transformation would embrace Indigenous ways of knowing and adopt a similar position to that taken at the World People's Conference on Climate Change and the Rights of Mother Earth (2010: para. 3):

The capitalist system has imposed on us a logic of competition, progress and limitless growth. This regime of production and consumption seeks profit without limits, separating human beings from nature, creating an arresting domination of the natural world, and transforming everything into commodities: water, earth, the human genome, ancestral cultures, biodiversity, justice, ethics, the rights of peoples, and life itself.

Within Indigenous worldviews, harmony with nature can only come about if there is equity among humans and a 'recovery, revalorization, and strengthening of the knowledge, wisdom, and ancestral practices of Indigenous Peoples ... [which recognizes the] indivisible, interdependent, complementary and spiritual relationship [with Earth]' (World People's Conference, 2010: para. 8): 'Some First Nation and Aboriginal communities (for example the Inuit and Lakota of North America) have models of respectful environmental or ecological use' (Schmitz, Matyók, Sloan and James, 2012: 2). The Indigenous Peoples' Restorative Network (IPRN) provides an overview of traditional ecological knowledge (IPRN, 1995a) as well as resources regarding Indigenous networks (IPRN, 1995b).

There is a 'legitimate academic role in higher education' (Hart, 2009: 27) to teach decolonizing methodologies and practices in which First Nations Peoples can 'see themselves' in the scholarship (Smith, 1999; see also Chinn, 2007; Iseke-Barnes, 2008). This would inevitably include course content on the history of colonization and First Nations' experiences and knowledge in course texts, lecture presentations and group discussions. Decolonization calls for a recognition and valuing of 'foundational aspects to Indigenous knowledge, such as spirituality intertwined with the land' (Hart, 2009: 27). It is in the context of spirituality and the human relationship to the environment that Indigenous values, beliefs and practices find common ground, though from very different roots, with other ecospiritual approaches to social work theory and practice.

Spirituality and Social Work

Few scholars question the strong religious and spiritual roots of social work in Britain and North America. Introductory texts refer to the significance of the Charity Organization Societies and Settlement Houses and the influence of the Social Gospel Movement in the emergence of the social work profession (for example, Morales and Scheafor, 1995; Van Wormer, 1997). Religion and spirituality continued to have an influence on social work scholarship and practice into the 1960s, when the growing secularism in society at large, such as the decline in church attendance (Bibby, 1987; Henerey, 2003), was mirrored by the profession (Graham, Coholic and Coates, 2007). Social work became increasingly secular as it sought professional status and distanced 'itself from its Christian charitable foundations [and was displaced by a] deep rooted, historical antipathy toward religion amongst social work in Western societies' (Holloway, 2007: 4). Fears about proselytizing (Canda and Furman, 1999; Drouin, 2002) and concerns about inadequate theory development and practice guidelines (Holloway, 2007) also contributed to this decline.

Recent interest in the area of spirituality and social work in North America, and perhaps beyond, was initiated by Ed Canda and Leola Furman's groundbreaking scholarship (Canda 1988; Canda and Furman, 1999, 2010). According to Besthorn (2002: 6), the 'focus of this new developmental phase has tended, generally, to be on broadening the definition of the religious/spiritual construct so as to make it more inclusive and honoring of diverse religious and nonreligious traditions'. The literature has included a call for increased sensitivity to the important part played by religion in social work history (see, for example, Graham et al., 2007; Lowenberg, 1988) and awareness of the role spirituality plays in the lives of people in many cultures, including people in more secular societies (see also Canda, 1998).

Scholarship on spirituality has been growing and contributing to increased attention to religion and spirituality in social work education and practice in various countries: in the USA (Canda, 1988; Canda and Furman, 1999), the United Kingdom (Henerey, 2003; Holloway, 2007), Canada (Coholic, Cadell and Nichols, 2008; Coates, Graham, Swartzentruber and Ouellette, 2007; Coholic, 2005; Graham, 2006), Australia (Gray, 2008; Lindsay, 2002), and New Zealand (Nash and Stewart, 2002). In social work, the importance of attending to spirituality has been demonstrated in several fields and levels of practice: for example, in cross-cultural practice (Al-Krenawi and Graham, 2003; Weaver, 1999), in work with children in fostercare (Coholic, 2011), in palliative care (Cadell and Marshall, 2007), in community development (Todd, 2009) and in social justice (Hodge, 2007). A number of scholars have made a distinct connection between spirituality and environmental issues, including Besthorn (2002), Coates (2003), Dylan and Coates (2012), Lysack (2012), Mary (2008) and Zapf (2009). They are opening the profession to a new and broadened framework for professional theory and practice.

Additionally, spirituality has opened a space for considering the importance of place (Zapf, 2009) and the environment in the spirituality of many peoples and cultures. While understandings of spirituality are diverse, the celebration of that diversity and critiques of traditional individualistic social work theory and practice are based on considerations of interdependence, holism and diversity. They have initiated a welcoming of alternative frameworks that challenge the imperialism of Western epistemology, the oppression that flows from it (see, for example, Coates et al., 2007; Gray et al., 2008) and its inability to value alternative paradigms (see Barker, 1990).

The holistic focus of spiritually oriented scholars, such as Canda and Furman (2010) and Coates (2003), challenges not only the environmental and political conservatism of religion (Sherkat and Ellison, 2007) but also points to, as Besthorn's (2002: 6) prescient article notes, an alliance between ecology and spirituality. Ecospirituality has the potential to reconceptualize the commitment and values of social work to move 'beyond the dualism in the western philosophical project and its own practice models' to merge spirituality and environmental justice with the profession's traditional emphasis on social justice and personal growth. This serves not only to broaden social work beyond a preoccupation with the social, but also to decolonize professional thinking and shift away from the pre-eminence of individualism and dualism, and the unquestioned acceptance of progress, efficiency and modernity that hamper and prevent effective work across cultures and make it difficult for social workers to fulfil their role as agents of change (see Gray et al., 2008).

Environment and Social Work

Popular interest in the environment has steadily grown in recent decades such that the environmental movement has been called the 'largest, most densely organized political cause in human history' (Brown, 1995: xiv). Aided by the globalization of communication, people in all parts of the world are increasingly aware of the growing concern about environmental changes, and the current and potential threats to human and global well-being. This concern is revealed in the millions of small, locally oriented focus groups and large globally influential organizations, such as Greenpeace, World Watch and Kairos, and international structures, such as the Kyoto Protocol and the Intergovernmental Panel on Climate Change (IPCC) (2007) (see Hawken, 2007; Turner, 2007).

A number of scholarly publications have drawn attention to the severe negative impacts of environmental destruction and industrial practices (see Cohen et al., 2008; Gosine and Teelucksingh, 2008) on Indigenous Peoples. Examples are numerous but include relocation, water pollution and ill health as a consequence of mining operations on the traditional territory of Indigenous Peoples (Canadian Ecumenical Jubilee Initiative, 2000), deforestation (Pulido, 1996), toxic dumping (Rogge, 1994), radiation poisoning (Dawson, 1994; Korstrom, 1998) and mercury poisoning (Shkilnyk, 1985). Frequently governments would collude with large corporations to exploit natural resources without reasonable and adequate compensation to Indigenous Peoples who were displaced or negatively impacted. The structural adjustment programmes of the International Monetary Fund (IMF) and World Trade Organization (WTO) that demanded opening natural resources to international markets frequently contributed to these injustices (Hofrichter, 1993; Westra and Wenz, 1995). Similar exploitation was reported in the documentary *Hungry for Profit* (Richter, 1984) that exposed the coerced displacement of Indigenous farmers in support of corporate agribusiness. In Canada, Australia and the USA, struggles to secure resolution of violations are ongoing (see, for example, Behrendt, 2003; Ross, 2003; Wilson and Yellow Bird, 2005). An outstanding issue in Canada is the struggle of the Lubicon Cree to secure compensation for the pollution and exploitation of gas and oil from the Alberta Tar Sands (Amnesty International, 2010). What this scholarship reveals is the direct relationship of environmental degradation to social injustices experienced by Indigenous Peoples, and others.

A major force in the United States is the environmental justice movement led by the United Church of Christ's Commission on Racial Justice (Chavis and Lee, 1987) whose work identified the 'pervasive reality of racism' as racialized communities were 'disproportionately harmed by industrial toxins on their jobs and in their neighborhoods' (Bullard, 1993: 15). While initially the focus was local, concern spread to other communities in the USA and internationally as risky technologies and waste disposal were transferred to nations in the Global South. Greenpeace advocates labelled this as 'toxic colonialism' (Koné, 2010) and works by such authors as Hofrichter (1993) and Pulido (1996) brought attention to the role of international financial institutions in the social injustices created by environmental degradation. Bullard (1993) argues the environmental justice movement brought issues of social inequality and power imbalances into the larger environmental movement and underscored the importance of connecting environmental and social justice issues.

The wide disciplinary interest in environmental issues, such as climate change, habitat destruction and species extinction, has resulted in a multidisciplinary perspective among scholars regarding discussions of causes, consequences and restorative actions. Critiques of the lack of effective action point to the need to break free of the domination of progress, profit and efficiency that blind many to the severity of social and environmental injustices. Detailed reviews across many disciplines – articulated by Berry (1988), Capra (1982), Clark (1989), Dryzek, (2005), Godrej (2001), Hamilton (2003), Jarman (2007) and Spretnak (1997) – critiqued the socioeconomic system for relentlessly extracting resources and exhausting the rehabilitative capacities of Earth (see also Diamond, 2005; Glavin, 2006; Greenberg, 2010; Korten, 2009). Despite the many benefits modern society has provided, there has been a dark side to growth as modern life has also produced an 'intrinsically destructive relationship to nature' (Christopher, 1999: 361) and poor and Indigenous Peoples suffer disproportionately more from the negative impacts of climate change.

Several social work scholars have raised the need for attention to environmental justice (Besthorn, 2002; Coates, 2003; Hoff and McNutt, 1994; Rogge, 1994; Zapf, 2009), and the corresponding social injustices (Dylan and Coates, 2012). While there are differences among environmental justice communities, as Suagee (2002: 1) points out, due to the legal status, collective rights and 'cultural ties to the environment' of Indigenous Peoples, there are similarities. For example, in the First National People of Colour Environmental Leadership Summit's (1991: 1) affirmation of the 'sacredness of Mother Earth, ecological unity and the interdependence of all species, and the right to be free from ecological destruction', scholars have identified the need to break free of the domination of progress, profit and efficiency that blind many to the severity of social and environmental justices. Decolonizing efforts include exposing the values, beliefs and destructive practices that have contributed not only to the exploitation of Indigenous Peoples and their traditional territories, but also to the benefits of elitist economic priorities and methods accruing to the Global North. A good example is the substantial efforts of the Indigenous Environmental Network to oppose the development of the Alberta Tar Sands and related pipelines in Canada (see, for example, Indigenous Environmental Network, 2011). The contemporary movement to 'Decolonize Wall Street' that exposed the gross financial inequality in society can be seen as an effort to decolonize the pervasive economic rationality dominating global governance.

Ecospiritual Social Work as Decolonizing Practice

All three discourses emerged in reaction to the devastating consequences of modern economic and political practices, and critique the severe shortcomings of the colonizing worldview of modernity that dominates the world economy, popular culture and international politics. Several scholars, including Coates (2003), Gladwin, Newbury and Reiskin (1997), Lerner (2003), Scharmer (2003), and Indigenous scholars such as Gregory (2008) and Smith (1999), argue that modernity's constraints pervade the public and private understanding such that the root cause of most social and environmental exploitation is 'in our thinking' or more correctly, as Scharmer (2003: 4) puts it, in 'how we don't [think]'. For their part, Indigenous, environmental and spiritual approaches have directly challenged neo-liberal assumptions and values – faith in endless progress, the economic growth imperative, rampant consumerism and modern technology (see Catton and Dunlap, 1997; Coates, 2003) – that lead to the exploitation of people and the planet for profit (see Hart, 2009). Decolonizing practice questions these most fundamental assumptions and considers environmental and social problems to be the 'logical and unavoidable consequences of modern … capitalism, industrial technology, individualistic morality, and mechanistic science' (Christopher, 1999: 361).

Scholars in many fields (for example, biology – Benyus, 1997; philosophy – Berry, 1999; science – Capra, 1982; economics – Korten, 2009; theology – O'Murchu, 1997; and ecofeminism – Spretnak, 1997) have proposed an alternative set of foundational values and beliefs with the potential to free humans 'from the straightjacket of modernity and markets' (Elshof, 2010: 75). This framework, variously referred to as cultural and spiritual consciousness (Korten, 2006), ecological consciousness (Chefurka, 2011), conscious evolution (Sahtouris, 1998), the good life (Hart 2002), living well (World Peoples Conference, 2010) and global consciousness (Earley, 1997), shares foundational assumptions based on interdependence between humans and between humans and the non-human world; responsibility for self, others and the environment; connectedness of all things; and boundaries or limits to natural resources (see Coates, 2003; Hart, 2008; Hubbard, 1998; Macy, 1990). These assumptions inform ecospiritual approaches which seek to provide a sense of meaning and purpose to human life (see Canda and Furman, 2010; Coates et al., 2007) and may be seen to define a proper role for humans in relationship to one another and the planet, at heart reflecting a relational worldview.

Ecospiritual approaches believe that efforts to build a just and sustainable future must be founded 'on the awareness of the connections that bind us to each other, to all life and to all life to come' (Orr, 2009: 125). Orr (2009: ix) argues that every individual is 'stitched to a common fabric of life, kin to all other life forms … Each … is part of a common story that began three billion years ago'. Teasdale (1999: 2) sees humanity at the threshold of a new age that will reflect 'the deeper foundation of a new universal society' based upon 'a consensus of experience on the common elements present in every viable form of spiritual life' (Teasdale, 1999: 5). Individual identity and well-being are considered to be connected to the well-being of the Earth and future generations. They find expression in the principles of Indigenous helping articulated by Hart (2009) – respect, sharing, balance, harmony, relationship and responsibility. The responsibility is both personal and collective (Morton, 2007) in view of the impact of human behaviour on other people and Earth.

Ecospiritual approaches develop and augment interdependence, diversity and an inclusive framework that incorporates psychological, social, environmental and spiritual elements and enables social workers to build on the assets of modernity (such as scientific knowledge and communication) yet also see through its constraints (such as exploitation and greed). Decolonization discourses seek to understand how colonialism fosters gross inequality and seeks to rectify persistent inequalities. They critique modernity and point to the need for a holistic worldview though they retain core modern ideas of human rights and social justice. Such integration expands the purview of mainstream social work enabling it to more effectively engage issues of social marginalization and economic exploitation that impact on all people, and Earth more generally.

Decolonization Process

While ecospiritual approaches offer an alternative to modernity, decolonization requires all people to arrive at their own 'regimes of truth' (Smith, 1999). A way forward to the 'decolonizing of all minds' (Gregory, 2008: 14) can be found in the decolonizing processes advocated by Indigenous Peoples. One of the first steps in decolonization is recognizing and celebrating cultural diversity. This often takes the form of acknowledging the validity and significance of alternative – non-scientific and non-Western – frameworks and worldviews. The goal of decolonization is to weaken entrenched points of view in non-Indigenous minds and embed paradigms that expose and balance exploitive non-Indigenous views. Closely related to this is the recognition that one has been colonized (see Yellow Bird, 2012) and that one's life has been dramatically distorted as a result. This is the beginning of a critical consciousness that may continue to be developed in subsequent steps.

A third step involves developing a historical perspective. Building on Green (2002: 32), learning what happened to Indigenous Peoples, and to those who are poor and marginalized, can aid understanding of the way in which 'present conditions emerge from historical yet continuing relations of privilege and subordination'. Green (2002) further suggests it is essential to see events experienced by Indigenous Peoples, and other oppressed groups, in the context of colonial history, rather than view the consequences of colonization on people, such as individual pathology, as devoid of context or as isolated incidents. It is vital for both the colonizer and colonized to explore how colonialism persists in political and social life and impacts upon daily life (Gregory, 2008; Memmi, 1965).

A fourth step stresses the importance of seeing how human lives are controlled and to understand the sources of information or discourses upon which they have based their identity and understanding of events (Dempsey and O, 2003).

Modernity's emphasis on the relationship between consumerism and identity is a case in point. While discourses, such as environmentalism, spirituality and Indigenous social work all share a similar worldview, they might have competing political projects.

A fifth step in the decolonization process involves individuals examining the desires and identity they have inherited and internalized – from *inter alia* the media, education and daily interaction. Dempsey and O (2003: para. 18) point out that 'decolonizing the self requires extreme honesty' and critical self-reflection. For both non-Indigenous and Indigenous Peoples, the attainment of a critical consciousness requires that people learn about their complicity in 'racist-sustained oppression' (Green, 2002: 31) and exploitive practices. This is the responsibility about which Hart (2009) speaks. Individuals and groups need to explore how the way they choose to live often sustains 'oppressive ideology' (Dempsey and O: para. 20) and discriminatory practices. Hence to become effective actors and allies in processes of decolonization there must be 'decolonization of all minds' (Wilson and Yellow Bird, 2005: 2). For non-Indigenous Peoples, an exploration of their own beliefs, assumptions and knowledge, and how they have benefited from and been complicit in, the colonizing, dehumanizing and othering of Indigenous Peoples is imperative.

A sixth step involves changing the language we use to describe another's experience: the 'language of deficiency and dysfunction' does not fit Indigenous Peoples' 'survival and resistance … to oppressive conditions' (Nadeau and Young, 2006: 91). Nadeau and Young (2006: 90) use the term education instead of therapy or healing to shift the focus from the victim-oppressor relationship to resistance and survival: to restore 'sacred vitality' referring to Indigenous Peoples' 'feeling of energetic connection with [their] own sacredness, with the earth, and with others in community, a feeling of being fully alive'. Many First Nations Peoples use traditional ceremonies to restore 'sacred vitality' while many non-Indigenous people may use strengths-based models (Saleebey, 2009).

Ecospiritual approaches are interdisciplinary drawing upon scientific analyses, social and environmental history and Indigenous knowledges. As decolonizing approaches, they are markedly different from mainstream theory as they are, by definition, inclusive, holistic and spiritual and seek to bring together rather than polarize diverse perspectives. Ecospiritual approaches recognize the interdependence of all life forms and the importance of finding ways to share Earth's resources. Their aim is a higher level of human existence where people think and live in more empathic ways (Wilber, 2007). The Universal Declaration of the Rights of Mother Earth argues humans have responsibilities to each other and Earth that are essential for the flourishing of both (World People's Conference, 2010). In ecospiritual approaches, this awareness reflects a shift in consciousness away from the duality of anthropocentrism toward ecocentrism where emphasis is on humans achieving harmony in their *relationship* with Earth. They emphasize that a first step is the transformation of individual consciousness – the decolonization of human minds (Wilson and Yellow Bird, 2005) and this precedes community and social transformation (Baskin, 2009; Graham, 2011).

Interweaving Discourses, Goals and Projects

Since the 1990s, in separate discourses, the importance of attending to spirituality and the physical environment in social work practice has been growing among social work scholars who challenge the foundational assumptions of the profession (Besthorn, 2002; Coates, 2003; Faver, 2010; Hanrahan, 2011). The social work literature on Indigenous social work, ecology and spirituality emphasizes the importance of interdependence, interconnectedness and holism, all of which are central concepts in Indigenous epistemology. Where these three discourses overlap provides a critical opening, an integrative framework of ecospiritual approaches that transform social work's understanding of the person-environment relationship and the world in which we exist (see, for example, Baskin, 2011; Canda and Furman, 2010; Wilson, 2009). From an ecospiritual decolonizing perspective, the profession can 'decolonize the mind' (Gregory, 2008; Smith, 1999; Wilson and Yellow Bird, 2005) of mainstream social workers (see Smith, 1999) so they are better able not only to become more effective allies in the political and social struggles of Indigenous Peoples, but also more effective practitioners and educators by not inadvertently oppressing others through misguided conceptualizations and methods of practice.

Further, the United Nations' Declaration of Human Rights (1948) and Declaration of the Rights of Indigenous Peoples (2007) are consistent with social work's anthropocentric codes of ethics that focus on the key values of *human* dignity and worth, and *human* rights and social justice: 'Social justice encompasses the satisfaction of basic needs, fair access to services and benefits to achieve *human* potential, and recognition of individual and community rights' (Calma and Pridey, 2011: 147 emphasis added). Social injustice is defined in terms of damage to human interests and points to environmental racism's focus on the very close relationship between environmental degradation and the social problems affecting human well-being (Bullard, 1993, 2002; Hulme, 2011). While similarities exist among Indigenous, spirituality and environmental discourses, a way forward is neither automatic nor unproblematic as human social action is required to resist and transform colonial patterns of thinking and acting. Decolonizing efforts can have different objectives and take different forms. Their associated movements have different political goals which, at times, may work against one another.

Indigenous – Social Work – Discourse

As shown above, Indigenous social work is intentionally political (Hart, 2009) as it concerns Indigenous Peoples' efforts to reclaim their roots, values and ways of knowing and practices that support their development and existence. Mainstream social work has failed to address this political need effectively. Indigenous Peoples' decolonization objectives include getting society to recognize their collective legal rights to land claims and to secure reasonable compensation for resource extraction from their territories (Amnesty International, 2010; Green, 2002). Efforts to reclaim Indigenous lands and celebrate Indigenous traditions, languages, cultures and ways of knowing are forms of decolonizing practices whereby Indigenous Peoples attempt not only to seek sovereignty, that is, the freedom to govern themselves – political decolonization – but also to throw off the yoke of internalized oppression and overcome the trauma of dehumanization and 'unresolved generational pain and shame' (Dempsey and O, 2003: para. 4). Indigenous decolonizing endeavours also include critiques of capitalism and international trade arrangements, and see capitalism as aided and abetted by imperialism: 'the system of control which secured ... markets and capital investments' and simultaneously involved the 'exploitation and subjugation of indigenous peoples [*sic*]' (Smith, 1999: 21). For Indigenous Peoples, the imperialistic roots of capitalism continue to thrive today, perpetuating inequities and reinscribing historic injustices.

Decolonizing practice includes opposition to oppressive policies but is more than anti-oppressive practice. It includes the development of Indigenous social work education programmes and practice frameworks but is more than add-on courses. It involves the exploration of the relationship between social and health problems, including suicide and the lingering psychological trauma of residential schools, social isolation, poverty and loss of cultural identity which involves more than piecemeal programmes (see, for example, the Royal Commission on Indigenous Peoples, 1996; Wilson and Yellow Bird, 2005). The Indigenous Peoples' movement wants nation states to recognize their legal and historical rights to land, sovereignty and self-determination (Coon-Come, 1996) and to allocate resources to ensure a healthy quality of life for all the Indigenous Peoples of the world. This requires wealthy people in the Global North to support the equitable reallocation of economic resources. As former National Chief of the Assembly of First Nations in Canada Mathew Coon-Come asked of the Canadian citizenry, politicians and constitutional authorities: 'Are [you] willing to allow First Nations peoples to share the wealth?' (Green, 2002: 31)

Sharing the wealth is one of the areas where governments and many sectors of society may disagree. The resolution of land claims, sovereignty and resource issues, and effective responses to reduce the impact of climate change on Indigenous Peoples (see World People's Conference, 2010), necessitate a significant shift in resource allocation by national and international governing bodies. While goals of social and ecological justice are shared with the spiritual and environmental discourses, disagreements may arise concerning policy priorities. For example, should government funds go toward settling Indigenous land claims (social justice) or protecting endangered species and establishing protected habitat (environmental justice)? Should the royalties from resource extraction be targeted toward environmental restoration and greenhouse gas reductions, or toward Indigenous land claim settlements?

While land claims and self-government unite Indigenous people engaged in reclaiming their traditional territories and regaining control over their daily lives, decolonization also requires power sharing, where the goals of the colonizer and colonized are in accord. The anti-globalization movement extols small government and the importance of the local in eschewing capitalism and the power of global corporates and financial markets. In this sense, its goals are in accord with the Indigenous Peoples' and environmental movements' fight for social and environmental justice respectively. However, the agreement on foundational values may dissolve when decisions must be made to allocate or redistribute the increasingly limited economic resources for Indigenous welfare.

Environmental – Social Work – Discourse

Social work scholars have challenged the anthropocentricity of social work (Besthorn, 2002; Coates, 2003; Mary, 2008; Zapf, 2009), critiqued the dehumanizing effects of 'regimes of truth' (Smith, 1999), and discussed injustices arising from environmental destruction as human rights issues (Tester, 2012; Calma and Priday, 2011). Coates (2003), Graham (2006), and Hoff and Polack (1993), among other social work scholars, suggest there is much that social work – environmentalists – can learn from life-sustaining Indigenous cultures. For example, Hulme (2011) critiques the pervasive influence of the IPCC, which, as Giddens (2009: 24) notes, 'is not simply a scientific body, but a political and bureaucratic one' with enormous power and influence. Hulme (2011: 178) argues for the importance of learning not only from science but also from Indigenous teachings on 're-thinking the value of consumption'. By learning from different understandings, humans can bridge disciplinary boundaries and 'reimagine' how they live on Earth. He goes on to argue for a broad interdisciplinary understanding of social work and the environment within which the contribution of Indigenous knowledges can be recognized and respected.

Environmental scholarship in social work recognizes that human well-being is dependent upon the resources and regenerative capacities of Earth. This leads attention to anthropocentric concerns of environmental racism, human rights, habitat destruction, overharvesting and pollution (see Eckersley, 1992; Tester, 2012). It can extend toward ecocentric concerns based on the intrinsic value of all life forms and implications for human behaviour, such as Deep Ecology. Many social work scholars see intimate connection between environmental and spiritual issues – ecospirituality (Besthorn, 2002; Coates, 2003; Mary, 2008; Zapf, 2009).

However, environmentalists may have different objectives in localities, such as Indigenous lands, where land claims, industrial development and employment and skill development opportunities oppose conservation and the preservation of pristine areas from development. This is a challenge in both the Global North and Global South where decisions are made regarding land, traditionally used by Indigenous Peoples, without consulting them. This may be particularly sensitive when traditional hunting-and-gathering practices come up against environmental efforts to preserve threatened and endangered species. Further, traditional Indigenous livelihoods, such as hunting and trapping, may run afoul of animal rights activists challenging what they see as inhumane practices (see Tester, 2012).

Spirituality – Social Work – Discourse

Spirituality and the sacredness of the physical environment have been core elements in Indigenous ways of knowing for millennia. Their importance has been recognized as essential elements in the healing of Indigenous Peoples from the effects of colonization which included, in all regions of the planet, their displacement from their traditional lands, and for many, the severing of ties to their ancestors, traditions and identity. An essential step has been called 'decolonizing of the mind'. This implies more than political independence and self-government. It is a form of healing as 'people separate themselves from hegemonic ideologies ... [and] think critically and rewrite their historical, cultural, and material experiences' (Gregory, 2008: para. 1). Decolonizing the mind is not merely an individual undertaking but involves supportive and cooperative relationships through which Indigenous people re-story their experiences so as to develop an understanding that liberates them from past oppressive influences and enables them to discover their personal and cultural truth (Gregory, 2008).

Major disagreement may occur between environmental and religious groups advocating a stewardship model when human need is perceived to take precedence over long-term environmental well-being. A situation may arise when stewardship (inherently anthropocentric) may lead to short-term social benefits displacing long-term environmental advantage. While spiritual and religious groups, such as Kairos and Development and Peace, support Indigenous efforts to oppose mining operations that pollute their traditional lands, will they support changes to international trade agreements that call for concessions from the Global North to offset the exploitation that is inherent in global neoliberal capitalism?

Conclusion

Decolonization relies upon humans' ability to sustain hope by locating explanations of the history of social problems and articulating a story that provides meaning and guidance for responsible and co-creative, collective, transformative action in the present. The idea here is that understanding and re-storying the past can heal past trauma and enhance human well-being in the present. At the same time, an essential element in the decolonizing agenda is to recognize and celebrate diversity and work with fellow decolonizing activists without 'dominating, redefining or essentializing' (Green 2002: 33). As a crosscutting perspective, ecospiritual approaches attempt to restore hope and meaning, as they celebrate cultural diversity and build on the interdependence of all things. Inclusive spiritualities can provide a 'moral context' (Pulido, 1998, 721) to support transformational social action and change. Individualized, cognitive arguments alone might not provide adequate personal or political motivation but social movements that have brought about transformational social action and change, such as those led by Gandhi, King, Chavez, Tecumseh, Chief Seattle and Malcolm X indicate that 'individuals and societies can be transformed by collective (and individual) spiritual consciousness and action' (Pulido, 1998: 721–2). Spiritual agreements that recognize and engage the diverse spiritualities of others might be more powerful and desirable, and perhaps even more enduring and sustainable, than political pacts and can lead to action in support of social and ecological justice (see Lysack, 2012). While the three discourses have objectives that may, at times, be in conflict, decolonization offers hope for a future where social justice is present for Indigenous Peoples and, by extension all peoples, and where environmental justice is not only a foremost motivation but also a tangible reality.

References

Adelson, N. (2005). The embodiment of inequity: Health disparities in Aboriginal Canada. *Canadian Journal of Public Health*, 96, S45–S61.

Al-Krenawi, A. and Graham, J.R. (eds). (2003). *Multicultural Social Work in Canada: Working with Diverse Ethno-Racial Communities*. Toronto, ON: Oxford University Press.

Amnesty International. (2010). *From Homeland to Oil Sands: The Impact of Oil and Gas Development on the Lubicon Cree of Canada*. Ottawa: Amnesty International [Online]. Available at: http://www.amnesty.ca/lubicon/?p=527 [accessed: 12 October 2011].

Barker, J. (1990). *The Business of Paradigms* [film]. Available from Charthouse International Learning Corporation, 221 River Ridge Circle, Burnsville, MN. 55337.

Baskin, C. (2002). Circles of resistance: Spirituality in social work practice, education and transformative change. *Currents: New Scholarship in the Human Services*, 1(1), 2–9.

Baskin, C. (2006). Indigenous world views as challenges and possibilities in social work education. *Critical Social Work* 7(2) [Online]. Available at: http://www.uwindsor.ca/criticalsocialwork/aboriginal-world-views-as-challenges-and-possibilities-in-social-work-education [accessed: 3 April 2011].

Baskin, C. (2011). *Strong Helpers' Teachings: The Value of Indigenous Knowledges in the Helping Professions*. Toronto, ON: Canadian Scholars Press.

Behrendt, L. (2003). *Achieving Social Justice: Indigenous Rights and Australia's Future*. Annandale, NSW: Federation Press.

Benyus, J. (1997). *Biomimicry: Innovation Inspired in Nature*. New York: William Morrow.

Berry, T. (1988). *The Dream of the Earth*. San Francisco, CA: Sierra Club.

Besthorn, F.H. (2002). Expanding spiritual diversity in social work: Perspectives on the greening of spirituality. *Currents: New Scholarship in the Human Services*, 1(1) [Online]. Available at: http://wcmprod2.ucalgary.ca/currents/files/currents/v1n1_besthorn.pdf [accessed: 3 April 2011].

Bibby, R. (1987). *Fragmented Gods: The Poverty and Potential of Religion in Canada*. Toronto, ON: Irwin.

Brown, L. (1995). Ecopsychology and the Environmental Revolution: An environmental forward. In T. Roszak, Gomes, M. and Kanner, A. (eds), *Ecopsychology: Restoring the Earth, Healing the Mind*. San Francisco, CA: Sierra Club Books, xiii–xvi.

Bruyere, G. (2007). Making Circles: Renewing First Nations ways of helping. In J. Coates, Graham, J.R., Swartzentruber, B. and Ouellette, B. (eds), *Spirituality and Social Work: Selected Canadian Readings*. Toronto, ON: Canadian Scholars Press, 259–72. Originally published in L. Dominelli, Lorenz, W. and Soydan, H. (eds). *Beyond Racial Divides: Ethnicities in Social Work Practice*. Aldershot: Ashgate, 213–27.

Bullard, R. (1993). *Confronting Environmental Racism: Voices from the Grassroots*. Cambridge, MA: South End Press.

Bullard, R. (2002). *Environmental Justice in the Twenty-First Century* [Online]. Available at: http://www.ejrc.cau.edu/ejinthe21century.htm.[accessed: 3 April 2011].

Cadell, S. and Marshall, S. (2007). The (re)construction of self after the death of a partner to HIV/AIDS. *Death Studies*, 31(6), 537–48.

Calma, T. and Priday, E. (2011). Putting Indigenous human rights into social work practice. *Australian Social Work*, 64(2), 147–55.

Canadian Ecumenical Jubilee Initiative. (2000). *Sacred Land, Scarred Land* [Documentary]. Canadian Ecumenical Jubilee Initiative: Toronto.

Canda, E.R. (1988). Conceptualizing spirituality for social work: Insights from diverse perspectives. *Social Thought*, 14(1), 30–46.

Canda, E.R. and Furman, L.E. (1999). *Spiritual Diversity in Social Work Practice: The Heart of Helping*. New York: Free Press.

Canda, E.R. and Furman, L.D. (2010). *Spiritual Diversity in Social Work Practice* (2nd edn). New York: Oxford University Press.

Capra, F. (1982). *The Turning Point*. New York: Simon & Schuster.

Carniol, B. (2005). *Case Critical: Social Services and Social Justice in Canada* (5th edn). Toronto, ON: Between the Lines Press.

Catton, W. Jr. and Dunlap, R. (1997). A new ecological paradigm for post-exuberant sociology. *American Behavioral Scientist*, 24(1), 15–47.

Chavis, B. and Lee, C. (1987). *Toxic Wastes and Race in the United States*. New York. Commission on Racial Justice United Church of Christ.

Chefurka, P. (2011). Home economicus, home ecologicus. *Mother Pelican: A Journal of Sustainable Human Development*, 7(3) [Online]. Available at: http://www.pelicanweb.org/solisustv07n03page9.html [accessed: 3 April 2011].

Christopher, M, (1999). An exploration of the 'reflex' in reflexive modernity: The rational and pre-rational social causes of the affinity for ecological consciousness. *Organizations and Environment*, 12(4), 357–400.

Chinn, P. (2007). Decolonizing methodologies and Indigenous knowledge: The role of culture, place and personal experience in professional development. *Journal of Research in Science Teaching*, 44(9), 1247–68.

Clark, M. (1989). *Ariadne's Thread: The Search for New Modes of Thinking*. New York: St. Martin's Press.

Coates, J. (2003). *Ecology and Social Work: Toward a New Paradigm*. Halifax, NS: Fernwood Press.

Coates, J., Graham, J., Swartzentruber, B. and Ouellette, B. (eds). (2007). *Spirituality and Social Work: Selected Canadian Readings*. Toronto, ON: Canadian Scholars Press.

Cohen, B., Basmajian, S., Rosenberg, D. G., Lentin, M., Lee, A., Winestock, P. and Pell, R. (2008). *Toxic Trespass: How Safe Are Your Children?* Montreal: National Film Board of Canada.

Coholic, D. (2005). The helpfulness of spiritually influenced group work in developing self-awareness and self-esteem: A preliminary investigation. *The Scientific World Journal*, 5, 789–802.

Coholic, D. (2011). Exploring the feasibility and benefits of arts-based mindfulness-based practices with young people in need: Aiming to improve aspects of self-awareness and resilience. *Child and Youth Care Forum*, 40(4), 303–17.

Coholic, D., Cadell, S. and Nichols, A.W. (eds). (2008). *Special Issue of the Journal of Religion, Spirituality and Social Work – Social Thought*, 27(1–2), 1–3, 41–6, 123–5, 167–70.

Coon-Come, M. (1996). *Remarks of Grand Chief Mathew Coon Come*. Canada Seminar, 28 October 1996. Harvard Centre for International Affairs and Kennedy School of Governance [Online]. Available at: http://www.nativeweb. org/pages/legal/coon_come.html [accessed: 26 October 2011].

Diamond, J. (2005). *Collapse: How Societies Choose to Fail or Succeed*. Toronto, ON: Viking.

Dawson, S. (1994). Navajo Uranium Workers and the Environment: Technological disaster as survival strategies. In M. Hoff and McNutt, J. (eds), *The Global Environmental Crisis: Implications for Social Welfare and Social Work*. Brookefield, VT: Avebury.

Dempsey, O. and O, D. (2003). Decolonizing the self. *The Peak* [online], 113(10) [Online]. Available at: http://www.peak.sfu.ca/the-peak/2003–1/issue10/fe-decolself.html [accessed: 20 December 2011].

Drouin, H. (2002). Spirituality in social work practice. In F.J. Turner (ed.), *Social Work Practice: A Canadian Perspective* (2nd edn), Toronto: Prentice Hall, 33–45.

Dryzek, J. (2005). *The Politics of the Earth: Environmental Discourses*. New York: Oxford University Press.

Duran, B. and Duran, E. (2000). Applied Post-Colonial Research and Clinical Strategies. In M. Battiste (ed.), *Reclaiming Indigenous Voice and Vision*. Vancouver, BC: UBC Press, 86–100.

Dylan, A. and Coates, J. (2012). The spirituality of justice: Bringing together the eco and the social. *Journal of Religion and Spirituality in Social Work*, 31(1–2), 128–49.

Earley, J. (1997). *Transforming Human Culture*. Albany: SUNY Press.

Eckersley, R. (1992). *Environmentalism and Political Theory: Toward an Ecocentric Approach*. Albany: SUNY Press.

Elshof, L. (2010). Changing Worldviews to Cope with a Changing Climate. In R. Irwin (ed.), *Climate Change and Philosophy: Transformational Possibilities*. New York: Continuum Press, 75–108.

Faver, C. (2010). Seeking our place in the web of life: Animals and human spirituality. *Journal of Religion and Spirituality in Social Work*, 28(4), 362–78.

First National People of Colour Environmental Leadership Summit. (1991). *Principles of Environmental Justice* [Online]. Available at: http://www.ejnet. org/ej/principles.html [accessed: 21 October 2011].

Giddens, A. (2009). *The Politics of Climate Change*. Bristol: Polity Press.

Gladwin, T., Newbury, W. and Reiskin, E. (1997). Why Is the Northern Elite Mind Biased against Community, the Environment and a Sustainable Future. In M. Bazerman and Messick, D. (eds), *Environment, Ethics and Behavior*. San Francisco: New Lexington Press, 234–74.

Glavin T. (2006). *Sixth Extinction: Journeys among the Lost and Left Behind*. New York: St. Martin's Press.

Godrej, D. (2001). *The No-Nonsense Guide to Climate Change*. Toronto, ON: New Internationalist Publications.

Gosine, A. and Teelucksingh, C. (2008). *Environmental Justice and Racism in Canada: An Introduction*. Toronto, ON: Edmond Montgomery Publications Limited.

Graham, J.R. (2006). Spirituality and social work: A call for an international focus of research. *Areté*, 30(1), 63–77.

Graham, M.A. (2011). Change of heart in song. Keynote presentation at the *6th North American Conference on Spirituality and Social Work*, Washington, DC, June.

Graham, J., Coholic, D. and Coates, J. (2007). Spirituality as a Guiding Construct in the Development of Canadian Social Work: Past and present considerations. In J. Coates, Graham, J.R., Swartzentruber, B. and Ouellette, B. (eds), *Spirituality and Social Work: Selected Canadian Readings*. Toronto, ON: Canadian Scholars Press, 47–64.

Graveline, J. (1998). *Circle Works: Transforming Eurocentric Consciousness*. Halifax, Nova Scotia: Fernwood Press.

Gray, M. (2008). Viewing spirituality in social work through the lens of contemporary social theory. *British Journal of Social Work*, 38(1), 175–96.

Gray, M., Coates, J. and Yellow Bird, M. (eds). (2008). *Indigenous Social Work around the World: Towards Culturally Relevant Education and Practice.* Aldershot: Ashgate.

Green, J. (2002). Decolonizing in the era of globalization. *Canadian Dimension,* 36(2), 31–3.

Greenberg, P. (2010). *Four Fish: The Future of the Last Wild Food.* New York: Penguin.

Gregory, J. (2008). *Decolonization: A Process* [Online]. Available at: http://juliangregory.weebly.com/decolonization-a-process.html [accessed: 12 October 2011].

Hamilton, C. (2003). *Growth Fetish.* Sydney, AU: Allen & Unwin.

Hanrahan, C. (2011). Challenging anthropocentrism in social work through ethics and spirituality: Lessons from studies in human-animal bonds. *Journal of Religion and Spirituality in Social Work: Social Thought,* 30(3), 272–93.

Hart, M.A. (2002). *Seeking Mino-Pimatisiwin: An Aboriginal Approach to Helping.* Halifax, Nova Scotia: Fernwood Press.

Hart, M. (2008). Critical Reflections on an Aboriginal Approach to helping. In M. Gray, Coates, J. and Yellow Bird, M. (eds), *Indigenous Social Work Around the World: Toward Culturally Relevant Social Work Practice.* Aldershot: Ashgate, 129–40.

Hart, M.A. (2009). Anti-Colonial Indigenous Social Work: Reflections on an Aboriginal approach. In R. Sinclair, Hart, M.A. and Bruyere, G. (eds), *Wicihitowin: Aboriginal Social Work in Canada.* Halifax, Nova Scotia: Fernwood Press, 25–41.

Hawken, P. (2007). *Blessed Unrest: How the Largest Movement in the World Came into Being and No One Saw It Coming.* New York: Viking Press.

Henderson-Youngblood, J. (2000). Aukpachi: Empowering Aboriginal Thought. In M. Battiste (ed.), *Reclaiming Indigenous Voices and Vision.* Vancouver: UBC Press, 248–78.

Henerey, N. (2003). The reality of visions: Contemporary theories of spirituality in social work. *British Journal of Social Work,* 33(8), 1105–13.

Hodge, D. (2007). Social justice and people of faith: A transnational perspective. *Social Work,* 52(2), 139–48.

Hoff, M. and McNutt, J. (eds). (1994). *The Global Environmental Crisis: Implications for Social Welfare and Social Work.* Brookefield, VT: Avebury.

Hoff, M. and Polack, R. (1993). Social dimensions of the environmental crisis: Challenges for social work. *Social Work,* 38(2), 204–11.

Hofrichter, R. (ed.). (1993). *Toxic Struggles: The Theory and Practice of Environmental Justice.* Gabriola Island, BC: New Society Publishers.

Holloway, M. (2007). Spiritual need and the core business of social work. *British Journal of Social Work,* 37(2), 265–80.

Houpt, S. (2011). Marketing the aboriginal housing crisis, *The Globe and Mail,* 10 December: A5.

Hubbard, B. (1998). *Conscious Evolution: Awakening Our Social Potential.* Novato, CA: New World Library.

Hulme, M. (2011). Meet the humanities. *Nature Climate Change,* 1, 177–9.

Indigenous Environmental Network (2011). *US Tribal Leaders Present President Obama with Mother Earth Accord Opposing Keystone Xl* [Online]. Available at: http://www.ienearth.org/news/us-tribal-leaders-present-president-obama-with-mother-earth-accord-opposing-keystone-xl.html [accessed: 29 February 2012].

Indigenous Peoples' Restoration Network (IPRN). (1995a). *Traditional Ecological Knowledge* [Online]. Available at: http://www.ser.org/iprn/default. asp [accessed: 12 October 2011].

Indigenous Peoples' Restoration Network (IPRN). (1995b). *Organizations and Communities* [Online]. Available at: http://www.ser.org/iprn/org.asp. [accessed: 12 October 2011].

Iseke-Barnes, J. (2008). Pedagogies for decolonizing. *Canadian Journal of Native Education,* 31(1), 123–48.

Intergovernmental Panel on Climate Change (IPCC). (2007). *Climate Change 2007: Synthesis Report. A Contribution of Working Groups I, II, and III to the Fourth Assessment Report of the Intergovernmental Panel on Climate Change.* [Core Writing Team, Pachauri, R.K. and Reisinger, A. (eds)]. Geneva: IPCC [Online]. Available at: http://www.ipcc.ch/publications_and_data/ar4/syr/en/ contents.html [accessed: 5 August 2011].

Jarman, M. (2007). *Climate Change.* Halifax, Nova Scotia: Fernwood Press.

Johnston, B. (2003). *Ojibway Heritage.* Toronto, ON: McClelland and Stewart.

Keevil, G. (2011). Folio: Attawapiskat. *The Globe and Mail,* 10 December, A10-A11.

Koné, L. (2010). Toxic colonialism: The human rights implications of illicit trade of toxic waste in Africa [Online]. Available at: http://www.consultancyafrica. com/index.php?option=com_contentandview=articleandid=473:toxic-colonialism-the-human-rights-implications-of-illicit-trade-of-toxic-waste-in-africaandcatid=91:rights-in-focusandItemid=296 [accessed: 30 October 2011].

Korstrom, G. (1998). Deline Poisoned? Past area mining linked to cancer. *Northern News Service,* 23 March [Online]. Available at: http://arcticcircle.uconn.edu/ SEEJ/Mining/korstrom.html [accessed: 12 October 2011].

Korten, D. (2006). *The Great Turning: From Empire to Earth Community.* San Francisco, CA: Kumarian Press and Berrett-Koehler.

Korten, D. (2009). *Agenda for a New Economy: From Phantom Wealth to Real Wealth.* San Francisco, CA: Berrett-Koehler.

Lerner, M. (2003). Editorial: Closed hearts, closed minds. *Tikkun,* 18(5), 7 [Online]. Available at: http://www.tikkun.org/article.php/Lerner [accessed: 12 December 2011].

Lindsay, R. (2002). *Recognizing Spirituality: The Interface between Faith and Social Work.* Perth, WA: UWA Press.

Lowenberg, F. (1988). *Religion and Social Work Practice in Contemporary American Society*. New York: Columbia University Press.

Lynn, R. (2001). Learning from a 'Murri Way'. *British Journal of Social Work*, 31(6), 903–16.

Lysack, M. (2012). Building capacity for environmental engagement and leadership: An ecosocial work perspective. *International Journal of Social Welfare*, 21, 1–10 [Online]. Available at: http://onlinelibrary.wiley.com/doi/10.1111/j.1468–2397.2011.00854.x/pdf. [accessed: 20 December 2011].

Macy, J. (1990). The Ecological Self: Postmodern ground for right action. In D.R. Griffin (ed.), *Sacred Interconnections*. Albany: SUNY Press.

Manuel, G. and Posluns, M. (1974). *The Fourth World: An Indian Reality*. Toronto, ON: Collier-Macmillan.

Mary, N. (2008). *Social Work in a Sustainable World*. Chicago, IL: Lyceum Books.

Memmi, A. (1965). *The Colonizer and the Colonized*. Boston, MA: Beacon Press.

Miller, J. (2001). *Skyscrapers Hide the Heavens: A History of Indian-White Relations in Canada* (3rd edn). Toronto, ON: University of Toronto Press.

Morton, T. (2007). *Ecology without Nature*. Boston, MA: Harvard University Press.

Morrisette, V., McKenzie, B. and Morrissette, L. (1993). Towards an Aboriginal model of social work practice. *Canadian Social Work Review*, 10(1), 91–108.

Morales, A. and Scheafor, B. (1995). *Social Work: A Profession of Many Faces* (7th edn). Toronto: Allyn & Bacon.

Nadeau, D. and Young, A. (2006). Educating Bodies for self-determination: A decolonizing strategy. *Canadian Journal of Native Education,* 29(1), 87–101.

Nash, M. and Stewart, B. (2002). *Spirituality and Social Care: Contributing to Personal and Community Well-Being*. Philadelphia: Jessica Kingsley.

O'Murchu, D. (1997). *Quantum Theology: Spiritual Implications of the New Physics*. New York: Crossroads.

Orr, D. (2009). *Down to the Wire*. Toronto, ON: Oxford.

People of Color Environmental Leadership Summit. (1991). *Principles of Environmental Justice* [Online]. Available at: http://www.ejrc.cau.edu/princej.html.[accessed: 12 October 2011].

Pulido, L. (1996). *Environmentalism and Economic Justice*. Tucson: University of Arizona Press.

Pulido, L. (1998). The sacredness of 'Mother Earth': Spirituality, activism, and social justice. *Annals of the Association of American Geographers*, 88(4), 719–23.

Richter, R. (Producer) (1984). *Hungry for Profit* [Documentary]. New York: WNET Television.

Rogge, M. (1994). Environmental Injustice: Social welfare and toxic waste. In M. Hoff and McNutt, J. (eds), *The Global Environmental Crisis: Implications for Social Welfare and Social Work*. Burlington, VT: Ashgate, 53–74.

Ross, D. (2003). *Reviewing the Land Management Process: Some Common Ground at a Point in the Process: A Report on the Collaboration between*

Alcoa Wagerup and Yarloop/Hamel Residents. Bunbury, Western Australia: Edith Cowan University.

Royal Commission on Aboriginal Peoples. (1996). *The Final Report of the Royal Commission on Aboriginal Peoples*. Ottawa, ON: Canada Communications Group.

Sahtouris, E. (1998). *Conscious Evolution: Awakening the Power of our Social Potential*. Novato, CA: New World Library.

Saleebey, D. (2009). *The Strengths Perspective in Social Work Practice* (5th ed.). Boston: Pearson Education, Inc.

Scharmer, C. (2003). *The Blind Spot of Leadership: Presencing as a Social Technology of Freedom* [Online]. Available at: http://www.ottoscharmer.com/docs/articles/2003_TheBlindSpot.pdf.[accessed: 12 October 2011].

Schmitz, C., Matyók, T., Sloan, L.M. and James, C. (2012). The relationship between social work and environmental sustainability: Implications for interdisciplinary practice. *International Journal of Social Welfare*, 21, 1–9 [Online]. Available at: http://onlinelibrary.wiley.com/doi/10.1111/j.1468–2397.2011.00855.x/pdf [accessed: 20 December 2011].

Sherkat, D. and Ellison, C. (2007). Structuring the religion-environment connection: Identifying religious influences on environmental concern and activism. *Journal for the Scientific Study of Religion*, 46(1), 71–85.

Shkilnyk, A. (1985). *A Poison Stronger than Love: The Destruction of an Ojibwa Community*. New Haven, CT: Yale University Press.

Sinclair, R. (2004). Aboriginal social work education in Canada: Decolonizing pedagogy for the seventh generation. *First Peoples Child & Family Review*, 1(1), 49–61.

Sinclair, R. (2009). Identity or Racism? Aboriginal transracial adoption. In R. Sinclair, Hart, M.A. and Bruyere, G. (eds), *Wícihitowin: Aboriginal Social Work in Canada*. Halifax, Nova Scotia: Fernwood Press, 89–112.

Sinclair, R., Hart, M.A. and Bruyere, G. (eds). (2009). *Wícihitowin: Aboriginal Social Work in Canada*. Halifax, Nova Scotia: Fernwood Press.

Smith, L.T. (1999). *Decolonizing Methodologies: Research and Indigenous Peoples*. New York: Zed Books.

Spretnak, C. (1997). *The Resurgence of the Real: Body, Nature and Place in a Hypermodern World*. Harlow: Addison-Wesley.

Suagee, D. (2002). *Dimensions of Environmental Justice in Indian Country and Native Alaska*. Resource Papers Series, Second National People of Colour Environmental Leadership Summit – Summit 2. Atlanta: Environmental Justice Resource Centre [Online]. Available at: http://www.ejrc.cau.edu/summit2/IndianCountry.pdf.[accessed: 12 October 2011].

Teasdale, W. (1999). *The Interspiritual Age: Practical Mysticism for the Third Millennium*. Council on Spiritual Practices [Online]. Available at: http://www.csp.org/experience/docs/teasdale-interspiritual.html [accessed: 23 August 2011].

Tester, F. (2012). Climate Change as an Issue of Human Rights. In M. Gray, Coates, J. and Hetherington, T. (eds), *Environmental Social Work*. Aldershot: Ashgate, 102–18.

Todd, S. (2009). Mobilizing Communities for Social Change: Integrating mindfulness and passionate politics. In S. Hick (ed.), *Mindfulness and Social Work*. Chicago: Lyceum Books, 171–87.

Turner, C. (2007). *The Geography of Hope: A Tour of the World We Need*. Toronto, ON: Vintage Canada.

United Nations' Declaration of Human Rights. (1948) [Online]. Available at: http://www.un.org/en/documents/udhr/[accessed: 12 October 2011].

United Nations Declaration of the Rights of Indigenous Peoples. (2007) [Online]. Available at: http://www.un.org/esa/socdev/unpfii/documents/DRIPS_en.pdf [accessed: 12 October 2011].

Van Wormer, K. (1997). *Social Welfare: A World View*. Chicago: Nelson-Hall.

Weaver, H. (1999). Indigenous people and the social work profession: Defining culturally competent services. *Social Work*, 44(3), 217–25.

Weaver, H. (2004). The elements of cultural competence: Applications with Native American clients. *Journal of Ethnic and Cultural Diversity in Social Work*, 13, 19–35.

Westra, L. and Wenz, P. (eds). (1995). *Faces of Environmental Racism: Confronting Issues of Global Justice*. London: Rowman & Littlefield.

Wilber, K. (2007). *Integral Spirituality: A Startling New Role for Religion in the Modern and Postmodern World*. Boston: Integral Books.

Wilson, C. (2001). Review of Smith, L.T. (1999). *Decolonizing methodologies: Research and Indigenous Peoples* [New York: Zed Books]. *Social Policy Journal of New Zealand*, 17, 214–17.

Wilson, S. (2009). *Research is Ceremony: Indigenous Research Methods*. Halifax, Nova Scotia: Fernwood.

Wilson, W. and Yellow Bird, M. (2005). (eds). *For Indigenous Eyes Only: The Decolonization Handbook*. Santa Fe, NM: School of American Research Press.

World People's Conference on Climate Change and the Rights of Mother Earth (2010). Peoples Agreement [Online]. Available at: http://pwccc.wordpress.com/2010/04/24/peoples-agreement/[accessed: 12 October 2011].

Yellow Bird, M. (2004). Cowboys and Indians: Toys of genocide, icons of colonialism. *Wicazo Sa Review*, 19(2), 33–48.

Yellow Bird, M. (2012). Neurodecolonization: Using mindfulness practices to delete the neural networks of colonialism. In Waziyatawin, and Yellow Bird, M. (eds), *For Indigenous Minds Only: A Decolonization Handbook* (2nd edn). Sante Fe, NM: School of American Research.

Zapf, M.K. (2009). *Social Work and the Environment: Understanding People and Place*. Toronto, ON: Canadian Scholars Press.

Chapter 4

Why Decolonized Social Work is More than Cross-Culturalism

Ann Joselynn Baltra-Ulloa

To put my story in context, I am a Chilean Mapuche woman who came to Australia as a refugee and tried to 'fit in' by assimilating to a culture and way of life that – as a colonized individual – I was led to believe was not only superior to my Indigenous culture but offered me and my family a safer way of life. Assimilating was a tool for deflecting the pain I felt when I thought of my own Indigenous heritage as something I had lost, or that had been damaged and was no longer relevant in Australia, something that had compromised my safety and my survival. Alschuler's (1996) reference to Memmi's (1973) analysis of the process of assimilation resonated for me:

> at first the colonized seeks to assimilate into the colonizer's society, the colonized experiences 'self-rejection', 'self-hatred', and 'shame' as [s]he attempts assimilation. The colonized finds in the colonizers a model of all that is worthy, prestigious, honorable, powerful, and wealthy ... equaling this model to the point of disappearing in it. (Alschuler, 1996: 514–15)

'Fitting in' via assimilation was a process of rejecting myself. It was not until I travelled back to Chile in 1995 that I began the journey I am currently on: realizing that, in Australia, I was living a life not as myself. My true self laid waiting for me in my culture, which remained rich, vibrant and relevant, a living organism in me. Reconnecting with *my* people, our land, our traditions, our rituals and our values has felt more fulfilling to me than any other act of assimilation I have attempted in Australia. I felt reborn in my peoples' passion to politicize their struggles and rid themselves of colonization. Today, I feel profoundly spiritually connected to them and our land and, while I live in Australia, I no longer question how guided, welcomed and safeguarded I am by the Mapuche spirit.

In Australia, I work predominantly with people of refugee background and therein lies my interest in 'cross-cultural' social work practices. I use the term 'people of refugee background' in respect for what I have learnt through dialogue with the people with whom I have worked over the years. I have learnt that, for many people of refugee background, once safety is secured, a home becomes a possibility, with connection and belonging to a welcoming community in which they are valued. This makes 'being a refugee' no longer part of their personal

identity or what 'defines' their place in society. However, for many of those
with whom I have worked, the experience of having 'been a refugee' – having
experienced human rights violations – shapes personal and social identity, and
daily life. It becomes part of one's historical context, which evolves over time,
particularly as experiences are contextualized and reconnection with positive
aspects of humanity takes place.

The extent to which people are defined and influenced by their historical context
depends on how much their history, lived experience, culture, values and beliefs
are acknowledged, respected, integrated and understood by society. These points
of view are as much shaped by my Mapuche culture and my own experiences as a
'person of refugee background' as they are by my work, which is a way of life for
my family and me. We eat with 'clients', visit one another at home, look after one
another's children, nurse one another through illness, and learn from one another.
We fall out and reconcile, run workshops together for our communities, lobby for
change, write government submissions, have obligations to our communities and
house those the government later deports. In essence, we are *in* each other's lives.
All this felt intuitively 'normal' to me, perhaps because I grew up being taught that
we are all of *Mapu* – land – and we are all *Che* – people – interconnected by our
human need to give and receive help.

Until I formalized my social work training and became a professional social
worker with Australian qualifications I never questioned this intuitive way of life
but the contradictions experienced during my social work training have endured
through my years of practice. We were trained to believe we were 'the good guys':
caring, sensitive, aware, competent, ethical, agents of social justice and change,
and, above all, capable of empowering ourselves and others. This seemed an
ill-fitting cloak from the very beginning, uncomfortable and burdensome when,
'in the job', I was essentially being paid to support and promote a new form of
colonialism – a 'fitting in' to a system that values individualism, discourages
collective care for collective issues, prefers to control, survey and judge people. I
was to do this by managing risk, reporting my activities, withdrawing my services
if people did not comply, and timing my availability. I was to know at all times
what to do. I was to keep an emotional distance, avoid conflict and never ever
speak of befriending a 'client'.

In 1993, Meemeduma presented a paper on *Reshaping the Future Cultural
Sense and Social Work* at a national social work conference in Newcastle, Australia.
She argued it was not enough for social work to remain conceptually incarcerated
by an obsession with how the 'other' is. Social workers needed to turn their gaze
on themselves, know themselves first before they sought to know the 'other'.
Likewise, I believe social workers will continue to support the marginalization
of Indigenous, immigrant and refugee communities around the world if they do
not focus on the why and how of what they do. This chapter is the product of my
personal journey and reflections, my context thus far, and the thoughts that have
occurred as a result of turning the gaze inwards on myself and outwards toward
social work. The more I read about social work, speak to people and hear stories

about it, and the more conferences I attend, the more I am convinced my journey is not that far removed from what many social workers encounter – and grapple with – when they think of what they know as 'social work', what they do as social workers, how they do it and why. This chapter aims to make 'invisible norms' explicit using the lenses of 'Whiteness', 'privilege' and 'power' in the context of work with Aboriginal Peoples in Australia and other ethnic minorities, such as 'people of refugee background'.

The invisibility of concepts like Whiteness in social work is scattered through the social work literature. In essence, this literature defines Whiteness as an ideology, a silent mainstream, dangerously and pervasively setting invisible benchmarks against which everyone is measured. Whiteness eludes obvert discussion while it nevertheless dictates how people should live, advantaging one way of thinking, one way of being and doing above all others. There is Moreton-Robinson's (2000, 2004) work on Whiteness within Indigenous representation and feminism; Gair, Thomson, Miles, and Harris's (2003) work on the challenge of decolonizing social work education in Australia; Young's (2004) emphasis on the invisibility of Whiteness in social work theory and practice; Pease's (2010) unmasking of the source of white privilege; Walter, Taylor and Habibis's (2011) exploration of Whiteness in Australian social work; Razack's (2002, 2005, 2009) regular contributions in exposing Whiteness within international social work teaching and practice; and Mwansa's (2011) historical account of the crisis of relevance of Western social work education in Africa. From this literature, one might conclude that the limited number of articles focusing on Whiteness in social work, particularly in Australia, is the product of a concerted attempt by the status quo to dilute any focus on itself.

Pon (2009) calls this a form of 'new racism' and what I often refer to as the 'politics of silence' that prevails in places like Australia, infiltrating society and thus social work thinking and practice. 'New racism' colours the sociopolitical landscape, not through overt violent, physical threats, or verbal insults to people of colour, but rather through covert rhetoric under the guise of 'nationalism' and 'cultural preservation' (Pon, 2009: 61), political correctness and, at times, even silence. This new form of racism is particularly apparent in Australia where we think of multiculturalism as an undisturbed accomplishment by a non-racist, cultureless society that welcomes difference and finds peaceful ways to coexist in harmony (Gray and Allegritti, 2003). If difference is ever too far removed from the silent norm in Australia, as is the case with Muslims, we do not speak of their negative portrayals as racism (Masanauskas, 2011a). We call on multiculturalism to dilute any inference to racism in public discourse and opt to highlight 'happy' individual instances in which being a Muslim in Australia is apolitical – a simple personal choice void of sociocultural perceptions and influences, whether negative or positive.

Interrogating what diversity does or does not constitute, and the questioning of who gets to decide what diversity is and is not, is at the heart of a critical multiculturalism that Australia has yet to embrace. New racism in Australia promotes a looking away from Whiteness and thus acts to discriminate on grounds which are never openly associated with 'race' (Pon 2009) but rather focus on fearing difference. If the project of decolonization were to gain momentum, indeed 'indigenizing' social work would need to be about recasting social work theory and practice as 'a form of resistance and a medium of transformation from externally imposed to locally developed models of practice and solutions … [that] include local cultures' (Gray and Allegritti, 2002: 325). However, this is not just simply about making Western social work fit local contexts by 'being good, doing the right thing, mobilizing virtue but rather [about a fundamental] change of what it means to be human … [social workers] need to theorize how to give up power' (Moreton-Robinson, 2011, pers. comm., 8 August). This fundamental change is what will transcend the status quo where currently assimilation and misappropriation of local knowledge underpins what is currently called 'cross-cultural, culturally sensitive' practice. There is mounting evidence that social workers can no longer speak of crossing cultures as something they do with the relative assurance that it works (Abrams and Moio, 2009; Dean, 2001; Park, 2005; Sundar and Ly, 2013; Yan, 2008). For the most part, cross-cultural approaches to social work practice have been designed, developed and evaluated by Western social workers in the belief they are effective helpers across multiple cultural contexts though they know very little about whether or not the recipient of their help would agree. A decolonized social work would involve a critical stance on these issues – a stance no longer content with assuming that a 'crossing' of cultures is relevant or even possible. A decolonized social work calls for a view of the world as interrelated and co-dependent, a world where the redressing of inequality can only happen if there were solidarity, accountability and a commitment to both unveiling Whiteness and staying implicated in its critique.

Debunking Cross-Cultural Social Work Practice

In exploring the evolution of 'cross-cultural' social work practice, a critique of the term 'cross-cultural' is offered to build on Gray and Coates (2008) exploration of this contested theoretical terrain concerning issues of diversity within social work. Historically, cross-cultural social work has been defined as 'any working relationship in which two or more of the participants differ with respect to cultural background, values and lifestyles' (Sue et al., 1982: 47).

   In Australia, since World War II, with mass immigration and the changes to the status of Aboriginal Australians, social work has faced a growing concern with working 'cross-culturally'. In a review of writings on diversity, ethnicity and 'race' in Australian social work between 1947 and 1997, McMahon (2002: 173) traced concerns about 'working cross-culturally' to social work's attempt to respond to rapidly evolving social policies that shifted the focus from 'protection and assimilation to self-determination, multiculturalism and reconciliation'. From within the profession, the Australian Association of

Social Workers (AASW Code of Ethics, 1999) positioned culture as central to its description of one of social work's key responsibilities to clients of 'culturally and linguistically diverse backgrounds' (CALD), namely, 'cultural awareness'. It stated social workers would acknowledge the significance of culture in their practice by recognizing the effect of their own culture on their practice, acquiring knowledge of the cultural 'other', while remaining 'sensitive to difference' (AASW, 1999: 15–16). Practice framed around this responsibility was named 'culturally sensitive practice'. The assumptions underlying these statements are multiple.

First, social workers are implicitly expected to know their own culture. However, which cultures are alleged to be known by social workers is not made clear – is personal culture presumed to be known? Is there a presumption that there is a social work culture to be known? These aspects remain silent.

Secondly, somehow, social workers are unreservedly thought of as able to identify how culture affects their practice. Which culture is supposed to have an influence on practice is again not made clear, and how a social worker is able to identify how culture affects practice is also left unsaid. All the while the social worker is also expected to acquire cultural knowledge about the 'other' – what cultural knowledge is deemed necessary for acquisition is not stipulated. In addition, as an act of absolute skill mastering, the social worker is assumed to be able to juggle all this while remaining 'sensitive to difference'. Which difference the social worker needs to be sensitive to and how this sensitivity is accomplished is left unqualified. The most potent assumption made is that there is no need to ask *why* at any stage of this process, the 'culturally sensitive practitioner' needs to know how to do culturally sensitive practice but she or he remains immune to having to ask why the need exists.

More recently, the 2010 edition of the AASW Code of Ethics has continued to position culture at the centre of what constitutes working with people of non-Western backgrounds. However, the preferred model for practice has been renamed 'culturally competent, safe, and sensitive practice' (AASW, 2010: 17). Similarly to how cultural awareness was defined in the 1999 code, the latest version builds on prior attempts to define the preferred model of culturally sensitive practice by broadening culturally competent, safe and sensitive practice to sensitivity to and respectfulness of religious and spiritual worldviews; mindfulness of meaning making differences around issues of confidentiality across client groups; accessibility to services via the use of interpreters; promotion of culturally aware and culturally competent practices; inclusion of community Elders in shaping Indigenous practice; collaborative relationships with clients; and the promotion of anti-racist and anti-oppressive practice principles challenging racism and other forms of oppression. The predicaments that remain, and which are exemplified by the AASW's Code of Ethics (2010), are threefold.

The First Predicament: Culture as Static

First, the word 'culture' is defined as 'ways of life, and shared values, beliefs and meanings common to groups of people' (Quinn, 2009: 266, cited in AASW Code of Ethics, 2010: 43). This continues the tradition in the West of speaking of culture as static, ahistorical and decontextual. Australian social work is not alone in this predicament. Matsumoto and Juang (2004) note the word 'culture' is used interchangeably in many Western countries with concepts such as ethnicity, 'race' and nationality. The North American National Association of Social Workers' (2001: 9) Standard of Cultural Competence Practice document defines culture as the 'totality of ways of behaving that get passed on from generation to generation'. Becker (1986: 12) defines culture as 'concerted activity based on shared ideas and understanding'. These definitions conceive of culture as a cluster of defined categories and characteristics shared by groups of people which, over time, can present in different contexts but which do not change. Thus, culture is a confusing, ambiguous, static and contested term that, despite its elusive nature, social workers continue to force into a fixed meaning (Dean, 2001; Gray, Coates and Yellow Bird, 2008; Park, 2005).

Postmodernism has lent a hand in moving away from one-dimensional fixed meanings. Postmodernists define culture as a social and individual construction (Dean, 2001; Laird, 1998). Accordingly, Laird (1998: 28–9) states that culture is 'always contextual, emergent, improvisational, transformational ... political; above all, it is a matter of ... language, of discourse'. This notion of culture as a concept defined through 'discourse' has emerged in the social work literature as 'a key signifier of difference', more specifically of 'racial difference' (Park, 2005: 13). Culture, as a signifier of racial difference, continues to be attributed to 'non-white people' (Pease, 2010: 111). The racially different are spoken of as a minority. Minorities in Western societies are seen as marginal and, therefore, isolated from the 'mainstream'. This isolation translates into social deficit or social disadvantage. A concern for developing cross-cultural, culturally competent, safe and sensitive practices has emerged in the West from this context in which social workers speak of culture as socially and individually constructed, and thus in constant flux. One would argue, however, this idea of culture in constant flux is often used as an attack by the colonizer on the 'simple and primitive' Indigenous culture (Chilcott, 2011). Meanwhile, culture is related primarily to racial difference, accredited to non-white people, with racial difference regarded as a social deficit (Ling, 2004; Nimmagadda and Cowger, 1999; Nye, 2006; Patni, 2006; Pease, 2010; Williams, 2006).

The Second Predicament: A Deficit View of Those Non-White

The second predicament is that cultural competence has been allocated enormous significance in working with the 'cultural other' in social work without much thought to the origins of this priority and whether or not its genesis is in clients' needs. The literature on cultural competence, not just in social work but across many other disciplines like psychology, education, nursing and medicine, has grown considerably (Gentlewarrior, Martin-Jearld, Skok and Sweetser, 2008; Lynch and Hanson, 2004; National Health and Medical Research Council, 2006; Patni, 2006; Weaver, 1999). Harrison and Turner (2011) trace the origins of this priority in Australia to the development of a national push for a culturally competent workforce to meet the needs of an increasingly multicultural society. Australia has followed a similar trajectory towards cultural competence as the USA where it came about because the civil rights movement challenged the Eurocentric, deficit-focused view of coloured people (Abrams and Moio, 2009).

The priority given to cultural competence in Australia has arisen as a response to the ongoing sociocultural, political, economic and environmental assault on Aboriginal communities. These assaults have included the Northern Territory intervention in which the racial discrimination act was suspended to allow governments to impose, on Aboriginal communities only, income management strategies. The intervention was at first presented as a crisis intervention in which the government was responding to irresponsible, inadequate parenting and rampant child sexual abuse in Aboriginal communities (Perpitch, 2010). Disguised as a 'closing the gap' initiative, to date, it has resulted in the obliteration of all existing forms of self-governance and self-determination in many Aboriginal communities. Many social workers were employed and deployed by the government, flown into remote Aboriginal communities, to be part of 'the intervention'. Many returned to share stories of guilt at the obvious disparities between the service professions' professed values of empowerment and social justice and the intent of 'the intervention'. The uneasiness many in the human services sector and in the community felt as a result of these assaults on Aboriginal Australians has, to date, resulted in a reinvigorated commitment to culturally competent practices. It has not, however, resulted in the suspension of 'the intervention'. Australian politicians continue to regularly flood public discourse with 'good outcome' stories to appease the public and reassure Australians that the colonizers' project is undoubtedly justified (Perth Now, 2011).

The underlying assumption in Australia is that the only way to meet the needs of the 'culturally different other' is to cross cultures and to do so competently. Noteworthy is the assumption that the helping professional does the crossing with the goal of bringing 'them' back to the dominant 'us'. Further, consensus on defining what standards of practice are required to be deemed 'culturally competent' is seldom reached and the notion of 'crossing cultures' remains easier to imagine than to attain in practice (Yan and Wong, 2005). As Guthrie (2009) points out, what is regarded as cultural competence in one context may not be regarded as such in another, so even aiming for a standardized set of 'know hows' in practice would not overcome the challenges of diverse meanings across divergent contexts.

The most concerning aspect of the conundrum faced in holding onto cultural competency as a social work practice approach and core skill is the notion that social workers can actually 'cross cultures', via whatever sets of competencies, and thus overcome or bridge cultural differences. This points to an underlying assumption, rooted in racism, that the social worker is superior and thus eminently capable of overcoming all obstacles to reach the cultural 'other'. Social workers hold onto the belief that culturally sensitive services to clients of non-Western backgrounds can be provided even though their contexts are different, the meaning given to culture is contested and inherent sources of power and privilege reinforce the dominance of Western culture (Gray et al., 2008; Pease, 2010). It is difficult to conceive of a 'crossing of cultures' while the profession is not only 'raced' but also measured, in countries like Australia, against 'the invisible norm of Whiteness' (Moreton-Robinson, 2004: viii).

The Third Predicament: Invisibility of 'Whiteness'

The third impediment faced in continuing to favour 'cross-cultural' approaches to practice is 'Whiteness', an ideology blinding people to what is essentially a silent and invisible mainstream benchmark against which everyone is measured. To move beyond 'cross-culturalism' would require an unpacking of 'Whiteness' and how it propels the power and privilege of some groups in society above, and at the cost of, others. Indigenization as 'a form of resistance and a medium of transformation' (Gray and Allegritti, 2002: 325) offers this opportunity because it surfaces the sources of power and privilege and offers a 'vantage point' from which to examine practice from an historical and 'access' perspective. In other words, it asks who actually gets to ask the critical questions that shape interactions and what and who is left in and out of this cross-cultural practice discourse (Rossiter, 2005). A necessary precursor to any resistance to and transformation from the status quo is an examination of racism as a tool and outcome of 'Whiteness' (Briskman, 2008).

Cultural competence and its messages and promise of crossing cultures safely and sensitively promotes 'othering' by positioning the skills and knowledge of social workers above the skills and knowledge of clients. As such, it is a form of 'new racism' (Pon, 2009) and an instrument and product of 'Whiteness'. New racism moves away from overt discrimination based on biology to discrimination based on cultural difference. It is a form of racism connected to the assumed superiority of Western culture. Crossing cultures safely and sensitively via culturally competent practices does not 'theorize power or critique systems of [privilege, power and] oppression such as racism, sexism, ageism, heterosexism, and ableism' (Sakamoto, cited in Pon, 2009: 59) because to do so would mean having to acknowledge and do something about who gets to exercise the power to define the 'other'.

The sustainability of 'Whiteness' as an ideology informing culturally competent and culturally sensitive cross-cultural practices depends on remaining silent and passive about who gets to define whom. The most silent, pervasive and invisible source of detraction from the theorizing of power and privilege in social work is 'Whiteness' (Walter, Taylor and Habibis, 2011). A thorough examination of 'Whiteness' in Gray et al. (2008), particularly Chapter 6 where

Briskman deconstructs social work by adopting a 'Whiteness' perspective, reveals that 'Whiteness' acts as a 'default standard' (Sue, 2006: 15) against which all other races and ethnic groups are measured. When people do not measure up, they are problematized, made into minorities and seen as inferior to the problem solvers and experts with 'know-how'.

Social work in the West was built on 'Whiteness' (Sakamoto, 2007). This is why context is so important to the decolonization project because without first understanding the profession's history, social workers cannot hope to understand their effect on the contexts in which they operate. Devoid of this understanding, they remain unaware of a critical question they must ask themselves in this debate: can you be competent in someone else's culture and, in the long run, which culture are social workers being asked to be competent at? Are social workers really expected to practice in terms of other people's cultures indefinitely or is there an underlying expectation, propelled by Whiteness, that eventually everyone will promote Western culture and Western forms of culturally competent social work? If social work's context is one of 'Whiteness', cultural competency as the preferred tool for culturally sensitive practice would still position cultural 'others' outside this invisible norm (Pon, 2009). In essence, cultural competence as an attempt to practise safely and sensitively across cultures functions as 'new racism' in that it is blind to its context and thus perpetuates disengagement with 'Whiteness' and immobilizes a theorizing of the handover of power.

Cross-Cultural Social Work as an Instrument of 'Whiteness'

As an approach, cross-cultural social work via culturally safe, sensitive and competent practice feels as though it promotes 'the right – politically correct – recipe' because it seems to reject racism. However, it only rejects overt racism, the kind of 'blatant racism' (Simpson, 2008: 141) social workers have been socialized not to tolerate, such as racist language, race-derived violence and overt acts of race-related discrimination. Cross-cultural social work via culturally safe, sensitive and competent practice does not deal with racism or expose 'white privilege' and, therefore, continues to advantage one way of being, one way of thinking and one way of doing above all others, thereby maintaining the status quo and the privilege and power embedded in the dominant group. Nowhere is this more visible than in work with 'people of refugee background' and Aboriginal Australians. In these practice contexts, 'Whiteness' dictates how people live despite, in the case of Aboriginal Australians, having been on their land for centuries before the white colonizers arrived. There is little recognition of people's history and Aboriginal sovereignty over their land. Aboriginal people are considered unable to function in contemporary Australia without government intervention, while 'people of refugee background' are often spoken of as burdens to the taxpayer (Masanauskas, 2011b). 'Whiteness' functions freely by stripping people of context, history and agency, and hindering any opportunity to 'think together' (Simpson, 2008: 140).

Colour blindness is another tool which 'Whiteness' deploys to strip people of their context, history and agency. Colour blindness has been accepted as a way of not being racist or of ignoring 'race' by seeing only people with infinite individual potential despite their differences. Colour blindness acts to detract attention from the structural forces that 'Whiteness' has designed and developed to propel certain groups ahead of others.

During a lecture to a community work class recently, I spoke of 'Whiteness' and found myself apologizing for the use of the word as it clearly made most students in the audience uncomfortable. The students argued with me, a challenge I welcomed, that being 'of colour' in Australia was not the same as being 'of colour' in the USA. For them, Australia was somehow immune to racial intolerance and friction because Australians had long declared their society to be multicultural. I then posed the question: I wonder if an Aboriginal person would agree with you on this? Deafening silence ensued.

At the time, I felt compelled to reduce my personal discomfort with their resistance by apologizing for my use of 'Whiteness' given they were all 'white' students. My discomfort derived first from a perceived need to be liked and accepted by my students, an institutional pull to be politically correct and the inevitable influence of 'Whiteness' in convincing all in the classroom that the discussions were only about the colour of individuals' skins. Political correctness in this context means silence: say little or nothing to make people uncomfortable, accept that one can never be sure offence will not be taken. Therefore, it is best to say nothing to remain civil and avoid possible confrontation. Secondly, the students felt compelled to ignore racism in Australia because, for the most part, they would be criticizing a system designed to privilege them as 'white' students. Underlying these dynamics, all were social workers and in Australia social work 'has yet to fully engage with an understanding of itself as racialized and to explore what this might mean for practice' (Young, cited in Walter et al., 2011: 12).

On another occasion, I accompanied a family who had recently arrived from Africa to a meeting with the principal of their children's school. This family had wanted to raise the issue of what they perceived as the preferential treatment of 'white' families in the school. I sat with this family while they asked the principal why it was they never received invitations from their children's teachers to participate in parent help or working bees around the school. Further, they described how this situation had left them feeling excluded and discriminated against by the school community. The principal proceeded to explain that, while he acknowledged their feelings of exclusion, he had no perception of this situation from his perspective because, to him, all families were welcomed at the school. The response from the mother came quickly: 'Maybe because we're black you think we can't help'. The dismissal of this family's lived experience meant that only the perception of the principal stood as relevant. No space became available in this interaction to consider that, perhaps, to a 'black' family, the absence of an invitation to participate in the school community meant racism was at play. In this case, colour blindness as an agent of 'Whiteness' acted to dismiss the experiences of this family as racialized.

Finally, as an advocate for an Aboriginal Tasmanian family experiencing homelessness, I witnessed how a support service, run and managed by social workers, decided 'race' was to play no role in helping this family secure a permanent home. While there were many systems to support Aborigines experiencing homelessness, this particular service had decided this family was 'Australian enough' not to need the 'extra' referral. The family was not consulted on the design and delivery of the intervention. All this became known to the family and myself during the first lease application process when the real estate agent rang concerned that perhaps we had 'ticked the wrong box' on the lease form as they had not been informed by the support service that they would be dealing with a family of Aboriginal descent. Needless to say, homelessness continued to be experienced but the next port of call, at the request of the family, was the anti-discrimination commission.

Moving beyond Cross-Culturalism

Contributing to the decolonization of social work via indigenization, a transformation that involves replacing externally imposed models with locally developed models of practice and solutions that include local cultures (Gray and Allegritti, 2002), would involve addressing the fundamental challenge 'Whiteness' presents: decontextualized encounters with people. If 'Whiteness' were to be made visible and social workers were to accept that cross-culturalism was not decolonized social work, they would need to make context visible, not just the context of 'other' but their own context as well. A contextualized social work encounter would then involve reciprocal learning facilitated by deep listening – of 'self' and 'other', a space where people seeking help would define the help they wanted rather than a space where the helper determined what was needed, how the need would be met and when. So, in the case of 'people of refugee background' and Aboriginal Australians, they would tell social workers what they wanted from them and whether they wanted them involved at all in the helping and, if so, what the nature of the 'helping' they required might be. There would be a special kind of discourse around these interactions where the common practice would be that there were no recipes or rigid formulae – only ongoing learning from one another through meaningful relationships. 'Clients' and social workers would work in partnership to design, develop and test what might work for them, in their context, in their particular situation rather than expert workers busily designing and implementing what they considered to be the help the 'client' was seeking. This would be a practice of evoking a 'third space' (Bhabha, 1994) where the encounter would be contextualized giving meaning to histories, cultures and values, and developing new and unique ways of *doing* social work. Social workers would share with 'clients' what their organizational contexts – and their associated imperatives – imposed on the kind of help they were able to offer and, therefore, the form of social work practice they could offer. They would take care to notice how and why all cultural contexts, all histories and all positionalities of power and privilege made them uncomfortable with 'not knowing' one another and how their organizational contexts contributed to reinforce this dynamic. If cognizant of the intersection between cultural norms, values, ideologies and individual experience, and open to sharing all that the 'other's' world brought to the social work encounter, then social workers might reach a space of co-construction, engagement and joint action (Freire, 2003; Penn and Frankfurt, 1994; Yan and Wong, 2005).

The key tool for this type of engaged transformed practice is dialogue as 'a form of struggle … not chitchat' (Lerner and West, 1996: 266). Dialogue demands social workers situate their theories and practices within history to surface the present lived experience of racism – conceiving of ways in which power and privilege are not shared with the client but rather given up for the sake of a relevant and transformational encounter. Dialogue calls for a collective search for a dynamic and complex understanding of 'race' and its persistent effects, valuing the contributions that all experiences make to a collective or shared understanding. In an organizational context, dialogue would entail a willingness to confront and engage with direct conflict because, as a tool of 'Whiteness', political correctness has swayed many in a professional environment to avoid conflict as harmful, and only ever violent – or leading to violence – when, in fact, it is by working through conflict that the possibilities for transformative dialogue, capable of delivering concrete change, is opened up (Simpson, 2008). Contextualized encounters via dialogue might threaten the sense of self and material power with which 'Whiteness' has seduced social workers. Not all people would be willing or eager to see their lives as racialized. In essence, 'this process [is best] … undergirded by an ethic of care' (Simpson, 2008: 143) where care was received by the 'cared for' as care (Gray, 2010).

An Ethic of Care as a Final Move from Cross-Culturalism

In making context visible, it is also important to consider that 'Whiteness', as an ideology protecting the concentration and exclusionary accumulation of power and privilege, is not only about the colour of one's skin or about 'race'. It is also about class, gender, sexuality, age, religion, physical ability and values: 'Whiteness' manifests at the intersection of these forms of oppression in 'advantage or subordination' (Pease, 2010: 117) and often invites a binary between 'white' and 'non-white', as Pease (2010: 118) attempts to tease out:

> There is a tendency [in thinking about whiteness] to locate all non-black people as white. Some racial minorities who may not be as disadvantaged as black people may be regarded as white, even though they are relatively disadvantaged compared to white people. The question is whether recognizing diversity within

whiteness takes away the focus off white dominance. Although white people do not all have the same degree of access to white privilege, the notion of white privilege per se is not negated, just complicated.

Further, it is also worth noting:

> The colonizers ... necessarily live the privileges of their role in the colonial drama at the expense of the colonized. The idea of a neutral colonial, living in harmony with all in the colony at no one's expense and without special privileges does not exist ... It is not possible to live in the colony as a member of the [colonialist] culture without such privileges being bestowed ... all types of colonizers ... share a knowledge that their privilege depends on the exploitation and misery of the colonized. (Alschuler, 1996: 504)

Therefore, while Whiteness is as an ideology protecting the concentration and exclusionary accumulation of power and privilege, manifesting at the intersection of multiple forms of oppression, it must also be understood as an act of colonization by the non-neutral colonizer. Razack and Jeffery (2002: 266) advocate an 'integrated approach to oppression', however, not before social work was capable of identifying itself and its notion of caring as racialized – a product of the 'benevolent' colonizer who refutes Whiteness, 'den[ies] the privilege they enjoy' (Memmi, in Alschuler, 1996: 505) and seeks instead to identify with the role of humanitarian.

As previously stated, a move beyond cross-culturalism, via contextualized social work encounters using dialogue as a tool of practice must 'be undergirded by an ethic of care' (Simpson, 2008: 143) as a moral and political frame of reference to help social workers decolonize their actions and think of the centrality of relationships, reciprocity and mutuality as crucial to human coexistence (Featherstone, 2010; Gray, 2010). Thus, an ethic of care offers yet another ingredient in this effort to decolonize. If social work were to be decolonized it would think of Whiteness as impacting on the capacity of social workers to care for all people, including caring for how and why they do what they do in social work. In decolonized social work caring would be about ensuring all people recognized that care was not just about being 'cared for' but also about 'caregiving' (Featherstone, 2010).

An ethic of care in decolonized social work would be invested in the capacity of every human being to give and receive care as equal members of and actors in a just society. As such it is linked to the politics of care and our duty as citizens (Gray, 2010; Sevenhuijsen, 1998; Tronto, 1993). Therefore, social workers would no longer think of cross-culturalism as necessary, nor would they think of cultural sensitivity or cultural competence as tools for practice, but rather would be invested in ensuring people 'care for' one another and are 'cared for' by others in the sense that these values underlie community life but with the knowledge that there might be varying cultural expectations surrounding caring for one rather than another. In this dynamic, what each person brings to their interactions with others would be valued and each interaction would be unique because being able to care and be cared for could only be defined during the interaction with one another within a particular cultural context. The process could not be universalized or standardized, however. It could only be contextual – decolonized of external factors and cognizant of all things being interrelated and thus Indigenous.

Conclusion

Decolonized social work as more than cross-culturalism would involve the exposure of 'Whiteness' as an ideology that has infiltrated the way social work is thought about in the West. The belief that cultures could be crossed through cultural sensitivity and cultural competence has acted as a seductive and powerful diversion from a focus on the 'whys' of social work practice with marginalized groups such as Aboriginal Australians and 'people of refugee background'. These approaches have become a tool of the status quo, further reinforcing the marginalized nature of these communities and moving away from social justice. Beginning the transformation, and thus beginning the decolonization of social work, would require social workers to turn their gaze back to who they are as a profession, how they think of 'others' and how they conceptualize practice. Context becomes a core component of decolonized practice: social work encounters that are context focused would not only bring to the surface professional intentions, power and privilege, but would also facilitate dialogue. Through dialogue social workers would have an opportunity to learn about themselves and their clients. Contextualized via dialogue, these encounters would be framed by an ethic of care that fundamentally challenged the notion that care was in the eye of the caregiver only. Caring in contextualized decolonized social work would be about ensuring that everyone had the capacity and the means by which to give and receive care.

References

Abrams, L. and Moio, J. (2009). Critical race theory and the cultural competence dilemma in social work education. *Journal of Social Work Education*, 45(2), 245–61.

Alschuler, R. (1996). Oppression, liberation and narcissism: A Jungian psychopolitical analysis of the ideas of Albert Memmi. *Alternatives: Global, Local, Political*, 21(4), 497–523.

Australian Association of Social Workers (AASW). (1999). *Code of Ethics*. Canberra: AASW.

Australian Association of Social Workers (AASW). (2010). *Code of Ethics*. Canberra: AASW.

Bhabha, H. (1994). *The Location of Culture*. New York: Routledge.

Becker, H.S. (1986). *Doing Things Together: Selected Papers*. Evanston, IL: Northwestern University Press.

Briskman, L. (2008). Decolonizing Social Work in Australia: Prospect or illusion. In M. Gray, Coates, J. and Yellow Bird, M. (eds), *Indigenous Social Work around the World: Towards Culturally Relevant Education and Practice*. Aldershot: Ashgate, 82–93.

Chilcott, T. (2011). Teachers bring dying language home. *The Courier-Mall*, 10 September 2011 [Online]. Available at: http://www.couriermail.com.au/ipad/ teacher-brings-worrongo-language-home/story-fn6ck51p-1226133451763 [accessed: 21 September 2011].

Dean, R.G. (2001). The myth of cross-cultural competence. *Families in Society: The Journal of Contemporary Social Services*, 82(6), 623–30.

Featherstone, B. (2010). Ethic of Care. In M. Gray and Webb, S.A. (eds), *Ethics and Value Perspectives in Social Work*. Basingstoke: Palgrave, 73–84.

Freire, P. (2003). *Pedagogy of the Oppressed*. Translated by M.B. Ramos. Continuum: New York.

Gair, S., Thomson, J., Miles, D. and Harris, N. (2003). It's very 'white' isn't it! Challenging mono-culturalism in social work and welfare education. *Advances in Social Work and Welfare Education*, 5(1), 37–52.

Gentlewarrior, S., Martin-Jearld, A., Skok, A. and Sweetser, K. (2008). Culturally competent feminist social work practice: Listening to diverse people. *Affilia*, 23(3), 210–22.

Gray, M. (2010). Moral sources: Emerging ethical theories in social work. *British Journal of Social Work*, 40(6), 1794–811.

Gray, M. and Allegritti, I. (2002). Cross-cultural practice and the indigenisation of African social work. *Social Work/Maatskaplike Werk*, 38(4), 324–36.

Gray, M. and Allegritti, I. (2003). Towards culturally sensitive social work practice: Re-examining cross-cultural social work. *Social Work/Maatskaplike Werk*, 39(4), 312–25.

Gray, M. and Coates, J. (2008). From 'Indigenization' to Cultural Relevance. In M. Gray, Coates, J. and Yellow Bird, M. (eds), *Indigenous Social Work around the World: Towards Culturally Relevant Education and Practice*. Aldershot: Ashgate, 13–30.

Gray, M., Coates, J. and Yellow Bird, M. (eds). (2008). *Indigenous Social Work around the World: Towards Culturally Relevant Education and Practice*. Aldershot: Ashgate.

Guthrie, H. (2009). *Competence and Competency-Based Training: What the Literature Says*. Adelaide: National Centre for Vocational Education Research.

Harrison, G. and Turner, R. (2011). Being a 'culturally competent' social worker: Making sense of a murky concept in practice. *British Journal of Social Work*, 41, 333–50.

Laird, J. (1998). Theorizing culture: Narrative Ideas and Practice Principles. In M. McGoldrick (ed.), *Re-Visioning Family Therapy*. New York: Guildford, 20–36.

Lerner, M. and West, C. (1996). *Jews and Blacks: Let the Healing Begin*. New York: Grosset/Putnam.

Ling, H.K. (2004). The search from within: Research issues in relation to developing culturally appropriate social work practices. *International Social Work*, 47(3), 336–45.

Lynch, E. and Hanson, M.J. (2004). *Developing Cross-Cultural Competence: A Guide for Working with Children and Their Families*. Baltimore, MD: Paul H. Brookes Publishing Co.

Masanauskas, J. (2011a). Protesters clash at anti-Muslim rally in Melbourne, *Herald Sun*, 15 May 2011 [Online]. Available at: http://www.adelaidenow. com.au/ipad/protesters-clash-at-anti-muslim-rally in-melbourne/story-fn6t2xlc-1226056442139 [accessed: 20 September 2011].

Masanauskas, J. (2011b). Some refugees in Australia sending welfare payments abroad. *Herald Sun*, 22 June 2011 [Online]. Available at: http:www.heraldsun. com.au/news/some-refugees-in-australia-sending-welfare-payments-abroad/ story-e6frf7jo-1226079532616 [accessed: 29 July 2011].

Matsumoto, D. and Juang, L. (2004). *Culture and Psychology*. Belmont, CA: Thomson and Wadsworth.

Mwansa, L.K. (2011). Social work education in Africa: Whence and whither? *Social Work Education*, 30(1), 4–16.

McMahon, A. (2002). Writing diversity: Ethnicity and race in Australian Social Work, 1947–1997. *Australian Social Work*, 55(3), 172–83.

Meemeduma, P. (1993). Reshaping the future: Cultural sense and social work. Paper presented at the National Social Work Conference, September, Newcastle, Australia.

Memmi, A. (1973). *Liberation*. Philadelphia, PA: Pennsylvania State University.

Moreton-Robinson, A. (2000). *Talkin' up to the White Woman*. Queensland, Australia: University of Queensland Press.

Moreton-Robinson, A. (2004). *Whiteness, Epistemology and Indigenous Representation: Whitening Race*. Canberra: Aboriginal Studies Press, 75–88.

Moreton-Robinson, A. (2011). *Conversations on Whiteness*. Post-graduate seminar series presentation. School of Sociology and Social Work: University of Tasmania, Hobart, 8 August 2011.

National Association of Social Workers (NASW). (2001). *Standard of Cultural Competence Practice*. Washington, DC: NASW.

National Health and Medical Research Council. (2006). *Cultural Competency in Health: A Guide for Policy, Partnerships and Participation*. Canberra: Commonwealth of Australia.

Nimmagadda, J. and Cowger, C.D. (1999). Cross-cultural practice: Social worker ingenuity in the indigenisation of practice knowledge. *International Social Work*, 42(3), 261–76.

Nye, C. (2006). Understanding and misunderstanding in cross-cultural practice: Further conversations with Suwanrang. *Clinical Social Work Journal*, 34(3), 303–17.

Park, Y. (2005). Culture as deficit: A critical discourse analysis of the concept of culture in contemporary social work discourse. *Journal of Sociology and Social Welfare*, 32(3), 11–33.

Patni, R. (2006). Race-specific vs. culturally competent social workers: The debates and dilemmas around pursuing essentialist or multicultural social work practice. *Journal of Social Work Practice*, 20(2), 163–74.

Pease, B. (2010). *Undoing privilege: Unearned Advantage in a Divided World*. London: Zed Books.

Penn, P. and Frankfurt, M. (1994). Creating a participant text: Writing, multiple voices, narrative multiplicity. *Family Process*, 33, 217–31.

Perpitch, N. (2010). Intervention is devastating Aboriginal people, *The Australian*, 16 November 2010 [Online]. Available at: http://www.theaustralian.com. au/news/nation/intervention-is-devastating-for-aboriginal-people/story-e6frg6nf-1225954051484 [accessed: 21 September 2011].

Perth Now. (2011). Gillard says NT intervention working. *Perth Now*, 9 June 2011 [Online]. Available at: http://www.perthnow.com.au/gillard-says-nt-intervention-working/story-fn6mhb6v-1226072595862. [accessed: 21 September 2011].

Pon, G. (2009). Cultural competency as new racism: An ontology of forgetting. *Journal of Progressive Human Services*, 20(1), 59–71.

Quinn, M. (2009). Towards anti-racist and culturally affirming practices. In J. Allan, Briskman, L. and Pease, B. (eds), *Critical Social Work: Theories and Practices for a Socially Just World* (2nd edn). Crows Nest, NSW: Allen & Unwin, 91–104.

Razack, N. (2002). A critical examination of international student exchanges. *International Social Work*, 45(2), 251–65.

Razack, N. (2005). 'Bodies on the move': spatialized locations, identities, and nationality in international work. *Social Justice*, 32(4), 87–104.

Razack, N. (2009). Decolonizing the pedagogy and practice of international social work. *International Social Work*, 52(1), 9–21.

Razack, N. and Jeffery, D. (2002) Critical race discourse and tenets for social work. *Canadian Social Work Review*, 19(2), 257–71.

Rossiter, A. (2005). Discourse analysis in critical social work: From apology to question. *Critical Social Work*, 6(1) [Online]. Available at: http://www. uwindsor.ca/criticalsocialwork/discourse-analysis-in-critical-social-work-from-apology-to-question [accessed: 12 May 2008].

Sakamoto, I. (2007). An anti-oppressive approach to cultural competence. *Canadian Social Work Review*, 24(1), 105–18.

Sevenhuijsen, S. (1998). *Citizenship and the Ethics of Care*. London: Routledge.

Simpson, J. (2008). The color-blind double bind: Whiteness and the (im)possibility of dialogue. *Communication Theory*, 18, 139–59.

Sue, D.W. (2006). The Invisible Whiteness of Being: Whiteness, white supremacy, white privilege, and racism. In M. Constantine and Sue, D.W. (eds), *Addressing*

Racism: Facilitating Cultural Competence in Mental Health and Educational Settings. New Jersey: John Wiley & Sons, 15–30.

Sue, D. W., Bernier, J.E., Durran, I., Feinberg, L., Pedersen, P., Smith, E.J. and Vasquez-Nuttal, E. (1982). Position paper: Cross-cultural counseling competencies. *The Counseling Psychologist*, 10, 45–52.

Sundar, P. and Ly, M. (2013). Multiculturalism. In M. Gray and Webb, S.A. (eds), *Social Work Theories and Methods* (2nd edn). London: Sage, 126–36.

Tronto, J.C. (1993). *Moral Boundaries: A Political Argument for an Ethic of Care*. New York: Routledge.

Walter, M., Taylor, S. and Habibis, D. (2011). How white is social work in Australia? *Australian Social Work*, 64(1), 6–19.

Weaver, H.N. (1999). Indigenous people and the social work profession: Defining culturally competent services. *Social Work*, 44(3), 217–25.

Williams, C. (2006). The epistemology of cultural competence. *Families in Society: The Journal of Contemporary Social Services*, 87(2), 209–20.

Yan, M.C. (2008). Exploring the meaning of crossing and culture: An empirical understanding from practitioners' everyday experience. *Families in Society: The Journal of Contemporary Social Services*, 89(2), 282–92.

Yan, M.C. and Wong Y.R. (2005). Rethinking self-awareness in cultural competence: Toward a dialogic self in cross-cultural social work. *Families in Society: The Journal of Contemporary Social Services*, 86(2), 181–8.

Young, S. (2004). Social Work Theory and Practice: The invisibility of whiteness. In A. Moreton-Robinson (ed.), *Whitening Race: Essays in Social and Cultural Criticism*. Canberra, Australia: Aboriginal Studies Press, 104–18.

PART II
Practice: From the Bottom Up

Chapter 5

Community-Based Social Work in Cuba

Lourdes de Urrutia Barroso and David Strug

Social work in Cuba evolved at the end of the 1990s in response to emergent social problems on the island. Policy makers designated social workers to serve as agents of community transformation and provide services for 'at-risk populations' in poor communities. Unlike Western definitions of community as geographically located or interest based, a community in Cuba is defined numerically as comprising 250 houses and 750 inhabitants. Hence the terms community and neighbourhood are synonymous in Cuba.

'Agent of community transformation' refers to the social worker's role in assessing the service needs of vulnerable 'at-risk' groups as defined by Cuban social policy makers. These groups include young people who are not in school or are unemployed, older people living alone on meagre resources, mothers with low birth weight children and poor families (Ferriol et al., 1997; Torres, 1993).

This chapter describes social work in Cuba, where social workers engage mainly in mobilizing communities to address their own needs and problems (Uriarte, 2002). This contrasts strongly with social work in the United States – and elsewhere – focused largely on helping individuals and families.

Brief Decolonized History of Cuba (1492–1959)

The estimated size of the Indian population in Cuba prior to the arrival of the Spaniards ranges from 16,000 to 600,000 (Pérez, 2006). The largest was the Arawak population, followed by the Taíno and Ciboney. Columbus arrived in Cuba in 1492 and by the mid-1550s, the Indian population numbered less than 3,000. Indians had been absorbed, killed by the Spaniards or died of illnesses brought by their Iberian colonizers. Massacre was the primary means of conquest and terror was used to control the Indian population (Pérez, 2006). Suicide was a common form of Indian protest.

The Spaniards imported slaves from Africa, at first in small numbers to serve as domestic servants, and in the eighteenth and nineteenth centuries, in the tens of thousands to work in the sugar cane fields (Cluster and Hernández, 2006). By the 1830s, slaves represented 40 per cent of Cuba's population and this percentage was even higher in the eastern part of Cuba. A large slave population was ruled over by the Spanish and subsequently Creole elite. Whites proclaimed themselves superior to slaves whom they controlled through force and violence. Afro-Cuban cultural beliefs developed, including *santería*, a religion that mixes African and Christian traditions and practices. It remains strong in Cuba to this day and is a legacy of colonial slavery (Cluster and Hernández, 2006).

By 1898, Cuba had won its war of independence from Spain, but in 1899 the United States assumed formal possession of and occupied the island. The USA ceded control of Cuba in 1901, but retained the perpetual right to intervene through the Platt Amendment, named after US Senator Orville H. Platt (Pérez, 2006), which the Cubans were forced to incorporate into their constitution. US private investment grew enormously in the twentieth century, especially in sugar production, which was vital to the Cuban economy. The USA exercised control over Cuban economic, political and social life through the twentieth century until the Cuban revolution of 1959. Throughout the 1950s, the proximity of the USA and Cuban dependence on US imports kept the United States as a frame of reference for Cuba (Pérez, 2006).

Extreme poverty grew in the years leading up to the revolution in 1959 resulting in unhealthy living conditions, high rates of illiteracy and unemployment, and urban slums around the capital, Havana. Charitable and philanthropic organizations provided social assistance to the growing poor population in Cuba throughout the 1930s (De Urrutia Barroso and Muñoz Gutiérrez, 2006). Social work was not an organized profession in Cuba prior to the 1940s. The first Cuban school of social work was established at the University of Havana in 1943, though it was not a degree programme, and ended when the university closed its doors in 1956, due to social turmoil leading up to the Cuban revolution (De Urrutia Barroso and Muñoz Gutiérrez, 2005).

Cuban Revolution (1959–1989)

The dictatorship of Fulgencio Batista was toppled on 1 January 1959 by a revolutionary movement which soon mobilized workers, peasants and other sectors of society. The Cuban revolution of 1959 was one of the most remarkable phenomena in the history of Latin America (Kaplan, 2009) and one of the most profound social transformations ever seen in the Americas (Fagen, 1969). The leaders of the new government introduced laws that restructured society and promoted egalitarianism. Cuba transformed its political culture, socialized its economy, redistributed its wealth, and mobilized its population to address illiteracy, poor health and other social and economic problems. These reforms were created at the national level and implemented locally through a top-down decision-making process. Community leaders and grassroots organizations were vehicles for implementing national policies and programmes, such as polio eradication.

From the beginning of the revolution, Cuba promoted a social policy based on social equity and provided universal access to services, with the government fully responsible for the funding of social entitlements (Uriarte, 2002). Cubans expected that the revolutionary government would likewise assume responsibility for social services but Cuba's post-revolutionary government did not see a need for professional social workers because its economic and social programmes were designed to provide universal access to education, employment, healthcare, housing and nutrition, and remove rural-urban disparities. Powerful mass organizations, especially the Federation of Cuban Women (FMC), were created after the revolution and entrusted with a variety of public health, educational and security functions within the community (De Urrutia Barroso and Muñoz Gutiérrez, 2006; Diaz-Briquets, 2002).

By the 1970s, however, national leaders decided that Cuba needed trained social workers to assist healthcare professionals in bolstering the country's public health infrastructure as it had deteriorated considerably due to the emigration of large numbers of health professionals at the time of the revolution (Bravo, 1998). In 1973, the Cuban Ministry of Public Health (MINSAP) established two-year technical training institutes at 14 locations across the country to prepare social work technicians to assist doctors, nurses and other healthcare professionals in hospitals and medical clinics. Students received little information about community practice as part of this training but were prepared for practice in medical centres, rather than neighbourhood health clinics (Fierro, 1988). This changed, however, as Cuban medicine became more community-based in the late-1970s. Cuban social work was evolving in response to the particular economic, political and social transformations unfolding in the years following the revolution. It was not based on British or US models.

A small number of social workers were trained at government ministries, such as the Ministry of Work and Social Security, to provide assistance to people on benefits, including pension and disability payments. They were not trained nor hired to provide family counselling or to work with delinquent youth, the elderly, or other at-risk populations at this stage as addressing the psychosocial problems of individuals and families was considered a global enterprise. Multiple sectors of society, including teachers, doctors, psychologists and sociologists and, to a lesser degree, social workers in healthcare and untrained 'empirical social workers' were employed by national, provincial and municipal authorities to function as 'agents of transformation'. 'Empirical social workers' were quasi-volunteer community members affiliated with mass community organizations who provided informal guidance and support to delinquent youth, older persons living alone and other at-risk individuals whom they linked to grassroots organizations for help. They were called 'empirical social workers' because they were guided by practical experience rather than theory.

Emerging Social Problems and the Development of Social Work in Cuba (1989–2000)

A major economic crisis resulted from the breakup of the former Soviet Union in 1989 and was exacerbated by a tightening of the US economic embargo against

Cuba. The resulting social problems prompted a change in social work education in the 1990s and led to the government's deployment of large numbers of young, government-trained social work paraprofessionals for work in poor communities.

Economic Crisis

The collapse of the former Soviet Union devastated Cuba's fragile economic base due to its dependence on the Soviet Union for most of its foreign trade (Strug, 2006). Without economic assistance from the Soviet Union, Cuba's economical survival was threatened. Soviet aid was important because of the USA's trade embargo and Cuba's isolation in the Western hemisphere (Domínguez, 1978).

The economic crisis had a catastrophic impact on living standards and led to worsening economic and social conditions, including rising unemployment, increased poverty and social differentiation. Cubans refer to this period of economic crisis as 'The Special Period in Time of Peace,' which lasted through the mid-1990s (Cole, 2002). Economic class differences sharpened from 1989 to 1998, threatening social cohesion (Burchardt, 2002). Real average wages in 1989–1998 declined precipitously (Comisión Económica para América Latina y el Caribe (CEPAL), 2000), as did salaries in the state sector. For many people income was insufficient to meet basic household needs (Togores González, 1999) and Cuba became a less egalitarian society as segments of the urban and rural populations began to live in poverty (Espina Prieto, 2004, 2010). The crisis had an especially deleterious impact on young people for whom it became much more difficult to find work and go to university. The crisis also had a harmful effect on the elderly population and single mothers.

The economic crisis forced the government to abandon its policy of universal access in favour of programmes targeted at the most vulnerable populations, such as nutrition programmes for single mothers (Barbería, Briggs and Uriarte, 2004; García Álvarez and Anaya Cruz, 2010). Nevertheless, Cuba remained committed to a policy of universal access to education, including primary, secondary, technical or pre-university education and special education for those who needed it.

Cuba's leaders created a number of social programmes and centralized investment projects at the end of the 1990s as part of a campaign called 'The Battle of Ideas', aimed at improving social indicators that had deteriorated during the Special Period (Everleny Pérez Villanueva and Pavel, 2010). One of these was a training programme for social workers in community practice with at-risk populations.

Neighbourhood Movement

A top-down decision-making process for the implementation of health and other local programmes, which had been in place since the beginning of the revolution, faltered with the economic crisis of the Special Period. The *barrio* or neighbourhood as a geographical and social space took on greater importance because government had fewer resources to distribute at the local level and lacked transportation to bring resources to poor outlying communities. This stimulated community members living in these neighbourhoods to develop local support systems. Natural helping networks developed spontaneously as members of poor communities sought to survive economically (Ramírez, 2004).

The dire economic situation led Cuba's leaders to initiate programmes to mobilize community members to find their own solutions to their economic, environmental and social problems. This was the start of the so-called 'neighborhood movement' (Dilla, 1999). In 1988, Fidel Castro created the Group for the Integral Development of the Capital (GDIC), which implemented 'transformation workshops' in socioeconomically marginalized neighbourhoods. These workshops gathered together professionals from both within and outside the community to work in a coordinated way with grassroots organizations and community members to identify the main problem areas in the neighbourhood – usually housing – and mobilize community and outside resources to address them (Uriarte, 2002).

Community leaders and a wide-ranging group of professional organizations participated in the neighbourhood movement, including architects, psychologists, sociologists, engineers and urban planners, as well as non-government organizations (NGOs), like the Canadian International Development Agency (CIDA). Cuba's leaders determined that it was important to include professionals of diverse backgrounds to work in an integrated way with the community to address the effects of the crisis on the well-being of community members, and the deterioration of housing, health and sanitation in the community. The neighbourhood movement involved community development and social planning with professionals promoting partnerships between community groups and individual community members to identify key problems and find strategies to address those problems.

At about the same time as the GDIC started its work in Havana, the Cuban constitution called for the creation of regional 'people's councils' (*consejos populares*) to bridge the gap between municipalities and local communities, address the economic, social and medical needs of community members under their jurisdiction and administer resources to address these needs (Roman, 2003). Comprising community delegates, mass organizations and administrative bodies, people's councils played a key role in the neighbourhood movement.

Neighbourhood Movement and Social Work Reform

Mass organizations and neighbourhood transformation workshops alone were unable to address the growing number of problems among alienated youth, single mothers and older persons living alone with few resources. The government's growing concern over the impact of the economic crisis on the most vulnerable sectors of the population increased the importance of the neighbourhood as the locus for intervention. The achievements of the neighbourhood movement led

Cuba's leaders to reform social work education to train more social workers for community practice.

In 1998, the Ministry of Public Health and the Federation of Cuban Women charged the University of Havana with the task of starting an education programme to prepare social workers for community practice (De Urrutia Barroso and Muñoz Gutiérrez, 2006; Strug and Teague, 2002). The university responded by creating a five-year university degree programme called 'The Social Work Concentration in Sociology' to broaden the community practice skills and educational horizons of social workers, the majority of whom had graduated from two-year technical training institutes for social workers in public health discussed earlier. The concentration programme was situated in the Department of Sociology at the University of Havana, because the government and university determined this department best suited to train 'agents of transformation' for practice with vulnerable populations in the community. Policy makers and social work educators sought transformatory rather than ameliorative and 'assistentialist' practice ('assistentialist' was a term used to refer to the tradition of social work practice in Cuba and other Latin countries, where intervention was limited to *assisting* the individual). 'Agents of transformation' worked with community members, leaders, grassroots organizations and municipal authorities to facilitate change.

The University of Havana began to train practitioners who could – with sufficient preparation – work with the community to promote self-improvement and link members to resources outside the neighbourhood via popular councils and municipal agencies (De Urrutia Barroso and Muñoz Gutiérrez, 2006). The concentration programme taught students how to engage with individuals, families and groups, and stimulate community involvement in local programmes. Students were also taught about the special needs of single mothers with scarce resources, adolescents at risk for substance abuse and delinquency, and elderly people living in crowded conditions with extended family members.

At the turn of this century, the government developed a number of specialized paraprofessional schools to 'rapidly train' students in the areas of education, health and social work. These schools were important because they gave young people the opportunity to study beyond the twelfth grade, in addition to training them to provide important services in the community. In the year 2000, government leaders and the Union of Communist Youth (UJC) directed the University of Havana to create the country's first paraprofessional social work school at Cojímar, outside Havana, for youth between the ages of 17–21 years. The paraprofessional social work training programme differed from the Sociology Concentration in Social Work described above in that its purpose was to 'rapidly train' thousands of young government social workers for deployment in communities throughout the country. It did not offer a university degree as did the concentration programme at the University of Havana. These paraprofessional training programmes prepared graduates for community-based practice in the face of growing social inequality with disadvantaged and vulnerable groups, such as youth at risk, juvenile delinquents and people with disabilities.

Eventually the government created five social work training schools across the country. The first cohort of students was selected for training by the youth wing of the Communist Party of Cuba (Union of Young Communists or UJC) in cooperation with officials from the University of Havana. They were young people from poor neighbourhoods who had passed the twelfth grade but had not been admitted to the university, or found employment. A more representative body of students was selected for training in subsequent years.

Beginning as a six-month programme, it was later extended to two years. By international – Western – standards, a two-year paraprofessional qualification does not equate to a professional degree in social work which, in Australia, for example, is a four-year degree qualification taught by social work qualified academics with a PhD in social work but it was ideally suited to the needs of local communities in Cuba.

Professors at the university and government policy makers worked closely together in considering the kind of education students needed to be effective as community workers. The preparation of the curriculum for the social work programme was the responsibility of faculty at the University of Havana. To prepare students for community work, students studied applied social work, i.e., direct practice skills, social and community psychology, urban sociology, social prevention and community work, social communication and present-day Cuban socialist society, among other topics (De Urrutia Barroso and Muñoz Gutiérrez, 2005). The programme, though sociologically oriented, was taught by faculty from diverse disciplines, including, sociology, psychology, law and social communication. This was done in order to expose students to various disciplines relevant to the work that graduates would perform in the community.

Students who graduated from the schools of social work were assured of work in the community and a good salary by the government. Social work school graduates, who were named *emergentes*, were required to work in their own communities – insiders – once they had finished their training (Clarke, 2000). They were named *emergentes* because they addressed *emergent* social problems, such as child malnutrition, school absenteeism and the elderly's need for economic and social assistance (Barthelemy, 2004).

Though the focus of the training programme for *emergentes* was community work, initially policy makers in government and social work educators at the University of Havana were not sure of the best way to deploy graduates in the community. Over time, and with experience, government officials together with educators in psychology, social work, law and other disciplines discovered how to educate more than 40,000 graduates (De Urrutia Barroso and Muñoz Gutiérrez, 2005). It was not unusual for the government and the university to collaborate in preparing students for work in fields important to the development of the country nor is it unusual in the USA where often social work students get jobs in the public sector to carry out the mandates of the government.

For the most part, social work education in Cuba has comprised 'rapid training' in community-based practice in the two-year training programmes at the special schools for young social work students described above rather than the undergraduate Bachelor of Social Work degrees as the accepted international qualification for social work (IFSW/IASSW Education Standards, 2004). However, in recent years, all the universities of the country have offered a postgraduate specialty in social work for university social work graduates and graduates in related disciplines; the Universities of Villa Clara and Camaguey now have master's programmes in community social work.

'National Social Work Program': Social Workers in the Community

Created in 2000, the 'National Social Work Program' was an initiative of Cuba's top political leadership. Its municipal and provincial branches fell under the jurisdiction of the Cuban Council of State, a legislative body headed by the president of Cuba, which provided the resources needed to carry out the programme's mission. Comprising graduates from the *emergentes* programme and youth who occupied leadership positions in community organizations, the programme's directorate helped to define its aims and goals, one of which was for the newly trained *emergentes* to identify and gather information about young persons in poor communities who were neither attending school nor working. Cuba's leaders were particularly concerned about the views of this sector of the population. Leaders worried that a sector of the youth population, who were not in school and out of work, might feel alienated from society and question whether the government really wanted to find collective solutions to the challenges facing the country (Domínguez, 2005).

The National Social Work Program and social policy makers decided that social work needed to become multisectoral to make it more dynamic and community oriented. Therefore, social workers were expected to coordinate their practice more closely with community members and leaders, with family doctors, healthcare centres, municipal and regional authorities, and professionals from different ministries to support community-oriented interventions. Social work educators and policy makers considered the work carried out by the first graduates of the rapid training schools for youth started in 2000 as overly 'assistentialist,' since they were too dependent for their direction on community leaders, municipal officials and popular council leaders. They were unable to act independently or to fulfil their role as agents of community transformation adequately.

Recent Developments (2000 onwards)

To address these concerns, in 2004 the National Social Work Program better integrated social workers into the organizational structure of the community by placing them in the communities where they lived, thereby promoting their role as insiders. Working inside the community allowed social workers to focus their attention on local problems and resources. If several social workers lived in the same neighbourhood, some were permitted to work outside their home community, but still within the municipality in which they resided. The advantage of this was that the social workers' knowledge about fellow community members, their way of life and local social organizations thus facilitated their ability to create community support networks. Furthermore, the community viewed the resident social worker as one of their own with equal investment in improving community life, especially for at-risk members. Resident social workers were the subjects and objects of the community transformation they were attempting to bring about.

Since 2008, the National Social Work Program's directorate has directed social workers to address the increasingly wider array of social problems and to work with diverse target populations, including children with educational problems, dysfunctional families and families with limited economic and material resources. Their activities have been linked increasingly to the work of the popular councils, allowing them to interact more effectively with local and regional decision-makers as well as with community members. Increased contact with popular councils and municipal bodies has enabled them to better comprehend the service needs of individuals, groups and families and serve as channels of communication between the community and external state structures. Social workers evaluate how social policies are implemented at the local level and the extent to which they reach individuals with special needs. The social workers' knowledge about the quality of services received from non-state providers allows them to give feedback to the state about community members' satisfaction with the services provided, thus further legitimizing their role in the eyes of community members. This has led to the implementation of new services for older people and mothers of children with disabilities and of low birth weight children.

Despite the attempt to better integrate social workers into the life of the community, their role is sometimes limited by overly centralized decision-making processes. This is problematic, because top-down government decision-making compromises social workers' capacity to facilitate effective community development and address the unique needs for services in particular communities (Gray and Mubangizi, 2010). Community development requires simultaneous action and coordination at both the micro (local) and macro (public policy) levels (Bhattacharyya, 2004). As noted earlier, until the late-1980s, Cuba had a top-down decision-making structure for introducing change at the community level. Though this has changed to a degree, top-down decision-making still occurs in some instances, defeating the purpose of the National Social Work Program, which acknowledges that not all communities and community members have the same characteristics and needs. For example, the central government has established low-cost cafeterias for poor people in communities across Cuba but they are not always ideally located. Sometimes they are placed far from where those who need them happen to live, or sometimes they are too difficult for elderly people or people with disabilities to get to. In such cases, community social workers attempt to mobilize networks of neighbours and grassroots organizations to provide services for those whose needs cannot be met by centrally planned services. This example of the central government's effort to provide subsidized nutrition for older persons suggests the tendency to impose interventions in a top-down fashion has not been completely eliminated.

Examples of Social Work in the Community

The community of Manzanillo in Granma province provides an example of the multisectoral nature of social work as practitioners engage with municipal officials, representatives of the Communist Party of Cuba (CPC) and community members to increase the availability of social services. At the same time, social workers in Manzanillo have worked with officials from the Ministry of Public Health to have defunct medical offices reopened. Also, they have arranged for government offices to be open at a more convenient time for community members than was previously the case. Social workers were instrumental in arranging for an extension of the community's network of telephone services to promote communication within and outside the community and, through working with local authorities, in ensuring that those communities with water storage problems receive a guaranteed supply of water brought in by special trucks carrying potable water.

In the city of Bayamo, social workers carried out a community needs assessment in partnership with the community's leadership; organized public discussions about how best to meet the social service needs of community members; worked with government officials, community members and grassroots organizations on how best to engage young people in meaningful activities and dealt with the antisocial behaviours of some youth; and addressed the community's need for healthcare services. In the rural districts of Bayamo, like La Piedra, social workers have held weekend community workshops which have become a social event to which community members bring their families to engage in discussions – led by the social worker – about problems that need to be addressed. They engage professionals in the community to lend their expertise in working on community projects.

Social workers are engaged in projects coordinated with the regional popular councils of Las Tunas and Holguin where informal leaders have emerged and been encouraged to work with formal community leaders. In the rural regions of Las Tunas, social workers identified a number of vulnerable women living in an economically and socially precarious situation due to the frailty of their marital relationships and initiated a programme to teach these women how to sew and preserve food to enhance their economic survival skills.

Abel Santamaría is a neighbourhood on the periphery of the city of Santiago with water supply problems and high rates of unemployment and juvenile delinquency. With the assistance of the Communist Party and other government institutions, social workers instituted social transformation workshops in which neighbourhood members analysed the community's problems and attempted to address them by themselves, if possible. The social worker and community leaders take issues the community cannot resolve on its own, for example, scarcity of construction materials for housing, to the appropriate popular council and municipal authorities and demand the authorities address these issues. Such actions strengthen ties between the social worker, the community and local government.

The kind of social work experiences noted above show that the social worker helps the community come together to address its problems. Though the social worker remains central to the process, his or her presence in the neighbourhood is an incentive to community members to seek local solutions to local problems. It is an incentive because the community recognizes the role of the social worker in encouraging its members to come together to solve its problems. The community believes the social worker has the critical training and analytic skills necessary to help and observes the social worker doing so.

Each community now has an elaborate needs assessment conducted by the social worker, which includes a profile of social problems and needs, resources available for addressing them and a plan to resolve them. Working relationships between social workers and community representatives have improved. Social workers in coordination with the National Social Work Program organize what are called 'Workshops for Systematizing Social Work Practice', which are in place in all Cuban municipalities. The purpose of the workshops is to bring community members into the process of identifying and solving social problems. These workshops are important learning experiences for the social workers who attend them on a weekly or biweekly basis. Among the topics these workshops address are the integration of ex-prisoners' to family and community, and personalized attention to children with rare illnesses and behaviour problems.

Economic and Social Change and Social Work in Cuba

In April 2011, the Sixth Congress of the Cuban Communist Party approved a series of guidelines for future economic and social development, for the purpose of promoting greater economic efficiency and increased worker productivity. Cuba is now in the process of a transition from a socialist economy in which almost all of the means of production are in the hands of the state, to one which is encouraging some state workers to become owners of small private enterprises, such as beauty parlours, small restaurants, repair shops of all sorts, and stores for the production, processing and sale of agricultural products and foods. It is these kinds of services that are becoming privatized, absorbing available workers from the state sector. This transition is being introduced gradually and the basic sectors of the economy and social services remain in the hands of the state. The state has made it clear that it will not abandon its responsibility for the economic and social protection of workers unable to move into the private sector (Rendón Matienzo, 2011). However, this economic transition will not be without tensions and contradictions. It will be harder for some people to move into the emerging small private business sector. Some may lack the necessary skills for this type of work. This will add a new task for the social worker to identify, in a timely fashion, those workers for whom moving to the private sector might be difficult so they can be incorporated into the workforce with the help of state institutions and the community.

The transition will have an impact on social work. While Cuba has made advances in the development of social work over the last decade, the future of the National Social Work Program with its membership of more than 40,000 *emergentes* is uncertain. The government is in the process of incorporating the National Social Work Program – previously an independent body – into the Ministry of Work and Social Security as a result of the economic changes noted above. How exactly this incorporation will affect social work remains to be seen.

Relevance of Cuba's Community-Based Social Work Approach to the USA and Other Countries

The development of a community-based social work approach in Cuba reflects that country's post-revolutionary development, its political economy, socialist ideology and collective value system (Estrada, 2003). Therefore, it cannot be transferred easily or serve as a role model for capitalist countries with a more individualistic value system (Backwith and Mantle, 2009). However, social workers in other countries may benefit from learning about social work in Cuba, even though it may not serve as a role model. Sectors of the social work profession in countries with a radical, politically progressive critical social work approach– in theory anyway – such as Australia and Canada (Allan, Pease and Briskman, 2003; Carniol, 2010) may be interested in learning about social work in Cuba, because Cuban social work is community-based, socially oriented, and is a product of the Cuban revolutionary process. Sectors of the social work profession in Canada may be interested in learning about Cuban social work as some elements of how First Nations attempt to practise social work are similar to Cuba's community-based approach. In some Aboriginal communities, native resident social workers are both subjects and objects of the transformation they are trying to bring about within the community (Sinclair, Hart and Bruyere, 2009), as is the case in Cuba where most social workers are expected to live and work in their community of origin.

Cuba's community-based social work approach shares similarities with an older model of community organization developed in the USA in the 1960s (Dunham, 1958; Rothman, 1968). That model promoted community building, locality development and the mobilization of community members to decide their goals and strategies. It encouraged neighbourhoods to increase their capacity for development. However, this model of community building is no longer in ascendancy in social work in the USA. Although there are community development projects in the USA and elsewhere, based on aspects of the older model, they do not necessarily involve professional social workers (Butcher, Banks, Henderson and Robertson, 2007; Dudley St. Neighborhood Initiative, 2010; Harlem Children's Zone Initiative, 2011).

The social work profession in other countries may be interested in learning how Cuba, an economically poor country of only about 11 million people, has trained and deployed more than 40,000 social workers for practice in their community of origin with targeted vulnerable populations. They may want to learn how the National Social Work Program uses a multisectoral approach to coordinate social work practice with community members and leaders, grassroots organizations and regional and municipal authorities.

The adoption of a neo-liberal economic policy in Western democratic countries, along with the global economic downturn, has resulted in fewer available resources to meet the service needs of vulnerable groups in those countries. Neo-liberalism fosters globalization, marketization and entrepreneurship (Martínez and García, 1996) and has been associated with the reduction of public expenditure on social services and the transfer of resources from the public to the private sector. Western democracies that follow neo-liberal economic policies face what Giroux (2010) referred to as the 'neo-liberal juggernaut', which disproportionately empowers the wealthy.

Most Western democratic governments have restructured social services – though social spending has increased – for addressing the needs of vulnerable populations out of economic necessity during this same period (Månsson and Proveeyer-Cervantes, 2005). This has made the targeted delivery of services to at-risk individuals the major focus for the social work profession in these countries so Cuba is no different in this respect.

Because of the country's underproductive economy and the global economic downturn, Cuba faces increasing difficulty in maintaining the disproportionately large segment of its national budget that it devotes to social entitlements. Cuba's leaders are trying to discern how the government might continue to provide the broadest possible access to social services for its citizens, while finding innovative ways to target particularly vulnerable groups (Sexto, 2011). Targeting particular sectors of society with special needs is not new in Cuban social policy but is receiving renewed attention in light of the country's economic difficulties. In Cuba, targeting special needs groups is not associated with privatization as it is in countries with neo-liberal economies.

All Cubans have access to free healthcare and public education. They are eligible for government-sponsored pensions and a variety of subsidies, including for meals and day care for children of working mothers (Uriarte, 2002). Homelessness does not exist, although good housing is in short supply. Unemployment is typically low (less than three per cent) as government employs most workers. However, underemployment is a problem (Index Mundi, 2009) and poverty has increased as nominal wages have not kept up with the consumer price index (Pérez, 2008). It is estimated that 20 per cent of the population in urban areas lives in poverty (Espina Prieto, 2004, 2010) but critical or extreme poverty resulting in wide-scale malnutrition, poor health, illiteracy and insecurity is kept at bay by the government-provided social safety net (Zabala-Argüelles, 2010).

Cubans expect their leaders to maintain a social safety net. This contrasts with the situation in the USA where the neoconservative decades since 1975 have eroded citizens' confidence that political leaders will support their rights to healthcare, housing and social welfare benefits. War expenditures in the USA, deregulation, tax cuts, privatization and the use of deficits to shrink the public sector have harmed the economy and placed vulnerable communities, especially poor blacks and Hispanics, at increased risk for a variety of psychosocial problems, including delinquency, incarceration and substance abuse. Sixteen per cent of US citizens – 49 million – live in poverty and 15 million are out of work. More than 58 million are without healthcare (Morgan, 2011). The population in extreme poverty in metropolitan neighbourhoods, where at least 40 per cent of Americans live below the poverty line, rose by one third from 2000 to 2009 (Brookings, 2011).

Community action programmes to address social problems in the USA have always been limited by an ethos of individualism rather than collectivism as in Cuba. Community interventions are implemented in a conservative, politically regressive environment (DeFilippis, Fisher and Shragge, 2010). Hopps and Pinderhughes (1996) suggested that the US government promoted an ethos of individualism because it was consonant with the US capitalist economic system. In the more socially activist years of the 1930s and 1960s, social work in the USA was more preoccupied than it is today with community action and social reform (Reisch and Andrews, 2002).

Budget cuts in England and elsewhere are having a negative impact on the delivery of health and human services at a time when vulnerable populations in those countries are most in need of services (British Association of Social Workers, 2010). Similar cutbacks like these have not occurred in Cuba. Managerial approaches and defunding of social services in Great Britain and in other Western democracies have produced a crisis in the social work profession (Ferguson, 2008; Ferguson and Lavalette, 2007). In England, community services are shutting down. Deep cuts in the defunding of civil-society institutions, including in the budgets of social workers and youth services that do valuable work with young people, have contributed to recent mob violence in London, which brought punitive action by the Coalition government. This comes at a time when Britain's youth unemployment rate is over 20 per cent (Sennett and Sassen, 2011). The social work profession in the UK is fighting back against the state's assault on the delivery of social services to populations in need of assistance through the creation of organizations like the Social Work Action Network (SWAN). Such organizations challenge the dominant pro-market, scapegoating agendas of the new Coalition government through the formation of alliances with citizens to challenge service cutbacks (SWAN, 2011).

Neo-liberal processes and values tend to shrink the welfare state and discredit and undercut state and collective responses to the kinds of problems individuals, groups and communities increasingly face (McDonald and Marston, 2002). The restructuring of community social services has had a negative impact on the delivery of social services in Canada and other Western democracies (Transnational Institute, 2006) making it difficult to maintain 'a sense of social responsibility, voluntary spirit, and participatory culture' (Baines, 2010: 11). This contrasts with Cuba's encouragement of a culture of participation which social workers help to promote at the local level.

Neo-liberal restructuring in Canada has left local governments with a diminished capacity to meet the needs of community members while government has distanced itself from direct service delivery to vulnerable populations. This is in sharp contrast to the situation in Cuba where local and regional government has played an increasing role in supporting the service needs of community members. The Canadian government has advanced an agenda of individualized and privatized views of social problems (McKeen, 2007) in contrast to Cuba where such privatized roles are non-existent. Social workers and movements in Canada have begun to react against these approaches as they have in the UK (Carniol, 2010; Ferguson, 2008; SWAN, 2011).

While Cuban social work education and training programmes focus on community practice, the opposite is true in the USA where growing numbers of students enter social work schools to receive credentials to allow them to practise as private mental health practitioners (Gibelman, 2004) due to the greater prestige and income associated with clinical practice with individuals than with marginalized groups or communities. In the USA, community practice is no longer taught as a discrete method (Pippard and Bjorklund, 2003) and social work educators are asking how the scope and prominence of community practice might be increased and curricula revised to help students think more critically about social problems (Thomas, O'Connor and Netting, 2011).

In Australia, Mendes (2009) has noted that professional social work education and discourse has relegated community development to the margins and suggests that social work educators should offer examples of community development interventions in small group skill sessions in their classrooms. Cuban social work educators have experience in doing just that.

Until recently, community work approaches had all but disappeared in the UK social work curriculum (Ward, 2002).The British Association of Social Workers (BASW) has called for reform of social work education to prepare workers to address the needs of vulnerable populations. They may wish to find out how Cuban social work educators prepare their students for this. Some members of the social work profession in Great Britain assert that teaching of the social sciences has become marginalized while a narrow, functional competencies approach has been imposed on social work education (Garrett, 2010). A UK review has proposed a series of proficiencies for social workers in England, including the ability to reflect on and take account of the impact of inequality, disadvantage and discrimination on those who use social work services and their communities (Health Professions Council, 2011).

Even though they may view Cuban social work practice and education as very different from the way social work is taught and practised in their countries, social work educators developing community curricula in Canada, Great Britain, the USA and other countries might wish to examine how their Cuban counterparts have incorporated community-oriented methods and practice skills into their social work curricula. They could learn how Cuban social workers have worked with community leaders and regional and municipal authorities to promote community development.

Social work in Cuba is unique, because it reflects that country's particular historical development as a post-revolutionary socialist country that has undergone many societal transformations since 1959. The Cuban community-based social work approach described herein, as intended, provided a pragmatic response to emerging social problems by quickly training and deploying thousands of government social workers for practice in poor neighbourhoods. The institutionalization and professionalization of social work in Cuba has taken place only in the last 20 years in contrast to the USA and many other countries. For all of these reasons, the Cuban social work model is different from that which exists in other countries.

Decolonizing Social Work: The Cuban Context

Decolonizing social work is concerned with the effects of Western colonization on social work and its impact on Indigenous and local peoples (see Introduction to this book). Among the attributes of a decolonizing social work approach are the recognition of Indigenous disadvantage, the realization of Indigenous rights and a focus on the promotion of community strengths (Briskman, 2008). Though Cuba's Indigenous population was killed off in the early years of the conquest, ideas relating to decolonizing social work are nevertheless relevant because many Cubans still have an Indigenous Afro-Cuban heritage. Decolonization involves recognizing and learning from this in the development of Cuban social work. Hence, it might be asked, to what extent does social work in Cuba share characteristics of a decolonizing social work approach? Does it concern itself with processes that promote disadvantage in the communities in which it works, and with self-determination of community members? Is Cuban social work practice collaborative and is it carried out in a bottom-up fashion?

Cuban social work does have a number of decolonizing aspects. Cuban social work education trains students to work with community members, grassroots organizations and regional authorities to enhance the collective strength of the community. The National Social Work Program encourages social workers to practise in their communities of origin and to organize discussions with community members concerning problems in the neighbourhood. Social workers support the community in expressing its need for services at the regional and municipal levels. Social workers thereby serve as a bridge between the local community and the wider society. However, Cuba's community-based social work approach remains a work in progress and is still evolving in its role of promoting the collective actions of the community. Centralized decision-making and top-down implementation of programmes are a legacy of the revolution, which sometimes limits the social worker's role, as this chapter has shown.

Significance of Cuban Social Work

The institutionalization of Cuban social work has had both practical and symbolic significance for the country and its leadership. More than 48,000 *emergentes* and university postgraduates have worked with thousands of at-risk individuals in communities throughout Cuba over the years. The creation of social work programmes was part of 'The Battle of Ideas' campaign mentioned earlier, which promoted revolutionary renewal through Cuba's belief in the power of ideology to strengthen the socialist revolution. The Battle of Ideas was conceived at a time when some individuals inside the country questioned whether Cuba's leadership and Cuban socialism could survive in the face of the economic crisis of the Special Period (Font, 2008; Yamaoka, 2004). Cuba's leaders could point to the work of thousands of social workers as proof that they were addressing the needs of the most socioeconomically disadvantaged segments of the population and that government was providing socially meaningful work to thousands of young social workers whom Fidel Castro referred to colourfully as 'doctors of the soul' (Durand, 2005).

Conclusion

Social work in Cuba is a work in progress and the profession has yet to evolve emancipatory, participatory strategies to enhance its role in promoting the collective actions of the community. Nevertheless, the National Social Work Program has enhanced the professional status of social work in Cuba as social workers have made important contributions in providing services to at-risk populations. Community members increasingly perceive them as engaged community change agents. While social work higher education has advanced in recent years, the economic and social changes occurring in Cuba are likely to affect the trajectory of Cuban social work in as yet unforeseen ways.

The Cuban social work community and the social work communities in other countries can benefit from learning about one another's approaches. Social workers from Cuba, the USA and elsewhere can share educational methods, research strategies and theoretical advances. This exchange can contribute to the internationalization of social work and the infusion of international content into the social work curriculum.

References

Allan, J., Pease, B. and Briskman, L. (eds). (2003). *Critical Social Work: An Introduction to Theories and Practice*. Sydney: Allen & Unwin.

Backwith, D. and Mantle, G. (2009). Inequalities in health and community-oriented social work: Lessons from Cuba? *International Social Work*, 52(4), 499–511.

Baines, D. (2010). Neoliberal restructuring/activism, participation and social unionism in the nonprofit social sciences. *Nonprofit and Voluntary Sector Quarterly*, 39(1), 10–28.

Barbería, L., Briggs, S. de Souza, and Uriarte, M. (2004). The End of Egalitarianism? Economic inequality and the future of social policy in Cuba. In J.I. Domínguez, Omar-Everleny Pérez Villanueva, O.E. and Barbería, L. (eds), *The Cuban Economy at the Start of the Twenty-First Century*. Cambridge, MA: Harvard University, 297–318.

Barthelemy, S. (2004). El trabajo social: Misión transformadora. *Granma* [Online]. Available at: http://www.granma.cubaweb.cu/2004/01/24/nacional/articulo02. html [accessed: 24 January 2004].

Bhattacharyya, J. (2004). Theorizing community development. *Journal of the Community Development Society*, 34(2), 5–34.

Bravo, E.M. (1998). *Development within Underdevelopment: New Trends in Cuban Medicine*. La Habana, Cuba: Editorial José Martí.

Briskman, L. (2008). Decolonizing Social Work in Australia: Prospect or illusion. In M. Gray, Coates, J. and Yellow Bird, M. (eds), *Indigenous Social Work around the World: Towards Culturally Relevant Education and Practice*. Aldershot: Ashgate, 83–93.

British Association of Social Workers (BASW). (2010). *Budget Cuts that Fail to Protect Social Work Risks Lives* [Online]. Available at: http://www.basw.co.uk/ media/budget-cuts-that-fail-to-protect-social-work-risks-lives/ [accessed: 11 November 2011].

British Association of Social Workers (BASW). (2011). *Developing a Single College of Social Work* [Online]. Available at: http://www.basw.co.uk/ campaigns/college/developing-a-single-college-of-social-work/ [accessed: 15 September 2011].

Brookings. (2011). *The Re-Emergence of concentrated poverty: Metropolitan trends in the 2000s* [Online]. Available at: http://www.brookings.edu/ papers/2011/1103_poverty_kneebone_nadeau_berube.aspx [accessed: 11 November 2011].

Burchardt, H. (2002). Social dynamics in Cuba. *Latin American Perspectives*, 29(3), 57–74.

Butcher, H., Banks, S., Henderson, P. and Robertson, J. (2007). *Critical Community Practice*. Bristol: The Policy Press.

Carniol, B. (2010). *Case Critical: Social Services and Social Justice in Canada* (6th edn). Toronto, Ontario: Between the Lines.

Clarke, S. (2000). *Social Work as Community Development: A Management Model for Change*. Aldershot: Ashgate.

Cluster, R. and Hernández, R. (2006). *The History of Havana*. New York: Palgrave Macmillan.

Cole, K. (2002). The process of socialist development. *Latin American Perspectives*, 29(3), 18–39.

Comisión Económica para América Latina y el Caribe (CEPAL) (2000) *La Economía Cubana: Reformas estructurales y desempeño en los noventa* (2nd edn). México: Fondo de Cultura Económica.

DeFilippis, J., Fisher, R. and Shragge, E. (2010). *Contesting Community: The Limits and Potential of Local Organizing*. New Brunswick, NJ: Rutgers University Press.

Diaz-Briquets, S. (2002). The Society and Its Environment. In R.A. Hudson (ed.), *Cuba: A Country Study*. Washington, DC: Hudson, Library of Congress, 89–156.

De Urrutia Barroso, L. and Muñoz Gutiérrez, T. (2005). Development of social workers in Cuba: Professionalism and practice. *Cuadernos del Centro de Estudios Avanzados Multidisciplinares*. Brasilia: Brasilia University, Year V-No 19.

De Urrutia Barroso, L. and Muñoz, T. (2006). *El trabajo social en Cuba, una disciplina científica en construcción. Experiencias de profesionalización luego de* 1959 in *Lecturas sobre historia del trabajo social*. La Habana, Cuba: Editorial Félix Varela.

Dilla, A.H. (1999). Cuba: Virtudes e infortunios de la sociedad civil. *Revista Mexicana de Sociologia*, 61(4), 129–48.

Domínguez, J.I. (1978). Cuban foreign policy. *Foreign Affairs*, 57(1), 83–108.

Domínguez, M.I. (2005). Cuban Youth: Aspirations, social perceptions, and identity. In J.S. Tulchin, Bobea, L., Espina Prieto, M.P. and Hernández, R. (eds), *Changes in Cuban Society since the Nineties*. Washington, DC: Woodrow Wilson International Center for Scholars, 155–70.

Dudley St. Neighborhood Initiative. (2010). *History* [Online]. Available at: http://www.dsni.org/history.shtml [accessed: 8 July 2011].

Dunham, A. (1958). *Community Welfare Organization: Principles and Practice*. New York: Thomas Y. Crowell Co.

Durand, C. (2005). Cuba today: A nation becoming a university. *MRZine* [Online]. Available at: http://mrzine.monthlyreview.org/2005/durand131005.html [accessed: 3 November 2011].

Espina Prieto, M. (2004). Social Effects of Economic Adjustment: Equality, inequality and trends toward greater complexity in Cuban society. In J.I. Domínguez, Omar-Everleny Pérez Villanueva, O.E. and Barbería, L. (eds), *The Cuban Economy at the Start of the Twenty-First Century*. Cambridge, MA: Harvard University, 209–44.

Espina Prieto, M. (2010). Looking at Cuba today: Four assumptions and six intertwined problems. *Socialism and Democracy*, 24(1), 95–108.

Estrada, N. (2003). *Identidad y* ética *professional*. Paper presented at the *III Encuentro, Internacional de Trabajo Social*, Habana, Cuba.

Everleny Pérez Villanueva, O. and Pavel, V.A. (2010). Cuba's economy: A current evaluation and several necessary proposals. *Socialism and Democracy*, 24(1), 71–93.

Fagen, R.F. (1969). *The Transformation of Political Culture in Cuba*. Stanford, CA: Stanford University Press.

Ferguson, I. (2008). *Reclaiming Social Work: Challenging Neo-Liberalism and Promoting Social Justice*. London: Sage.

Ferguson, I. and Lavalette, M. (eds). (2007). *International Social Work and the Radical Tradition*. Birmingham, UK: Venture Press.Fierro, L.D. (1988). Reflexiones acerca de la formación docente de la trabajadora social Psiquiátrica. *Temas de Trabajo Social*, 10(2), 25–37.

Ferriol, A., Carriazo, O., Echavarría, U., et al. (1997). *Efectos de políticas macroeconómicas y sociales sobre el rol del estado en la experiencia cubana*. Buenos Aires, ARG: CLASCO.

Font, M. (2008). *Cuba and Castro: Beyond the battle of ideas. Changing Cuba, Changing World* [Online]. Available at: http://www.scribd.com/doc/31269283/Changing-Cuba-in-a-Changing-World [accessed: 3 November 2011].

García Álvarez, A. and Anaya Cruz, B. (2010). Relación entre desarrollo social y económico. In O.E.P. Villanueva (ed.), *Cincuenta años de la economía cubana*. La Habana, Cuba: Editorial de Ciencias Sociales, 274–331.

Garrett, P. (2010). Examining the 'conservative revolution': Neoliberalism and social work education. *Social Work Education*, 29(4), 340–55.

Gibelman, M. (2004). *What Social Workers Do* (2nd edn). Washington, DC: NASW Press.

Giroux, H. (2010). *Youth in the age of moral and political plagues. Z-Net* [Online]. Available at: http://www.zcommunications.org/a-society-consumed-by-locusts-by-henry-giroux [accessed: 16 September 2011].

Gray, M. and Mubangizi, B. (2010). Caught in the vortex: Can local government community development workers succeed in South Africa? *Community Development Journal*, 45(2), 186–97.

Harlem Children's Zone Initiative. (2011). *The HCZ project* [Online]. Available at: http://www.hcz.org/about-us/the-hcz-project [accessed: 11 November 2011].

Health Professions Council. (2011). Consultation on draft standards of proficiency for social workers in England. [Online]. Available at: http://www.hpcuk.org/assets/documents/100035F9ConsultationondraftstandardsofproficiencyforsocialworkersinEnglandFINAL

Hopps, J.G. and Pinderhughes, E.B. (1996). Social Work in the United States: History, context, and issues. In M.C. Khinduka, S.K. and Midgley, J. (eds), *Profiles in International Social Work*. Washington, DC: NASW Press, 163–79.

Index Mundi. (2009). Cuba unemployment rate [Online]. Available at: http://www.indexmundi.com/cuba/unemployment_rate.html [accessed: 8 November 2011].

International Federation of Social Work/International Association of Schools of Social Work (IFSW/IASSW). (2004). *Global standards for social work education and training* [Online]. Available at: http://www.iassw-aiets.org/index.php?option=com_contentandtask=blogcategoryandid=28andItemid=49 [accessed: 15 September 2011].

Kaplan, F. (2009). 1959: The Year Everything Changed. Hoboken, NJ: John Wiley & Sons.Månsson, S. and Proveeyer-Cervantes, C. (eds). (2005). *Social Work in Cuba: Achievements and Prospects*. La Habana, Cuba: Universidad de la Habana.

Martínez. E. and García, A. (1996). *What is neo-liberalism? A brief definition for activists* [Online]. Available at: http://btw.mayfirst.org/sites/default/files/ whatisneo-liberalism_7230.pdf [accessed: 15 September 2011].

McDonald, C. and Marston, G. (2002). Fixing the niche: Rhetorics of the community sector in the neo-liberal welfare regime. *Just Policy*, 26, 7–20.

McKeen, W. (2007). The national children's agenda: A neo-liberal wolf in lamb's clothing. *Studies in Political Economy*, 80, 151–73.

Mendes, P. (2009). Teaching community development to social work students: A critical reflection. *Community Development Journal*, 44(2), 248–62.

Morgan, D. (2011). New census data raise number of poor to 49 million [Online]. Available at: http://www.reuters.com/article/2011/11/07/us-usa-poverty-idUSTRE7A634M20111107 [accessed: 8 November 2011].

Pérez, L.A., Jr. (2006). *Cuba: Between Reform and Revolution* (3rd edn). New York: Oxford.

Pérez, O.E. (2008). La economía en Cuba: Un balance actual y proyecciones necesarias. *Boletín Cuatrimestral*. La Habana, Cuba: Centro de Estudios de la Economía Cubana.

Pippard, J. and Bjorklund, R. (2003). Identifying essential techniques for social work community practice. *Journal of Community Practice*, 11(4), 101–16.

Ramírez, R. (2004). Factores que contribuyen al éxito o fracaso de proyectos comunitarios. Experiencias el en barrio Pogolotti, la Habana, Cuba. *Boletín del Instituto de la Vivienda*, 19, 181–245 [Online]. Available at: http://redalyc. uaemex.mx/pdf/258/25805011.pdf [accessed: 9 September 2011].

Reisch, M. and Andrews, J. (2002). *The Road Not Taken: A History of Radical Social Work in the United States*. New York: Brunner-Routledge.

Rendón Matienzo, F. (2011). Llama presidente cubano a cambiar de mentalidad en bien del socialismo. *Agencia Cubana de noticias* [Online]. Available at: http:// contacto-latino.com/view/?u=http%3A%2F%2Fnews.google.com [accessed: 9 September 2011].

Roman, P. (2003). *People's Power: Cuba's Experience with Representative Government*. Lanham, MD: Rowman and Littlefield.

Rothman, J. (1968). Three Models of Community Organization Practice. In F. Cox, Erlich, F.M., Rothman, J. and Tropman, J. E. (eds), *Strategies of Community Organization*. Itasca, IL: F.E. Peacock, 3–26.

Sennett, R. and Sassen, S. (2011). *Cameron's broken windows*. New York Times, A19.

Sexto, L. (2011). Kafka and the master's eye [Online]. Available at: http:// progreso-weekly.com/2/index.php?option=com_content&view=article&id=2 858:kafka-and-the-masters-eye&catid=36:in-cuba&Itemid=54 [accessed: 26 October 2011].

Sinclair, R., Hart M.A. and Bruyere, G. (2009). *Wicihitowin: Aboriginal Social Work in Canada*. Halifax, NS: Fernwood Books.

Social Work Action Network (SWAN). (2011) [Online]. Available at: http://www.socialworkfuture.org/ [accessed: 15 September 2011].Strug, D. (2006). Community-oriented social work in Cuba: Government response to emerging social problems. *Social Work Education*, 25(7), 749–62.

Strug, D. and Teague, W. (2002). New directions in Cuban social work education: What can we learn? *Social Work Today*, 18, 8–11.

Thomas, M.L., O'Connor, M.K. and Netting, F.E. (2011). A framework for teaching community practice. *Journal of Social Work Education*, 47(2), 337–52.

Togores González, V. (1999). *Cuba: Efectos sociales de la crisis y el ajuste económico en los 90s': Balance de la economía Cubana a finales de los 90s*. La Habana, Cuba: Universidad de La Habana.

Torres, J. (1993). *Pobreza: Un enfoque para Cuba*. Havana: INIE

Transnational Institute (2006). *Participatory Budgeting in Canada* [Online]. Available at: http://www.tni.org/archives/newpol-docs_pbcanada [accessed: 15 September 2011].

Uriarte, M. (2002). *Cuba: Social Policy at the Crossroads: Maintaining Priorities, Transforming Practice*. Boston, MA: Oxfam America.

Ward, D. (2002). Groupwork. In R. Adams, Dominelli, L. and Paynes, M. (eds), *Social Work: Themes, Issues and Critical Debates* (2nd edn). London: Palgrave MacMillan, 149–58.

Yamaoka, K. (2004). Cuba's social policy after the disintegration of the Soviet Union: Social development as legitimacy of the regime and its economic effectiveness. *The Developing Economies*, 42(2), 305–33.

Zabala-Argüelles, M. (2010). Poverty and vulnerability in Cuba today. *Socialism and Democracy*, 24(1), 109–26.

Chapter 6
Social Work Practice with Mexican Americans

Flavio Francisco Marsiglia

In the United States *Hispanic* and *Latino* are umbrella terms used to identify more than 50 million individuals living within its contemporary borders, connected through language, culture and geography to the Spanish colonial experience of North, Central and South America, and the Caribbean. Hispanics – or Latinos – are the largest ethnic minority in the United States and, for more than 400 years, have had an uninterrupted presence in the lands today forming the USA (Henderson, 2011). While there are cultural and linguistic similarities among the Latino/Hispanic subgroups, national origin, history, socioeconomic status, immigration and acculturation, among other factors, produce a rich diversity within this ethnic minority (Delgado, 2007). This chapter focuses on Mexican Americans, the largest Latino subgroup in the USA, accounting for two-thirds of all Latinos in the country (Yznaga, 2008).

Mexican Americans have a long and complex history. The USA and Mexico share almost 2,000 miles (3,218 km) of *frontera*, the longest international border separating a developed and developing country in the world. Gloria Anzaldúa (1987: 3) described the US–Mexico border as *'una herida abierta donde el tercer mundo raspa contra el primero y sangra* [an open wound where the Third World grates against the first and bleeds]'. The terminology and imagery of the 'borderlands' expresses and vividly captures the experience of Indigenous Peoples that have been colonized on three occasions – first by Spain, then by Mexico and later by the USA. Historically, the term 'borderlands' was used by officials of the Spanish empire (until 1821) and later by the independent Mexican Republic (until 1846) to identify the northernmost reaches of their colonial possessions (Johnson and Graybill, 2010). Already inhabited and controlled for centuries by various groups of Indigenous Peoples prior to the three periods of colonial invasion, the borderlands later became the contemporary US states of Arizona, California, Colorado, New Mexico, Oregon, Texas and Utah. Mexicans and Mexican Americans in the borderlands see themselves predominantly as *mestizos* – a people resulting from the amalgamation of Indigenous Peoples with Spanish colonizers and their descendants (Menchaca, 2007). In the1960s, the Chicano movement proudly embraced the Indigenous roots of Mexican Americans and started to decolonize the *mestizo* identity (Harley, 2010).

The international border in the Southwest USA, the rich cultures of its inhabitants, their languages and the way in which communities organized and governed themselves have changed, adapting and resisting different waves of colonialism over time. These experiences are summarized in a popular saying among elder Mexican Americans of the Southwest: 'We did not cross the border, the border crossed us.' Contemporary Mexican migration into the USA is not restricted to the Southwest. Today there are Mexican American communities in all states of the union but the largest concentration of Mexican Americans continues to be in the borderlands (Henderson, 2011).

The lives of Mexican Americans are intrinsically connected to border and border crossing narratives, to the duality of having roots in two countries, speaking two languages, and having a contemporary ethnic minority status. Spanish-language television, radio, printed press and all sorts of online bilingual and bicultural sites make Mexican American culture extremely vibrant and the antithesis of a Diaspora culture. Most Mexican Americans – regardless of their generational status and even those who have never lived in 'old Mexico' – tend to live transnational lives (Smith, 2000). Mexican and Mexican American cultures are intertwined and alive on both sides of a historically fluid but increasingly well-guarded border. Transnational Mexican American culture is vibrant, dynamic and very much alive on both sides of the border. Border communities, however, face ongoing social, political and civil rights challenges.

Social work as a profession has had a mixed record in responding to the unique needs of the Mexican American community and has only a limited understanding of the culturally specific natural ways of helping Mexican Americans (Patterson and Marsiglia, 2000). At times, social workers have allied themselves to oppressed communities or, at other times, perpetuated dominant hegemonies and inequitable distributions of power and privilege, approaching culture as a deficit (Gorski, 2007; Park, 2005; Yellow Bird, 2008). In those instances, social work has played a social control role and perpetuated the colonization of the peoples of the borderlands (Sinclair, 2004). This chapter presents cross-cultural practice as one of the first steps toward decolonizing practice. The concept of transnationalism requires further exploration in order to advance the decolonization of social work practice and research.

Transnationalism

Though the concept of transnationalism has been mainstreamed since the early 2000s, the practices associated with transnationalism have always existed among immigrants (Portes, 2001). Transnationalism is 'the process by which transmigrants, through their daily activities, forge and sustain multi-stranded social, economic and political relations that link together their societies of origin and settlement, and through which they create transnational social fields that cross national borders' (Basch, Glick Schiller and Blanc-Szanton, 1994: 6).

Transnational life includes practices and relationships that link immigrants and their descendants in the USA with Mexico (Smith, 2000). The contemporary movement of migrants is often traced back to the *Bracero Program* (1942–1964) through which the US Government contracted millions of Mexican nationals to work seasonally in agriculture for low wages to address the labour needs of US agriculture. The *Bracero Program* provided the foundations for the contemporary transnational movement of Mexican workers (Bohem, 2011). Global capitalism has strengthened transnationalism by allowing the free circulation and exchange of goods across the US–Mexico border. The North America Free Trade Agreement (NAFTA) has lifted barriers for the commerce of goods between the two countries but the border has become more unwelcoming for workers entering the USA from Mexico and other Latin American countries.

International migration is one of the most hotly debated contemporary social issues in the USA. Documented and undocumented Mexican immigrants have felt the rise in anti-immigrant sentiment and policies, which have exacerbated access and equity challenges experienced by all Mexican Americans and other Latinos (Delgado, 2007). In states such as Arizona, Alabama and Georgia, the anti-immigrant rhetoric has been translated into state-sponsored anti-immigrant and nativist laws that often disproportionally affect Mexican and Mexican American residents in those states (Galindo, 2011). Prejudice and discrimination compound the stress of immigrants dislocated from their extended families resulting in an increase in mental health issues such as anxiety, depression and other emotional challenges (Furman and Negi, 2007; Furman et al., 2009; Yznaga, 2008). For example, Post Traumatic Stress Disorder (PTSD) has been found to be associated with the often treacherous migration experience of trying to cross the US–Mexico border (Delgado, 2007).

Despite these challenges, Mexican American families and communities are blossoming across the country. Besides individual resilience, protective urban and rural enclaves provide a sense of belonging along with opportunities to expand the migrants' social networks and overcome some of the barriers to maintaining transnational relationships with their extended families in Mexico (Domínguez and Lubitow, 2008). Although a socially vulnerable group, transnational migrants generally live productive and healthy lives and achieve their goal of securing a better future for their children (Furman and Negi, 2007). The positive health and behavioural indicators of Mexican and Mexican American migrant communities have been referred to as the 'Mexican paradox' given the difficulties and challenges they face (Albright et al., 2011). However, according to migration selection theory, healthier members of a community tend to migrate and acculturation studies show the protective force of culture of origin tends to weaken after the first generation (Portes and Rivas, 2011). Paradoxically, discrimination might account for the counterintuitive educational attainment of Mexican Americans, which peaks among second-generation children of immigrants, but declines for the third and fourth generations – the grandchildren and great-grandchildren of immigrants (Telles and Ortiz, 2008). Thus, there is a need to better understand the resilience that comes from culture and the factors that may erode their positive effects over time. Social work has an important role to play in conducting such research and in informing the design and evaluation of interventions to strengthen existing assets and reduce or eliminate the risks of transborder migration.

Transculturalism and Social Work

A transcultural perspective to practice and research challenges social workers to address the experience of Mexican American communities in transcending borders. A transborder and transcultural lens is helpful in assessing the assets and challenges of Mexican American families and individuals. Some factors and experiences will be shared with other individuals, families and communities while others will be unique to the Mexican American experience in part due to these communities' historical and contemporary experiences with immigration and transculturalism. The Mexican American community, like other racial and ethnic communities, is highly diverse. Among other factors, differences in socioeconomic status, educational attainment, generational and acculturation status, language proficiency, religion and location (urban or rural) are key factors within a transcultural perspective.

Transcultural or Transborder Families

Extended families provide important emotional and financial support even when members live on different sides of the border. The migration experience tends to weaken the bond to Mexico over time, with transborder connections and related social networks eventually disappearing. Geographic proximity or distance from the ancestral home does not provide sufficient information about the strength of extended family support systems. Completion of a bi-national genogram has been found to be beneficial in helping Mexican American migrants work through the stress associated with migration and acculturation processes (Yznaga, 2008). The genogram provides unique insights into the history of the client as well as essential information for culturally grounded interventions. For example, for some being apart from extended family members in Mexico might result in isolation among immigrant nuclear families but for others transborder communication and bidirectional support might continue over time (Fitzgerald, 2009).

Acculturation

Differences in acculturation among family members can present challenges and lead to family conflict (Delgado, 2007). Understanding how families manage to reconcile differences in acculturation and retain high levels of health and mental health is important to effective intervention. Acculturation is a process by which immigrants and their children adopt the values, beliefs, customs and lifestyles of their new country of residence. Immigrants are faced with the task of adapting to this new receiving culture, while also choosing which aspects of their heritage culture they wish to retain (Berry, 2006). Acculturation is a process of cultural acquisition that is most salient for first-generation immigrants (those born outside the receiving country) and second-generation immigrants (those born in the receiving country but raised by foreign-born parents). Given that later generations of the descendants of immigrants generally integrate themselves into the receiving culture, they often may lack the elements of their culture of origin, although second- and third-generations may wish to socialize into their culture of origin, a process that has been identified as 'enculturation' (Berry, 1994). These acculturation or enculturation perspectives could be less applicable to a transnational and transcultural community, such as Mexican Americans. As a predominately *mestizo* people, Mexican Americans of the Southwest USA live where some of their ancestors lived. However, it is important to remember that the Southwest was and is home to numerous nations of Indigenous Peoples. Although there is a shared history of colonialism, some tribes may not fully share the Chicano movement's interpretation of the *mestizo* experience (Harley, 2010). For example, the Apache fought the Mexican army to keep them out of Apache territory and there are several bi-national tribes with large numbers of their members residing in Mexico and the USA (for example, Tohono O'odham, Yaqui Pascua and Apache). This complex history needs to be addressed as part of the decolonization process at the community and academic levels on both sides of the international border.

Acculturation and enculturation need to be placed within the historical processes of annexation and colonialism which gave birth to the minority status of Mexican Americans. Existing acculturation and enculturation paradigms may not necessarily capture the transcultural experiences of Mexican American individuals, families and communities. The acculturation process is not linear and does not take place in a vacuum. For example, young Mexican Americans may have high levels of perceived discrimination from mainstream society which will affect their acculturation process and sense of belonging (Kulis, Marsiglia and Nieri, 2009). Acculturating youth may also experience a sense of rejection from their communities of origin due to their fast pace of acculturation, in those cases interventions might support enculturation (Yoon, Hacker, Hewitt, Abrams and Cleary, 2011).

US Social Services System vis-à-vis *Mexican American Culture*

There are various assets and challenges associated with the transcultural experience of Mexican Americans which surface in the social services arena. First, the values and practices of the US social service system often conflict with the values and culture of Mexican Americans: the US focus on individualism may conflict with Mexican American collectivism. The strong emphasis on individual goals in the USA and family goals among Mexican Americans would render individualistic intervention modalities problematic for many ethnic minorities. In addition, the more linear and direct communication styles of white, middle-class North Americans might alienate Mexican Americans accustomed to more traditional, indirect and sometimes circular communication styles and threaten the effectiveness of insight-oriented interventions (Furman et al., 2009). Secondly, Mexican American values differing from mainstream US culture include *personalism* – preference for working with people rather than institutions; *confianza* – strong levels of trust and intimacy in a relationship; and *spiritualism and fatalism* – the belief that there are other forces at work and individuals are not fully in control of their destinies (Añez et al., 2008; Furman et al., 2009). Thirdly, mainstream US ideas of anonymity and equality may conflict with Mexican Americans' cultural identity with a study reporting that 80 per cent of Mexican Americans value their cultural *mestizo* heritage as much as or more than their identity as US Americans (Delgado, 2007). Thus in order to build a strong and decolonizing working relationship with Mexican Americans, early recognition of the unique, amalgamated Mexican and Indigenous values and norms important to them is essential (Añez et al., 2008).

Given social work is a profession with strong Eurocentric theoretical and methodological roots (Wong et al., 2003) the cultural competence paradigm has failed to address cultural disparities, in part because it is based on non-Indigenous approaches (Pon, 2009). Mexican American communities and other oppressed groups have survived oppression in many of its forms, including colonization, over the centuries not because of social work but because of their Indigenous community supports. Natural helping is one specific Indigenous way of helping that has provided strength and courage to continue to challenge oppressive conditions.

Natural Helping

Many Mexican Americans in the USA have maintained strong community and mutual aid networks through natural helping practices despite experiencing adverse social, economic and political conditions (Patterson and Marsiglia, 2000). This 'natural', informal, non-professional social support helps mediate health and mental health problems (Patterson et al., 1992) and enables Mexican American individuals and families cope with stress and maintain high levels of well-being. Natural helping among Mexican Americans far outdates formal, professional social work intervention. Thus Mexican Americans appear to be able to maintain pro-social tendencies even when experiencing high acculturative stress, as a result of direct, face-to-face helping in emergencies and emotionally charged situations (McGinley et al., 2010). These pro-social attitudes and behaviours and corresponding social networks have kept communities healthy and, over time, have provided a safety net for immigrants. Current anti-immigrant legislation and climate are challenging the strength of such networks.

Anti-Immigration Laws and Well-Being

Although constitutional law suggests that the courts should uphold minority rights, Mexican Americans have historically been marginalized in the court systems because immigration law falls under federal government jurisdiction (Johnson, 2009). Detainees' basic legal and human rights are not being met in an ever-changing and rapidly growing immigration system (London, 2010). A history of marginalization, coupled with widespread anti-Mexican sentiment among the general public, has supported widespread changes to immigration law (Johnson, 2009; London, 2010). While US courts have consistently ruled that the federal government has jurisdiction and responsibility over migration issues, as early as 1976 courts started to rule in favour of individual states having limited regulatory powers (Medina, 2011). The most notorious piece of state immigrant legislation (Arizona's SB-1070) has sought criminal enforcement powers over undocumented citizens (Medina, 2011), which more than half of registered US voters support (London, 2010). Such bills have not safeguarded the USA against terrorists and have had a negative impact on Mexican American communities and other Latino populations (Vasquez, 2011).

The result – and perhaps intent – of recent immigration laws is to keep poor people of colour out of the USA (Johnson, 2009). It is projected that the future reforms will include harsher and more stringent laws for future immigrants (London, 2010). Social workers need to be aware of and knowledgeable about US immigration policy, especially its impact on the emotional, psychological and physical health of affected clients and communities and its immediate detrimental implications for families, particularly children, when immigrants are harassed or detained (Vasquez, 2011). Children born in the USA of immigrant parents, affected by the stress of being part of a 'mixed' family, begin to exhibit behavioural health, learning and discipline problems at school (Dreby, 2010). Anti-immigrant sentiment contributes to Latinos' mistrust of law enforcement agencies, avoidance of health and behavioural health services, non-participation in educational activities and marginalization in the informal labour market (Vasquez, 2011). Some Mexican American immigrant families risk imprisonment and deportation while others move to states with more lenient immigration laws. Because the anti-immigrant and pervasive anti-Mexican American sentiment has been found to be related to the ongoing economic downturn (Diaz, Saenz and Kwan, 2011), these discriminatory attitudes will likely not change in the foreseeable future. Living in an environment of widespread prejudice leads to chronic stress, despite the individual resilience, and strong family and community bonds characteristic of the Mexican American population (Campa, 2010; Crosnoe, 2005; Flores et al., 2008; Furman et al., 2009). Social work has a role in supporting immigrant networks and natural helping systems mounting community-based resistance to discriminatory and unjust laws and legal practices (Bender, Negi and Fowler, 2010). Social workers need to develop innovative strategies to change oppressive social conditions. Culturally competent services and competent social work practitioners (Vidal de Haymes and

Kilty, 2007) are of little use in a system where state and federal laws deny Mexican Americans access to services (Dettlaff and Earner, 2007).

Suggested Intervention Strategies

Culturally Relevant Services

The delivery of culturally competent services requires a culturally and linguistically competent workforce. This means social workers working with Mexican American clients know and understand their culture and speak their language – Spanish and English (Furman et al., 2009). Culturally responsive services with Mexican American clients: (i) identify and integrate family members and friends of clients in engagement, assessment and treatment processes (Añez et al., 2008), which might include *compadres, comadres* and other ritualistic forms of social kinship; (ii) adapt the language and content of intervention programmes to resonate better with Mexican and Mexican American cultures and cosmologies (Bernal and Rodríguez, 2009); (iii) focus on strengthening families, communities and individuals (Furman et al., 2009); (iv) broaden the concept and definition of the nuclear family to include the roles played by extended and extra-familial individuals focusing not only on the individual's functioning in the family but also what families – and significant others who are not necessarily blood relatives – do for individuals; (v) base services in the social fabric of Latino communities (Delgado, 2007); and (vi) work with Indigenous helpers – such as *promotoras* – so as to increase the cultural relevance of interventions and retain Mexican American participation (Bernal and Rodríguez, 2009).

Health Services

There is a historical hesitancy in many Mexican American communities to use health and behavioural health services now more pronounced due to rising anti-immigrant attitudes and discriminatory immigration policies (Casas and Cabrera, 2011). The US healthcare system is difficult to navigate for English-speaking US citizens, even more so for those whose first language is not English (Delgado, 2007). Mexican Americans are less likely to seek treatment from mental health providers who judge them (Furman et al., 2009) and often prefer Indigenous or culturally grounded forms of treatment from folk healers – *curanderos* (*curanderismo* is the use of folk healers) (Padilla and Villalobos, 2007). Mexican Americans in need of long-term in-home healthcare have been found to be reluctant to use US health services (Herrera et al., 2008). While use of US in-home healthcare services might vary, social workers need to be aware of cultural barriers and Mexican Americans' preference for family-based care (Padilla and Villalobos, 2007). Many tend to use traditional and mainstream health services, with the latter increasing with acculturation (Vega, Kolody and Aguilar-Gaxiola, 2001). Bilingual or bicultural community-based lay health advisors – *promotoras* – appear to play an important role in supporting people through the care continuum from natural helping to mainstream medical treatment (Ayala et al., 2010). Social work can play an important role in supporting these processes by working with communities and Indigenous lay workers to take a leadership role in advocating for equitable access to quality care (Marsiglia and Kulis, 2009).

Interestingly, disparities in access to mental health services between Latinos and the rest of the US population are almost completely eliminated when the clients' culture and language are integrated in service delivery protocols (Añez et al., 2008). This speaks to the need for social workers and allied health professions to educate students in culturally grounded practice approaches. One way to do this is by facilitating the use of bilingual and bicultural *promotoras* – paraprofessionals – to help ease the stresses associated with a complex healthcare system (Padilla and Villalobos, 2007; Sánchez, 2007). Agencies can also respond by using integrated models that combine physical and mental health centres and providing bilingual staff members (Furman et al., 2009). Lastly, educating social workers to view culture as a strength rather than a barrier to quality healthcare might enhance their potential to provide culturally responsive services and thereby increase Mexican American uptake (Schur and Albers, 2010).

Social Work Education

Due to renewed anti-immigrant sentiments in the USA (for example, Arizona, Georgia, Utah and Alabama state immigration laws), it is important that social work education programmes at all levels (that is, Bachelor, Masters and Doctoral) emphasize a human and civil rights-focused curriculum. Research conducted in states where the most stringent anti-immigrant laws have been enacted shows that university students in those states reflect similar perceptions of Mexican Americans as their communities (Diaz et al., 2011). Increasing students' awareness of and access to accurate information is essential. Social workers should be familiar with state and federal laws impacting upon Mexican immigrants' and Mexican Americans' access to services (Dettlaff and Earner, 2007). Indeed, at the most fundamental level, the solution to advancing culturally grounded services with Mexican American communities is to improve the US social work education system. While social work students believe it is important to know how to serve this population, less than half think they are prepared to do so (Furman et al., 2009). The same study found that only three per cent of Master of Social Work graduates were Latinos, showing a great need for universities to enhance their recruitment of bilingual and bicultural students. The new generation of professionals need to be educated about the complexities of transnational and transcultural communities. The Mexican American case offers fruitful opportunities for learning and for making the profession more responsive to the cultural needs of clients. This learning process should start with the knowledge that exists within communities,

Indigenous service providers and the needs and assets identified by community members. The next generation of students should identify their role in dialogue with community members and a variety of service providers (professional and paraprofessional). Transnational alliances between the USA and Mexico will allow for such dialogue to take place on both sides of the border and to integrate perceptions and ideas from both countries and produce transnational and transcultural interventions.

Case Study: Familias Sanas

Familias Sanas (Healthy Families) is a psychosocial intervention implemented and tested with low-income Mexican American mothers at a community-based clinical setting. The programme was designed to reduce health disadvantages among Mexican American women by supporting them to take an active role in the management of their health and encouraging them to advocate for themselves. *Familias Sanas* was implemented at a prenatal clinic located at a major urban hospital in a large southwestern US state. The efficacy of the intervention was evaluated through a randomized controlled trial measuring the participants' rate of postpartum visits along with other relevant well-being measures. Initial findings showed a significant effect of the intervention, with participants in the experimental group returning for their postpartum clinic visit at a statistically significant higher rate in comparison with the control group. This culturally tailored programme positively influenced care access, adherence and outcomes. One of the reasons for *Familias Sanas'* success was its responsiveness to Mexican American spiritual and cultural beliefs related to health, such as the importance and influence of social support from family and friends, and beliefs in the power of faith over illness, and or about the supernatural roots of illness.

The *Familias Sanas* intervention was designed to bridge the culture gap between Mexican Americans and the US healthcare system, and to reinforce among pregnant women the importance of the postpartum visit and of caring for their health. *Familias Sanas* used Prenatal Partners (PP) – or *Compañeras* – as cultural brokers who showed participants how to navigate the health system, encouraged them to advocate for themselves and their children, helped them improve communication with providers and get answers for all their health-related questions. The Prenatal Partner's role was designed after the *promotoras de salud* – health promoters' – model, also known as community health workers (CHWs) or lay health educators (Williams, 2001). *Promotoras* have been broadly used to address various health problems in ethnically diverse communities across the USA, as well as internationally. Because these workers are often members of the community in which they work, they have been shown to be effective in providing culturally and linguistically appropriate health education for underserved populations (Deitrick et al., 2010). In the *Familias Sanas* project, however, a hybrid model was used. The PPs were MSW students who were bilingual, bicultural and from the community. The intervention took place at the Women's Health Clinic in a large urban public hospital, where the PPs met with participants, usually in the waiting room.

Although the PPs in this study were recruited social work students and social workers often provide counselling to clients, *Familias Sanas* is not a traditional social work intervention. In this study, patients in need of counselling were referred to community resources. The PPs received training from the study manager in recruiting, engaging and retaining participants, and in ways to support participants and encourage them to be active in their own health decisions. Results showed that 73 per cent of the intervention group attended the postpartum visit compared with 51 per cent of their peers in the control group (χ^2=17.880, 1df, p=.000). The chances of women in the intervention group attending the postpartum visit were 2.5 times those of their control group peers. The intervention was found to be cost-efficient and easily replicable with trained lay workers without a university affiliation (Marsiglia, Parsai and Coonrod, 2010).

Conclusion

This chapter discussed social work practice with Mexican heritage communities in the USA. The introductory historical background provided a context for the unique assets and challenges present within Mexican American communities and the need for culturally grounded social work as a part of a long tradition of community-based helping and resilience under oppressive conditions and a first step in decolonizing practice. Lessons from social work practice with Mexican Americans suggest that practitioners can mediate between the two cultures, be competent in both cultures and, ideally, fluent in English and Spanish. Social work practitioners' ethnic background and professional experience may not be sufficient for effective practice. If they cannot interpret or understand cultural assets and value conflicts, practitioners would do well to seek the assistance of cultural experts already located in the community. The case study illustrated a form of culturally grounded social work where the professional social worker supported Indigenous or natural helping approaches. Social workers can play an important role as consultants and supporters of culturally grounded services. Moving away from the centre of the service delivery system and working in the background can be an effective strategy for decolonizing social work. By becoming familiar with community-based natural helping networks and belief systems, practitioners develop increased effectiveness at accessing communal or family oriented types of helping and connecting them – when needed – to more individualistic types of interventions used by many of the agencies for which they work.

References

Albright, K., Chung, G., De Marco, A. and Yoo, J. (2011). Moving Beyond Geography: Health practices and outcomes across time and place. In L.M. Burton, Kemp, S.P., Leung, M., Mathews, S.A. and Takeuchi, D.T. (eds), *Communities, Neighborhoods, and Health: Expanding the Boundaries of Place*. New York: Springer, 127–43.

Añez, L.M., Silva, M.A., Paris, M. Jr. and Bedregal, L.E. (2008). Engaging Latinos through the integration of cultural values and motivational interviewing principles. *Professional Psychology: Research and Practice*, 39, 153–9.

Anzaldúa, G. (1987). *Borderlands/La Frontera. La Nueva Mestiza*. San Francisco, CA: Spinsters/Aunt Lute.

Ayala, G.X., Vaz, L., Earp, J.A., Elder, J.P. and Cherrington, A. (2010). Outcome effectiveness of the health advisor model among Latinos in the United States: An examination by role. *Health Education Research*, 25, 815–40.

Basch, L.G., Glick Schiller, N. and Blanc-Szanton, C. (1994). *Nations Unbound: Transnational Projects, Post-Colonial Predicaments, and Deterritorialized Nation States*. Langhorne, PA: Gordon and Breach.

Bender, K., Negi, N. and Fowler, D.N. (2010). Exploring the relationship between self-awareness and student commitment and understanding of cultural responsive social work practice. *Journal of Ethnic and Cultural Diversity in Social Work*, 19, 34–53.

Bernal, G. and Rodríguez, M.M.D. (2009). Cultural adaptation of treatments: A resource for considering culture in evidence-based practice. *Professional Psychology: Research and Practice*, 40, 361–8.

Berry, J.W. (1994). Acculturation and Psychological Adaptation: An overview. In A. Bouvy, van de Vijver, F.J.R., Boski, P. and Schmitz, P. (eds), *Journeys into Cross-Cultural Psychology*. Berwyn, PA: Swets and Zeitlinger, 129–41.

Berry, J.W. (2006). *Immigrant Youth in Cultural Transition: Acculturation, Identity, and Adaptation across National Contexts*. Mahwah, NJ: Erlbaum.

Bohem, D.A. (2011). U.S.-Mexico mixed migration in an age of deportation: An inquiry into the transnational circulation of violence. *Refugee Survey Quarterly*, 30, 1–21.

Campa, B. (2010). Critical resilience, schooling processes, and the academic success of Mexican Americans in a community college. *Hispanic Journal of Behavioral Sciences*, 32, 429–55.

Casas, J.M. and Cabrera, A.P. (2011). Latino/a immigration: Actions and outcomes based on perceptions and emotions or facts? *Hispanic Journal of Behavioral Sciences*, 33, 283–303.

Crosnoe, R. (2005). Double disadvantage or signs of resilience? The elementary school contexts of children from Mexican immigrant families. *American Educational Research Journal*, 42(2), 269–303.

Deitrick, L.M., Paxton, H.D., Rivera, A., Gertner, E.L.J., Biery, N., Letchner, A.S., Lahoz, L.M., Maldonado, E. and Salas-López, D. (2010). Understanding the role of the *promotora* in a Latino diabetes education program. *Qualitative Health Research*, 20, 386–99.

Delgado, M. (2007). *Social Work with Latinos: A Cultural Assets Paradigm*. New York: Oxford Press.

Dettlaff, A.J. and Earner, I. (2007). The intersection of migration and child welfare: Emerging issues and implications. *Protecting Children*, 22, 3–7.

Dreby, J. (2010). *Divided by Borders: Mexican Migrants and Their Children*. Berkeley, CA: University of California Press.

Diaz, P., Saenz, D.S. and Kwan, V.S.Y. (2011). Economic dynamics and changes in attitudes toward undocumented Mexican immigrants in Arizona. *Analysis of Social Issues and Public Policy*, 11, 300–13.

Domínguez, S. and Lubitow, A. (2008). Transnational ties, poverty, and identity: Latin American immigrant women in public housing. *Family Relations*, 57, 419–30.

Fitzgerald, D. (2009). *A Nation of Emigrants: How Mexico Manages Its Migration*. Berkeley, CA: University of California.

Flores, E., Tschann, J.M., Dimas, J.M., Bachen, E.A., Pasch, L.A. and de Groat, C.L. (2008). Perceived discrimination, perceived stress, and mental and physical health among Mexican-origin adults. *Hispanic Journal of Behavioral Sciences*, 30(4), 401–24.

Furman, R. and Negi, N.J. (2007). Social work practice with transnational Latino populations. *International Social Work*, 50, 107–12.

Furman, R., Negi, N.J., Iwamoto, D.K., Rowan, D., Shukraft, A. and Gragg, J. (2009). Social work practice with Latinos: Key issues for social workers. *Social Work*, 54, 167–74.

Galindo, R. (2011). The nativistic legacy of the Americanization era in the education of Mexican immigrant students. *Educational Studies*, 47, 323–46.

Gorski, P.C. (2007). *Good intentions are not enough: A decolonizing intercultural education*. EdChange. Hamline University [Online]. Available at: http://www.edchange.net/publications/intercultural-education.pdf [accessed: 25 November 2011].

Harley, G. (2010). The curandera of conquest: Gloria Anzaldúa's decolonial remedy. *Aztlán: A Journal of Chicano Studies*, 35, 135–61.

Henderson, J.T. (2011). *Beyond Borders: A History of Mexican Migration to the United States*. Malden, MA: Blackwell.

Herrera, A.P., Lee, J., Palos, G. and Torres-Vigial, I. (2008). Cultural influences in the patterns of long-term care use among Mexican American Family caregivers. *Journal of Applied Gerontology*, 27, 141–65.

Johnson B.H. and Graybill, A.R. (2010). *Bridging National Borders in North America: Transnational and Comparative Histories*. Durham, NC: Duke University Press.

Johnson, K.R. (2009). The intersection of race and class in U.S. immigration law and enforcement. *Law and Contemporary Problems*, 72, 1–35.

Kulis, S., Marsiglia, F.F. and Nieri, T. (2009). Perceived ethnic discrimination versus acculturation stress: Influences on substance use among Latino youth in the Southwest. *The Journal of Health and Social Behavior*, 50, 443–59.

London, J. (2010). Immigration policy from 2010 to 2020. *Aztlán: A Journal of Chicano Studies*, 35, 177–83.

Marsiglia, F.F. and Kulis, S. (2009). *Diversity, Oppression, and Change: Culturally Grounded Social Work*. Chicago, IL: Lyceum Books.

Marsiglia, F.F., Parsai, M. and Coonrod, D. (2010). *Familias Sanas*: An intervention designed to increase rates of postpartum visits among Latinas. *Journal of Health Care for the Poor and Underserved*, 21, 119–31.

McGinley, M., Carlo, G., Crockett, L.J., Raffaelli, M., Torres-Stone, R.A. and Iturbide, M.I. (2010). Stressed and helping: The relations among acculturative stress, gender, and prosocial tendencies in Mexican Americans. *Journal of Social Psychology*, 150, 34–56.

Medina, M.I. (2011). *Symposium on Federalism at Work: State Criminal Law, Non-citizens and Immigration Related Activity – an introduction* [Online]. Available at: http://ssrn.com/abstract=1843401 [accessed: 25 November 2011].

Menchaca, M. (2007). Latinas/os and the mestizo racial heritage of Mexican Americans. In J. Flores and Rosaldo, R. (eds), *Companion to Latino/a Studies*. Oxford: Blackwell, 323–31.

Padilla, Y.C. and Villalobos, G. (2007). Cultural responses to health among Mexican American women and their families. *Family and Community Health*, 30, S24–S33.

Park, Y. (2005). Culture as deficit: A critical discourse analysis of the concept of culture in contemporary social work discourse. *Journal of Sociology and Social Welfare*, 32(3), 11–33.

Patterson, S. and Marsiglia, F.F. (2000). 'Mi casa es su casa': A beginning exploration of Mexican Americans' natural helping. *Families in Society: Journal of Contemporary Human Services*, 81, 22–31.

Patterson, S.L., Memmott, J.L., Brennan, E.M. and Germain, C.B. (1992). Patterns of natural helping in rural areas: Implications for social work research. *Social Work Research and Abstracts*, 28, 22–8.

Pon, G. (2009). Cultural competency as new racism: An ontology of forgetting. *Journal of Progressive Human Services*, 20(1), 59–71.

Portes, A. (2001). Introduction: The debates and significance of immigrant transnationalism. *Global Networks*, 1, 181–93.

Portes, A. and Rivas, A. (2011). The adaptation of migrant children. *The Future of Children*, 21, 219–46.

Sánchez, M.S. (2007). Mexican American women's pathways to health. *Family and Community Health*, 30, S43–S52.

Schur, C.L. and Albers, L.A. (2010). Language, sociodemographics, and health care use of Hispanic adults. *Journal of Health Care for the Poor and Underserved*, 7, 140–58.

Sinclair, R. (2004). Aboriginal social work education in Canada: Decolonising pedagogy for the seventh generation. *First Peoples Child and Family Review*, 1, 49–61.

Smith, T. (2000). *Foreign Attachments: The Power of Ethnic Groups in the Making of American Foreign Policy*. Boston, MA: Harvard University Press.

Telles, E.E. and Ortiz, V. (2008). *Generations of Exclusion: Mexican Americans, Assimilation and Race*. New York: Russell Sage Foundation.

Vasquez, Y. (2011). Perpetuating the marginalization of Latinos: A collateral consequence of the incorporation of immigration law into the criminal justice system. *Scholarship at Penn Law*. Paper 373 [Online]. Available at: http://lsr. nellco.org/upenn_wps/373 [accessed: 23 November 2011].

Vega, W.A., Kolody, B. and Aguilar-Gaxiola, S. (2001). Help seeking for mental health problems among Mexican Americans. *Journal of Immigrant Health*, 3, 133–40.

Vidal de Haymes, M. and Kilty, K.M. (2007). Latino population growth, characteristics, and settlement trends: Implications for social work education in a dynamic political climate. *Journal of Social Work Education*, 43, 101–16.

Williams, D.M. (2001). La promotora: Linking disenfranchised residents along the border to the U.S. health care system. *Health Affairs*, 20, 212–18.

Wong, Y.R., Cheng, S., Choi, S., Ky, K., Leba, S., Tsang, K. and Yoo, L. (2003). Deconstructing culture in cultural competence: Dissenting voices from Asian-Canadian practitioners. *Canadian Social Work Review*, 20(2), 149–67.

Yellow Bird, M. (2008). Terms of Endearment: A brief dictionary for decolonizing social work with Indigenous Peoples. Postscript. In M. Gray, Coates, J. and Yellow Bird, M. (eds), *Indigenous Social Work around the World: Towards Culturally Relevant Education and Practice*. Aldershot: Ashgate, 271–91.

Yoon, E., Hacker, J., Hewitt, A., Abrams, M. and Cleary, S. (2011). Social connectedness, discrimination, and social status as mediators of acculturation/ enculturation and well-being. *Journal of Counseling Psychology*. Advance online publication. doi: 10. 1037/a0025366.

Yznaga, S.D. (2008). Using the genogram to facilitate the intercultural competence of Mexican immigrants. *The Family Journal*, 16, 159–65.

Chapter 7

From Trauma to Triumph: Perspectives for Native Hawaiian and Māori Peoples

Noreen Mokuau and Peter J. Mataira

Native Hawaiian and Māori are Indigenous Peoples with roots in the Pacific islands of Hawai`i and New Zealand, respectively. There are approximately 449,000 Native Hawaiians living in the USA, mainly in the states of Hawai`i and California (US Census Bureau, 2006–2008). Approximately, 565,329 Māori reside in New Zealand and 72,000 in Australia (Statistics NZ, 2006). An estimated 20,000–23,000 New Zealanders live in the USA, 15 per cent – approximately 3,500 – of whom are Māori. The majority of Native Hawaiians and Māori are of multiracial backgrounds but regard their native heritage as their dominant identity. Despite their diversity, Native Hawaiians and Māori share cultural values and practices and, like other Indigenous Peoples, their history bears significant similarities in regards to historic trauma. This chapter examines the trajectory of historic trauma for Native Hawaiians and Māori and explores how they are using cultural strengths and resilience to 'rise from the trauma', despite continuing challenges. For too long, settler governments, society and social workers have viewed Native Hawaiians and Māori through a problem-focused lens, which negates the good work and collective progress of these groups, including their historical leaders. This chapter adopts Wesley-Esquimaux and Smolewski's (2004) five areas of impact to frame the discussion of historic trauma and 'rise' to triumph. The model addresses cultural strengths that contribute to this transition and their implications for Indigenous social work practice.

Historic Trauma

Historic trauma has been defined as the cumulative emotional and psychological wounding over the lifespan and across generations, emanating from massive group trauma (Brave Heart, 2000; Takini Network, n.d.). The members of a cultural group experience unhealthy or maladaptive consequences, such as health disparities in heart disease and cancer, low life expectancies and substance abuse, and these consequences become endemic to society and likely are carried forth into successive generations (Halloran, 2004). Arriving in several waves of migration to their island homelands, Native Hawaiians (300–800AD) and Māori (1300AD) created isolated, thriving island societies predicated on unique cultural systems

(Chadwick et al., 2007; Office of Hawaiian Affairs, 2011; Taonui, 2006). However, the arrival of British explorer Captain James Cook, for Native Hawaiians in 1778 and Māori in 1769, brought dramatic changes and devastating consequences for these native peoples, which continue to influence these populations in troubling ways. Wesley-Esquimaux and Smolewski (2004) identified five areas of historic trauma for Indigenous Peoples, including Native Hawaiian and Māori cultures:

1. *Physical* through the introduction of infectious diseases, the decimation of Indigenous Peoples, and intergenerational stress.
2. *Cultural* through religious transformation and cultural destruction of native cultures and belief systems.
3. *Economic* through a violation of native stewardship of land and removal of people from environmental systems.
4. *Sociopolitical* through the introduction of alien governing and social structures and diminishing cultural values and mores.
5. *Psychological* through the marginalization of native people, an eradication of their social selves, and an undermining of their personal and group autonomy.

Physical Impact: Depopulation

Historical records indicate that for thousands of years prior to Western contact, Native Hawaiians were robust and healthy, living in a sustainable ecology with a clearly delineated social structure (Bushnell, 1993; Pukui et al., 1979). The arrival of Captain Cook in 1778 with the sailor and merchant population brought the introduction of infectious diseases for which Native Hawaiians had no immunity, and a massive decline of the population ensued. European diseases unknown to this population, such as venereal disease, smallpox, measles and influenza, decimated this group. It is estimated that the Native Hawaiian population ranged from 300,000 to 1 million in 1778, yet less than 100 years later in 1853, the first census tabulation showed only 71,000 remained (Nordyke, 1989; Stannard, 1989).

Likewise, prior to British settlement, the Māori population was estimated to be 200,000–250,000 (Orange, 1987; Statistics NZ, 2006), although some historical accounts put this figure around 1 million (Harawira, 1998). With the abundance of fertile lands and rich food supplies, this higher estimate could have been sustained (Taylor, 1974). Within a century of contact, Māori experienced rapid depopulation. Cumulative effects of disease, including typhoid, tuberculosis, polio and influenza, along with the protracted Land Wars (1840s–1870s), precipitated cultural decay leading to fears of genocide (Grace, 1901; Simon and Smith, 2001). Historical reports indicate that between 1857 and 1874, the Māori population declined by 16 per cent, and, by 1896, Māori numbers had fallen from 200,000 to 42,113. The tribes in remote areas away from British contact fared best.

Cultural Impact: Erosion of Spiritual Systems

Traditional Hawaiian cosmography is founded on ideas of genealogical linkages of the spiritual realm, nature and people. In this manner, all parts of the world are related by birth and, as such, constitute a single indivisible lineage (Kame`eleihiwa, 1992). Kame`eleihiwa (1992) suggests this cosmography is reflected in three lessons: (i) caring for the land (Mālama `Āina); (ii) separation of the male element from the female element (`Aikapu); and (iii) chiefly mating by incest (Nīaupi`o). While many societies have prohibitions against incest, in historical times incestuous relationships ensured the continuation of familial lines, and political and economic power (Wikipedia, 2011).

With the arrival of missionaries in Hawai`i in 1820, new standards, with an emphasis on Christian doctrines and beliefs, were forced upon populations. The Native Hawaiian cosmographic view of relationships was replaced by a fundamentally different Christian perspective of a single God, separate from nature and people. The fundamental change to subscribing to one God changed the way in which Indigenous people viewed their relationship with their land and other people. The imposition of Christian prescriptions altered the fabric of family life, brought about the decline of native languages and led to the discontinuation of traditional cultural practices and art forms, such as the *hula*.

Through the late-1800s, Māori embraced Christianity with a degree of acceptance and caution. Indeed, many did convert to the Church of England and the Roman Catholic faith and new syncretic religions arose, combining aspects of Christian and traditional Māori beliefs. These new religions – notably Ratana, which formed in 1925, Ringatū in 1868, and Pai Marire and Hauhau in 1863 – were headed by charismatic, well-versed, bilingual Māori chiefs, known as the 'Prophets' (Binney, 1990). Later they would become formidable powerful forces uniting expressions of Māori political sovereignty. In large measure, Māori acceptance of Judeo-Christian beliefs was the accommodation of their *taongo matauranga tuku iho* – knowledge from the heavens – and Old Testaments principles embedded in ritual practice. Infused into Māori cosmology, today these Christian values are the accepted norm. Māori public gatherings – *hui* – proceed and conclude with prayer – *karakia* – and acknowledgement of the Judeo-Christian God. Life for Māori is a constant shifting between states of sacredness – *tapu* – or heightened levels of conscience, and the commonplace – *noa* – or state of normalcy, where balance is the goal (Marsden, 2003; Mataira, 2000a). Having a 'bad day', or encountering new daily experiences, requires *karakia* for guidance, instruction and protection (Marsden, 2003).

Economic Impact: Dispossession of Land

The traditional system of land tenure in Native Hawaiian culture was based on relationships of gods, chiefs and the people, and not on Western conceptualizations of individual 'ownership'. In general, the chiefs held the lands in trust for the gods and had the responsibility to create conditions for the people to steward the land in ways that would provide food and resources for all. Under the reign of King Kamehameha III (1825–1854), land stewardship in Hawaiian culture underwent significant change. With the threat of foreign powers seeking occupation of the islands, and guided by foreign advisors, King Kamehameha III instituted land reform in 1848 called the Māhele (Kame'eleihiwa, 1992). In premise, this was intended to ensure that Native Hawaiians had land through its allocation to the king (crown lands), chiefs (konohiki lands), revenue for the government (government lands) and commoners (kuleana lands) (Chinen, 1958). However, Native Hawaiians did not understand the idea of 'ownership', were cash-poor and unfamiliar with rules and procedures for land claims. Thus, the result of the Māhele was that foreign land ownership escalated and lesser chiefs and commoners ended up with less than one per cent of the land (Hasager and Kelly, 2001).

In 1862, the British Crown Settler government in New Zealand enacted the Native Land Act laws to transfer Māori land to British land speculators and migrant settlers by forceful conversion of collective traditional customary land rights into individual title. The established Native Land Courts, therefore, gave entitlement power to 'any Māori' – those the Crown named on the land deed – and the right to sell land on the open market, thereby negating the government's right of pre-emption under the 1840 Treaty of Waitangi. The ensuing Land Wars (1845–1872), resulting from a combination of impassioned Māori resistance and the extraordinary tactical build-up of British militia, was heightened in the early1860s by the introduction of the New Zealand Settlements Act, which gave further powers to confiscate lands belonging to Māori tribes deemed to be in rebellion, or suspected of aiding or abetting those resisting the intent or substance of imposed British Imperialist law. By 1896, an estimated 56 million acres of Māori land was annexed, effectively stripped through elicit and unfair practices, dubious purchase agreements and confiscation laws. A further 6 million acres was annexed between 1897 and 1910 and, by the mid-1920s, Māori held a mere 5 million (7 per cent) of the 66.5 million acres they once owned. On the surface there was no denying the Treaty of Waitangi and ensuing land laws, including the Native Lands Act and Settlement Act, were ruses to obfuscate Māori legitimacy to claims to their ancestral birthright. Clearly, the British had no semblance of deference or intent on honouring their Treaty partnership obligations. Rather, by force, the intent was to fragment and overpower systematically and superciliously. The rhetoric of Māori political, social and economic resistance still resonates five generations later (see Awatere, 1984; Sharples, 2008; Smith, 2007; Sykes, 2011; Walker, 1996, 2004).

*Sociopolitical Impact: Overthrow of the Hawaiian Monarchy and Threats to Māori Sovereignty (*tino rangatiratanga*)*

Traditional ruling structures in Native Hawaiian culture show the 'king was the … head of the government; the chiefs below the king, the shoulders and chest. The priest of the king's idol was the right hand and the minister of the interior the left hand of the government' (Malo, in Cordy, 2000: 55). The momentum of foreign land ownership in the mid-1850s led to changes that resulted in the overthrow of the Native Hawaiian monarchy in 1893. Queen Lili`uokalani was dethroned and imprisoned by North Americans who sought to gain greater political influence over the islands with the support of a heavily armed US military (Fuchs, 1961). After the overthrow, a provisional government was established that seized control of crown and government lands and took action to annex Hawai`i to the USA (Mokuau and Matsuoka, 1995). The provisional government was established by those who wanted to end the authority of the Queen and argued strongly for annexation to the USA. With annexation, political authority and valuable land resources would become more readily available to non-Hawaiians. Hawai`i was annexed in 1898 despite opposition from many Native Hawaiians.

The social, political and economic impact of land loss on the fabric of traditional Māori society caused major long-term consequences, including detrimental effects on future generational spiritual and psychological well-being. Today, such loss has manifested in familial and tribal separation and a degradation of a Māori sense of wellness (Durie, 1998; Te Puni Kokiri, 2010) and many Māori have lost contact with their ancestral lands, with perhaps as many as 30–40 per cent of adult Māori with no knowledge or ownership of their traditional lands (Moeke-Pickering, 1996). Also, the prevailing system has led to a complex and decimating fragmentation within the family, and long-lasting impact on life expectancy. In 2005–2007, reports showed that the Māori male life expectancy at birth was 70.4 years in comparison to 79 years for non-Māori. Female life expectancy at birth was 75.1 years for Māori women and 83.0 years for non-Māori (Statistics NZ, 2010).

Psychological Impact: Loss of Cultural Identity

An essential element of Native Hawaiian identity is the affiliated nature of relationships in which a person is defined by a collective rather than an individual identity (Ewalt and Mokuau, 1995). A person defines and identifies him or herself by the quality of his or her relationships with family, the community, the environment and the spiritual realm. The pronounced value of collective identity and cohesiveness underscores a structured social order, where each person knows his or her role and place, and contributes to the welfare of the entire community. The destruction of the traditional Native Hawaiian society as evidenced by historical events led to the marginalization of its people and an insidious loss of collective identity. The erosion of traditional beliefs brought confusion, doubt and a loss of personal identification with a culture (Pukui et al., 1979). For many, the loss of cultural identity and esteem precipitated feelings of despair and hopelessness (Blaisdell, 1989).

For Māori, cultural identity is linked inextricably to psychological well-being and a sense of self-worth. Conversely, depopulation, land loss and the decaying social fabric led to psychological despair (Walker, 2004). Patterns of mental health, since the mid twentieth century, clearly show psychological stress (Kingi, 2005, 2007). Only recently was cultural alienation, poverty, unemployment, the breakdown of cultural traditions and failures of the education system for Māori considered contributors to psychological stress (Edmonds, Williams and Walsh, 2000). A recent overview of health trends in New Zealand showed that, since the mid-1980s, disparities between Māori and non-Māori have increased in areas of life expectancy, cancer mortality and cardiovascular illness. Equally disturbing are trends showing that, in areas where Māori reside, health needs are high and access to appropriate health services remains low (NZ Ministry of Health, 2010).

Rise to Triumph: A Decolonizing Approach

Shoulders of Our Historic Leaders

While there is clear evidence of historic trauma, Native Hawaiian and Māori peoples have drawn upon cultural strengths to deal with past challenges. The strengths perspective postulates that the positive qualities or strengths of an individual, group, family and community can be put to use to solve personal and social problems. As Saleebey (2002: 14) observes, 'trauma and abuse ... may be injurious but they may also be sources of challenge and opportunity'. A related concept is resilience, which emphasizes that recovery from adversity is aided by protective factors that offset risk (Kirst-Ashman and Hull, 2006). During the time of historic trauma, many native leaders were heedful of the negative impact of multiple risk factors and events and worked vigilantly to create systems of care that would provide protection for their people. It is on the broad shoulders of these historic leaders that present and future generations stand.

For Native Hawaiians, there are many leaders who carved a notable role in history, but in particular, the husband and wife team of King Kamehameha IV and Queen Emma, and the last royal monarch Queen Lili`uokalani are highlighted for their enduring legacies. In 1859, in context of massive depopulation from diseases, King Kamehameha IV and Queen Emma established a hospital to address the needs of Native Hawaiians as well as foreigners (Kanahele, 1999). The hospital has grown over the years, and today is the single largest acute care facility in the state of Hawai`i serving Native Hawaiians and all people of Hawai`i. Hardwired into the Queen's Medical Center is the Native Hawaiian Health Program with its special attention to the health disparities still afflicting the native population today (The Queen's Health System, 2009). In 1909, another notable Hawaiian leader, Queen Lili`uokalani, with great concern for future generations of her people, and with particular consideration for children and families, established a private foundation for their care. In keeping with her intentions, the Queen Lili`uokalani Children's Center, a social service agency, was created for the welfare of orphaned and destitute children, with preference to Hawaiian children (Queen Lili`uokalani Children's Center, 2011). These royal leaders, who lived amid historic trauma and devastation, used their position and influence to establish organizations that today continue to serve all people, with special attention to Native Hawaiians. Fundamental to these organizations are resilience and protective factors derivative of the culture, including the integration of Native Hawaiian values and practices, such as 'ohana (family), kokua (helping) and lokahi (unity), the governance and participation of Native Hawaiian leaders, and strong ties with the Native Hawaiian community.

While remaining strong and resilient in their efforts to rise beyond the debilitating effects of historic cultural trauma, Māori *esprit de resistance* manifested impressively through multiple levels of transformative leadership. From the wholesale rejection of the Treaty of Waitangi by signatory chiefs in the mid-1840s to the post-colonial political, economic, social and intellectual entrepreneurs, their focus has always been on development and the preserving of *tino Ranagtiratanga* (sovereignty) rights. These rights were coalesced through genealogy (*whakapapa*), knowledge (*Matauranga* Māori), language (*reo*), artistic expression (for example, *kapa haka*) and the emergence of highly sophisticated Māori/non-Māori (hybrid) constructs and models of practice. Perhaps the most recognized illustration of Māori resolve and need to find common ground was penned by Sir Apirana Ngata in his 1940s proverb (*whakatauaki*) 'E Tipu e Rea', Grow up on Tender Child (see Keelan, 2002). Ngata emphasized the three pillars central to maintaining family, individual and community health and well-being. As one of the most prominent Māori political leaders and Indigenous social entrepreneurs (Mataira, 2000b; Rata, 2004) of the twentieth century, he emphasized the importance of striving to achieve the highest academic accolades, and holding onto cultural identity through honouring ancestral connections and knowledge of genealogy, and using this knowledge to guide future decision-making. He stressed the need to build resilience through strong personal testimonies of faith in *Te Atua* (the Creator, God). Ngata understood these pillars to be critical to maintaining optimal balanced, healthy physical, psychological and spiritual lifestyles throughout the lifespan. Recognizing the challenges, he also understood the persistent and ongoing nature of the problems that would afflict ensuing generations. Clearly today Māori leadership remains resolute and committed to the legacy of colonial resistance and to the cause of Tino Rangatiratanga (Māori sovereignty) as it was during and before the time of Ngata and the Young Māori Party movement of the early 1900s. A demonstration of this was captured recently when Māori political leader Hone Harawira was unceremoniously ousted from Parliament during his swearing in speech in 2011. He was ejected amidst his angry protests for citing his allegiance, first and foremost, to the Treaty of Waitangi, an act deemed by Parliamentary Speaker of the House to be unlawful. Harawira's claim was that it was within the 'lore' of his people and within his rights as a descendant of the Northern Māori tribes (Tai Tokerau) of Aotearoa (Harawira, 2011).

The legacies of historic leaders, along with a host of other variables, including personal fortitude, familial support, political advocacy and community partnerships, all contribute to Native Hawaiians and Māori 'rising from the trauma'. The culturally based solutions – building cultural strengths and resilience (Mokuau, 2011) – might be seen as a decolonizing approach to counteract the worst vestiges of historical trauma.

Counteracting Physical Impacts on Population Growth

Population demographics in Hawai`i began to change as foreign labourers were brought to Hawai`i for the growing sugar industry in the mid-1800s. Since 1900 the rate of population has grown 2.3 per cent with continued in-migration and natural increases (Nordyke, 1989). The depopulation clearly evident in history began to shift as Native Hawaiians experienced high interracial marriages with various groups, including (i) immigrant labourers from countries such as China, Portugal, Japan, Korea and the Philippines from the mid-1800s; (ii) US citizens during annexation in 1898, territory status in 1900 and statehood in 1959; (iii) Pacific Islanders from US associated jurisdictions, such as American Samoa and Guam; and (iv) US military personnel since World War II (Braun, Mokuau and Browne, 2010; Nordyke, 1989).

Due to high rates of interracial marriages and births, the census for Native Hawaiians today has increased to approximately 401,000 in the USA (US Census Bureau, 2001). Of these, approximately 140,000 indicated they were full-blood Native Hawaiian and 261,000 were part-blood Native Hawaiian. Although there is variation in blood quantum, census estimates today exceed the conservative census estimate of 300,000 Native Hawaiians at pre-contact in 1778.

The twentieth century saw a resurgence of Māori vitality contrasting the long decline during the nineteenth century. This reversal was due to a combination of factors, including changes in census reporting, intermarriage, improved living conditions and a strong Māori advocacy presence in social policy and programme reforms. Census figures since 1901 show increases in Māori population numbers. By 1921, Māori rates increased at a higher rate than European (Pakeha), although the Pakeha population received considerable increments from immigration (Te Ara, 2011). By 2021, the Māori population is projected to grow from 586,000 reported in 2001 to 749,000 representing a 28 per cent increase. Although annual Māori growth is projected to slow from 1.4 per cent to 1.2 per cent by 2021, overall it is predicted that the Māori population will continue to grow at a faster pace than the total New Zealand population (Statistics NZ, 2010).

Cultural Resilience and Spiritual Resurgence

During the 1800s, Christianity permeated native society, and was largely supported by Native Hawaiian royalty. Cultural practices, anchored in traditional cosmography and spirituality, such as *lua* (martial arts), were outlawed and went 'underground' to be practised in secret by a few (Paglinawan, Eli, Kalauokalani and Walker, 2006). At some point, however, traditional Native Hawaiian spirituality experienced resurgence. While it is difficult to ascertain the chronological period, it can be argued that it was always evident, albeit with less visibility and attention. Since the 1970s, there are clearly visible indications of Native Hawaiian cultural and spiritual revival. Exploratory research shows that Native Hawaiians today are diverse in their definition and practice of religion and spirituality, with some subscribing to Christianity, others to traditional Native Hawaiian spirituality, yet others to a combination of Christian and traditional Hawaiian spirituality, while still others adhere to other religious doctrines (Mokuau, 2011). Cultural practices, with roots in Native Hawaiian cosmography and spirituality, including *lua*, *hula* (dance), *oli* (chant), ocean navigation, aquaculture-fishponds and agriculture-taro fields, are surging in distinction among Native Hawaiians and other peoples today.

A Māori sense of identity is connected intricately to ancestral lands and recognized and delineated not just as tribal geopolitical boundaries, but within the context of spiritual and relational laws, as Mother, Nurturer and Giver of life (Barlow, 1991; Pere, 2006). It is the intervention as well as the remedy to achieving and sustaining optimal family, communal and individual well-being. As such, every generation is obligated to safeguard and care for land and natural resources as *Kaitiaki* (guardians), inheritors and obligators entrusted to protect the environment (Selby, Moore and Mulholland, 2010). Land is the life-blood and its loss coupled with depopulation as the 'double-negative' spurred positive effort to revitalize.

Undoing Disparate Economic Impact: Some Evidence of Change

While the situation for Native Hawaiians today is far improved over the period of the *Māhele* in 1848, commonly defined economic indicators still show Native Hawaiians with significant disparities when compared with other groups in regards to variables such as poverty, median household income (Keahiolalo-Karasuda and Speck, 2010) and high numbers of working Native Hawaiians who are still homeless (Allen, 2007). Education is seen to be linked to economic achievement, and again, while it is acknowledged that educational disparities continue, modest changes are noted. For example, at the University of Hawai'i at Mānoa, the largest public university in Hawai'i, increases are noted in the Native Hawaiian student population. In 1984, 4.9 per cent of the university student population was Native Hawaiian (Ka'u, 1986); in 1999, 8.8 per cent (undergraduates) and 6.4 per cent (graduates); and in 2010, 14.3 per cent (undergraduates) and 11.3 per cent (graduates) were Native Hawaiian (Office of Student Equity, Excellence and Diversity, 2011). Another economic indicator, home ownership, shows similar rates for both the total state population at 58 per cent as well as Native Hawaiians at 54 per cent (Keahiolalo-Karasuda and Speck, 2010).

According to a 2003 report of the Global Entrepreneurship Monitor (GEM, 2003), if the Māori were a nation of sovereign people, they would be the fourth most entrepreneurial in the world. While the country has much to redress in terms of overall economic disparities, Māori people have excelled as one of the world's most entrepreneurial populations and, as the GEM points out, Māori exceed all others in total early stage entrepreneurial activity with 17.1 per cent starting a business compared with 13.3 per cent of non-Māori. Perhaps not surprisingly more Māori women (83.1 per cent) identified themselves as opportunity entrepreneurs compared with 30 per cent of Māori men, suggesting they were more apt to take advantage of opportunities than their male and non-Māori counterparts. This is reflected among women in developing countries where they too are significant players in small business enterprise building and social entrepreneurship. Their involvement in micro-enterprise activities is particularly evident in less developed countries like the Philippines, Sri Lanka and Vietnam (Tambunan, 2009). Mohammad Yunus (1999), in his noted work with microfinance and the Grameen Bank, reiterated the critical role of women given that their instinctual nurturing capacities lend themselves to developing successful small business enterprises for the sake of their families. Today Māori entrepreneurs are a significant contributor to the Māori commercial asset base and Māori participation in the New Zealand economy adds value to New Zealand's Gross Domestic Product (GDP) (De Bruin and Mataira, 2003; Te Puni Kokiri, 2010).

Sociopolitical Sovereignty and Federal Recognition

Efforts to reclaim a Hawaiian government began immediately after the overthrow of the monarchy in 1893. However, progress on sovereignty has been made in recent decades. Today there is strong evidence of Native Hawaiians seeking to reclaim an Indigenous land base that would serve as a foundation to sovereignty (Mokuau and Tauili`ili, 2011). Such efforts have resulted in the Apology Resolution of 1993 in which the US government acknowledged and apologized for the illegal overthrow of the Native Hawaiian monarchy in 1893. Efforts have also led to the Native Hawaiian Government Reorganization Act of 2009 and support from President Barack Obama's administration granting federal recognition to Native Hawaiians (NativeHawaiians.com, 2009). Despite such movement, there are still polarizing issues that jeopardize sovereignty, such as the sale of ceded lands – those lands of the 1893 monarchy that were ceded to the government during annexation. In 2009, the US Supreme Court ruled that the State of Hawai`i had the right to sell 1.2 million acres of ceded land. However, the Office of Hawaiian Affairs continues to argue that the state cannot sell ceded lands until there is resolution around the Native Hawaiian Government Reorganization Act (Guedel, 2009; Kim, 2009). There are several Native Hawaiian organizations that are not in agreement with the direction and precepts of federal recognition, asserting that it continues the 'wardship' status of Native Hawaiians within the US government and there are non-Hawaiian critics who indicate that federal recognition is race-based and jeopardizes the basic principles of the USA (Kelly, 2002; Starr, 2009). The progress on sovereignty is not minimized by conflict and debate, but rather, accentuates the commitment and tenacity of many people to seek resolution for Native Hawaiian people, the Indigenous people of Hawai`i.

Since the rapid population decline of the late-1800s, the Māori population has markedly increased. Census figures from 2006 put the Māori population at 565,329 representing14.6 per cent of New Zealand's overall population. The Māori population is highly urbanized (84 per cent) with 24 per cent of all Māori living in the Auckland metropolitan area. Although the national population is older (median age of 35.9 years), Māori are relatively younger (median age of 22.7 years). Studies show kinship groups continue to be significant and important to Māori knowledge, sense of belonging and well-being, even among the highly urbanized populations (Pakura, 2005). *Whānau* is the core unit and central medium for the transmission of intergenerational knowledge and cultural norms and provides a key role in expressing identity and developing opportunities. Thus, for Māori, 'to connect' and 'to belong' are best observed when at regular social gatherings. The question asked is not 'Who are you?' or 'What do you do?' but 'Where are you from?' This predicates relationships being built on tribal kinship and land connections through iterations of one's rivers, mountains, *waka* (canoe) and genealogy. Given demographic trends showing that investing in the realization and revitalization of Māori potential is critical to ensuring New Zealand's overall sustainable future, there is recognition today that, by 2051, the Māori population will increase to 800,000 or 22 per cent of New Zealand's total population.

Psychological Healing through Strengthening Cultural Identity

Theorizing about the loss of cultural identity during periods of historic trauma links psychological problems, such as collective depression among Native Hawaiians today, to historic trauma (Kaholokula, 2007). This is uppermost in the decolonization discourse where discussions about the strengthening of cultural identity through connections to spatial and spiritual space (Oneha, 2001), ties to families and communities, regular engagement in cultural practices (Kana'iaupuni, Malone and Ishibashi, 2005), learning of native languages (Mokuau and Tauili'ili, 2011) and relationships with native elders (Browne, Mokuau and Braun, 2009) are paramount. Underscoring this discussion is the importance of the revival of traditional Native Hawaiian cosmography which emphasizes the relational importance of the person, family, community, environment and spiritual realms. Growing cultural identity originates in the valuing and practice of cultural ways and traditions in ways that fit people's day-to-day lives (Mataira, Matsuoka and Morelli, 2006).

Cultural identity is an important contributor to Māori physical, spiritual, relational and psychological well-being. Identifying with one's culture instils and affirms a sense of belonging and security. A strong cultural identity reveals strong links to positive outcomes in Māori health and education providing access to social networks which then help to support shared values and aspirations. Strengthening Māori social networks is important to breaking down barriers and building local tribal social capital (Williams and Robinson, 2004). Cultural identity expressed negatively creates stereotypes and barriers leading to social exclusion and intolerance. Today New Zealand is a diverse, pragmatic, global nation comprising many cultures. While people may describe themselves as 'New Zealanders', how they define their 'New Zealand-ness' varies. It is clear, however, that Māori culture represents a significant part of the nation's identity and the New Zealand psyche. Māori symbols, art, music, film, sport and literature reflect the country's strong global identity.

Implications for Indigenous Social Work Practice

Indigenous social work involves the development of culturally relevant social work for, with and by Indigenous Peoples (Gray, Coates and Yellow Bird, 2010). The commitment to culture as central to Indigenous social work requires an understanding of diverse peoples and solidifies the mandate for their participation. Native Hawaiians and Māori, like other Indigenous Peoples, share the experience of historic trauma through its negative impacts across the lifespan and across generations. Emerging out of historic trauma will require the incorporation of cultural strengths and the recognition of peoples' cultural resilience. McCormick (1995/1996) identifies aspects fundamental to healing and recovery for Indigenous Peoples: (i) balance of the physical, mental, emotional and spiritual dimensions; (ii) emphasis on the interconnectedness between family, community, culture and nature; and (iii) transcendence of the individual (in Wesley-Esquimaux and Smolewski, 2004). Wesley-Esquimaux and Smolewski (2004) add that the fragmented parts of the past, present and future must also be reintegrated to facilitate emergence out of historic trauma.

Implications for social work practice with Native Hawaiians and Māori begins with the understanding that they have common roots in a history of trauma, may share tenets of balance, interconnectedness, transcendence and spatial time as noted above, but may express their cultures in different ways. With such recognition, decolonizing social work practice with Indigenous Peoples should explore unique qualities and intragroup variance as well as shared cultural traits. For Native Hawaiian and Māori peoples, emerging from trauma will require awareness of historic trauma as well as the need for promoting and preserving cultural strengths and resilience. Social workers practice cultural relevance when they partner with Native Hawaiian and Māori peoples to integrate history with present and future perspectives, and emphasize cultural strengths, such as spirituality, sovereignty and language resurgence. There is growing information on culturally based solutions for Native Hawaiians (Mokuau, 2011) and Māori (Royal, 2007) founded on cultural values and practices, bound by the teachings of elders, and inclusive of Native leadership (see Chapter 10 in this volume).

While there is evidence of a 'rise' from trauma for these populations, social workers must address the continuing challenges and significant disparities that continue to exist today. For Native Hawaiians, disparities include low life expectancy, high rates of death from cancer and high rates of incarceration and for Māori, high rates of admission to psychiatric hospitals, family disintegration and violence, and unemployment. Clearly, to bring improvement in Native Hawaiian and Māori health, and to eliminate health inequities and economic disparities, the root causes of inequality must be addressed to reverse major structural oppressions, including the elimination of spiritual beliefs and practices, the minimization of native languages, values and norms, and the illegal possession of land. Colonization and racism which underpin these disparities are forces driving both the differential distribution of economic determinants and the differential outcomes associated with socioeconomic measures and health.

Implications for social work education with Native Hawaiians and Māori emphasize the incorporation of Indigenous models. One conceptual framework for education proposed by Native Hawaiian elder Richard Paglinawan is called *hana lima* (work with the hands) and is based on the premise that insight comes from experience, and learning occurs when one observes, listens and works with the hands (Duponte et al., 2010). Duponte et al. (2010) suggests that this model provides an experiential learning format that integrates thoughts and feelings within the context of a culture-based curriculum.

Social work education in New Zealand has undergone significant transformation since the 1990s government overhaul of the tertiary education sector. With universities, polytechnics and Māori education providers like Te Whare Wananga o Aotearoa are responding proactively to government and community calls for more accountability to Iwi Māori, the need for more professionally qualified, biculturally competent social workers has arisen. This has been given impetus, among other things, by the success of Matua Whangai, family group conferencing, Whanau Ora and Marae-based health programmes. Whare Wananga (Māori universities) now account for 44 per cent of Māori attending tertiary education institutions (Hook, 2007)

As a response to planning Māori future directions, the fourth Hui Taumata Mātaurangayasdas|Mayadas – Māori Knowledge Summit held in 2004 greatly added to the advancement of Māori success. Geared toward the global knowledge economy, five broad themes emerged: (i) relationships for learning, (ii) an enthusiasm for learning, (iii) balanced outcomes for learning, (iv) future planning, and (v) being Māori (Durie, 2004). The question of knowledge and education are central to culture, as Hook (2007: 11) states:

> What is Mātaurangayasdas|Mayadas Māori? Others have intimated that what is taught in the Māori Wānanga is not pure and has become contaminated with the learning of Europeans, which, in my opinion, is totally appropriate. Somehow within the mind of many Māori has arisen the idea that, 'there is your knowledge and then there is mine, and that mine is just as good as yours.' The facts are that not all knowledges are equivalent, and that truth has no preference when it comes to ethnicity. However, it is not the place of a government agency to define truth and what is appropriate learning for Māori.

Government may define expectations, but exactly how those expectations are met should be up to Māori to decide. The answer seems to lie intrinsically in understanding knowledge as a boundless, synergistic tool for re-empowerment and liberation. What this means and what matters most is not who has proprietary claims over knowledge but how knowledge is best applied and used. Its relevance, respectfulness and valuing of positive outcomes are central to any Indigenous pursuit of autonomy, self-determination and sovereignty.

Conclusion

The United Nations Declaration on the Rights of Indigenous People (United Nations, 2008) asserts that the over 370 million Indigenous Peoples worldwide are free and equal to other peoples, and by that right can freely determine their political status and pursue their economic, social and cultural development. While the Declaration promotes these notions, they are not binding under international law and states that occupy the lands of Indigenous Peoples continue to violate or ignore Indigenous Peoples' rights. Social work can assume a pivotal role in advancing precepts of the Declaration in practice and education. Assuring the rights of Native Hawaiians and Māori, like all Indigenous people, requires a binding agreement among social workers that there are many ways to know and live in our world, and that all ways are deserving of respect and honour. With that, social workers can enhance the evolution of trauma to triumph.

A'ohe pau ka 'ike i ka hālau ho'okahi – Not all knowledge is taught in one school (Pukui, 1983: 24).

References

Allen, J. (2007). *Homeless in paradise* [Online]. Available at: http://www.isreview. org/issues/53/homeless.shtml [accessed: 9 October 2011].

Awatere, D. (1984). *Maori Sovereignty*. Auckland, NZ: Broadsheet.

Barlow, C. (1991). *Tikanga Māori: Key Concepts in Māori Culture*. Oxford: Oxford University Press.

Binney, J. (1990). Ancestral Voices Maori Prophet Leaders. In K. Sinclair (ed.), *The Oxford Illustrated History of New Zealand*. Auckland, NZ: Oxford University Press.

Blaisdell, K. (1989). Historical and cultural aspects of Native Hawaiian health. *Social Process in Hawai'i*, 32, 1–21.

Braun, K.L., Mokuau, N. and Browne, C.V. (2010). *Life Expectancy, Morbidity, and Health Practices of Native Hawaiian Elders*. Honolulu, HI: University of Hawai'i Myron B. Thompson School of Social Work – Hā Kūpuna: National Resource Center for Native Hawaiian Elders.

Browne, C.V., Mokuau, N. and Braun, K.L. (2009). Adversity and resiliency in the lives of Native Hawaiian elders. *Social Work*, 54, 253–61.

Brave Heart, M.Y.H. (2000). Wakiksuyapi: Carrying the historical trauma of the Lakota. *Tulane Studies in Social Welfare*, 21–2, 245–66.

Bushnell, O.A. (1993). *The Gifts of Civilization: Germs and Genocide in Hawai`i*. Honolulu, HI: University of Hawai`i Press.

Chadwick, O.A., Kelly, E.F., Hotchkiss, S.C. and Vitousek, P.M. (2007). Pre-contact vegetation and soil nutrient status in the shadow of Kohala Volcano, Hawaii. *Geomorphology*, 89, 70–83.

Chinen, J.J. (1958). *The Great Mahele*. Honolulu: University of Hawai`i Press.

Cordy, R. (2000). *Exalted Sits the Chief: The Ancient History of Hawai`i Island*. Honolulu, HI: Mutual Publishing.

De Bruin, A. and Mataira, P.J. (2003). Indigenous Entrepreneurship. In A. De Bruin and DuPois, A. (eds), *Entrepreneurship: New Perspectives in a Global Age*. Aldershot: Ashgate, 169–84.

Duponte, K., Martin, T., Mokuau, N. and Paglinawan, L. (2010). Ike Hawai'i: A training program for working with Native Hawaiians. *Journal of Indigenous Voices in Social Work*, 1, 1–24.

Durie, M. (1998). Tirohanga Maori, Maori Health Perspectives. In M. Durie (ed.), *Whaiora: Maori Health Development* (2nd edn). Auckland, NZ: Oxford Press, 66–80.

Durie, M. (2004). *Increasing Success for Rangatahi in Education Insight, Reflection and Learning Māori Achievement: Anticipating the Learning Environment*. Hui Taumata IV. Turangi/ Taupo [Online]. Available at: http://www.massey. ac.nz/massey/fms/TeMataTau/Publications [accessed: June 2011].

Edmonds, K., Williams, S. and Walsh, A. (2000). Trends in Māori mental health. *Australian and New Zealand Journal of Psychiatry*, 34(4), 677–83.

Ewalt, P. and Mokuau, N. (1995). Self-determination from a Pacific perspective. *Social Work*, 40, 168–75.

Fuchs, L. (1961). *Hawai`i Pono: A Social History*. San Diego, CA: Harcourt Brace Jovanovich.

Global Entrepreneurship Monitor (GEM). (2003). *Global Report*. Ewing Marion Kauffman Foundation [Online]. Available at: http://www.gemconsortium. org/download/1311968642808/ReplacementFINALExecutiveReport.pdf [accessed: 12 June 201].

Grace, A. (1901). *Tales of a Dying Race*. London: Chatto & Windus.

Gray, M., Coates, J. and Yellow Bird, M. (eds). (2010). *Indigenous Social Work around the World: Towards Culturally Relevant Education and Practice*. Burlington, VT: Ashgate, 1–10.

Guedel, G. (2009). *For Native Hawaiians, An Apology does not Return the Land* [Online]. Available at: http://www.nativelegalupdate.com/2009/04/articles/ for-native-hawaiians-an-apology-does- [accessed: 9 October 2011].

Halloran, M.J. (2004). *Cultural maintenance and trauma in indigenous Australia.* Paper presented at the 23rd Annual Australia and Aotearoa New Zealand Law and History Society Conference, Perth, Western Australia.

Harawira, H. (1998). Short history of Maori struggle. Speech to the Asia Pacific Solidarity Conference, Sydney, April [Online]. Available at: http://www.greenleft.org.au/node/17167 [accessed: 12 June 2011].

Harawira, H. (2011). *New oath call after Hone* [Online]. Available at: http://www.nzherald.co.nz/politics/news/article.cfm?c_id=280andobjectid=10738585 [accessed: 5 March 2012]. Also available at: http://www.youtube.com/watch?v=Q4XiTjOtjpE [accessed: 5 March 2012].

Hasager, U. and Kelly, M. (2001). Public policy of land and homesteading in Hawai`i. *Social Process in Hawai`i*, 40, 1–31.

Hook, G.R (2007). *A Future for Māori education Part II: The reintegration of culture and education.* MAI Review. Wellington [Online]. Available at: http://www.review.mai.ac.nz/ [accessed: 2 July 2011].

Kaholokula, J.K. (2007). Colonialism, Acculturation, and Depression among kānaka maoli of Hawai`i. In P. Culbertson, Agee, M.N. and Makasiale, C. (eds), *Penina uliuli: Confronting Challenges in Mental Health for Pacific Peoples.* Honolulu, HI: University of Hawai`i Press, 180–95.

Kame`eleihiwa, L. (1992). *Native Land and Foreign Desires: Pehea lā e pono ai?* Honolulu, HI: Bishop Museum Press.

Kanahele, G.S. (1999). *Emma: Hawai`i's Remarkable Queen.* Honolulu, HI: The Queen Emma Foundation.

Kana`iaupuni, S.K., Malone, N. and Ishibashi, K. (2005). *Ka huaka`i: Native Hawaiian Educational Assessment.* Honolulu, HI: Kamehameha Schools, Pauahi Publications.

Ka`ū. (1986). *Ka`ū: University of Hawai`i Hawaiian Studies Task Force Report.* Honolulu, HI: University of Hawai`i Hawaiian Studies Task Force.

Keahiolalo-Karasuda, R. and Speck, B. (2010). *Post-High Update* 2010. Honolulu, HI: Kamehameha Schools Research and Evaluation.

Keelan, J. (2002). *E Tipu e Rea: A framework for Taiohi Māori development.* Wellington: Ministry of Youth Affairs [Online]. Available at: http://www.myd.govt.nz/documents/about-myd/publications/e-tipu-e-rea/e-tipu-e-rea.pdf [accessed: 10 June 2011].

Kelly, A.K. (2002). A field guide to the Akaka bill(s). *Honolulu Weekly*, 12(5), 5–6.

Kim, L. (2009). *U.S. Supreme Court overturns ruling preventing the sale of ceded lands* [Online]. Available at: http://www.hawaiinewsnow.com/story/10105160/us-supreme-court-overturns-ruling-preventing-[accessed: 9 October 2011].

Kingi, T.K. (2005). *Māori Mental Health: Past Trends, Current Issues, and Māori Responsiveness.* Massey University, Wellington: Te Pumanawa Hauora/Te Mata o te Tau Research School of Public Health.

Kingi, T.K. (2007). The Treaty of Waitangi: A framework for Māori health development. *New Zealand Journal of Occupational Therapy*, 54(1), 4–10

Kirst-Ashman, K.K. and Hull Jr., G.G. (2006). *Understanding Generalist Practice* (4th edn). Belmont, CA: Thomson Brooks/Cole.

McCormick, R. (1995/1996). Culturally appropriate means and ends of counselling as described by the First Nations people of British Columbia. *International Journal for the Advancement of Counselling*, 18(3), 163–72.

Marsden, M. (2003). The Woven Universe: Selected writings of Rev Māori Marsden. In C. Royal (ed.), *Otaki. Mauriora ki te Ao/Living Universe.* Masterson, New Zealand: The Estate of Māori Marsden, 60–62.

Mataira P.J. (2000a). Mana and Tapu: Sacred knowledge, sacred boundaries. In G. Harvey (ed.), *Indigenous Religion: A Companion.* Aldershot: Ashgate, 99–112.

Mataira P.J. (2000b). Maori entrepreneurship: The articulation of leadership and the dual constituency arrangements associated with Maori enterprise in a capitalist economy. Unpublished PhD thesis. Auckland, NZ: Massey University at Albany.

Mataira, P.J., Matsuoka J. and Morelli P. (2006). Issues and Processes in Indigenous Research. In *Huilili: Multidisciplinary Research on Hawai`i Well-Being*, vol. 2. Honolulu, HI: Kamehameha Schools.

Moeke-Pickering, T. (1996). *Maori Identity within whanau: A Review of Literature.* Hamilton, NZ: University of Waikato.

Mokuau, N. (2011). Culturally based solutions to preserve the health of Native Hawaiians. *Journal of Ethnic and Cultural Diversity in Social Work*, 20, 1–16.

Mokuau, N. and Matsuoka. J. (1995). Turbulence among a native people: Social work practice with Hawaiians. *Social Work*, 40, 465–72.

Mokuau, N. and Tauili`ili, P. (2011). Native Hawaiians and Samoans. In E.W. Lynch and Hanson, M.J. (eds), *Developing Cross-Cultural Competence: A Guide for Working with Children and Their Families* (4th edn). Baltimore, MD: Brooks Publishing Company, 365–91.

NativeHawaiians.com (2009). *Obama administration supports Akaka bill* [Online]. Available at: http://www.nativehawaiians.com/?p=50 [accessed: 8 February 2010].

New Zealand Ministry of Health. (2010). *Shifting Māori Health Needs: Māori Population Trends, Health Service Needs, and Medical Workforce Requirements – Issues Arising* [Online]. Available at: http://www.maorihealth.govt.nz/moh. nsf/indexmh/shifting-maori-health-needs?Open [accessed: 12 June 2011].

Nordyke, E.C. (1989). *The Peopling of Hawai`i.* Honolulu, HI: University of Hawai`i Press.

Office of Hawaiian Affairs. (2011). *Federal recognition for Native Hawaiians* [Online]. Available at: http://www.oha.org/nhgra/pdfs/ FedRecBookletFINALWeb.pdf [accessed: 27 May 2011].

Office of Student Equity, Excellence and Diversity. (2011). Enrollment Graphs. (Available from Author, Queen Lili`uokalani Center for Student Services, Room 413, 2600 Campus Road, Honolulu, Hawai`i 96822).

Oneha, M. (2001). Ka mauli o ka `āina a he mauli kānaka: An ethnographic study from a Hawaiian sense of place. *Pacific Health Dialog*, 8, 299–311.

Orange, C. (1987). *The Treaty of Waitangi*. Wellington, NZ: Allen & Unwin.

Paglinawan, R., Eli, M., Kalauokalani, M. and Walker, J. (2006). *Lua: Art of the Hawaiian Warrior*. Honolulu, HI: Bishop Museum Press.

Pakura, S. (2005). The Family Group Conference 14-Year Journey: Celebrating the successes, learning the lessons. Paper presented at the IIRP's Sixth International Conference on Conferencing, Circles and other Restorative Practices. Penrith, New South Wales, Australia, 3–5 March.

Pere, R. (2006). Nga Kawai Rangatira o Wheke Kamaatu. The Eight Noble Tentacles of the Great Octopus of Wisdom. Keynote Address. 10th Australasian Conference on Child Abuse and Neglect. Wellington, New Zealand, 14–16 February.

Pukui, M.K. (Translator). (1983). *Ōlelo no`eau: Hawaiian Proverbs and Poetical Sayings*. Honolulu: Bishop Museum Press.

Pukui, M.K., Haertig, E.W., Lee, C.A. and McDermott, J. (1979). *Nānā i ke kumu*: *Look to the Source*. Honolulu, HI: Hui Hānai.

Queen Lili`uokalani Children's Center. (2011). *Queen Lili`uokalani Children's Center* [Online]. Available at: http://www.qlcc.org/ [accessed: 2 June 2011].

Rata, E. (2004). Leadership Ideology in Neo-Tribal Capitalism. In D.E. Davis (ed.), *Political Power and Social Theory*, vol. 16. Boston, MA: Emerald Group Publishing Limited, 43–71.

Royal, T.A.C. (2007). The purpose of education: Perspectives arising from Mātauranga Māori. Report prepared for the Ministry of Education 2005. Version 4 [Online]. Available at: http://www.mkta.co.nz/assets/educationpurposev.4.pdf [accessed: 10 June 2011].

Saleebey, D. (ed.). (2002). *The Strengths Perspective in Social Work Practice* (3rd edn). Boston, MA: Allyn & Bacon.

Selby, R., Moore, P. and Mulholland, M. (eds). (2010). Māori and the Environment: Kaitiaki. Wellington, NZ: Huia Publishers.

Sharples, P. (2008). Maori leadership. Presentation at Auckland University, 18 August 2008 [Online]. Available at: http://youtu.be/ELVBBGe3Sr4 [accessed: 21 October 2011].

Simon J. and Smith, L.T. (eds). (2001). A Civilising Mission: Perceptions, and Representations of a Native School System. Auckland, NZ: Auckland University Press.

Smith, M. (2007). Interview with New Zealand Center for Political Research, 21 October 2007 [Online]. Available at: http://www.nzcpr.com/weekly104.htm [accessed: 20 October 2011].

Stannard, D. (1989). *Before the Horror: The Population of Hawai`i on the Eve of Western Contact*. Honolulu, HI: Social Science Research Institute, University of Hawai`i.

Statistics NZ. (2006). *Census Report* [Online]. Available at: http://www.stats.govt.nz/Census/2006CensusHomePage.aspx [accessed: 10 June 2010].

Statistics NZ. (2010). *Social Report. Wellington* [Online]. Available at: http://www. socialreport.msd.govt.nz/notes-references/technical-details.html [accessed: 10 June 2010].

Starr, P. (2009). Long-ago collapse of Hawaiian monarchy described as U.S.-assisted regime change. *CNSNews.com* [Online]. Available at: http://www. cnsnews.com/public/content/article/aspx?RsrcID=52224 [accessed: 11 February 2010].

Sykes, A. (2011). *Interview on Te Karere – Television New Zealand* [Online]. Available at: http://youtu.be/iDcmaSKQED0 [accessed: 20 October 2001].

Takini Network. (n.d.). *Welcome to Takini's historical trauma* [Online]. Available at: http://www.historicaltrauma.com/ [accessed: 4 February 2011].

Tambunan, T.T.H. (2009). *SME in Asian developing countries.* London: Palgrave.

Taonui, R (2006). *Canoe traditions: Te Ara – Encyclopedia of Aotearoa New Zealand* [Online]. Available at: www.TeAra.govt.nz/NewZealanders/ MaoriNewZealanders/CanoeTraditions/en [accessed: 12 June 2011].

Taylor, R. (1974). *Te Ika a Maui, or, New Zealand and Its Inhabitants.* Wellington: A. H. & A.W. Reed (cited in Te Ara – Encyclopedia of New Zealand) [Online]. Available at: http://www.teara.govt.nz/en/conservation-a-history/2 [accessed: 10 July 2011].

Te Ara. (2011). *Pākehā fertility and mortality* [Online]. Available at: http://www. teara.govt.nz/en/population-change/3 [accessed: 27 July 2011].

Te Puni Kokiri. (2010). *Tirohanga Ohanga mō Te Moana a Toi: Māori Entrepreneurs in TeMoana ā Toi and New Zealand for 2001 and 2006* [Online]. Available at: http://www.tpk.govt.nz/en/in-print/our-publications/publications/ [accessed: 12 June 2011].

The Queen's Health Systems. (2009). *Native Hawaiian Health Program* [brochure]. Honolulu, HI: The Queen's Health Systems.

United Nations. (2008). *United Nations Declaration on the Rights of Indigenous Peoples* [Online]. Available at: http://www.un.org/esa/socdev/unpfii/ documents/DRIPS_en.pdf [accessed: 4 November 2011].

US Census Bureau. (2001). *The Native Hawaiian and Other Pacific Islander Populations:* 2000. Washington, DC: US Census Bureau.

US Census Bureau. (2006–2008). S0201. *Selected Population Profile in the United States American Community Survey.* Washington, DC: US Census Bureau.

Walker, R. (1996). *Nga Pepa a Ranginui: The Walker Papers.* Melbourne, VIC: Penguin Books.

Walker, R. (2004). *Ka Whawhai Tonu Matou: Struggle without End.* Auckland, NZ: Penguin Books.

Wesley-Esquimaux, C.C. and Smolewski, M. (2004). *Historic Trauma and Aboriginal Healing.* Ottawa, Ontario: Aboriginal Healing Foundation.

Wikipedia. (2011). *Incest* [Online]. Available at: http://en.wikipedia.org/wiki/ incest [accessed: 15 June 2011].

Williams, T. and Robinson, D. (2004). Social capital and philanthropy in Maori society. *The International Journal for Not-for-Profit Law*, 6(2) [Online].

Available at: http://www.icnl.org/knowledge/ijnl/vol6iss2/special_4.htm. [accessed: 18 July 2011].

Yunus, M. (1999). *Banker to the Poor: Micro-Lending and the Battle against World Poverty*. New York: Public Affairs.

Chapter 8

Decolonized Social Work Practice in Jordan

Sahar Al-Makhamreh and Mary Pat Sullivan

This chapter presents and discusses the localization of social work knowledge and practice in Jordan and argues for its authentication to shape the future of social work in the Middle East. First it explores the history of colonization in Jordan and its consequent impact on the country's social and political systems. The development of professional social work, including education and training, is then described within the contemporary environment by considering, for example, the cultural and religious context of everyday life and social interactions, family structure, the impact of instability in the Middle East, immigration, economic challenges and increasing societal awareness of social problems. Finally, using hospital social work, Bedouin health programs, residential care leavers, care of older people and Iraqi refugees as examples, the development of culturally relevant social work practice is explored and discussed.

History of Colonization in Jordan

Jordan's history of colonization is very much embroiled in early empire building in the Middle East, the oil industry, the cold war, the Arab–Israeli conflict, and not least, the influential arm of the USA. Political, economic and sociocultural issues that permeated Transjordan during the demise of the Ottoman Empire and Britain's strategic attempt to build a modern administration following World War I have lingered throughout the following generations, the eventual declaration of an independent Hashemite Kingdom of Jordan in 1946 and well beyond (Barr, 2011; Hourani, 1991; Robbins, 2004).

The territory of Transjordan existed under the authority of the Ottoman Empire from the 1860s until the 1920s when the British Empire asserted itself in the lands of the Middle East. Under Ottoman imperialism, the relatively small population in Transjordan was culturally organized by means of kin, village or religious groups, and tribal norms and law. The residents, some of whom were semi-nomadic, survived from a subsistence economy and the Empire collecting taxes and supplying resources, security and certain economic initiatives (for example, Hijaz Railway) (Hourani, 1991; Robbins, 2004). Importantly, the trade economy was supported by the Arab and Bedouin inhabitants moving between the east and west banks of the Jordan River and between what are now the borders of Syria, Iraq and Saudi Arabia. In addition, the Empire facilitated the settlement of communities of Circassians and Chechens in the region of Amman to cultivate commercial development.

The collapse of the Ottoman Empire following World War I presented a strategic opportunity for the Anglo-French objective to develop modern states in the Middle East under their authority. The 1916 Sykes-Picot Accord ostensibly drew a map for the region – post-war influence for Transjordan, Palestine and Iraq to be designated to the British, and responsibility for Syria and Lebanon given to the French (Barr, 2011). As Robbins (2004: 13) states: 'From its very inception as an entity Transjordan's value, not for its own sake but as a buffer and a bridge among lands of inestimably greater importance, was recognized'. By 1920, Britain had begun its work to establish a separate state (that is, not to be part of the new Jewish national home). Arab leadership in Transjordan was given to Abdullah, a member of the Hashemite clan, Amman was designated the capital, local political administration was organized, and funds were transferred annually to develop the military and stimulate economic development. British representatives held senior positions in the administrative sanctum to act as 'advisors' in areas of importance, and educated and experienced Palestinians were recruited to lower positions in the civil service. With the development of the Arab Legion, a British soldier was appointed as commander.

It is worth digressing from the historical overview for a moment to highlight two important issues that acted as a backdrop for activities in Transjordan and neighbouring lands during these early years. First, Britain's confident attempt to build a sophisticated political and economic independent state was continually influenced and modified by ongoing challenges within the entire Arab region and the ever-present Arab–Israeli conflict. Additionally, Transjordan's own internal disputes and power struggles meant that His Britannic Majesty's Government continued to assert itself by, for example, setting conditions for the release of fund transfers (Robbins, 2004). Secondly, the culture of imperialism embracing Europe at that time meant countries such as Jordan were helpless to defend their identity against the primacy of British interest to maintain regional and world power (for example, control of oil) – and thus cultivate these people to save them from a life of peasantry (Hourani, 1991).

With the arrival of World War II, Transjordan stood alongside Britain against the Germans. By the time the war ended, however, a 'decolonization bandwagon' coupled with post-war economic exhaustion meant that Britain's interest became Transjordan's independent status. According to Robbins (2004), Britain was no longer a superpower nor capable of acting as the leader state of the Middle East, and Abdullah had finally successfully united state and leader. In May 1946, a new Anglo-Transjordanian treaty saw the creation of the Hashemite Kingdom of Jordan. However, the new kingdom remained dependent on an annual subsidy from Britain (but with relaxed conditions attached to the funds), British officers continued to command Jordan's army and Palestinian civil servants were replaced by Transjordanians as much as this was possible. Political conflict in the Middle East did not abate at this time, and thus Britain (and others) maintained their involvement to try and find a resolution to the Arab disputes, a perceived threat from Communist Russia and the challenges of a Jewish state.

With Hussein's ascension to the throne in 1953, Jordan was confronted with a host of complex challenges, including continued internal and external political instability, economic problems, Palestinian refugees and an anti-British sentiment among younger generations. Indeed, Arab nationalists within the region were determined to secure full sovereign independence and shed its European colonialist history (Robbins, 2004). Most significantly, the 1950s witnessed Jordan establishing relationships, particularly with Egypt, Saudi Arabia and Syria, which eventually secured financial support. Thus the creation of Arab solidarity reinforced unnecessary ties to Britain, and in 1957 the Anglo-Jordanian treaty was abolished.

Despite its newly independent status, Jordan continued to maintain and or develop relationships with the West. For Jordan this was a welcomed necessity in light of ongoing political fragility within the region, and for the West, this was an opportunity to continue to exert power, particularly over those nations that posed a threat (for example, Iraq).

Within a continuing tradition of international aid from both the West and the East, Jordan has continued to evolve its administrative structures and public service to develop, for example, financial aid for low-income families, healthcare and education. A vast network of non-government organizations and charities act as a subsidy to ensure priority areas of need are met, and services are delivered using models from the West and regional neighbours. For most, however, the Arab tradition of family and tribal solidarity remains and this natural form of helping is positively respected by helping professionals and negatively reinforced by the government's non-interventionist approach. Thus the sustainability of much of Jordan's social system rests primarily, as it did in the past, on the family and the international community. What becomes evident and relevant in social work's development is a pervasive tension between the necessary presence of the West and its colonial influence juxtaposed against the progress being made to cultivate local responses to social need and injustice.

The Cultural Context and 'Informality' within Jordanian Society

The modern state of Jordan is located in a strategic position in the Middle East sharing borders with Syria, Iraq, Saudi Arabia, Israel and Palestine (National Population Committee, 2000) and covering an area of approximately 88,778 sq km. Jordan is a low to middle income country, although economic indicators show it fares better than most other countries in this income category with a reliance on income from tourism, agriculture and service industries (Al-Makhamreh and Lewando-Hundt, 2011; Ibrahim, 2010). The Hashemite Kingdom of Jordan is a constitutional monarchy headed by King Abdullah II and enjoys a relatively free political environment. The Prime Minister and Central Cabinet oversee a variety of ministries, including national defence, education, social welfare and infrastructure development (Robbins, 2004). According to the country's constitution, all citizens have equal rights and duties regardless of their religious or tribal affiliation (Droeber, 2003).

The majority of Jordan's 5,230,000 citizens are Sunni Muslim with a very small Shia minority. Christians comprise 5–8 per cent of the population and there are smaller numbers from religious groups such as Druze and Bahais. In terms of non-Arab populations, there are small numbers of people originating elsewhere, including Circassians, Chechens, Armenians and Kurds. These minority groups incorporate some of the cultural attributes of the wider society (Bureau of Near Eastern Affairs, 2004; Department of Statistics, 2007; Sheikh and Gatrad, 2000). As previously mentioned, all Jordanian citizens have equal rights and duties regardless of their religious affiliation (Droeber, 2003). Freedom of religion is vital in Jordan and still plays a major part in influencing and organizing social and political life (Higher Council for Science and Technology General Secretariat, 2001; Sheikh and Gatrad, 2000).

In Jordanian society, as in many Arab societies, people are typically characterized as town dwellers (*madanein*), villagers (*fellahein*) or Bedouin desert dwellers (*badow*). The vast majority of Jordanians are settled in large urban areas, including Amman, the capital.

Familiar in popular culture, the Bedouin comprise only 5 per cent of the Jordanian population. The Badia (أدب) (the root bada meaning 'to be clear', 'come to light') is the place where the Bedu (ودب) live and is the name commonly given to the arid lands of the Middle East (Al-Makhamreh, Hasna and Al-Khateeb, 2011). The number of Bedu living in the Badia has sharply declined since the introduction of the new Ottoman land laws in the mid eighteenth century, which abolished communal ownership of the land that was a basic component of their nomadic lifestyle (Al-Smairan, 2006). Although primarily nomadic in the past, they are now relatively settled in small villages and employed in waged labour, the army and teaching (Hasna et al., 2010). Bedu society is based on tribal organization characterized by collectivism and loyalty to family, clan and tribe (Al-Makhamreh, Hasna et al., 2011). Their community structure is based on tribes (asheirah), subdivided into clans of extended families (hamoulah), which are then divided into principal families (fakhd) (Dutton and Shahbaz, 2008).

The structured divisions of family remains significant throughout Jordan given Arabs, in general, are descendants from various tribes that migrated throughout the centuries. Social relationships belong to and are controlled by tribes and families, and these do not follow religious affiliations. Tribal or village leaders (sheikh or mwktar) also play a vital informal role in mediating (wasita) social conflicts (Al-Nakshbandy, 2001).

Typically, the restriction of women's participation in public life has been challenged by indirect strategies of resistance aimed at permitting women access to information and resources. More formally, current national policy in Jordan, supported by women in the Royal Family and other elite groups, is working towards developing and improving women's rights and participation in public events. As a member of the Convention on the Elimination of all Forms of Discrimination Against Women (CEDAW), Jordan and other key players are working actively to empower women. For example, they are engaging women specifically in lower income groups in the process of socioeconomic development. However, as a patriarchal Muslim society, perceptions and practices in terms of gender division are only slowly changing and women's participation in political and economic life remains weak – even though their educational levels are among the highest in the region (Al-Nakshbandy, 2001; Information and Research Centre King Hussein Foundation, 2011; Seijaparova et al., 2004). The strength of a family's authority is very apparent in how husbands and or parents play a vital part in influencing a woman's social interactions, relationships and engagement in the labour force – if at all. Not surprisingly then, some professions have been deemed more suitable to women (for example, teaching, nursing and social work) and, here too, the division of labour is gendered with women working as subordinates to men. It has been noted that Christian Arab women, whose relationships are also culturally scrutinized, experience less restricted social interactions. This was exemplified by the establishment of the Jordanian Women's Federation in 1954 by a Christian advocate (Al-Nakshbandy, 2001).

Family honour is another important feature of tribal and family life in Jordan. For a woman, all her behaviour is expected to honour her family (Darwazeh, 2002; El-Kharouf, 1999) and the highly valued reputation of an individual, family and tribe is expected to guide conduct. More recently, the Jordanian Women's Union has played an active role in raising awareness around women's issues, including domestic abuse and honour crimes. However, both religious and cultural sensitivities in Jordanian society have had a tremendous impact, highlighting the limits of established legal and social intervention in the instance of, for example, honour killings. Honour killings, the responsibility of an entire tribe, are often carried out by young men. Younger males are chosen to conduct the killing given current law dictates imprisonment for young men must be limited to six months followed by a period in residential care. The recognized tribal response is for members (sometimes including representatives from other tribes) to go to the victim's family and apologize to show them respect (*attwa*). Some families will not accept the apology and threaten revenge which may lead to the taking of another life in the perpetrator's family (Husseini, 2009). Following considerable debate by government representatives, the Royal Family, judicial representatives, women's organizations and international human rights groups, there is now a move to treat honour crimes with harsher penalties.

Both males and females are raised to take the responsibilities for their children and other family members (El-Kharouf, 1999). However, older members of the family and or tribe have the privilege of gaining respect and high status regardless of their gender or tribal affiliation (Al-Makhamreh, 2005). Interestingly, women who are granted a good status enjoy more liberty when they old. For example, the Holy Quran sets out the basic principles for care of older people:

Lord decrees that you worship none but him and be kind to your parents. If either or both of them attain old age in your lifetime, Say not to them a word of contempt, nor repel them, but address them in terms of honor. And out of kindness, lower to them the wing of humility, and say: 'My Lord, Bestow on them, Your mercy even as they cherished me in childhood.' (chapter 17, verse 23 and 24)

Common within this patriarchal society is the expectation that the eldest male child assumes family control when the older parent is no longer able. He is also charged with responsibility for decision-making and care.

Thus the organization of social life in Jordan remains bound within the family, including gendered roles and ascribed status. Social problems, for the most part, are managed informally by families, kin, religious leaders or the tribe. As Ibrahim (2010: 85) states: 'interdependent support among vertical and horizontal kin is a social and religious obligation'. For many, formal systems of care are stigmatizing and are viewed as only necessary for the less privileged or marginalized.

Preparing for Social Work Practice

Traditionally, social work provision in Jordan tended to focus on supporting those who were disadvantaged due to, for example, poverty or physical disability, family conflict, including domestic abuse, and community development (Al-Makhamreh, 2005; Brosk et al., 2000). Despite challenges of recognition and status, there is some encouraging evidence to attest social work is rapidly expanding.

In 2008, the British Council commissioned a study to identify where social workers were employed and what their daily practice entailed. Employers included 39 non-government organizations (NGOs), 14 hospitals and four social workers hired by mental health rehabilitation programmes. The main beneficiaries of social work intervention tended to focus on children and families, including families 'at risk', orphans, domestic violence, youth anti-social behaviour and refugees. Specific roles for practitioners included psychosocial support, obtaining financial assistance, behaviour modification and liaison or referral to community supports (Mahara, 2008). For the first time, this study highlighted that social workers often lacked formal training, job descriptions were vague or absent (the exception being those employed by NGOs), practice was unregulated, services were poorly coordinated, those practising lacked the capacity to meet the increasing demands being placed on them and there was an absence of state support for social work (Cocks et al., 2009; Mahara, 2008; Sullivan, Forrester and Al-Makhamreh, 2010). Most importantly, this study documented how a heavy reliance on international funds to meet social needs hindered the development of a local and sustainable system of health and social care, supported by the delivery of professional social work. This undoubtedly reinforces the strain between a colonial legacy and current efforts by social workers to localize systems of care.

These issues remain a substantial challenge for social work. It is worth mentioning that in 2008 the plans to develop a Jordanian Social Work Association were launched and received governmental support. At the time of writing, key stakeholders were continuing to work with the Columbia University Middle East Research Center to implement a professional code of ethics in addition to mechanisms for ongoing professional training. To date, the Association and its related functions remain inactive and the government has not yet supported the registration or licensing of practitioners. Nevertheless, these limited achievements represent significant steps to localize social work in Jordan.

The social work academy in Jordan also remains an ongoing issue. The first social work diploma programme was established in 1965 at Princess Rahma University College. In 1998, the diploma was replaced with a baccalaureate programme. Since then, the University of Jordan and Hashemite University have developed programmes to provide undergraduate and post-qualifying training (Cocks et al., 2009; Mahara, 2008; Sullivan et al., 2010).

These programmes are delivered by the limited number of experienced social work academics and doctoral graduates (Mahara, 2008). The problem is being managed by hiring academics from related disciplines and sponsoring staff to obtain further research training in various Western countries (that is, UK, USA and Australia). In the absence of national standards for social work education most of the teaching materials are imported from Egypt, where academics there simply translated Western literature (Soliman and Abd Elmegied, 2010). Thus students receive a considerable amount of Western social work content that may or may not be relevant to the Jordanian context, and the emphasis is on didactic classroom instruction rather than field training. Here again, neocolonialism continues to exert a powerful influence on social work's development thereby sometimes limiting the progress of localization.

Concerns about teaching effectiveness and curriculum content have been raised in a number of local forums (Mahara, 2008; Sullivan et al., 2010). This issue has been accentuated in light of the need for localized knowledge and skilled practitioners to deal with the social problems emerging from the political crisis in the region and the socioeconomic challenges in Jordan. In response, a recent initiative was undertaken by the Ministry for Higher Education to review social work curricula and mechanisms for accreditation. Participants agreed on the need to increase the number of training hours spent by students in field training, to infuse the curricula with mental health and family interventions content and to include crisis intervention and research methods modules. Strategies to build partnerships with social work practitioners to deliver teaching and engage in research have also been established. Princess Rahma University College has also developed an innovative programme to link student volunteers with local community services as a method to increase practical social work experience.

Developing Culturally Relevant Practice: Example from Recent Developments in Social Work

As shown above, culture and religion shape everyday life in Jordan and lay the groundwork for help-seeking behaviours and a social work response. A requisite of any social work intervention is that it embraces such sensitivities, including both informal and formal relationships. Thus the localization of social work practice in Jordan has resulted in culturally relevant practice that strategically embeds relationships, religion and other Arab cultural norms to support those where traditional forms of helping are no longer sufficient or sustainable in light of a rapidly changing society. Localizing social work not only influences the construction of practice at the micro level, but may also have an impact on shaping larger policy frameworks (Al-Makhamreh, Hasna, et al., 2011; Munford and Sanders, 2010). However, evidence of the latter is less apparent given Jordan's very modest system of state welfare alongside a continued dependence on the international community.

Examples of Indigenous social work practices that have developed using formal and informal knowledge are becoming more visible in Jordan's health and social care community. A brief exploration of these examples reveals that Jordan is shedding many Western notions of social work (although still within its shadow), highlights its ongoing struggle to establish its capacity within the community and shows that an innovative culturally relevant form of practice is emerging.

Hospital Social Work

Social workers practice in Jordan's hospitals as members of the healthcare team, where they are usually the key liaison between the team and patients and their family. Here the sociocultural context is highly relevant with a particular emphasis on gender and religion. Religion, whether Muslim or Christian, plays an important part in coping with illness, explanations for ill health and suffering and problem resolution (Al-Krenawi and Graham, 2001; Al-Makhamreh, 2005; Droeber, 2003; Furman et al., 2004; Sheikh and Gatrad, 2000). For example, Al-Makhamreh's (2005) ethnographic study of hospital social work practice and Al-Krenawi and Graham's (2001) extensive exploration of Bedouin communities reinforce the belief that suffering teaches people about the power of God and this message is central to reducing their suffering on the Day of Judgement. Social workers are, therefore, skilled in using religious explanations to facilitate communication with patients. The following excerpt from Al-Makhamreh's (2005: 240) field notes from a military hospital demonstrates this central feature in practice.

> The social worker said: 'My brother, you know that illness is a test from our God and we have to thank him for everything, not only when we are happy, but also when we are sad'. He said, 'Thanks to God. God will always forgive us our sins and have mercy upon us.'

Gender and the use of informal, yet culturally acceptable language in practice is also an important feature. To avoid violating social taboos associated with unsupervised male-female interaction, practitioners will refer to patients and families using 'brother' or 'sister'. This fictive kin reference eliminates any perceived sexual threat or indiscretion.

Similarly, social workers trying to establish financial support for patients will use informal and religiously accepted practices, such as *Zakāt* and *Ṣadaqah*. Almsgiving or participation in charitable activities is considered noble practice in Arab culture and Islam (Al-Nakshbandy, 2001; Qutb, 2000; Sheikh and Gatrad, 2000). For patients with financial problems, social workers will, therefore, make a determination of who needs aid and ask for donations from formal and personal social networks. The social worker will also seek charitable donations to fund wheelchairs, commodes and other assistive technology needed for patient care. For the female social worker, this practice also permits her to exercise power indirectly rather than deal with male authority in the hospital administration. Interestingly, these gendered hospital roles are eliminated in military hospitals where rank supersedes gender or professional status.

In terms of hospital-based social work intervention, typically families are involved in all decision-making. As previously mentioned, adult family members in Arab societies, particularly parents and the eldest male figure are considered a source of wisdom and authority. This is relevant to the patient as well as the social worker (Al-Nakshbandy, 2001; El-Kharouf, 1999; Khasawneh, 2001). As a result, the social worker takes great care to involve the patient's family in all discussions and planning, and if the social worker needs to conduct a domiciliary visit, she will likely be accompanied by her husband or brother. Al-Makhamreh (2005: 243) quotes a hospital social worker describing her job:

> My husband and my family sometimes get involved in my job because it is sometimes risky and dangerous. For my safety, my husband drives me to a client's house. He has tried many times to find jobs for some clients or one of their family members.

In some instances, conservative cultural backgrounds would dictate that social work intervention could only be conducted by someone of the same gender as the following quote from a female amputee shows:

> My father would be the first to reject the idea of a man dealing with me and being with me in the same room or visiting my family at my house, especially if he is not a doctor or a nurse. That would create a great many problems. (Al-Makhamreh, 2005: 241)

Bedouin Health Programmes

In terms of localizing social work practice in Jordan, a number of recent initiatives have been addressing the development of culturally competent practice for Jordan's diverse population. The Bedouin, the Indigenous group of tribes in Jordan, live a settled lifestyle in villages in northeastern Badia, using agriculture to supplement income from other forms of employment, such as teaching. A loyal hierarchy of families, clans and tribes has reinforced a collective culture that has developed unique ways of living – not always viewed sympathetically by the dominant social group (Al-Makhamreh, Hasna, et al., 2011; Dutton and Shahbaz, 2008; Hasna et al., 2010).

A recent project aimed at improving access to healthcare for Bedouins included a field placement experience for social work and nursing students to develop culturally competent practice. A secondary aim was to expose students to a setting to further their understanding of health and social inequalities in rural communities. For seven weeks, social work and nursing students were given an opportunity to work alongside other healthcare professionals to conduct culturally sensitive assessments of need and develop interventions that were community-focused in light of the collective nature of the Bedouin. The field training was supplemented by lectures on topics such as the social determinants of health, household structures and strategies for intervention, and community service delivery.

After the completion of the training, five students were interviewed by academic staff to explore their understanding of culturally competent practice. The findings confirmed the value of field training and highlighted specific areas of student development for future interdisciplinary culturally competent practice. First, the opportunity to work alongside a health colleague challenged student preconceptions about the health and social care divide. The development of shared practice, particularly in a rural community setting, was viewed as relevant given the complexities of intervention due to family and tribal practices, deprivation and lack of formal resources. Secondly, the students were able to recognize the value of informality or *wasta* (to help others and prioritize needs in relation to relatives and friends), gender and religion, and how collective self-help is reflected in help-seeking behaviour. The following statement from a student captures the essence of the practice:

> When I told her to go to the police station to write a statement about the birth identity of her granddaughter, she looked strangely at me and said, '*I am not going make a scandal*'. I told her that she was the only relative for this 11 year old girl. '*What will happen to her if you die?*' She said that Allah will be taking care of her. I decided to ask one of the relatives in a senior position to help this woman. (Al-Makhamreh, Hansa, et al., 2011)

Residential Care Leavers

Child protection in Jordan is one of the oldest forms of social work. As a 'generational link', children are highly valued in an Arab Islamic society and child protection has received both political and royal prioritization. There are approximately 29 residential homes in Jordan accommodating up to 150 orphans, children from 'unknown families' or children who have been abused (Ibrahim, 2010).

Ibrahim (2010) conducted an in-depth investigation of the experiences of young Jordanians leaving care. One of the most significant findings was that care leavers lacked social or cultural preparation for coping with 'normal' life post-care. The care system, described as formal and bureaucratic, seemingly overlooked the importance of culture in the lives of these young people once they left care and their sense of belonging to the larger society. The transmission of values such as honour and shame, very much characteristic of this collective culture, are essential for membership in an in-group (that is, kin) (Al-Makhamreh, 2005; Ibrahim, 2010). However, young people who have been in care have experienced stigmatization, abandonment, dishonour and rejection by their family (that is, many not formally registered at birth). More importantly, they lack family (unknown or concealed), the cornerstone of Jordanian society, and therefore have no connection to extended family or tribe. Hence, the children in Ibrahim's study struggled to achieve a meaningful life, and above all, were forced to be independent in a society that values collectivism. It is worth pointing out here that systems of child welfare in Jordan are rooted in colonial practices whereby individualism, rather than collectivism, is valued.

The findings from this study have had important cultural implications for social work practice with children in care. Setting aside the significant issues for these children pre-care, attention to in-care and post-care has led to recommendations to alter practices to address exclusion and marginalization. In other words, how does a child return to the community and fulfil cultural expectations? Efforts to develop individualized care plans and leaving care plans to assist young people as they reintegrate, counselling, mentoring and network systems, financial support and 'open door' policies are being promoted to reduce the likelihood of poor outcomes in this context. However, the issue of 'identity' in absence of family and kin remains a challenge for this system of care and for Jordanian society as a whole.

Older People

Approximately 5.5 per cent of Jordan's current 6 million inhabitants are over the age of 60 (UN, 2009). This is expected to rise dramatically by 2050 to 15.3 per cent of the entire population. Reductions in mortality rates mean that life expectancy at birth is now 76 years for men and 81 years for women. These rapid demographic changes present substantial challenges at the macro level (for example, health and social care delivery) and for individuals and families (for example, disability and dependency), particularly in light of current socioeconomic conditions and changing family structures. At the time of writing, there were only 18 officially registered caring centres for older people in Jordan. The majority of these were public and private nursing homes (394 beds in total) that primarily care for the most marginalized groups – the poor, those without family and individuals with stigmatizing illnesses (that is, Alzheimer's disease) (Al-Makhamreh et al., 2011). Specialized healthcare services for older people were also not available despite high levels of chronic illness (Mahasneh, 2000).

The importance of intergenerational family relationships is reinforced when an older family member becomes ill or frail. Illness and disability in older age are considered a test from God, and people believe that acceptance and resilience leads to peace. It is expected that the family will provide care, and any form of institutional care is usually viewed negatively. Although many families are providing care, can the traditional forms of filial piety be sustained in light of smaller families, immigration, women working outside the home and challenging illnesses, such as Alzheimer's disease? And despite the moral incentive to care for older people bound in culture and traditions, a lack of public awareness on their needs (for example, dementia) and a poorly developed formal system of supports for older people and their family carers has meant that their quality of life may be deteriorating (National Council for Family Affairs, 2008).

A number of specific concerns have emerged in recent, albeit limited, research. For example, Attalah (1998) argued that, having achieved status within the family, older woman were finally empowered to speak their opinion (that is, challenge a decision made by a male family member). However, they also feared loneliness and those women who had not chosen their husband experienced more problems. Similar findings were identified by Abu Nahemh (1985). Al-Makhemrah (2010) addressed the widespread rejection of nursing home care even when families were faced with high levels of care and fatigue, frustration and strain. Qaddomi (1991) and Abu Nahemh (1985) drew attention specifically to the important, yet unacknowledged, issue of high levels of neglect. Finally, poor living conditions, lack of recreational facilities and psychological problems were also identified by Qaddomi (1991) and Mahafza (1993).

The National Strategy of Senior Citizens (2008) outlines six key directives to improve the quality of life of Jordan's older people. The directives address a range of issues, including older people's participation in public life, the maintenance of dignity, support for families to strengthen intergenerational relationships, public policy to address health and social care, geriatric and gerontological research development and the training of health and social care professionals to ensure quality care.

Relevant to the development of gerontological social work, the National Strategy draws specific attention to the social determinants of health and quality of life in older age. As such, public attitudes, family care, community outreach, advocacy and protection for the vulnerable are identified as targets for development and intervention. At the time of writing, the social work community is collaborating with colleagues in nursing and medicine to untangle the concerns and identify effective interdisciplinary approaches to address them.

Iraqi Migrants

The geographic situation of Jordan and its politically secure atmosphere has attracted a number of significant waves of refugees. The influx of Iraqi forced migrants was estimated to be about 450,000 or about 10 per cent of Jordan's 6 million inhabitants (Barnes, 2009). They are described as a diverse group socioeconomically, 20 per cent of households are headed by females and a high number professionally qualified (Johns Hopkins University Bloomberg School of Public Health et al., 2009). A significant number of Iraqis are also traumatized due to war, kidnapping, rape and torture (International Organisation for Migration, 2008). This new social phenomenon challenged existing humanitarian aid programmes and the overall infrastructure of the country. Most importantly, Jordan's experience of receiving Palestinian refugees influenced the government's decision to decline to be a signatory on the 1951 Geneva Convention Relating to the Status of Refugees, the key legal text outlining the rights of refugees and the obligations of the receiving state. Thus the legal status of these refugees is ambiguous (Fagen, 2007).

The Jordanian government does not recognize Iraqi refugees. Rather they are considered as 'guests' or 'visitors' despite the fact that it is unlikely they will return to their country of origin (Johns Hopkins University Bloomberg School of Public Health et al., 2009). A Memorandum of Understanding between the Jordanian government and the United Nations High Commissioner for Refugees (UNHCR, 2009) outlines the UNHCR as the body responsible for registering Iraqis as refugees and finding a 'durable solution for recognized refugees within six months' (that is, supporting their voluntary repatriation or resettlement in a third country (Chartland, Washington and El-Abed, 2008). In other words, integration into Jordanian society is not an option. However, many Iraqis are not prepared to register with the UNHCR, particularly those that have overstayed their visas (Al-Makhamreh and Lewando-Hundt, 2011; Chartland et al., 2008).

With a precarious legal status, Iraqis have been constrained in terms of restricting employment and housing. As a result, women and children are often forced to find employment because it is unlikely that they will be deported if reported to the police. Given Iraqis are raised in a patriarchal collective culture, women as breadwinners may pose a threat to traditional families. Since 2007 they have been given access to primary healthcare and education. A small number of NGOs also offer psychosocial and mental health support, assistance with food and other items, and so forth (Al-Makhamreh and Lewando-Hundt, 2011). Services to support the issues emerging from severe trauma are limited, however (International Organisation for Migration, 2008).

The need to develop culturally relevant social work practice for this population was identified by local practitioners who were often engaged in supporting families experiencing severe conflict owing to mental health and behavioural problems. First and foremost, and given their psychosocial isolation and vulnerability, the Iraqis have become easy targets for exploitation with no possible recourse. Secondly, they have very basic health and social care needs that have been complicated by the circumstances of their forced migration. And thirdly, their 'guest' status reinforces a total lack of stability, while lack of information and trust in service providers further complicates their plight (Al-Makhamreh and Lewando-Hundt, 2011).

A comprehensive review of the literature was conducted by Jordanian academics to inform the development of culturally relevant social work practice and expand understanding of the needs of Iraqis and possible intervention strategies. Al-Makhamreh and Lewando-Hundt (2011) argue that an ecological approach respectful of 'tradition' is necessary (that is, religious affiliation, age, gender and family structure). A community-based interdisciplinary partnership model was also identified as relevant to address multiple needs across a range of systems and a community focus providing an opportunity to work with natural networks, address issues of discrimination, safety and dignity. Finally, they suggest that social work is well positioned to advocate for policies to support a stronger civil society in Jordan, ensure basic rights are met and well-being among all refugees is fostered.

Al-Makhamreh and Lewando-Hundt (2011) provide a convincing example of attempts to decolonize social work using a systemic analysis of the 'problem' and recommending a multi-level approach for a localized form of intervention. Most importantly, this example moves social work beyond direct intervention to community development with international aid programmes in Jordan and to the more complex issues relevant at the policy level.

Conclusion

Although an independent state since 1946, Jordan continues to rely on its allies in the West and East to support the development of a civil society. The development of social work and the cultivation of Indigenous practice is occurring within a complex environment. Colonial structures remain, tensions within the Arab world continue, a heavy reliance on international aid exists and a large number of professionals have obtained their training in the West. Thus a post-colonial tension remains as the social work community exerts its identity, capacity and status in a rapidly changing society. And unfortunately, this long-established tradition of engagement with the West also has potential to undermine local developments to address oppressive systems of care.

This situation is being confronted, however. Ongoing exchanges with colleagues in the East and in North America and Europe have provided constructive opportunities for practitioners to critically consider and debate sources of knowledge and religious and cultural norms, and promote localized practice responsive to the needs of a diverse population. Efforts to expand social work education beyond Western models and to build a body of evidence to support the emerging models of localized practice are ongoing even though their sustainability often rests on post-colonial structures. Importantly though, the social work community is working strategically with international aid agencies and other Western partners to influence the shape of social care, confront ongoing oppression and identify priorities for development for the diverse population.

As Gray, Coates and Yellow Bird (2008) and Rankopo and Osei-Hwedie (2011) argue, local relevance is emerging. The Jordanian context has necessitated careful consideration of models of practice that support a collective society where family and kin take precedence over the individual and are the main source of social support. Alongside this consideration is the characteristic Muslim and patriarchal society and how this impacts on roles, interaction and decision-making. Lastly, the acceptance of 'informality' dictates a mode of conduct that is effective in facilitating the helping process.

Hospital social work, Bedouin health programmes, care of older people and Iraqi refugees provided four examples of rapidly advancing Indigenous social work practice in Jordan. Other examples are available and many more are evolving at this time, including an exploration of 'what works'. And despite the fact that the profession continues to work to gain official status in Jordan, including an articulation of its central focus in this context, the social work community remains committed to social justice and well-being for all citizens.

References

Abu Nahemh, H. (1985). Problems of the elderly in Jordan. Unpublished MA thesis, University of Jordan, Amman.

Al-Kateeb, E. (2011). A study of dementia in Jordan. Presentation at the Ageing and Alzheimer's Disease Workshop, Philadelphia University, Amman, 3 October.

Al-Krenawi, A. and Graham, J. (2001). The culture mediator: Bringing the gap between a non-western community and professional social work practice. *British Journal of Social Work*, 31, 665–85.

Al-Makhamreh, S. (2005). Social work as an emerging profession in the Middle East: An ethnographic case study of Jordan hospital social work. Unpublished PhD thesis, University of Warwick, UK.

Al-Makhamreh, S. (2010). The forgotten few: How can social work impact on the well-being of elderly people with dementia in Jordan? Presentation at *Ageing and Alzheimer's Disease Workshop*, Philadelphia University, 3 October.

Al-Makhamreh, S. and Lewando-Hundt, G. (2011). An examination of models of social work intervention for use with displaced Iraqi households in Jordan. *European Journal of Social Work*. Available online: 26 Jul 2011 DOI: 10.1080/13691457.2010.545770.

Al-Makhamreh, S., Hasna, F. and Al-Khateeb, E. (2011). The forgotten few: The social context of Ageing and Alzheimer's disease in Jordan. *Generations Review*, 12(2) *[Online]*. Available at: http://britishgerontology.org/DB/gr-editions-2/generations-review/the-forgotten-few-the-social-context-of-ageing-a-2.html [accessed: 13 May 2011].

Al-Makhamreh, S., Hasna, F., Lewando-Hundt, G., Smeiran, M. and Al-Zaroo, S. (2011). Localising social work: Lessons learnt from a community-based intervention amongst the Bedouin in Jordan. *Social Work Education: The International Journal*. Available online: 14 Sep 2011. DOI:10.1080/0261547 9.2011.610787.

Al-Smairan, M.H. (2006). Investigation of a hybrid wind-photovoltaic electrical energy system for a remote community. Unpublished PhD thesis, Coventry University, UK.

Attalah, K. (1998). The situation of elderly women in a changing Jordanian society. Unpublished MA thesis, University of Jordan, Jordan.

Barnes, A.E. (2009). *Realizing protection space for Iraqi refugees: UNHCR in Syria, Jordan and Lebanon*. New Issues in Refugee Research. Research Paper No. 167. Damascus: UNHCR [Online]. Available at: http://unhcr.org/4981d3ab2.html [accessed: 1 June 2009].

Barr, J. (2011). *A Line in the Sand: Britain, France and the Struggle that Shaped the Middle East*. London: Simon & Schuster.

Brosk, H., Qtaishat, M., Irshaid, H., Nandakumar A. and Shehata, I. (2000). Jordan National Health Accounts: Executive Summary Paper. Amman, Jordan: Partnerships for Health Reform Project [unpublished, in Arabic].

Bureau of Near Eastern Affairs. (2004). *Background Note: Jordan* [Online]. Available at: http://www.state.gov_e/r/[a/ei/bgn/3464.htm [accessed: 3 August 2011].

Chartland, G., Washington, K. and El-Abed, O. (2008). *An Assessment of Services Provided for Vulnerable Iraqis in Jordan*. Ramallah: AUSTCARE, Middle East Regional Office.

Cocks, A., Al-Makhamreh, S., Abuieta, S., Al-Aledein, J., Forrester, D. and Sullivan, M.P. (2009). Facilitating the development of social work in the Hashemite Kingdom of Jordan: A Jordanian/UK collaboration. *International Social Work*, 52(6), 799–810.

Darwazeh, N. (2002). *Gender and Democratization in the Arab World*. Workshop organized by the Regional Human Security Center, Institute of Diplomacy, Amman, Jordan, 11–13 March.

Department of Statistics. (2007). *Living Conditions in the Hashemite Kingdom of Jordan* [Online]. Available at: http://www.dos.gov.jo/sdb_pog_e/ehsaat/analytical/cover.htm [accessed: 3 July 2011].

Droeber, J. (2003). Woman to woman: The significance of religiosity for young women in Jordan. *Women's Studies International Forum*, 26(5), 409–24.

Dutton, R. and Shahbaz, M. (2008). *Jordan's Arid Badia: Deepening Our Understanding*. Amman: Jordan Badia Research and Development Centre.

El-Kharouf, A. (1999). An Investigation of Socio-economic, Demography and Cultural Factors Influencing Women's Employment Status: The Case of Employed and Non-employed Women in Amman. Unpublished PhD thesis, University of Bradford, UK.

Fagen, P. (2007). *Iraqi Refugees: Seeking Stability in Syria and Jordan*. Amman: Institute for the Study of International Migration and Centre for International and Regional Studies.

Gray, M., Coates, J. and Yellow Bird, M. (2008). Introduction. In M. Gray, Coates, J. and Yellow Bird, M. (eds), *Indigenous Social Work around the World: Towards Culturally Relevant Education and Practice*. Aldershot: Ashgate, 1–12.

Hasna, F., Lewando-Hundt, G., Al-Smairan, M. and Alzaroo, S. (2010). Quality of primary nursing care for Bedouin in Jordan. *International Journal of Nursing Practice*, 16, 564–72.

Higher Council for Science and Technology General Secretariat The Jordanian Scenario Project Until 2020. (2001). Report submitted to the Government of Jordan. Amman, Jordan: Higher Council for Science and Technology [unpublished, in Arabic].

Hourani, A. (1991). *A History of the Arab Peoples*. London: Faber and Faber.

Husseini, R. (2009). *Murder in the Name of Honour*. Oxford: One World Publications.

Ibrahim, R.W.Z. (2010). *Making the Transition from Residential Care to Adulthood: The Experience of Jordanian Care Leavers*. Unpublished PhD thesis, University of East Anglia, Norwich, UK.

Information and Research Centre King Hussein Foundation. (2011). *To be a girl in Jordan* [Online]. Available at: http://www.irckhf.org.jo/pages/prodetails. aspx?ID=29 [accessed: 13 May 2011].

International Organisation for Migration. (2008). *Assessment on Psychosocial Needs of Iraqis Displaced in Jordan and Lebanon. A Survey Report on Amman and Beirut* [Online]. Available at: http://www.iom.int/jahia/webdav/shared/… and…/report_psy_assessment.pdf [accessed: 5 June 2011].

Johns Hopkins University Bloomberg School of Public Health, UNICEF and WHO. (2009). *The Health Status of the Iraqi Population in Jordan* [Online]. Available at: http://www.unicef.org/jordan/jo_children_ HealthStatusofIraqisinJordan2009en.pdf [accessed: 12 March 2011].

Khasawneh, M. (2001). *Poverty Assessment Report: The case of Jordan* [Online]. Available at: http://www.erf.org.ef/html/Mohammed_Khasawneh.pdf [accessed: 16 December 2004].

Mahafza, W.A. (1993) Problems of Elderly in the Jordanian Nursing Homes. Unpublished MA thesis, Yarmouk University, Irbid.

Mahara Professional Consultancies in Development. (2008). Identifying the current situation of social work within the Jordanian context. Unpublished paper presented at Exploring the Reality Expanding the Vision, National Social Work Conference, Amman, Jordan, 7–8 October.

Mahasneh, S.M. (2000) Survey of the HEALTH of the Elderly in Jordan. *Medical Journal of Islamic Academy of Sciences*, 13(1), 39–48.Munford, R. and Sanders, J. (2010) Embracing the diversity of practice: Indigenous knowledge and mainstream social work practice. *Journal of Social Work Practice*, 25(1), 63–77.

National Council for Family Affairs (NCFA). (2008). *The National Strategy for Senior Citizens*. Amman, Jordan: NCFA.

National Population Committee. (2000) *Population Challenges and Sustainable Development in Jordan* 2000–2020. Amman: National Public Committee [in Arabic].

Qaddomi, K. (1991). The Problems of the Elderly in Light of the Variables of Sex, Marital Status and Residence. Unpublished MA thesis, Yarmouk University, Irbid.

Qutb, S. (2000). *Social Justice in Islam*. Oneonta, NY: Islamic Publications International.

Rankopo, M.J. and Osei-Hwedie, K. (2011) Globalization and culturally relevant social work: African perspectives on indigenization. *International Social Work*, 54(1), 137–47.

Robbins, P. (2004). *A History of Jordan*. Cambridge: Cambridge University Press.

Seijaparova, D., Pellekaan, J., Ingram, G., Chibber, A., Peters, K. and Hassan, F. (2004). *An evaluation of World Bank Assistance for Poverty Reduction, Health and Education: A Country Assistance Evaluation*. World Bank Operations Evaluation Department, Jordan [Online]. Available at: hhtp://www.wds.worldbank.org/servlet/WDS_Ibank_Servlet [accessed: 16 July 2011].

Sheikh, A. and Gatrad, A. (2000). *Caring for Muslim Patients*. Abingdon, Oxon: Radcliffe Medical Press.

Soliman, H.H. and Abd Elmegied, H.S. (2010). The challenges of modernization of social work education in developing countries: The case of Egypt. *International Social Work*, 53(1), 101–14.

Sullivan, M.P., Forrester, D. and Al-Makhamreh, S. (2010). Transnational collaboration: Evaluation of a social work training workshop in Jordan. *International Social Work*, 53(2), 217–32.

United Nations High Commissioner for Refugees (UNHCR). (2009). *Participatory Assessment* 2009: *Social Capital among Refugees in Jordan*. Amman, Jordan: UNHCR.

PART III
Education: Facilitating Local Relevance

Chapter 9

Decolonizing Social Work Education in Africa: A Historical Perspective

Linda Kreitzer

This chapter highlights the progress of social work education and practice in Africa from 1971 to 1990. It outlines the forces which have influenced and challenged the profession in its struggles to decolonize social work education and make social work practice more Afrocentric. Based on historical research, particularly documentary analysis of the conference proceedings of the Association for Social Work Education in Africa (ASWEA) between 1973 and 1986, it describes the dissatisfaction of African social work practitioners and academics with Western social work models and curricula, as well as the challenges to developing African-centred approaches. These conference proceedings are important historical records of the evolution of social welfare, social work education and the social work profession in Africa. The material in this chapter must be seen against the historical literature on indigenization in Africa – and what Indigenous means in the African context – beginning with Shawky's (1972) and Midgley's (1981) seminal work in this area (see Gray and Coates, 2008; Osei-Hwedie, 1993, 2002, 2007, 2008, 2011; Osei-Hwedie and Rankopo, 2008, 2012; Rankopo and Osei-Hwedie, 2011 for an outline of this debate, see also Chapter 1).

The author, while working on her PhD (Kreitzer, 2004), discovered the ASWEA documents and recognized their importance to social work education in Africa. There has not been an extensive analysis of these documents and this chapter examines the issues therein pertaining to the challenges of decolonizing social work. It presents an outsider's understanding in the hope that Africans will take on the work of an in-depth analysis of these documents in the future.

The European colonization of Africa goes back to the Greeks and Romans around 332 BC followed by the Arabian Islamic Caliphate in the early seventh century that expanded from North Africa to Sub-Saharan Africa. By the fifteenth century, Europeans had established forts along the coasts of Africa and were involved in the slave trade. The taking of African land by Europeans increased to a point that there was a need to divide up Africa in a more official way. The 1885 Berlin Conference fulfilled this task and by the early 1900s, all but two countries had been colonized by Europeans. By 1951, thanks to an initiative by the United Nations, countries became independent, with the majority becoming independent by 1980. The colonial era referred to herein extends approximately from 1885 to 1980.

Prior to colonization, family – and extended family – provided supportive structures for people in need (Apt and Blavo, 1997; ASWEA, 1974a). During the colonial era, some welfare services (literacy programmes, medical care, and child, youth and other remedial welfare services offered by departments of social welfare) were developed by missionaries and colonial administrators, in the process weakening traditional structures. Many of these colonial services remained after independence. One important colonial funding source was established in the USA through the Colonial Development Act of 1929 followed by the 1940 Colonial Development and Welfare Act to provide loans and grants to colonized countries for the development of their societies (Yimam, 1990). These funds were administered by local and district development committees and other government departments. As countries became independent and colonial funding ceased, many heads of countries realized that they had little money to fulfil their development plans (Shawky, in ASWEA, 1974a). In 1948, President Truman 'inaugurated the development age' (Rist, 2008: 71) and the world became divided between the developed and underdeveloped regions, with Africa considered part of the latter. Thus international agencies from the late-1950s onwards contributed to Africa's dependence on Western development agendas, external experts and foreign aid (Moyo, 2009).

In the early 1970s, spurred on by the International Association of Schools of Social Work (IASSW) eager to have representation in the African region, social work academics and practitioners formed the Association for Social Work Education in Africa (ASWEA). Many countries had membership (though South Africa was excluded) and were involved in the conferences. As part of its remit, ASWEA sought to: (i) address issues related to social work education, including dominance of Western social work curricula; (ii) provide opportunities for member schools to meet regularly to discuss social work's role in national development planning; and (iii) move forward in developing African-centred social work education for the continent (ASWEA, 1974a, 1976b, 1977, 1986). Between 1973 and 1986, ASWEA workshops and conferences highlighted issues relating to African social work education. Five conferences were held (ASWEA, 1974a, 1976b, 1981, 1985) and two directories were published: one of schools of social work (ASWEA, 1974b, 1982a) and the other of social welfare organizations (ASWEA, 1975a). Workshops and expert committee meetings were held to discuss particular issues in Anglophone and Francophone countries (ASWEA, 1975b, 1976a, 1977, 1978a, 1978b, 1979a, 1979b, 1982b) and various other papers were published (ASWEA, n.d., 1972a, 1972b, 1972c, 1973b, 1989), including two compilations of case studies for East and West Africa (ASWEA, 1973a, 1974c) and a pamphlet sketching the background of ASWEA (1986).

Past histories have led to generalizations about a large continent that remains diverse in terms of language, culture and nationalities (Maathai, 2009). Despite these differences:

African states have much in common, not only their origins as colonial territories, but [also] the similar hazards and difficulties they have faced. Indeed, what is so striking about the fifty-year period since independence is the extent to which African states have suffered so many of the same misfortunes. (Meredith, 2006: 14)

In light of this, what follows is a brief history of several African countries from independence to 1990, first from a political perspective before examining the evolution of social work education in Africa.

Events in East and West Africa 1957–1990

Most African countries gained independence in the 1960s and 1970s. Proud of their newly independent status, national planning and decolonization were high on the agenda of the newly elected governments (The South Commission, 1990). African leaders, such as Nkrumah in Ghana, Azikiwe and Awolowo in Nigeria, Kenyatta, Mboya and Odinga in Kenya, Neyere in Tanzania and Cabral in Guinea-Bissau, developed manifestos for African social policies, approaches and programmes. With the uneven influence of the USA and the Soviet Union, many of these leaders embraced socialist ideologies (Yimam, 1990). The societies they were called upon to govern were poor, highly unequal and largely illiterate. Rural-urban migration exacerbated widespread disease, along with inadequate housing and health services, and high rates of unemployment (Yimam, 1990). Many questioned whether colonial policies and programmes were sufficient for post-independent Africa. Believing that they would not stimulate nation building, many redefined the socioeconomic roles and functions of the state. At the Second United Nations Conference of African Ministers of Social Affairs held in Alexandria, Egypt in 1977 it was agreed:

Africa must proceed from remedial social action - foreign by nature and approach - to more dynamic and more widespread preventive and rehabilitative actions which identify ... with African culture in particular and with socio-economic policies of Africa in general. (UN, 1977: 6)

Thus began the search for an African model for social development. However, power struggles, corruption and foreign intervention became a substantive factor in Africa's lack of progress while colonialism persisted through the remaining colonial institutions, including social welfare (Midgley, 2010; Yimam, 1990). The excitement of Pan-Africanism was soon diminished by the reality of having to foot the bill for national development and mounting foreign debt. African countries borrowed heavily from international financial institutions (World Bank, International Monetary Fund (IMF) and the Global Agreement on Trade and Tariffs/World Trade Organization) to spearhead national planning and development initiatives. These international institutions, in particular the IMF, instigated Structural Adjustment Programs (SAPs) involving a focus on economic development and substantial reductions in social spending to force poor countries to pay back their debts (Holscher and Berhane, 2008; Konadu-Agyemang, 2000; Lewis, 2005; Maathai, 2009; Sewpaul, 2006). In 1980, disappointing socioeconomic performance of many countries in sub-Saharan Africa left the majority of their increasing populations living in absolute poverty: 'Out of 470 million people in Africa, 170 million lived below the poverty line; 85 million were severely malnourished; 160 million adults were illiterate, and only 30% of the population had safe drinking water' (Yimam, 1990: 10). Structural adjustment led to a decline in social welfare, health and education programmes. Government corruption, civil wars and the devastating effect of HIV and AIDS further added to Africa's slow development. Este's (1995: 25) Index of Social Progress found that African countries not only 'failed to provide more adequately for the basic needs of their populations in 1990 than in 1970, but they actually lost some of the social gains that had been achieved prior to 1970'. With rapidly declining economies, these countries faced serious financial and production crises which further aggravated social development. Referring to the decline as the 'worst crisis in the global economy since the Great Depression' (Loxley, 1983: 198), the World Bank blamed Africa's economic crisis on domestic policies and internal conflicts rather than foreign intervention (see also the Berg Report, Berg, 1982). In response, backed by the Organisation for African Unity (OAU), African leaders set out to develop a plan to increase Africa's self-sufficiency believing it was 'imperative to embark in earnest on a search for an African development paradigm that was not imitative of the dominant growth economics of the nation rather than the development of the people' (Adedeji, 2002: 6).

Called the Lagos Plan of Action (LPA) (1980), it led to the first 'realistic and comprehensive assessment of ... manpower [*sic*] needs and projected requirements' (ASWEA, 1982a: 117) for Africa's comprehensive development and social service agenda. While other strategies have emerged since then, all of these African initiatives 'were opposed, undermined and jettisoned by the Bretton Woods institutions and Africans were thus impeded from exercising the basic and fundamental right to make decisions for their future' (Adedeji, 2002: 4). Yimam (1990) identified several factors contributing to Africa's inability to withstand these external forces: (i) historical precedents; (ii) low level of understanding of the impact of external interventions; (iii) communication problems; (iv) population pressures; (v) natural phenomena, such as droughts and floods; (vi) political unrest, border conflicts and internal tensions, including ethnic tensions; and (vii) leadership 'crises', including government corruption. Despite these factors, colonialism was blamed continually for the slow progress of reform and development while external Western intervention and internal instability confounded attempts at Africanization:

It had become clear that Africa's persistent failure to decolonize its political economy by confronting the past and making necessary changes ... continued to impede its much needed socio-economic and political transformation. By trying to march towards its future hand-in-hand with its colonial, monocultural, low-productivity and excessively dependent and open economy, Africa has ensured no dignified future for itself. (Adedeji, 2002: 6)

Education in Africa

Added to these challenges was the effect of colonialism on education which, according to Ajayi, Goma and Johnson (1996: 3), was mainly Indigenous before colonization, as learning came from local sages 'knowledgeable about traditional history, laws, customs and folklore', moral teaching, and socialization at the elementary level. The second level involved learning traditional community values through an informal system of apprenticeship. Higher education was for training priests and rulers. The arrival of missionaries, and later the colonial states, brought Western education to Africa. This included sending Africans abroad to train them to teach and work in colonial institutions on their return (Midgley, 2010; Willinsky, 1998). Missionaries organized social services in Africa, brought medical services and education (literacy) and cared for needy children and families (Yimam, 1990). There are mixed opinions on the influence of missionaries with some seeing them as part of the colonization process through schools designed to 'civilize' Africans and convert them to Christianity (Ajayi et al., 1995; Willinsky, 1998) and others viewing them in a more positive light.

As regards higher education, African historicists report that the colonial institutional model exported from the Motherland (meaning England or France, as the case may be) led to the development of sub-Saharan African universities designed to meet colonial needs to produce a class of Africans – 'black' on the outside but European or 'white' on the inside – to staff its government institutions (Ashby, 1964; Boateng, 1982; van Hook 1994). Eurocentric education continued following independence. Ajayi et al. (1996) identified four colonial legacies in higher education and the changes needed to bring African universities under African control:

1. Educate people to uphold and respect traditional systems instead of training elites to uphold colonial administrations and in return exploit their own people.
2. Deliver African-centred rather than European curricula to address the needs of the country.
3. Change European-style hierarchical administrative and management structures in African universities to an African style of management with less hierarchy and more cost efficient.
4. Provide education for all Africans and not just elites.

However, as Osei-Hwedie (2007) noted, the situation was far more complex than this with universities increasingly concerned with developing an international profile, attracting international students and catering to African students wanting to work in Western countries.

The Emergence of Social Work Education in Africa

The first school of social work in Africa was established in South Africa. The South African Women's Federation funded a child guidance clinic at the Transvaal University College which led ultimately to the establishment of the first Department of Sociology and Applied Sociology at the University of Pretoria in 1931. In the same year, the University of Stellenbosch instituted its first degree course for social workers followed by the University of Cape Town in 1933 (Miller, 1968; Ntusi, 1995). The first school outside South Africa was established in Egypt in 1936 (Yimam, 1990). All followed developments in social work from the USA and Great Britain. At the same time, Africans continued to be sent to these countries for training focused on remedial social welfare provision and this affected the kind of social work education taught at African universities (ASWEA, 1977: 87). While the United Nations (1950, 1955, 1958, 1964, 1971) promoted the development of social work education to newly independent countries, Western schools of social work exported their curricula to these countries on the assumption that the duplication of the Western model of education would lead them to deliver appropriate social work programmes (Kendall, 1995). There was little critical thinking concerning whether these theories and practices were relevant to Africa until Shawky (1972) and Midgley (1981) opened discussions on the indigenization debate, that is, the relevance of imported social welfare and educational models. As one African academic stated:

> Just as Western-oriented social services were alien to the majority of people on the African continent, so were the type of planning approaches that produced these social services among other national programmes. The colonial administrators ... built institutions and employed approaches that had proved workable in their own mother countries. And since the mother countries were deemed to have superior systems, what motivation was there for developing new systems that were based on local conditions and local knowledge? It is only after independence that the majority in Africa began to see clearly that they were victims of foreign and alien systems that were detrimental to the development of the continent and its people. (ASWEA, 1981: 86)

By the 1970s, discontent was in the air and moves were afoot following the influence of the IASSW to establish an African social work association to address issues concerning social work education in sub-Saharan Africa.

Association for Social Work Education in Africa (ASWEA) 1973–1989

After independence, around 1956–1980, there were many social problems in Africa which were beyond the remit of social work education. The challenge to social work educators and practitioners in Africa was to establish a professional identity and develop a unique body of knowledge to meet the needs of Africans: 'The role of the social work profession to the major issues confronting Africans cannot be felt let alone being recognized if we ourselves are not clear of what is our professional identity and area of competence' (ASWEA, 1977: 65). At meetings in Ghana, Zambia and Egypt in the 1960s, discussion centred on moving from a remedial approach 'to one that fit the overall social development programmes [of African countries]' (ASWEA, 1974a: 16; see also Drake and Omari, 1962). There was a call for fresh interpretations of social work knowledge and dynamic approaches to establish the profession's important role in national development planning in Africa. Consequently, ASWEA was formed in Addis Ababa in 1971 (ASWEA, 1986). An impressive array of national and international organizations supported this initiative, including 55 social development institutions and 150 social work educators and social scientists. Thirty-four African countries were represented, as well as six non-African countries and six international organizations (Organization for African Unity, United Nations Commission for Africa, International Association of School of Social Work, International Council on Social Welfare, International Federation of Social Workers and African Centre for Applied Research and Training in Social Development). Funding for the Association came from Frederich Ebert Stiftung, the Ethiopian Government, Organization for African Unity, United Nations Economic Commission for Africa, UNICEF, International Planned Parenthood Association, International Association of Schools of Social Work, Canadian International Development Agency and the governments of Togo, Cameroon, Zambia, Egypt, Libya, Kenya and Nigeria.

Between 1971 and 1986, seminars and conferences were organized, encouraging debate on social work education in Africa. Twenty of these proceedings were published. The twenty-first document was a selection of readings from seminars collated by Seyoum Selassie from Ethiopia (ASWEA, 1989). The ASWEA *Journal for Social Work Education in Africa* had provided seven publications by 1986. Additionally, two volumes of case studies were produced: one for East Africa (ASWEA, 1973a) and another for West Africa (ASWEA, 1974c). A three-month staff exchange was organized in 1978–1979 so African social work educators could learn from one another concerning culturally appropriate and socially relevant social work education. A joint research project was established with the Centre for Coordination of Social Science Research and Documentation in Africa South of the Sahara (CERDAS) for ASWEA to produce a reader in social development in Africa (ASWEA, 1985: 57–67). However, by 1986 it had not materialized due to a 'lack of funds to cover honoraria, printing and distribution costs' (ASWEA, 1985: 61). The need to develop African social work curricula lay at the heart of ASWEA: 'the goal has been that of moving away from the curative approaches characteristic of social work in the developed countries of the West to what has been termed developmental social work or simply social development' (ASWEA, 1981: 85).

ASWEA's work in developing culturally relevant social work education is discussed below from information gathered from the aforementioned ASWEA conferences and workshops, and supported by case examples of social work academics and practitioners incorporating African content into the social work curriculum. Although South Africa was the first country to establish a school of social work, an important point to note is that South Africa was not a member of ASWEA and did not participate in any of these conferences. There are many reasons for this exclusion, including the fact that it was under the apartheid system. Therefore, the South African understanding of social work education was not part of these conference debates.

Challenges to Addressing African Social Needs through Western Social Work Education

Throughout ASWEA's 20-year history, conferences and workshops were held to debate and advance an African social work curriculum. However, ASWEA's failure to develop an African-centred social work curriculum and the lack of success was attributed to inter alia: (i) the colonial legacy; (ii) gap between educated Africans and the majority of Africans; (iii) social work's absence from national development planning; (iv) need for trained human resources for national development; (v) institutional changes following structural adjustment; (vi) lack of Indigenous teaching materials; (vii) inappropriate teaching styles; (viii) better use of social research; (ix) reorientation from social services to development and aid; (x) the establishment of a strong professional identity and powerful professional associations; and (xi) the tensions between social development and social welfare practice.

Colonial Legacy

The colonial legacy had a major impact on social welfare programmes in Africa. In turn, social work training was tied to colonial social welfare systems and based on Western curricula. As Shawky (in ASWEA, 1974a: 52–3) stated: 'Social welfare programmes designed to solve urban problems of highly industrialized countries were transplanted into African societies without serious examination of local priority needs and local approaches to problems and with little attempt towards their adaptation'. As most Africans 'lived in rural and peri-urban areas' (ASWEA, 1974b: 53) there was a need for social work methods that were preventative and developmental.

Social Work's Colonized Response: Do Nothing or Do the West

The rapporteur's report for the 1974 ASWEA conference identified complacency on the part of social work educators and practitioners in regards to being involved in social changes going on in Africa. In particular, he identified the need for educated social workers to learn from the masses. This included drawing from and understanding social traditions for practice (ASWEA, 1976b: 21). It also seemed easier for educators to continue with the Western curriculum and adapt accordingly instead of redoing the curriculum to make it more appropriate to the African context (ASWEA, 1974a), including a focus on teaching skills for rural development.

Social Work's Absence from National Development Planning

Some countries were slow in developing national development policies making it difficult for social workers to establish a role in social planning (ASWEA, 1974a). Hence social work educators and practitioners were often not invited to sit at the policy table. To rectify this, social work educators were encouraged by ASWEA to facilitate seminars and workshops that included politicians, social workers and the general public in an effort to enhance communication concerning national development planning. By the 1980s, there was a clear understanding that national policies needed to be reoriented towards: (i) promoting genuine community participation; (ii) empowering women; and (iii) taking action toward child survival and development (ASWEA, 1985). In order to do this appropriately trained personnel were needed.

Need for Trained Human Resources for National Development

In the early ASWEA documents, much was written about the need to train African social work educators and practitioners to deal with social needs post-independence: 'What Africa needs are social workers who are *relevantly* and, most importantly, *locally* trained, the kind of workers that can be regarded as being part of the cultural milieu and not strangers in their own work environment' (ASWEA, 1976b: 23). In 1974, the ASWEA conference for social development recommended that 'social work educators should provide a curriculum that is broad-based, relevant and meaningful to social situations and conditions of life in Africa; produce inner-directed social workers with initiative, creative capacity and imagination and who give effective services in situations of change and development' (ASWEA, 1974a: 13).

There was a need for trained social development workers to 'specifically play an important role in identifying problems related to development, setting up priorities, defining the different approaches to be used and involving themselves in overcoming these problems' (ASWEA, 1974a: 12). This required a change of paradigm and mind-set from the remedial and maintenance approach to a social development approach (Estes, 1995). In order for this to take place, training of social workers in the developmental approach was necessary and this included a critical look at the effectiveness of the remedial and maintenance-oriented colonial institutions.

Institutional Changes Following Structural Adjustment

In 1945, the *Crown Colonist* journal warned against transplanting social services institutions from Western countries to Africa but this happened anyway (ASWEA, 1976b). As a result, much of the training had centred on colonial institutions (ASWEA, 1977). To address this issue, governments, social policy planners and social workers needed to look critically at the relevance of these colonial social welfare institutions and to 'undertake interventions which support the objectives of social development, not rehabilitative modes of casework' (Laird, 2003: 259). If these were to change then the curriculum would have to change as well. There was encouragement to training local staff, who knew the community and society instead of sending them away for training, which would mean that social workers would be in tune with the needs of local communities (ASWEA, 1975b). As time went on, due to the effects of structural adjustment programmes, government spending on social welfare decreased and non-government organizations took on the role of providing social welfare services (Lewis and Wallace, 2000; Sankore, 2005; Wallace, 2004). Today, there are questions being raised as to the reasons for the huge increase in NGOs (around 25,000 groups are now qualified as international NGOs) and whether this is a healthy scenario for an equitable world (Onyanyo, 2005).

Lack of Indigenous Teaching Materials

From ASWEA's inception, there was recognition that most schools of social work were dependent on Western social work textbooks and case examples. Hence a top priority, and one of the first ASWEA projects, was the compilation of African case studies as the first step in decolonizing social work education and standardizing teaching materials across Africa. Although published in 1973/74, the case studies were unsuccessful due to distribution issues and lack of knowledge that they even existed and, in 1986, the problem remained. The development of local teaching materials is a critical factor in the transformation towards an African-centred social work. Along with the lack of African teaching material was the need for changes in teaching styles.

Inappropriate Teaching Styles

As part of the indigenization of social work training, one suggestion was to change the style of teaching to fit the oral and participatory traditions of Africa. Particularly, in social work education, lecturing and exams did not encourage critical and independent thinking (ASWEA, 1977: 32). In 1982, the need to evaluate the scope and content of, and teaching styles used in, social work education was highlighted once more (ASWEA, 1982b). Also, a constant suggestion was that teaching material and styles would benefit from social research.

Better Use of Social Research

The important role of research in social development training was a continual theme of the ASWEA conferences: 'Research and surveys need to be completed in order to provide the bases upon which a distinctively African form of social work can emerge' (ASWEA, 1974a: 13). National social science research councils were thought to be an answer to this. It was thought that social science research should be action oriented and interdisciplinary. It was also noted that, with more social science research conducted, the development of country-specific content in social work curricula in Africa was possible.

Reorientation from Social Services to Development and Aid

Generally, there was growing concern that development programmes for African countries by the international community were not working for Africa:

> A growing number of observers are beginning to perceive – sometime with a
> feeling of disgust – that so many of the efforts put in a large number of countries
> in the process of development have not assisted, up until now except to enrich
> further an already privileged minority, this without benefit for the underprivileged
> minority. (ASWEA, 1976b: 81)

By the 1980s, many social commentators in developing countries were critical of foreign aid seeing it as an economic instrument being used for political purposes to strengthen Western power over the rest of the world (ASWEA, 1982b). For social workers, the crucial issue was how to move from a colonial service-provision model to play a role in social development funded by foreign aid without compromising professional values. This meant a change of mind-set, attitude and practice from remedial and maintenance (social welfare) thinking to social development thinking. In practice, this meant that social workers had to be more proactive in building community capacity for self-sufficiency and growth (ASWEA, 1982b) and focusing on rural development (ASWEA, 1982b; Yimam, 1990). Community participation, interdisciplinary work, a focus on preventative work, community-based research and knowledge of and involvement with social policies created from national planning strategies were some of the necessary skills for the social development worker (ASWEA, 1976b, 1977, 1981, 1982b, 1985; Midgley, 2010; Yimam, 1990). It meant that professional associations needed to be established to offer genuine social policy advice to the government and this required an up-to-date understanding of African social realities.

The Establishment of a Strong Professional Identity and Powerful Professional Associations

The degree of respect for a profession is often determined by the strength of its professional associations. A common theme at several conferences was that the social work profession in Africa had failed to evolve a strong professional identity thus 'it was argued the profession had a very poor status in Africa' (ASWEA, 1977: 36). ASWEA (1977: 36) proposed:

> social work professional associations had to develop an identity by evolving theories, methods and skills of social work in Africa. In this activity, the developmental aspects of the profession should be accentuated while minimizing these borrowed methods and ideas whose relevance to the African social reality is only peripheral.

This change in thinking brought lively debate concerning social development and social welfare at ASWEA conferences.

Tensions between Social Development and Social Welfare

An ongoing debate during ASWEA's 20-year history was the tension between clinically-based Western models and community-based social development models for education and practice. In fact, in 1973, the umbrella term 'social development' had been accepted by most social workers on the continent who recommended that the term 'social welfare workers' be replaced with 'social development workers' (ASWEA, 1973a: iii). And yet, by the end of the 1970s, there was frustration that the concept of social development remained vague in spite of ongoing discussion at successive conferences (ASWEA, 1977). As a result, an expert group meeting was planned and followed in 1980 'to define the concept of social development in order to evolve "new approaches" which were likely to eliminate or reduce the pitfalls of past development strategies in Africa' (ASWEA, 1977: 63–4). A better understanding of what social development education might look like emerged:

> holistic in character and as such requires that the education and training of its practitioners be interdisciplinary ... It is equally important for students to be exposed to the various theories of change and development and be encouraged to engage in critical analysis of these theories in light of contemporary African realities. (ASWEA, 1981: 29)

The social welfare-social development debate had a major impact on the Association. ASWEA's executive planned to change the constitution and, among other things, was going to change the Association's name to the Association for Social Development Education in Africa (Yimam, 1990). This never happened as ASWEA was disbanded in the early 1990s as repeated attempts to revivify the association of the broad African region failed. In 1994, a new Association for East and Southern African Social Work Education was established at the IASSW Conference in Amsterdam with Lionel Louw from post-apartheid South Africa as its first president.

However, the proposed name change represented important progress towards a social development approach to national development planning in Africa. The tension between social development and social work was and continues to be a pivotal barrier in the progression of relevant social work education in Africa. And it is not only in Africa that this issue is highlighted. According to Midgley (2010: 194), 'advocates of developmental social work have not always offered a clear and coherent explanation of what developmental practice involves' and further research is crucial in understanding the relevance of this approach to social work practice.

It is clear in all of the conference proceedings that, from a critical – decolonization – perspective, given its allegiance to the IASSW, ASWEA never questioned the relevance of the social work profession per se to African cultures (see Gray and Allegritti, 2002, 2003; Gray et al., 2008). This unexamined assumption set into motion the continual struggle concerning appropriate social work curriculum instead of critical debate concerning the profession's relevance to the African reality.

Decolonization of Social Work: Innovations and Interventions

Despite ASWEA's attempts, no radical changes to the curriculum were made (ASWEA, 1977). However, two courses: one in family planning and welfare and one in rural community development emerged in ASWEA's 20-year history. What was important about these two courses was that they were created by Africans to address the developmental issues arising in Africa in the 1970s – population control – and in the 1980s – the mass poverty affecting many parts of Africa and the desperate need for rural community development workers. Dr Tesfaye, from Ethiopia (ASWEA, 1974a) set out his understanding of development priorities and proposed ways in which the social work curriculum might respond to these priorities (see Table 9.1). Below two country case examples are provided to highlight attempts to create African-centred social work education incorporating some of Dr Tesfaye's ideas.

Case Examples

In 1974, at the second ASWEA conference it was noted that two countries had changed their curriculum to be more African-centred: Mali and Zambia.

Table 9.1   Tesfaye's proposed curriculum

Development priorities	Curriculum content
Balance between social and economic development	Less remedial and more developmental and preventative
Citizen participation in national development	Community development
Education	Reduce illiteracy
Health	Interdisciplinary practice, nutritional education
Development and prevention	Integration into overall development plans and social work that anticipates social problems in order to minimize remedial services
Lack of trained social development workers	Multilevel training for development

Mali

From 1970 to 1972, Mali initiated an economic and social development plan that would lay the foundations for long-term development with social work integrated into these development plans. Mali had started out with a Francophone curriculum deemed inappropriate for training social workers in this new development plan, which aimed to advance rural development: 'the people of Mali had to return to their own origins and evaluate their potential with a view to developing it wisely' (ASWEA, 1974a: 61). (There is no ASWEA record of what the programme was like before this change). Social workers conducted a house-to-house survey, the findings of which led to the closure of the two schools of social work and the emergence of a new curriculum compatible with Mali's development priorities housed in a National Training Centre for Social Work and Community Development. This effectively transformed the curriculum from social work to community development and included law, economics, political science (social legislation), agriculture (livestock rearing), labour relations, accounting and home economics courses. Important to the curriculum was the health of the population with an emphasis on interdisciplinary work and cooperation within Africa. Although how many people were involved in social work in Mali in the early 1970s was not recorded, the ASWEA curriculum survey (ASWEA, 1982a) shows that social work training was still completed at the Centre National de Développement and was a four-year diploma programme. The programme kept many of the suggestions developed in the 1970s and was quite extensive. Presently, there is no social work degree at the University of Bamako and community development training is completed through international and national NGOs.

Zambia

In the curriculum survey (ASWEA, 1974b), Zambia offered a one-year certificate in community development that began in 1960 at the local college as well as a four-year Bachelor of Social Work at the University of Zambia that started in 1965. The Second National Development Plan (SNDP) of Zambia (1972–1976) included a chapter on social development with educational goals including: (i) self-sufficiency of the people implying the 'decolonization of attitudes and requirements and the development of an Indigenous capacity to identify and solve problems' (ASWEA, 1974a: 55); (ii) participatory democracy; (iii) village productivity committees; and (iv) participation in the continuing struggle for freedom in Africa through political and social citizen education (ASWEA, 1974a). In each of these areas, social workers had a role to play and, based on these goals, social work training in Zambia included: (i) supervised fieldwork with student involvement in village productivity committees (case studies for class use came from these committees); (ii) group work; (iii) conferences and meetings to examine how traditional problem-solving methods might be used more effectively so that cultural differences and controversies might be minimized; and (iv) curriculum review to encourage interdisciplinary and team teaching. This attempt to integrate national planning goals with the social work curriculum aimed to better equip Zambian social workers to interpret and respond to social problems in a developmental way. In 1982, the university had a more extensive four-year Bachelor of Social Work that included more content on Zambian society and rural sociology.

ASWEA Case Study Project

ASWEA's ongoing attempts to develop an African-centred social work curriculum included the use of Indigenous case studies in the classroom instead of Western case examples adapted to the African context. In cooperation with ASWEA, UNICEF and UNECA, seven countries (Ethiopia, Kenya, Malawi, Mauritius, Tanzania, Uganda and Zambia) were asked to send ten case examples from group and community work in their countries. The case studies (ASWEA, 1973b, 1974c) were to include a description of the case, the intervention and an analysis of how the case was handled. As it was the first compilation of its kind, this meant that African students could learn from African cases throughout East and West Africa.

Other Initiatives

Other African countries, including Kenya, Ethiopia, Uganda, Sudan, Mauritius, Ghana and Zambia, were attempting to indigenize their curriculum by encouraging students to write papers from original research in specific areas of social welfare or on particular social problems (ASWEA, 1976b). In his presentation on innovation in social work education at the 1977 conference, Nyirenda suggested a more integrated or interdisciplinary approach to social work education (ASWEA,

1977). Country examples from Egypt, Ethiopia, Togo, Zambia, Mauritius and Uganda reflected this trend. Fieldwork was extended from 12- to 17-week block placements: 'during these periods it is expected that students can absorb their settings and at the same time be able to apply whatever theories they have learnt' (ASWEA, 1977: 59). Zambian students had to do a 16-week rural placement.

The last two ASWEA conferences in 1982 and 1986 centred on the many crises in Africa during the 1980s since hunger, famine, drought, economic issues and political crises all affected social work training. Paramount was the training of social workers to work in rural areas to try and deal with some of the suffering. Three countries, Tanzania, Zimbabwe and Ethiopia, had incorporated rural development into their social work training. Zimbabwe, in particular, strengthened this area of social work in three ways: (i) revitalizing the curriculum development subcommittee; (ii) establishing a rural fieldwork unit; and (iii) creating a research unit (ASWEA, 1982a).

These examples show that, in the main, appropriate African-centred social work involved developmental social work, and in particular, rural community development but this did not necessarily accord with Western images of the professional social worker and, over the years, social workers remained urban-based and community development workers took over rural practice and had separate training institutions.

Conclusion

Former president of Zambia, Kenneth Kaunda, stated: 'Our great need is to educate people *for* Africa and not merely to educate people *from* Africa' (Yimam, 1990: 253 original emphasis). Despite the 20 years of ASWEA's activity surrounding social work education in Africa and, in particular, the development of a culturally relevant social work curriculum, there is still no agreement on Indigenous social work education and practice in Africa (Osei-Hwedie and Jacques, 2007). The colonial social welfare model was inappropriate to Africa where 80 per cent of people lived in rural areas during the 1960s and 1970s independence decades. The struggle to change the mind-set of social work educators and practitioners from a remedial and maintenance to a developmental approach was visible in ASWEA's conference proceedings and this was partly due to the fact that the social development concept was still being defined at these conferences. Midgley (2010: 194) suggests that 'to dismantle the system without having a clearly defined alternative in place could be disastrous' and this has been one of the main criticisms of the social development approach. Despite some country-specific attempts to indigenize the social work curriculum and incorporate a social development approach, by the end of the 1980s there had been very little progress and this was discouraging for the leaders in ASWEA (Dr Chibogu, Nigeria; Dr Ibo, Cote d' Ivoire; Dr Onyango, Kenya; Dr Tesfaye, Ethiopia; Dr Muzaale, Uganda; Mr Allouane, Tunisie; Professor Twagiramutara, Rwanda; Dr Selassie, Ethiopia; and

Dr Jazdowska, Zimbabwe). Why was it so difficult to decolonize and to develop an appropriate African social work curriculum broad enough for all countries to accept and flexible enough to adapt to country-specific contexts? Added to the barriers highlighted above from the ASWEA documents, more recent debates highlight barriers such as the: (i) idealization of Western social work knowledge (Kreitzer, Abukari, Antonio, Mensa and Kwaku, 2009); (ii) diversity within countries and ethnic and political tensions between countries; (iii) the brain drain (Engelbrecht, 2006); and (vi) the lack of critical debate on the appropriateness of the profession in Africa at all (Gray et al., 2008). Also, a social development approach, in many ways, goes against the present-day economic, political and social ideals of neo-liberalism: 'Instead of promoting capitalistic forms of enterprise, developmental social workers should campaign for social structural changes' (Midgley, 2010: 197) and this is not easy to do. The difficulties notwithstanding, one speaker at an ASWEA conference stated:

> At several conferences and expert group meetings African social work educators have lamentably talked about this lag between changing societal needs and the prevailing training approaches but have quickly found explanations in paucity of qualified teachers, shortage of funds and lack of local teaching materials. Needless to say, that these excuses are unacceptable. Africa must evolve its own approaches not only to social development, but also to the training of social welfare personnel. (ASWEA, 1977: 57)

As Gray et al. (2008) note, social work is a Western invention and the 'west is best' rationality permeates those societies in which it is practised. Even today, African social work students want a Western social work education and qualification and universities in Africa want to attract international students (Osei-Hwedie and Rankopo, 2008, 2012). The lack of respect for and understanding of social work's role in African countries by other professionals and the government is partly due to the profession's failure to decolonize and to adapt and respond to country-specific needs and problems. Western social work practice just does not fit Africa's cultures or the widespread poverty and urgent need for social development. Though excluded from ASWEA and this history of African social work, South Africa leads the way in social work and social development. Memunka's statement on social work in Africa in the 1970s rings true today:

> In my opinion the time has come for serious and critical re-examination of social work training in Africa ... Twentieth century Africa expects social work to be *creative* and *revolutionary*. In the context of the inter-disciplinary approach I see the profession of social work as a catalyst for the polarization of all shades of opinion relating to rural development. By virtue of their training, social workers should be able to make a positive contribution as members of inter-disciplinary development teams ... However, it is again necessary to reiterate my earlier concern that unless the *profession of social work is prepared to take a new path*,

social workers will for a long time to come remain ineffective in developing countries. (ASWEA, 1976b: 32, original emphasis)

Whether or not social workers were then and are now prepared to take a new path, questions as to the relevance of social work education and practice in Africa remain.

References

Adedeji, A. (2002). From the Lagos Plan of Action to the new partnership for African development and from the final act of Lagos to the constitutive act: Wither Africa? Keynote address prepared for the presentation at the African forum for envisioning Africa, Nairobi, 26–9 April.

Ajayi, J.F.A., Goma, L.K.H. and Johnson, G.A. (1996). *The African Experience with Higher Education*. Athens, GA: Ohio University Press.

Apt, A.A. and Blavo, E.Q. (1997). Ghana. In N.S. Mayadas, Watts, T.D. and Elliott, D. (eds), *International Handbook on Social Work Theory*. Westport, CT: Greenwood Press, 320–43.

Ashby, E. (1964). *African Universities and Western Tradition*. Cambridge, MA: Harvard University Press.

ASWEA. (n.d.). *An Effort in Community Development in the Lakota Sub-prefecture, Doc.* 1. Addis Ababa: ASWEA publication.

ASWEA. (1972a). *Community Services, Lakota Project Methodology, Doc.* 2. Addis Ababa: ASWEA publication.

ASWEA. (1972b). *The Important Role of Supervision in Social Welfare Organizations, Doc.* 3. Addis Ababa: ASWEA publication.

ASWEA. (1972c). *The Use of Films in Social Development Education, Doc.* 4. Addis Ababa: ASWEA publication.

ASWEA. (1973a). *Case Studies of Social Development in Africa, Vol.* 1. Addis Ababa: ASWEA publication.

ASWEA. (1973b). *Guidelines for Making Contact with Young People in Informal Groups in Urban Areas, Doc.* 5. Addis Ababa: ASWEA publication.

ASWEA. (1974a). *Relationship between Social Work Education and National Social Development Planning, Doc.* 6. Addis Ababa: ASWEA publication.

ASWSEA. (1974b). *Curricula of Schools of Social Work and Community Development Training Centres in Africa, Doc.* 7. Addis Ababa: ASWEA publication.

ASWEA. (1974c). *Case Studies of Social Development in Africa, vol.* 2. Addis Ababa: ASWEA publication.

ASWEA. (1975a). *Directory of Social Welfare Activities in Africa* (3rd edn). *Doc.* 8. Addis Ababa, ASWEA publication.

ASWEA. (1975b). *Report of ASWEA's Workshop on Techniques of Teaching and Methods of Field Work Evaluations, Doc.* 9. Addis Ababa: ASWEA publication.

ASWEA. (1976a). *Techniques d' Enseignement et methodes d'Evaluation des Travaux Pratiques, Doc.* 10. Addis Ababa: ASWEA publication.

ASWEA. (1976b). *Realities and aspirations of social work education in Africa, Doc.* 11. Addis Ababa: ASWEA publication.

ASWEA. (1977). *The Role of Social Development Education in Africa's Struggle for Political and Economic Independence, Doc.* 12. Addis Ababa: ASWEA publication.

ASWEA. (1978a). *The Development of a Training Curriculum in Family Welfare, Doc.* 13. Addis Ababa: ASWEA publication.

ASWEA. (1978b). *L'Elaboration d' un programme de formation en benêtre familial, Doc.* 14. Addis Ababa: ASWEA publication.

ASWEA. (1979a).*Guidelines for the Development of a Training Curriculum in Family Welfare, Doc.* 15. Addis Ababa: ASWEA publication.

ASWEA. (1979b). *Principes directeurs pour l'establissement d'un programme d'etude destine a la formation aux disciplines de la protection de la famille, Doc.* 16. Addis Ababa: ASWEA publication.

ASWEA. (1981). *Social Development Training in Africa: Experiences of the 1970s and Emerging Trends of the 1980s, Doc.* 17. Addis Ababa: ASWEA publication.

ASWEA. (1982a). *Survey of Curricula of Social Development Training Institutions in Africa, Doc.* 18. Addis Ababa: ASWEA publication.

ASWEA. (1982b). *Seminar on the organization and delivery of social services to rural areas in Africa, Doc.* 19. Addis Ababa: ASWEA publication.

ASWEA. (1985). *Training for Social Development: Methods of Intervention to Improve People's Participation in Rural Transformation in Africa with Special Emphasis on Women, Doc.* 20. Addis Ababa: ASWEA publication.

ASWEA. (1986). *Association for Social Work Education in Africa*. Addis Ababa: ASWEA publication.

ASWEA. (1989). *Social Development Agents in Rural Transformation in Africa: A Book of Selected Readings, Doc.* 21. Addis Ababa: ASWEA publication.

Berg, E. (1982). *Accelerated Development in Sub-Saharan Africa: An Agenda for Action*. Washington DC: World Bank.

Boateng, N.A. (1982). Western education and political leadership in Africa: The Ghana experience. Paper presented at the 5th National Conference on the Third World, Omaha, Nebraska, October.

Drake, S.C. and Omari, T.P. (1962). *Social Work in Africa*. Accra: Department of Social Welfare and Community Development.

Engelbrecht, L.K. (2006). Plumbing the brain drain of South African social workers migrating to the UK: Challenges for social service providers. *Social Work/Maatskaplike Werk*, 42(2), 127–46.

Estes, R.J. (1995). Social development trends in Africa, 1970–1994: The need for a new paradigm. *Social Development Issues*, 17(1), 18–47.

Gray, M. and Allegritti, I. (2002). Cross-cultural practice and the indigenisation of African social work. *Social Work/Maatskaplike Werk*, 38(4), 324–36.

Gray, M. and Allegritti, I. (2003). Towards culturally sensitive social work practice: Re-examining cross-cultural social work. *Social Work/Maatskaplike Werk*, 39(4), 312–25.

Gray, M. and Coates, J. (2008). From Indigenization to Cultural Relevance. In M. Gray, Coates, J. and Yellow Bird, M. (eds), *Indigenous Social Work around the World: Towards Culturally Relevant Education and Practice*. Aldershot: Ashgate,13–29.

Gray, M., Coates, J. and Yellow Bird, M. (eds). (2008). *Indigenous Social Work around the World: Towards Culturally Relevant Education and Practice*. Aldershot: Ashgate.

Holscher, D. and Berhane, S.Y. (2008).Reflections on human rights and professional solidarity. *International Social Work*, 51(3), 311–23.

Kendall, K. (1995). Foreword. In T.D. Watts, Elliott, D. and Mayasdas, N.S. (eds), *International Handbook on Social Work Education*. Westport, CT: Greenwood Press, xiii–xvii.

Konadu-Agyemang, K. (2000). The best of times and the worst of times: Structural Adjustment Programs and uneven development in Africa: The case of Ghana. *Professional Geographer*, 52(3), 469–83.

Kreitzer, L. (2004). *Indigenization of social work education and practice: A participatory action research project in Ghana*. Unpublished PhD thesis, University of Calgary, Alberta, Canada.

Kreitzer, L., Abukari, Z., Antonio, P., Mensah, J. and Kwaku, A. (2009). Social work in Ghana: A participatory action research project looking at culturally appropriate training and practice. *Social Work Education*, 28(2), 145–64.

Laird, S. (2003). Evaluating social work outcomes in sub-Saharan Africa. *Qualitative Social Work*, 2(3), 251–70.

Lewis, D. and Wallace, T. (2000). Introduction. In D. Lewis and Wallace, T. (eds), *New Roles and Relevance: Development NGOs and the Challenge of Change*. Bloomfield, CN: Kumarian Press, ix–xvii.

Lewis, S. (2005). *Race against Time*. Toronto, ON: House of Anansi Press.

Loxley, J. (1983). Review: The Berg report and the model of accumulation in Sub-Saharan Africa. *Review of African Political Economy*, 27/28, 197–204.

Maathai, W. (2009). *The Challenge for Africa*. New York: Pantheon Books.

Meredith, M. (2006). *The State of Africa: A History of Fifty Years of Independence*. Toronto, ON: Free Press.

Midgley, J. (1981). *Professional Imperialism: Social Work in the Third World*. London: Heinemann.

Midgley, J. (2010). The Theory and Practice of Developmental Social Work. In J. Midgley and Conley, A. (eds), *Social Work And Social Development: Theories and Skills for Developmental Social Work*. Oxford: Oxford University Press, 1–28.

Miller, P. (1968). Social work education and the international education act. *Social Work Education Reporter*, 16(2), 34–7.

Moyo, D. (2009). *Dead Aid: Why Aid Is Not Working and How There Is a Better Way for Africa*. New York: Ferrar, Straus and Giroux.

Ntusi, T. (1995). South Africa. In T.D. Watts, Elliott, D. and Mayadas, N.S. (eds), *International Handbook on Social Work Education*. Westport, CT: Greenwood Press, 261–79.

Onyanyo, M. (2005). NGO's pseudo governments or surrogates of western powers? *New African*, 443, 20–21.

Osei-Hwedie, K. (1993). The challenge of social work in Africa: Stating the indigenising process. *Journal of Social Development in Africa*, 8(1), 19–30.

Osei-Hwedie, K. (2002). Indigenous practice: Some informed guesses, self-evident and possible. *Social Work/Maatskaplike Werk*, 38(4), 311–23.

Osei-Hwedie, K. (2007). Indigenous Practice: Some informed guesses self-evident and possible. In K. Osei-Hwedie and Jacques, G. (eds), *Indigenizing Social Work in Africa*. Accra: Ghana Universities Press, 22–39.

Osei-Hwedie, K. and Rankopo, M.J. (2008). Developing Culturally Relevant Social Work Education and Practice in Africa: The case of Botswana. In M. Gray, Coates, J. and Yellow Bird, M. (eds), *Indigenous Social Work around the World: Towards culturally Relevant Education and Practice*. Aldershot: Ashgate, 361–86.

Osei-Hwedie, K. and Rankopo, M.J. (2012). Social Work in Developing Countries. In M. Gray, Midgley, J. and Webb, S.A. (eds), *The Sage Handbook of Social Work*. London: Sage, 723–39.

Rankopo, M.J. and Osei-Hwedie, K. (2011). Globalization and culturally relevant social work: African perspectives on indigenization. *International Social Work*, 54(1), 137–47.

Rist, G. (2008). *The History of Development* (3rd edn). New York: Zed Books.

Sankore, R. (2005). What are NGO's doing? *New African*, Aug/Sept, 443, 12–15.

Sewpaul, V. (2006). The global-local dialectic: Challenges for African scholarship and social work in a post-colonial world. *British Journal of Social Work*, 36, 419–34.

Shawky, A. (1972). Social work education in Africa. *International Social Work*, 15(1), 3–16.

South Commission. (1990). *The Challenge to the South: The Report of the South Commission*. New York: Oxford University Press.

United Nations. (1950). *Training for Social Work: An International Survey*. New York: United Nations.

United Nations. (1955). *Training for Social Work: Second International Survey*. New York: United Nations.

United Nations. (1958). *Training for Social Work: Third International Survey*. New York: United Nations.

United Nations. (1964). *Training for Social Work: Fourth International Survey*. New York: United Nations.

United Nations. (1971). *Training for Social Work: Fifth International Survey*. New York: United Nations.

United Nations. (1977). *Report of the 2nd African Ministers of Social Affairs*. New York: United Nations.

van Hook, M.P. (1994). Educational challenges in Southern Africa: Implications for social work. *International Social Work*, 37, 319–31.

Wallace, T. (2004). NGO dilemmas: Trojan horses for global neo-liberalism? *Socialist Registrar*, 40, 203–19.

Willinsky, J. (1998). *Learning to Divide the World: Education at Empire's End*. Minneapolis, MN: University of Minnesota Press.

Yimam, A. (1990). *Social Development in Africa 1950–1985: Methodological perspectives and future prospects*. Aldershot: Avebury.

Acknowledgement

I would like to thank Professor Nana Araba Apt, Professor of Sociology and Dean of Academic Affairs, Ashesi University, Ghana, Professor Mel Gray, School of Humanities and Social Science, University of Newcastle, Australia, and Dr Boniface Mgonja, Lecturer, Mzumbe University Tanzania for their contribution of important historical information for this chapter.

Chapter 10

Indigenizing the Curriculum: The Decolonization of Social Work Education in Hawai`i

Paula T. Tanemura Morelli, Peter J. Mataira and C. Malina Kaulukukui

Ua lehulehu a manomano ka `ikena a ka Hawai`i
Great and numerous is the knowledge of the Hawaiians
(Puku`i, 1983: 309)

The University of Hawai`i at Manoa School of Social Work came into being in 1936. The first four decades were devoted to establishing the school's foundation and national accreditation. In the 1970s, despite acute awareness of the needs of culturally diverse Hawaiian communities and a commitment to locally relevant social work practice, the school remained focused on Western service paradigms and developed its national and international reputation for expertise in inter alia empirical clinical practice (Fischer, 1973, 1976, 1978), sexual health (Gochros and Fischer, 1980; Mokuau, 1986) and community development (Sanders, 1982; Sanders and Fischer, 1988; Sanders and Matsuoka, 1989). By the 1990s, the importance of culturally relevant social work practice (Blaisdell and Mokuau, 1991; Fong and Mokuau, 1994; Matsuoka, 1991; Mokuau, 1995; Mokuau and Chang, 1991; Takeuchi, Mokuau and Chun, 1992; Untalan, 1991) and ageing and women's issues (Braun and Browne, 1997; Browne, Fong and Mokuau, 1994) were expressly part of the curriculum's focus, remaining, however, within the context of Western models of social work practice.

In 2005, after several failed attempts, the school set itself on a path to indigenization. This chapter describes a revolutionary process in which the school continues to indigenize the social work curriculum to make it more culturally relevant, a move which polarized faculty and community members. Indigenization refers to defining an identity and mission relative to the community to which the academy is accountable and is an important process in decolonizing the curriculum. The chapter examines the factors and processes that influenced this decision and the simultaneous efforts to engage in processes of discovery, learning, development and implementation while mindful of the larger questions: what is the value and significance of indigenizing social work education? How can social work education be indigenized? How will an indigenized social work education be assessed in light of mainstream professional social work standards nationally and internationally?

Following three years of sincere and passionate discussion and debate among faculty, students and community stakeholders, the Myron B. Thompson School of Social Work (MBTSSW) at the University of Hawai`i adopted its indigenization policy:

> Indigenization speaks to our commitment as a School to enhance social justice, equity and wellbeing for all under-represented, under-served, and marginalized people in Hawai`i, and throughout Asia and the Pacific. It honors our profession and challenges us to engage in efforts to (re)center professional social work education, training and research to align to Native Hawaiians values, principles and knowledge; to local customary ways; to traditional healing practices; and to developing a greater appreciation of our connectedness, as people, to the land and our environment.

> We believe indigenization is affirming of all knowledge systems that honor, respect, and advance the positive wellbeing and spiritual worth of all people, and protects the delicate natural resources of Hawai`i. To this end, our School is engaged in meaningful efforts to decolonize and critique dominant western approaches to social work and to encourage indigenous approaches that draw from the convergence of all knowledge sources with the aim of producing new concepts, theories, forms of analysis, and methods of practice. For faculty and staff, as we begin to engage in this process, we begin also our own journeys of self-discovery.

> Our mission, as a school, to engage in the active 'generation, transmission and application of knowledge in both western and indigenous forms, obligates us to produce well-rounded, versatile, professionally competent, culturally aware, students capable of working anywhere in the world. This calls on us to be inclusive, participatory, transparent, and respectful of all knowledge systems. Re-centering the School requires that we use science and technology, indigenous research methods, our human intellectual and spiritual experience, and our creative capacities to greatest effect, and, that we continue our active engagement in strengthening our relationships with the local community and the broader Pacific-Asian region. (Authored by Peter Mataira, Director of Indigenous Affairs, with guidance and input from the Kūpuna Council, and accepted by MBTSSW faculty, 20 April 2009)

Remarkably, the period 2006–2009 is distinguished by several school accomplishments, among them the following:

1. Naming the school in honour of Myron B. Thompson, or Pinky as he was affectionately called, a Native Hawaiian and World War II veteran and graduate of the University of Hawai`i, School of Social Work (UHSSW),

who made significant contributions to the field of social work in Hawai'i and began to indigenize local social work practice in the 1950s.

2. The well-received International Indigenous Voices in Social Work Conference.
3. Completion of the Alternative Reaffirmation Project, an option of the Council on Social Work Education's Educational Policy and Accreditation Standards (EPAS) (CSWE, 2008), which led to programme reaccreditation for seven years.
4. The reestablishment of the Hawaiian Learning Program.
5. The establishment of the online *Journal of Indigenous Voices in Social Work* (*JIVSW*), the name of which was changed to the *Journal of Indigenous Social Development* in 2011.

Pushing from the Edges: A Brief History

Since its inception in 1936, founders of the University of Hawai'i, School of Social Work and community constituents understood the necessity for locally relevant social work practice. While practices related to Native Hawaiians were supported, culturally relevant practice was not a primary focus. By necessity, the first four decades were devoted to establishing the school's foundation and accreditation to stand among the national social work programmes. Over the ensuing years, the State of Hawai'i's communities and social workers voiced the need for social work education to address Indigenous and local populations specifically. By 2005, the school described its mission as follows:

> The mission of the University of Hawai'i at Manoa School of Social Work is to contribute to the advancement of social work practice in its many forms for the purpose of preventing or resolving the most critical social problems. Within this general purpose, the school reaffirms social work's historic commitment to increase social justice and availability of opportunity of underrepresented and oppressed groups.

> The principle responsibility of the school is the generation, transmission, and application of knowledge that will benefit the State of Hawai'i. In addition, it is the school's responsibility to contribute knowledge for use by the profession as a whole. *In particular, it is the goal of this school to increase comprehension of the ways in which social policy, social work practice, and research can be improved through the understanding of Native Hawaiian and other Pacific Islander and Asian cultures of our communities, state and the Pacific Region.* (UHSSW Bulletin, 2005–06: 5)

The intention to address the social welfare needs of Native Hawaiian and Asian-Pacific region people was clearly stated in curriculum learning objectives but no concerted effort was made to define this intention, discover what it would involve and uniformly address its implementation. In a climate of diminishing resources, the discrepancies between the school's mission and educational practice was largely ignored and normalized. Like an elephant in the room, it was tacitly acknowledged but too difficult and enormous an undertaking to see through until 2002 when faculty sought opportunities to make progressive changes to the curriculum. In a series of three, off-campus, day-long strategic planning meetings (2002–2004), several initiatives were proposed to reorganize the curriculum around social justice and diversity issues with a focus on local perspectives. While the intent was positive, the meetings were difficult and faculty members were unable to agree on a way forward. As a result, enthusiasm waned and attention returned to daily academic priorities.

In 2005, the quest to indigenize social work education was re-introduced by the Dean, Jon Matsuoka, who, with like-minded faculty, organized and laid the foundation for the school's advisory board comprising respected individuals with expertise on local issues. The Kupuna Council was engaged to advise the board on Native Hawaiian needs and the school's name was changed.

In the ensuing years (2006–2009), faculty engaged in heated debates to locate and define the school's priorities during *holomua* meetings (or school retreats). The renewed discussions were stimulated and buoyed by: (i) national and international concerns about earth's sustainability; (ii) recognition of Indigenous People's deep knowledge of the reciprocal relationship between man [*sic*], earth and all life forms; and (iii) contemporary examples of capitalist greed run rampant without responsibility for human and environmental well-being. Simultaneously, during this period, faculty and staff worked in partnership with multiple community constituents engaging in direct indigenizing action, such as the *International Indigenous Voices in Social Work Conference* held in June 2007, which took over a year of targeted activity aimed at procuring necessary funding and volunteer help to support participants with travel, lodging and registration costs.

By 2009, the momentum to indigenize the social work programme was well established, and faculty reached consensus on a working definition that embodied the school's indigenizing mission. Despite substantial, ongoing challenges, the school has continued to indigenize the curriculum as discussed below.

Establishing Faculty Commitment to Indigenizing the Social Work Curriculum

In retrospect, the indigenization initiative relied upon strong school and community relationships, and a collective commitment to social justice. These positive relationships provided the goodwill for the arduous meetings – *holomua* – and difficult discussions, bolstered by the received wisdom and guidance of Indigenous elders, the international affirmation received and the national accrediting body's – CSWE – recognition of the importance of indigenization. These vital processes and relationships created the necessary conditions which empowered faculty to explore the purpose and meaning of indigenization and debate the methods by which the curriculum might be indigenized. Figure 10.1 depicts the process – timeline, activities and actions – that resulted in the school's active commitment to indigenize the social work curriculum.

Figure 10.1   MBTSSW continuing process of indigenizing social work education

Holomua: **Engaging in Difficult Discussions**

Five *holomua* were held between 2006 and 2008. These day-long planning sessions held off-campus involved open discussion to enlarge the debate and locate common ground. While the meetings were carefully planned and purposefully respectful, nurturing and supporting all perspectives, faculty expressed concern that standards of excellence would be diminished. Philosophical differences led to heated exchanges and confusion regarding the definition of indigenization, what indigenization would require of faculty and how it would affect curriculum and teaching practices. The *holomua* provided opportunities for safe communication, where faculty could share their varying perspectives, develop a deeper understanding of one another and work as a team, while entering into creative, progressive discussions, to explore possibilities and develop a vision. Initially, students and community more readily understood and accepted indigenization, while some faculty, especially those steeped in Western approaches, were resistant to change. Some feared that a shift towards indigenization would disempower and render their knowledge less relevant. Over time, however, hope for transformation, growth, healing and respect grew as a result of these meetings.

Despite the enormity of the task and the constant challenges of keeping up with daily academic work, faculty and community participants stayed on course. Faculty grew more comfortable with the uncertainty of the work in progress, demonstrating patience and commitment toward the larger vision of social justice until the inspiration for an international Indigenous social work conference emerged during the 2006–2007 *holomua*. It was envisaged that this conference would empower Indigenous people nationally and internationally to network and share Indigenous practices, knowledge and research.

Kupuna Council: Received Wisdom of Elders

Honouring and respecting the host Native Hawaiian culture by requesting their support and guidance was a significant priority. Six respected, knowledgeable social welfare practitioner-kupuna accepted the invitation to be part of the school's Kupuna Council. As far back as the 1950s and 1960s, several of these individuals, along with many who were no longer alive, pioneered the indigenization of social work methods by using Hawaiian approaches alongside Western social work methods in order to work effectively with Native Hawaiian clients. Some of these kupuna were part of the Culture Committee of Queen Liliuokalani Children's Center, which supported the publication of Nana I Ke Kumu (Look to the Source) (Puku`i, Haertig and Lee, 1979). This publication authored by Mary Kawena Pukui (1983) provides a rich and complex compilation of information about Hawaiian cultural traditions and offers guidance for how this knowledge can be used in the practice of social work. Mary Kawena Pukui was one of the first in her generation to revive Hawaiian practices that were abolished or repressed under the Western colonization of Hawai`i.

From the beginning, the Kupuna Council understood that this initiative was about creating fundamental changes in the way the school and faculty conceptualized and designed social work education. Year-long discussions examined the philosophy of indigenization and ways to indigenize the school's structures, processes and protocols, curriculum content and recruitment procedures and thus develop programmes that taught and reinforced skills in Native Hawaiian helping and healing. The meetings recognized the realistic limitations of what might be possible within higher education, specifically, the difficulties of achieving structural change.

The Kupuna Council held the philosophy that social work practice needed to be developed from the inside out. That is, social technologies should emanate from fundamental cultural properties and concepts related to socialization and development, health and healing, identity, family relationships and spirituality. Each of these elements should be incorporated into holistic approaches to prevent problems and restore health. In collective societies, social problems are highly contextualized, and not necessarily individualized. Thus processes of recovery and healing had to be inclusive of all predisposing environmental factors. Restoring balance in social relationships is central to generating positive health. Kupuna discussions recognized that traditional Native Hawaiian practices were being revitalized in ways that considered the realities of living within a Western context. Traditionally pure approaches to social work practice might be considered impractical and could be modified according to changing values, lifestyles and schedules while holding to core Indigenous values.

Members of the Kupuna Council not only summoned ideas regarding indigenization, but also affirmed and further developed those generated by the dean and faculty members. One of the first ideas to develop was the Hawaiian Learning Program to teach Native Hawaiian social work students about Indigenous practices of well-being and progressing toward educating non-Native Hawaiians (Dominelli, 2010; Gray and Coates, 2010). The Kupuna Council engaged in deep discussions, which became the foundation of the 9 April 2009 commitment to indigenization.

International Conference: Collective Affirmation

The International Indigenous Voices in Social Work (IIVSW): Not Lost in Translation conference convened in Makaha, Hawai`i (4–7 June, 2007) after over a year's work with communities, interdisciplinary partners and students. The conference brought together over 400 international participants from as far away as Africa, Australia, Aotearoa (New Zealand), Fiji, Japan, Papua New Guinea, Samoa, Tonga and Hawai`i. It further substantiated the relevance of the school's indigenization objectives and efforts to explore and develop ways in which values-based Indigenous knowledge and practice could be transmitted through educational programmes and research agendas to address critical social problems.

Student participation was an integral part of the conference. Twenty social work students participated in a course designed to involve them in learning about and contributing to the school's indigenization and conference development processes. Students rated participation in this course invaluable to a truer understanding of Indigenous Peoples' perspectives, issues facing Indigenous people globally and the potential for organized action to alleviate problems and improve their well-being.

The IIVSW conference published selected conference papers in the first volume of the *Journal of Indigenous Voices in Social Work* (*JIVSW*, February 2010). Equally important, the enthusiasm generated by the exchange of knowledge gave rise to Māori participants from New Zealand volunteering to take leadership in continuing the conference.

Alternative Reaffirmation Special Project

In 2007, under the Alternative Reaffirmation: Compliance Audit and Project of the Council on Social Work Education Commission on Accreditation (CSWE, 2004), the school submitted a reaffirmation compliance audit report and special project proposal: *Indigenization and the University of Hawai`i at Manoa School of Social Work: Exploring and Developing Concepts, Processes and Applications*. This special project proposal focused on indigenization, 'a subject of significance to the social work profession and the social work programme, related to the programme's mission, goals and object' (CSWE, 2008: 1):

> A focus on indigenization is a departure from a multicultural focus, within which a western base may pervade all other cultures. Indigenization means defining an identity and mission relative to the community to which the academy is accountable. In Hawai'i, we are accountable to Pacific constituencies that subscribe to divergent life philosophies. The primacy of the concepts of family and genealogy, propriety of traditional practices, wisdom of elders, intuitive intelligence, servant leadership, sense of place, environmental kinship and spirituality, collectivism, and restorative values over retribution are critical indigenous elements that support the sustainability of human well-being. We believe that these themes will guide us down a path to greater relevance – not only locally, but globally.

> The process of indigenization in an academic setting means developing and infusing new teaching and learning methods, which may include, e.g., offering courses co-taught by faculty and indigenous practitioners; a greater emphasis placed on 'collective' learning styles and the use of metaphor; the promotion of diverse and mixed research methods and indigenous ways of knowing, including participatory action methods; the development of new practicum opportunities at community-based non- government organizations; and a greater curricular emphasis placed on social policy and organic practices aimed at primary prevention. (MBTSSW, 2007: 81–3)

As a result of the faculty reaccreditation team's thorough and thoughtful report preparation, in 2009, both the BSW and MSW programmes received a full eight-year reaccreditation from the Council on Social Work Education, which is valid until 2018. CSWE's approval allows the school to explore and develop indigenization as a central tenet of the social work programme.

Defining Indigenization: A Transformative Process

One of the most difficult aspects of indigenization at MBTSSW was arriving at a definition that took account of purpose and process. The notion of indigenizing education within US academies has gained some momentum in the last 15 years, and, at the time of our exploration, was associated largely with environmental sustainability (Baines et al., 2003; Bowers, 1997a, 1997b, 2001; Jull, 2003; Korten, 2006). As early as 1972 onwards, social work educators internationally and nationally continued to recognize the importance of indigenization as a means of developing culturally relevant practice (Anucha, 2008; Cheung, 2007; Midgley, 1981; Nimmagadda and Cowger, 1999; Shawky, 1972; Yip, 2006; Yuen and Wang, 2002; see genealogy of the term in Gray and Coates, 2008: 13–29). More recent work by Māori, American Indian and Asian and Pacific Islander writers reaffirms the importance of indigenization by honouring and valuing cultural ways and explaining how Indigenous processes support cultural integrity, environmental resources and the re-empowerment of Indigenous Peoples (Gray et al., 2008; Kaomea, 2004; Mataira, 2006; Mataira, Matsuoka and Morelli, 2005; McGregor, 2004; McGregor, Morelli and Matsuoka, 2003; Wilson, 2004; Yang, 2004). In social work practice, current and former MBTSSW faculty members are among those who have made important contributions to the extensive literature focusing on various aspects of the intersection of culture and social work (Ka'opua, Gotay, Hannum and Bunghanoy, 2005; Mokuau, 2001; Morelli and Mataira, 2010).

In *holumua* discussions, the process of defining indigenization acknowledged that Indigenous scholars have long endured being ignored, discredited, suppressed and largely regarded as irrelevant or without merit by institutions and entities that hold sway (Mihesuah, 2004; Smith, 1999). It was, therefore, clear that our process of understanding and arriving at a working definition required Indigenous voices to form the foundation of, and redefine and add new dimensions to, our understanding of ways of knowing, practice and knowledge development in Indigenous social work.

MBTSSW's working definition of indigenization responds fully to the question of value and significance posed at the beginning of this chapter. Developed with guidance from the Kupuna Council and under the leadership of the Director of Indigenous Affairs, it was the subject of lengthy deliberation and critique. It now marks the way to address questions about the programme's progress in indigenizing and meeting standards of cultural relevance. While this is a major accomplishment, the challenges ahead are equally demanding.

Meeting the Challenges Ahead

From the beginning, a central goal for indigenizing social work education was recognition and inclusion of Indigenous and non-dominant paradigms of knowledge and practices with demonstrated effectiveness in dealing with social problems locally and internationally. One such endeavour, the Hawaiian Learning Program (HLP) taught in the MSW programme, was developed by Native Hawaiian social work instructors to integrate Native Hawaiian values, principles and practices into social work practice. The curriculum is an example of affirming the strengths of native and local people, actively changing oppressive practices, re-empowering communities to sustain themselves, and, thereby, contributing in significant ways to the development of social work knowledge and practice for local and international use. The HLP curriculum is taught by two seasoned Native Hawaiian MSWs, one of whom is a 'Living Treasure of Hawai`i', and requires a commitment on the part of students to engage and experience the essence of Native Hawaiian worldview, sense of place, values and cultural protocols related to respect, spirituality and healing, and to learn about how these ways may be applied in social work practice. The pedagogy is grounded in: (i) the `olelo no`eau (traditional saying, teaching), *'Ma ka hana, ka `ike'* (in the doing one learns, in doing comes knowledge); (ii) the importance of 'sense of place', as source of life, well-being, personal and collective identity, and more than can be explained verbally; (iii) teachings conveyed through *mo`olelo* (storytelling); and (iv) *kupuna* as bridges to understanding and activating knowledge. Students are involved in relationship building, that is, respectful interaction between themselves, faculty, community, culture and land and are asked to reach beyond the boundaries of their Western conceptualizations of well-being, spirituality and sustainable righteous living. This intensive course, offered initially to Native Hawaiian students, is currently open to all MSW students and is one example how the school is beginning to indigenize education.

While indigenization at the MBTSSW appears to be focused primarily on creating a complimentary curriculum or redeveloping the Western curriculum, a critical aspect of indigenization includes the recruitment and retention of students and faculty from underrepresented Indigenous groups, such as Native Hawaiians and Asian and Pacific region people. Recruitment and retention are longstanding and ongoing indigenization efforts within the University of Hawai`i though the complexities of this system-wide endeavour will not be discussed here. At the MBTSSW, students are among the most diverse on the UH Manoa campus. For example, the combined number of master's and doctoral students at MBTSSW (University of Hawai`i, 2011) is 53 per cent Asian and Pacific Islander and 30 per cent Caucasian as compared to the general population of graduate students at UH Manoa, which is 30 per cent Asian and Pacific Islander and 38.2 per cent Caucasian (Student Equity, Excellence and Diversity (SEED), 2011). The MBTSSW faculty (University of Hawai`i, 2011) is 74 per cent Asian and Pacific Islander (disaggregated: 26 per cent Native Hawaiian, 41 per cent Asian and 7 per cent other Pacific Islander) and 26 per cent Caucasian as compared to the larger UH Manoa campus, which is 60 per cent Caucasian and 31 per cent Asian and Pacific Islander (SEED, 2011). These figures obfuscate the fact that Native Hawaiians represent a mere 12.7 per cent of all UH Manoa graduate students, the lowest of all groups, and are among the lowest groups of minority faculty at 4.3 per cent. Thus, despite the diverse population of Hawai`i and efforts to indigenize the curriculum, Native Hawaiians and Asian-Pacific Islanders are underrepresented in the student body and faculty at UH Manoa.

In committing to the simultaneous challenges of indigenization, the school is realistically focusing on the work of specifically articulating the extent to which and how indigenization can take place within the curriculum, school policies and administrative practice. In November 2011, faculty identified five strategic priorities for the school: Global social justice; a 'Hawaiian place of learning' (HPL); collaboration; recruitment and retention; and technology development. These priorities align with the UH at Manoa's strategic plan (UH, 2011), which emphasizes the university's unique value as a 'Hawaiian place of learning' (HPL) contributing to a transformative teaching and learning environment. In light of the ways in which indigenization promotes and supports the 'lived values' of our Native Hawaiian homeland, faculty determined that integral to developing the school as a HPL was the need to:

1. Provide a rounding in Hawaiian history with particular attention to the historical trauma currently impacting on Native Hawaiian people.
2. Teach cultural competence with special attention to local cultures that make up our Hawaiian home and enhance current programming by offering specific courses on these diverse cultures, as well as ongoing infusion of ethnoculural content into each course in the school.
3. Create an inherently inclusive environment by providing opportunities for sharing and encouraging staff, faculty and students to explore and share their personal cultural histories.
4. Offer professional development for all (new) faculty members acknowledging the diversity of cultures unique to Hawai`i and giving special attention to the host culture.
5. Provide a variety of cultural resources to enhance cultural awareness.
6. Recognizes the critical importance of Place-Based Learning in our Hawaiian home and Native Hawaiian Peoples' connection to community, where, to be 'right' with our world is to keep our relationships with the sky, ocean, land, people and spirit-world true and honest.

Addressing all of these aspects, as well as evaluating indigenization outcomes, will not only be a most difficult undertaking with unforeseen challenges, it will also require continuous improvement and development. As Harvey (2003) advises, engaging in ethical and decolonizing behaviours, that is, acceptance and trust in Indigenous processes, requires transcending one's own perspectives and evolving toward culturally relevant meanings and ways of being. Whether we are truly able to meet these and other unforeseen challenges, only time will tell.

Transformative Lessons from Indigenization: Transformation in Progress

Our experience continues to teach us that the work of indigenizing social work education is a difficult, unpredictable journey with struggle, frustration and contention at every turn. Thinking about this experience and its relevance for other contexts, there is no single, prescribed path to indigenizing social work education.

AT MBTSSW, critical factors emerged as vital to sustaining the indigenization process; among the core lessons:

1. Indigenization must be established at the highest priority level in order to develop and deliver a socially just, competent, effective and culturally resonant social work education programme.
2. Social work educators need to be open to understanding the value of indigenization (how and why indigenization equates to social justice) and take leadership to educate others.
3. In order to continue developing and sustaining indigenization in social work, leadership needs to be inclusive and widespread, with leaders taking responsibility to educate others.
4. The quality, relevance and effectiveness of indigenized social work education must build in evaluation and renewal as part of the curriculum development process.

Unfortunately, leadership and momentum for valued proposals inevitably ebbs and flows with time and changing circumstances. Indigenous people knew this well, and provided their progeny with protocols to preserve their values, meaning and paths to well-being. The question is whether we can sustain the necessary long-term efforts to indigenize social work education successfully. Do we understand the significance of our indigeneity and remember that regardless of colour, creed or national background, we all originate from Indigenous ancestors and are all Indigenous to somewhere? Can we accept the challenge and responsibility to live in accord with Indigenous values and ways, which respect and honour the balance between and survival of all life forms on planet Earth? Do we understand fully what indigenization involves and are we willing to commit and do what it takes to indigenize social work education as a critical part of fulfilling that responsibility? The long-term answers to these questions will determine the ultimate fate of indigenization and our commitment to social justice at MBTSSW.

References

Anucha, U. (2008). Exploring a new direction for social work education and training in Nigeria. *Social Work Education*, 27(3), 229–42.

Blaisdell, K. and Mokuau, N. (1991). Kanaka Maoli: Indigenous Hawaiians. In N. Mokuau (ed.), *Handbook of Social Services for Asian and Pacific Islanders*. New York: Greenwood Press, 131–54.

Baines, J., McClintock, W., Taylor, N. and Buckenham, B. (2003). Using Local Knowledge. In H.A. Becker and Vanclay, F. (eds), *The International Handbook of Social Impact Assessment*. Cheltenham: Edward Elgar, 26–41.

Bowers, C.A. (1997a). Universities and the Culture of Denial. *The Culture Of Denial: Why the Environment Movement Needs a Strategy for Reforming*

Universities and Public Schools. New York: State University of New York Press, 35–93.

Bowers, C.A. (1997b). Rethinking the Ideological Foundations of an Educational Strategy. *The Culture of Denial: Why the Environment Movement Needs a Strategy for Reforming Universities and Public Schools*. New York: State University of New York Press, 95–142.

Bowers, C.A. (2001). *Elements of an Eco-Justice Curriculum: Educating for Eco-Justice and Community*. Athens, GA: The University of Georgia Press, 149–80.

Braun, K. and Browne, C. (1997). Cultural Values and Caregiving Patterns among Asian and Pacific Islander Americans. In D. Redbrun and McNamara, R. (eds), *Social Gerontology*. Westport, CT: Greenwood, 115–28.

Browne, C., Fong, R. and Mokuau, N. (1994). The mental health of Asian and Pacific Island elders: Implications for research and mental health administration. *Journal of Mental Health Administration*, 21(1), 52–9.

Cheung, J. (2007). Social work with Chinese characteristics: A study of the indigenization of social work education in China from a perspective of chaos theory. Unpublished doctoral thesis, University of Calgary, Canada.

Council on Social Work Education (CSWE). Commission on Accreditation. (2004). *Educational Policy and Accreditation Standards*. Alternative Reaffirmation: Compliance Audit and Project. Alexandria, VA: CSWE.

Council on Social Work Education (CSWE). Commission on Accreditation. (2008). *Educational Policy and Accreditation Standards*. Alternative Reaffirmation: Compliance and Audit Project. Alexandria, VA: CSWE.

Dominelli, L. (2010). Globalization, contemporary challenges and social work practice. *International Social Work*, 53(5), 599–612.

Fischer, J. (1973). *Interpersonal Helping: Emerging Approaches for Social Work Practice*. Springfield, IL: Charles C. Thomas.

Fischer, J. (1976). *The Effectiveness of Social Casework*. Springfield, IL: Charles C. Thomas.

Fischer, J. (1978). *Effective Casework Practice: An Eclectic Approach*. New York: McGraw-Hill.

Fong, R. and Mokuau, N. (1994). Not simply 'Asian Americans': Periodical literature review on Asians and Pacific Islanders. *Social Work*, 39(3), 298–305.

Gochros, H. and Fischer, J. (1980). *Treat Yourself to a Better Sex Life*. Englewood Cliffs, NJ: Prentice-Hall.

Gray, M. and Coates, J. (2008). From 'Indigenization' to Cultural Relevance. In M. Gray, Coates, J. and Yellow Bird, M. (eds), *Indigenous Social Work around the World: Towards Culturally Relevant Education and Practice*. Aldershot: Ashgate, 13–29.

Gray, M. and Coates, J. (2010). 'Indigenization' and knowledge development: Extending the debate. *International Journal of Social Work*, 53(5), 613–27.

Gray, M., Coates, J. and Yellow Bird, M. (eds). (2008). *Indigenous Social Work around the World: Towards Culturally Relevant Education and Practice.* Aldershot: Ashgate.

Harvey, G. (2003). Guesthood as ethical decolonising research method. *International Review for the History of Religions*, 50, 125–46.

Journal of Indigenous Voices in Social Work. (2010) [Online]. Available at: http://www.hawaii.edu/sswork/jisd/jivsw.

Jull, P. (2003). The Politics of Sustainable Development: Reconciliation in Indigenous hinterlands. In S. Jentoft, Minde, H. and Nilsen, R. (eds), *Indigenous Peoples: Resource Management and Global Rights.* Delft: Eburon Delft, 21–44.

Kaomea, J. (2004). Dilemmas of an Indigenous Academic: A Native Hawaiian Story. In K. Mutua and Swadener, B.B. (eds), *Decolonizing Research in Cross-Cultural Contexts: Critical Personal Narratives.* Albany: State University of New York Press, 27–44.

Ka'opua, L.S., Gotay, C.C., Hannum, M. and Bunghanoy, G. (2005). Adaptation to long- term prostate cancer survival: The perspective of elderly, Asian/Pacific Islander wives. *Health and Social Work*, 30(2), 145–54.

Korten, D.C. (2006). The Great Turning: From empire to earth community. *Yes! A Journal of Positive Futures*, 38, 12–18.

Mataira, P.J. (2006). *'Bridging the Gaps': Entrepreneurship, Enterprise and Education: the Revitalising of whanau Well-Being.* Auckland: Massey University, Albany Campus School Social Policy and Social Work.

Mataira, P.J., Matsuoka, J.K. and Morelli, P.T. (2005). Issues and processes in Indigenous research. *Hulili: Multidisciplinary Research on Hawaiian Well-Being*, 2(1), 35–45.

Matsuoka, J. (1991). Vietnamese Americans. In N. Mokuau (ed.), *Handbook of Social Services for Asian and Pacific Islanders.* New York: Greenwood Press, 117–30.

McGregor, D. (2004). Traditional Ecological Knowledge and Sustainable Development: Towards coexistence. In M. Blaser, Feit, H.A. and McRae, G. (eds), *In the Way of Development: Indigenous Peoples, Life Projects and Globalization.* Ottawa: Zed Books, 72–91.

McGregor, D.P., Morelli, P.T. and Matsuoka, J. K. (2003). An Ecological Model of Well-Being. In H.A. Becker and Vanclay, F. (eds), *The International Handbook of Social Impact Assessment.* Cheltenham: Edward Elgar, 108–26.Midgley, J. (1981). *Professional Imperialism: Social Work in the Third World.* London: Heinemann.

Mihesuah, D.A. (2004). Academic Gatekeepers. In D.A. Mihesuah and Wilson, A.C. (eds), *Indigenizing the Academy: Transforming Scholarship and Empowering Communities.* Lincoln: University of Nebraska Press, 31–47.

Mokuau, N. (1986). Human sexuality of native Hawaiians and Samoans. *Journal of Social Work and Human Sexuality*, 4(3), 67–80.

Mokuau, N. (1995). Pacific Islanders. In *Cultural Competence for Social Workers: A Guide for Alcohol and Other Drug Abuse Prevention Professionals Working with Ethnic/Racial Communities, Series 4*. U.S. Department of Health and Human Services, Substance Abuse and Mental Health Services Administration.

Mokuau, N. and Chang, N. (1991). Samoans. In N. Mokuau (ed.), *Handbook of Social Services for Asian and Pacific Islanders*. New York: Greenwood Press, 155–70.Mokuau, N., Hishinuma, E. and Nishimura, S. (2001). Validating a measure of religiousness/spirituality for Native Hawaiians. *Pacific Health Dialog: Journal of Community Health and Clinical Medicine for the Pacific*, 8(2), 407–16.

Morelli, P. and Mataira, P. (2010). Indigenizing evaluation research: A long-awaited paradigm. *Journal of Indigenous Voices in Social Work*, 1(2), 1–12.

Myron B. Thompson School of Social Work (MBTSSW). (2007). Indigenization and the University of Hawai`i at Mānoa School of Social Work: Exploring and developing concepts, processes and applications. Alternative Reaffirmation Project. Proposal submitted to the Council on Social Work Education Commission on Accreditation. Mānoa: School of Social Work.

Nimmagadda, J. and Cowger, C.D. (1999). Cross-cultural practice: Social worker ingenuity in the indigenization of practice knowledge. *International Social Work*, 42(3), 261–76.

Puku`i, M.K. (1983). `Ōlelo *No`eau: Hawaiian Proverbs and Poetical Sayings*. Honolulu: Bishop Museum Press.

Puku`i, M.K. and Elbert, S.H. (1986). *Hawaiian Dictionary*. Honolulu: University of Hawai`i Press.

Puku`i, M.K., Haertig, E.W. and Lee, C.A. (1979). *Nānā i ke kumu (Look to the Source)*. Honolulu: Hui Hānai.

Sanders, D.S. (ed.). (1982). *The Developmental Perspective in Social Work*. Honolulu: University of Hawaii School of Social Work.

Sanders, D.S. and Fischer, J. (1988). *Visions for the Future: Social Work and Pacific-Asian Perspectives*. Honolulu: University of Hawai`i School of Social Work.

Sanders, D.S. and Matsuoka, J.K. (1989). *Peace and Development: An Interdisciplinary Perspective*. Honolulu: University of Hawaii School of Social Work.

Student Equity, Excellence and Diversity (SEED). (2011). Newsletter. *Ethnic Diversity of UH Students*. December 2011. Honolulu: University of Hawai`i.

Takeuchi, D., Mokuau, N. and Chun, C. (1992). Mental health services for Asian Americans and Pacific Islanders. *Journal of Mental Health Administration*, 19(3), 237–45.

Shawky, A. (1972). Social work education in Africa. *International Social Work*, 15(1), 3–16.

Smith, L.T. (1999). Towards Developing Indigenous Methodologies: Kaupapa Maori research. In *Decolonizing Methodologies: Research and Indigenous Peoples*. Dunedin: University of Otago Press, 183–95.

University of Hawai`i School of Social Work (UHSSW). (2005–06). *Bulletin*. Honolulu: University of Hawai`i.

University of Hawai`i. (2011). *Achieving Our Destiny: University of Hawai`i at Manoa 2011–2015 Strategic Plan*. Honolulu: University of Hawai`i.

Untalan, F. (1991). Chamorros. In N. Mokuau (ed.), *Handbook of Social Services for Asian and Pacific Islanders*. New York: Greenwood Press, 171–82.

Wilson, A.C. (2004). Reclaiming Our Humanity: Decolonization and the recovery of Indigenous knowledge. In D.A. Mihesuah and Wilson, A.C., *Indigenizing the Academy: Transforming Scholarship and Empowering Communities*. Lincoln: University of Nebraska Press, 69–87.

Yang, H. (2004). Editor's Reflections: Academic Indigenization. *Peace and Conflict Studies* 11(1), 96–100.

Yip, K. (2006). Developing social work students' reflectivity in cultural indigenization of mental health practice. *Reflective Practice*, 7(3), 393–403.

Yuen-Tsang, A.W.K. and Wang, S. (2002). Tensions confronting the development of social work education in China: Challenges and opportunities. *International Social Work*, 45(3), 375–88.

Chapter 11

Challenging International Social Work Placements: Critical Questions, Critical Knowledge

Samantha Wehbi

Several authors contend that with the growing cultural diversity of Western societies comes the responsibility for social service providers to better prepare themselves to engage with their culturally diverse clients (Boyle and Barranti, 1999; John et al., 2003; Marmen and Delisle, 2003; Rebolloso Pacheco et al., 2003). Hokenstad, Khinduka and Midgley (1992: 187) note in their discussion of international social work, practitioners need to recognize that ethnic heterogeneity is 'the norm, not the exception'. As such, Nagy and Falk (2000: 57) argue 'the minimum requirement is that social workers should be prepared to work locally in an increasingly multicultural society'. International placements potentially contribute to this preparation by providing students with the opportunity to broaden their cultural horizons (Boyle, Nackerud and Kilpatrick, 1999; Pawar, Hanna and Sheridan, 2004; Webber, 2005). Moreover, as the discussion about the internationalization of social work continues to unfold, the important place of international placements is reaffirmed (Caragata and Sanchez, 2002; Healy, 2001; Pettys et al., 2005). This chapter aims to contribute to the discussion on the internationalization of social work education through a critical examination of international student placements. Specifically, it argues that exploration of students' initial choice to undertake overseas placements is crucial if the internationalization of social work is to avoid reproducing inequitable North–South power relations. As Razack (2000) and Drucker (2003) argue, efforts to internationalize social work must take into account these relations characterized by a history of colonialism and current-day imperialist practices.

The ideas presented in this chapter are based upon my reflections as a social work practitioner and researcher in Canada and in Southern contexts, including my own country of origin, Lebanon. Importantly, the ideas in this chapter are based on my ongoing involvement as an educator in Canada preparing students for international placements. Given social work's critically reflective approach, it is important to provide students with opportunities to examine their motivations for undertaking international placements critically *before* embarking on their travels in order to avoid to the maximum extent possible the reproduction of oppressive power relations. Given appropriate preparation, including critical knowledge on international social work, this chapter asserts the positive potential of international placements and social work practice taking account of and aiming to counter oppressive North–South relations.

Literature Review

In light of their increasing importance in social work education, there is a burgeoning scholarship on international field placements, even though this has mostly focused on the technical aspects of the experience. This literature has focused on three main areas: descriptions of international placement programmes, the links between cross-cultural competence and international placements, and students' reflections on their international experience. There is a growing US literature on the practicalities and mechanics involved in establishing international placement programmes (for example, Johnson, 2004; Panos, 2005; Panos et al., 2004; Pettys et al., 2005; Rai, 2004). Pettys et al. (2005) surveyed 21 schools of social work in the USA and found most students wanting an international placement were single, female, US citizens with emotional ties to the foreign country. Rai's (2004) study of 25 US schools found most students wanting to do an international placement had some overseas experience or friends or family in the destination country. Hence, given that international placements are seen primarily as vehicles for enhancing cross-cultural competence and communication, it is interesting to note those choosing international placements already had some overseas experience or friends or family in the destination country (for example, Boyle et al., 1999; Puig and Glynn, 2003; Traub-Werner et al., 2000). However, there is little critical analysis of cross-cultural competence in these accounts, a point I return to later in this chapter. Rather, their emphasis stayed at the descriptive level focusing on cultural norms and 'etiquette'. There is some agreement that the social work literature on cultural competence presumes a static notion of culture such that culture can be learned without immersion in particular ways of life (Gray, Coates and Yellow Bird., 2008; Park, 2005; Williams, 2006). Not only does this reinforce cultural stereotypes but the focus on culture has also replaced political discussions of race (Park, 2005). There is little critical analysis of power imbalances within and between cultures (Basu, 2004; Wong et al., 2003). Little attention is paid to issues of racism and white privilege, given the typical white student going on international field placements (Razack, 2002a).

A final area of emphasis in the literature on international field placements is students' experiences upon their return (for example, Heron, 2005; Pawar et al., 2004). In many international placement programmes the emphasis is on 'debriefing' and 're-entry issues' for returning students. Thinking critically about these issues and moving beyond discussions of 'reverse culture shock', Heron (2005) points to the need to integrate an analysis of globalization and colonialism in the debriefing sessions offered to returning students from international placements in sub-Saharan Africa. Students are given a framework to make sense of their experiences upon their return. However, this critical framework is important to impart to students prior to embarking on placement and not only once they are back home. Such a critical understanding of international social work requires an interrogation of social work's colonizing history and the imposition of Western social work on diverse cultures which is intensifying in this globalized era as seen in the international definition of social work and global education standards. As Gray and Webb (2008: 64) note, the rise of the discourse of global standards and definitions of social work betrays a lack of consideration of 'the dangers of applying liberal Eurocentric ideals'. Indeed, the motivations of students undertaking international placements need to be considered within this overall critical framework for interrogating social work's role and mission (Drucker, 2003).

Student Motivations for Undertaking International Placements

There is little critical discussion on students' motivations for international placements. Yet, considering social work's implication in perpetuating colonial and neocolonial discourses, 'critical attention is needed to how we teach global issues' (Razack, 2009: 9). In the face of over-emphasis of technical issues and the mechanics of international placements in the scholarship, there is a need to explore under-researched areas, such as the ways in which international students are received in the foreign country, their motivation for undertaking international placements and the impact of their placements on host organizations (Button et al., 2005; Goldstein and Kim, 2006; Lough, 2009). In reflecting on this gap and focusing on student motivations, I would suggest four possible reasons why social work students choose to undertake international placements (see Wehbi, 2009):

1. Fascination with other cultures.
2. Liking people of another country.
3. Making a difference.
4. Giving something back to their countries/cultures of origin.

Reason 1: Fascination with Other Cultures

In her study of social work students undertaking international placements, Barlow (2007: 246) notes that in their applications students express being 'drawn to wonder and mystery' of another culture. Fascination with other cultures could, potentiality, result in learning and reduce insularity within the profession. However, without critical awareness of social work's colonizing history, these placements could perpetuate cultural imperialism given the flow of students from North to South (Lough, 2009; Razack, 2002b). For example, one of my students who had completed an international placement in England commented that, unlike her classmates who had gone to Africa, she had not been in an 'exotic locale'. The culture of the 'other' is packaged as an exotic commodity to be consumed over a typically short period. In this sense, culture is understood as a simple combination of ingredients and mistakenly seen as characterizing an entire country (and sometimes continent): language, dress, music, food, religious customs and family structures among others (Narayan, 1997). In other cases, the culture of the 'other' is reified. For example, some students from former British colonies expressed their preference for doing an international placement in a Northern country fuelled by a fascination with the colonizers' cultures.

Because it is based on an unquestioned interest in other cultures, any information gained about international practice will be limited and will have the potential to reinforce oppressive relations. A pre-departure preparation programme would do well to integrate a component of critical self-reflection on the student's own cultural background through the lens of white privilege and anti-racism (Frankenberg, 1993; Williams, 1999). It is important to encourage students to problematize descriptive notions of culture and to seek an understanding of how power operates in defining cultural norms and relations between cultural groups. By providing students with a space to reflect critically on where their interest in other cultures may stem from and how a narrow conception of culture may in fact reinforce a limited understanding of culture, they might challenge misconceptions about international practice and gain more from their learning experience.

Reason 2: Liking People of Another Country

A second reason for undertaking international placements as expressed by some of my students is that they 'like' people of a particular country. This benevolent motivation is problematic in more ways than one. First, there may be an assumption of homogeneity that conceives of everyone from that country as being similar. The student expressing this sentiment might have had prior positive contacts with some individuals from this country, but this positive experience is shaped by intersecting social relations dependent on the social location of the student and her or his interlocutors. For example, the positive connection might be due to class or race affinities or due to the interplay of gender and sexual orientation. Or, this positive contact might have occurred in a tourist resort. This type of relationship is clearly not representative of all possible relationships that might be had in this country, but can be deceptive in making an unquestioning student think that she or he has established a good relationship with the 'locals'.

This reason may also reflect an ethnocentrism that neglects to critically examine the relationship between the student and the people she or he claims to like. Unequivocally, relationships as individuals are shaped by inequitable histories and contemporary practices between countries, ethnic groups and religious sects. It may simply be that the people the student claims to like may not like her or him back because of these inequitable practices. Any amount of 'goodwill' or benevolence may not transform a relationship marred by a history of colonial or other exploitative relations.

Preparation programmes for students undertaking international placements need to begin with knowledge and awareness of social work's colonizing history and the injustices perpetuated, not only in other parts of the world but also at home. In Canada, for example, Aboriginal people's experiences of social work are highly ambivalent, considering a history of colonization the impacts of which continue today in social work practices – a prominent example concerns child welfare (MacDonald and Attaran, 2007). This type of critical examination is a crucial part of the international placement experience because it has the potential to assist students in understanding the positive role they could potentially play in resisting oppressive conditions at home and abroad (Abram, Slosar and Wells, 2005).

Reason 3: Making a Difference

A third reason motivating some students to undertake an international placement is the perception that practising in another country would be more interesting than practising locally and would be a place where they could make a difference (Magnus, 2009). Once more, the idea that some places are more exotic than others and hence more interesting comes into play. Underlying this perception is the idea of 'us and them' that has been created between cultures. As Said (1978, 1993) argued in his explorations of inequitable North–South historical relations, colonizing nations have had the privilege of imposing on other nations an exotic image of adventure and exploration, and this image has invariably accompanied imperialism.

Students sometimes link their interest in another, typically Southern, country to the idea that they can 'make a difference' in an international placement whereas they would not be able to do this in a local placement. This reason hints at the charity perspective that has permeated the history of social work within North–South relations (Abram et al., 2005; Moldovan and Mayo, 2007). Hancock (1989: 19) argues that the danger in such a perspective is that it reinforces the belief that people in the South are 'fundamentally helpless victims of nameless crises, disasters and catastrophes, they can do nothing unless we, the rich and powerful, intervene to save them from themselves'. Chowdhry and Nair (2004) and Bush (2006) attribute this construction of powerlessness to colonialism and its views of Southern 'others' as inferior. Kapoor (2008) and Razack (2012) note that this historical construction continues today in practices of international development and aid. Moreover, such a perspective does not allow us to see how people use their agency to resist oppression (Wehbi, 2008). Ross-Sheriff (2006) provides an example in her critical study of Afghan women refugees. Her findings illustrate the many ways in which they used their individual agency actively to resist the injustices they were facing. A charity perspective does not allow students to work *with* communities but *for* them, thereby inadvertently reinforcing 'benevolent imperialism' (Razack, 2002b: 253) and missing out on opportunities to form alliances.

Moreover, the perception that social work students could make a difference 'elsewhere', and not 'here', renders invisible the interconnections between issues and the inequities that exist in the North as well. Social workers need look no further than the centuries of discriminatory treatment towards Indigenous Peoples in Canada, the USA and other Western nations. Globalization imposes the need to recognize the interconnections between North and South (Lyons, Manion and Carlsen, 2006; Midgley, 2000; Mohan, 2008). As Midgley (2000) and Mohan (2008) argued, globalization imposes the need for social workers to recognize the interconnections between North and South. Similarly, Lyons and colleagues (2006) prefaced their discussion of international social work with the assertion of the interconnectedness of local and global contexts and the need for social workers to ground their practice in an understanding of these interconnections. Hence, a local placement could afford students as much of an opportunity to make a contribution as would an international placement. However, it is also important to critically examine the idea that as individuals, social work students could make a difference. As such, a component of pre-departure preparation for students undertaking an international placement would be a critical exploration of the concepts of resistance, alliance-building and personal agency. Students could be encouraged to explore their expectations of their role and to critically examine the structural realities that circumscribe any contribution they could make. Far from calling for an abdication of personal responsibility, students should be given the opportunity to reflect critically on the extent of their agency before embarking on an international placement. In other words, students' perceptions of making a difference need to be deconstructed in ways that could help them to understand their own positionality in relation to the countries they are going to, their placement setting and broader North–South power relations.

Reason 4: Giving Something Back

Students with connections to the country where they want to do their placement talk of 'giving something back' to their countries of origin. Razack (2009) also notes that this is the case for students who enrol in international social work courses with the hope of being able to one day practice in their countries of origin. For me, the potential of 'giving back' to my country of origin was certainly an unquestioned assumption that I had to deconstruct over many years of practice. Simply put, we are not exempt from reproducing oppressive social relations by virtue of being originally from the country where we choose to practice.

At least two issues are important for students undertaking an international placement in their country of origin to reflect upon. First, it is important to help students reflect on how their positionality and connection to the North is likely to play out in their everyday relations. Students' own intersecting identities and positionalities along race, class, ethnicity, gender identity or other lines will situate them in historically specific ways within their countries of origin. In other words, their cultural affinities are not the only determinant of how their interventions will be received in their country of origin (Razack, 2009). Moreover, students may be seen as 'experts' whose knowledge trumps that of local residents simply by being Western educated. I have certainly been in situations in my country of origin where my Canadian education and residency status have granted me access to resources and treatment not available to my local colleagues, for example, being seen by funders as more of an 'expert' than my local colleagues on the local issues they deal with on a daily basis. Students' awareness – or lack thereof – of such differential treatment and how they deal with it is important in reinforcing or challenging potentially oppressive relations.

A second issue worthy of reflection is the dichotomization inadvertently reinforced between those who conduct international placements in their countries of origin and those seeking international placements in another country. At the beginning of a course on international social work, a white Canadian student asked me whether she believed a person could practise internationally in a country not their own, as she had been planning on going to Bangladesh. The underlying notion that those who were practising 'back home' could be better practitioners or would automatically have an anti-oppressive approach by virtue of being 'from there', did not necessarily allow for the building of genuine alliances or partnerships across cultural contexts. Putting aside for the moment earlier critiques of the idea of personal contribution, cultural heritage was not a guarantee that a student would be able to 'give something back'. Hence, a pre-departure preparation programme could engage all students in a reflection on how they are positioned in relation to the community where they would be practising and what this concretely might mean for their potential contributions and involvement.

Future Directions: Critical Knowledge for International Social Work

This chapter has argued for the need for students to examine their motivations to undertake an international placement in order to help prevent practices inadvertently reinforcing oppressive North–South relations. These arguments have implications for research and teaching in social work. More research is needed on the motivations behind international social work, as this could provide students with a reflective space in which to interrogate their reasons for seeking and undertaking international placements.

Along with continued research on international placements and student motivations, the field could be strengthened with the development of core critical knowledge areas integrated within specific courses (for example international social work or international practicum seminars) or the overall curriculum to guide teaching of international social work. The current preponderance of texts on international social work seems to place the emphasis on building students' knowledge of the internationalization of the profession, key international issues and how social work is practised in various cultural contexts (Cox and Pawar, 2006; Healy, 2001; Healy and Link, 2012; Lyons et al., 2006; Tice and Long,

2009). This is indeed important knowledge for students especially those from Northern contexts where social work has had a specific history of development that has varied across cultural contexts even within the North. The issues facing the profession, the need to internationalize, the relationship of social workers to international institutions and the social issues tackled will differ in other contexts where social work may be a young profession or not a profession at all. Students need to be made aware of these potential differences and alerted to the uniqueness of social work in relation to its cultural context. However, in addition to this available literature, much more scholarship is needed on a critical discussion of social work education for students interested in international social work (Haug, 2005). Specifically, the proposed critical knowledge areas for curriculum development would include not only a focus on international social issues, how the profession is organized and the issues facing social workers, but also on three core knowledge areas (see also Wehbi, 2008):

1. Knowledge of context of social issues, interventions and positionality of the social worker.
2. Knowledge of a politicized understanding of culture beyond cultural competence.
3. Knowledge of colonization and imperialism and their impacts as well as their links to social work.

Knowledge of Context

Critical practice hinges on the student social worker's ability to reflect on positionality vis à vis the placement context. Considering the impact of the broader context on social work, teaching about international issues must make room for these discussions (Anderson, 2006; Saleebey and Scanlon, 2005). However, current discussions of context within social work are often reduced to depoliticized understandings of 'cultural diversity'. As Bannerji (2000) notes, increased reliance on the concept of diversity has served the purpose of stripping away power differences from social relations, while maintaining distinctions between social groups. In other words, while there is recognition of diversity (for example, cultural diversity), there is no understanding that with this diversity come differences in access to power and privilege within a specific context.

A critical curriculum would introduce students to the social, economic, political, cultural and environmental context of their anticipated international placement. To address this question critically, this curriculum would begin from an understanding of how definitions of social work differ across contexts. As Gray and Fook (2004: 626) argue, approaches to practice vary across nations and, as such, our understanding of social work must be 'much more contextually oriented'. In addition, Webb (2003) cautions that there seems to be an erroneous and problematic belief within the scholarship that assumes a unified global framework of social work knowledge, perspectives, practice and values. Concretely, students would be encouraged to shed the assumption that the social work they had been taught would automatically be applicable across contexts and would need to conduct a thorough literature review of social work in the country to which they are going. Furthermore, examining this aspect of context means paying attention to the organizational contexts of practice and the relationship between the state and social workers, or those carrying out social work functions, whether or not they are in fact called 'social workers'.

In order to view these aspects critically, and reflect on their possible impact on interventions within the placement, students would be encouraged to develop an understanding of positionality, that is, on how the various elements of their personal and professional identity can have an impact on practice. Rather than an understanding limited to an additive description of elements of social location, such as class, gender identity, sexual orientation and so on, the social work educator's challenge is to push students further to a critical understanding, rather than simplistic insider-outsider frameworks. Such cultural essentialism fails to take account of the complexity of people's positionality and cultural affiliations within the broader sociopolitical context. People are always 'in relation' to a specific issue or in a specific context, never simply insiders or outsiders (Abu Lughod, 1991), and this relation has a crucial impact on the choice of appropriate social work intervention. Hence Razack (2009) notes that the complexity of positionalities and identities in transnational societies render social work discussions about intervention and how social workers are positioned in relation to international practice more nuanced. In other words, discussions of power across nations and peoples cannot simply be reduced to simplified – homogenized – stereotypes about the North or the South. A critical knowledge base would introduce students to the operation of power not only across, but also within nations based on historical and contemporary practices related to differences in sexual orientation, gender identity, race, religion, ethnicity and culture among other lines.

Knowledge of Culture beyond Cultural Competence

A critical perspective on international social work would alert students to their potential to reinforce cultural imperialism, 'othering' and a superficial understanding of culture (Asamoah, Healy and Mayadas, 1997; Basu, 2004; Said, 1993, 1997; Wong et al., 2003). Much discussion of culture has assumed a conception of culture as stable and monolithic (Dean, 2001; Ife, 2000; Wong et al., 2003). Park (2005) and Pon (2009) claim static and monolithic conceptions of culture amount to a new form of racism. Dean (2001: 624) notes the prominence of this framework in social work and critiques it as a 'flawed' understanding that assumes that social workers could develop competence in a culture other than their own. For her, this understanding reflects a 'belief that knowledge brings effectiveness and control [in practice]'.

A critical understanding of culture would alert students to unequal power relations and the context of culture within cross-cultural and international social work practice (Magnus, 2009; Tsang and George, 1998). Such an understanding of the context would require students to be constantly aware of their lack of competence as opposed to assuming that a culture can be known and that social workers could develop competence in this regard (Dean, 2001, see also Chapter 4). Being aware of their own lack of competence, students can be reminded that knowing a culture is never a fully accomplished feat as culture is ever-changing. Hence, instead of being taught the cultural customs and assumed norms of a particular culture as static 'knowns', students need to become aware of how cultural information is rooted within specific historical and contemporary conditions and social relations. Such knowledge would include a discussion not only of social differences within a particular culture (for example, such as those based on class) but is also inextricably linked to colonialism and imperialism and their impacts on culture.

Knowledge of Colonization and Imperialism

Another core area is critical knowledge of colonization and its historical and ongoing impact in inequitable North–South practices and relations, as well as the impact of globalization, and internationalizing forces within social work itself (Webb, 2003). There are tensions in developing locally relevant interventions in a profession which claims commonality across contexts (Gray and Fook, 2004). These tensions have been undergirded by assumptions of the universality and superiority of Western knowledge, social and cultural development and practice models. Abram et al. (2005), Midgley (2008) and Sewpaul (2006a) attribute these ideas to colonialism and imperialism and social work's involvement in these agendas.

A critical curriculum would introduce students to an understanding of the way in which Northern – foreign – aid and collaborations have been based historically on an individualistic charity perspective (Moldovan and Moyo, 2007) or to satisfy the wishes and needs of funders (Armstrong, 2004; Drucker, 2003; Kapoor, 2008; Markowitz and Tice, 2002) as opposed to genuine alliances promoting social justice. Philanthropic charity and foreign aid are politically infused and do not promote social justice especially since they are usually tied to conditions (Kapoor, 2008). An example of this has been the historical debt of the South combined with trade practices and structural adjustment programmes imposed by international financial institutions, such as the International Monetary Fund and the World Bank. Aid or loans are tied to conditionalities related to 'economic reforms', such as privatization, removal of 'trade barriers' and devaluation of currencies (Kawewe and Dibie, 2000; Manion, 2005; Polack, 2004; Sewpaul, 2006b).

Social work scholars have argued that this debt and current conditionalities are unjust and have inequitably served the interests of Northern countries and institutions (Manion, 2005; Polack, 2004). Moreover, Sewpaul (2006a) and Razack (2002b) contend that social work has played a role historically and in contemporary times in supporting colonial missions. This continues to be seen in

Northern social work's imperialist tendencies to assume a 'helping' or benevolent role in terms of international practice such as through placements or exchanges. Instead, Abram et al. (2005) note that international exchanges and placements should assist social work students to learn *from* the South about unjust North–South relations in order to resist 'professional imperialism' (173). In assisting with this learning, a critical knowledge base would include discussions of the need to adopt anti-colonial and decolonizing perspectives and approaches to social work. Briskman (2008), Lavallée (2009) and Baskin (2005) argue for a decolonizing approach to social work; this means the need to not only acknowledge social work's involvement in colonialism and imperialism but to also challenge the hegemony and assumed normativity of Western worldviews in social work theories, policy, research and practice.

Conclusion

This chapter has drawn out some of the concepts at the heart of the decolonization project through the examination of international students placements. A critical curriculum shifts the emphasis from how students can 'give back' or 'rescue' to what students need to learn about their nuanced and complex place in the nexus of North–South power relations and social work intervention as well as the potential role they could realistically play as allies. This is a crucial issue in decolonizing social work. The ideas presented in this chapter urge educators to believe in the potential of their students to contribute to resisting oppression. In so doing, they need to find ways and create spaces to assist students in critically examining their motivations for international placements and to provide a critical knowledge base from which to practice. Such a critical knowledge base is surely needed if we are to shift discourses surrounding international placements from helping and learning to be culturally competent to discourses of anti-colonialism, decolonization and global social justice.

References

Abram, F.Y., Slosar, J.A., and Wells, R. (2005). Reverse mission: A model for international social work education and transformative intra-national practice. *International Social Work*, 48(2), 161–76.

Abu-Lughod, L. (1991). Writing against Culture. In R.G. Fox (ed.), *Recapturing Anthropology: Working in the Present*. Santa Fe: School of American Research Press, 137–62.

Anderson, D.K. (2006). Mucking through the swamp: Changing the pedagogy of a social welfare policy course. *Journal of Teaching in Social Work*, 26(1/2), 1–17.

Armstrong, E. (2004). Globalization from below: AIDWA, foreign funding, and gendering anti-violence campaigns. *Journal of Developing Societies*, 20(1/2), 39–55.

Asamoah, Y., Healy, L.M. and Mayadas, N. (1997). Ending the international-domestic dichotomy: New approaches to a global curriculum for the millennium. *Journal of Social Work Education*, 33(2), 389–402.

Bannerji, H. (2000). The paradox of diversity: Construction of a multicultural Canada and 'women of color'. *Women's Studies International Forum*, 23(5), 537–60.

Barlow, C.A. (2007). In the third space: A case study of Canadian students in a social work practicum in India. *International Social Work*, 50(2), 243–54.

Baskin, C. (2005). Centring Aboriginal worldviews in social work education. *The Australian Journal of Indigenous Education*, 34, 96–106.

Basu, S. (2004). AIDS, empire and public health behaviorism. *International Journal of Health Services*, 34(1), 155–67.

Boyle, D.P. and Barranti, C. (1999). A model for international continuing education: Cross-cultural experiential professional development. *Professional Development: The International Journal of Continuing Social Work Education*, 2(2), 57–62.

Boyle, D.P., Nackerud, L. and Kilpatrick, A. (1999). The road less traveled: Cross-cultural, international experiential learning. *International Social Work*, 42(2), 201–14.

Briskman, L. (2008). Decolonizing Social Work in Australia: Prospect or illusion. In Gray, M., Coates, J. and Yellow Bird, M. (eds), *Indigenous Social Work around the World: Towards Culturally Relevant Education and Practice*. Aldershot: Ashgate, 83–93.

Bush, B. (2006). *Imperialism and Post-Colonialism. History: Concepts, Theories and Practice*. Toronto: Pearson Education Limited.

Button, L., Green, B., Tengnah, C., Johansson, I. and Baker, C. (2005). The impact of international placements on nurses' personal and professional lives: Literature review. *Journal of Advanced Nursing*, 50(3), 315–24.

Caragata, L. and Sanchez, M. (2002). Globalization and global need: The new imperatives for expanding international social work education in North America. *International Social Work*, 45(2), 217–38.

Chowdhry, G. and Nair, S. (2004). Introduction: Power in a Post-Colonial World: Race, gender, and class in international relations. In G. Chowdhry and Nair, S. (eds), *Power, Post-Colonialism and International Relations: Reading Race, Gender and Class*. New York: Routledge, 1–32.

Cox, D. and Pawar, M. (2006). 2006. *International Social Work: Issues, Strategies, and Programs*. New Delhi: Sage.

Dean, R. (2001). The myth of cross cultural competence. *Families in Society: The Journal of the Contemporary Human Services*, 82(6), 623–30.

Drucker, D. (2003). Wither international social work? A reflection. *International Social Work*, 46(1), 53–81.

Frankenberg, R. (1993). *White Women, Race Matters: The Social Construction of Whiteness*. Minneapolis, MN: University of Minnesota Press.

Goldstein, S.B. and Kim, R.I. (2006). Predictors of US college students' participation in study abroad programs: A longitudinal study. *International Journal of Intercultural Relations*, 30, 507–21.

Gray, M., Coates, J. and Yellow Bird, M. (eds). (2008). *Indigenous Social Work around the World: Towards Culturally Relevant Education and Practice*. Burlington, VT: Ashgate.

Gray, M. and Fook, J. (2004). The quest for a universal social work: Some issues and implications. *Social Work Education*, 23(5), 625–44.

Gray, M. and Webb, S.A. (2008). The myth of global social work: Double standards and the local-global divide. *Journal of Progressive Human Services*, 19(1), 61–6.

Hancock, G. (1989). *Lords of Poverty: The Power, Prestige, and Corruption of the International Aid Business*. New York: Atlantic Monthly Press.

Haug, E. (2005). Critical reflections on the remerging discourse of international social work. *International Social Work*, 48(2), 126–35.

Healy, L.M. (2001). *International Social Work: Professional Action in an Interdependent World*. New York: Oxford University Press.

Healy, L.M. and Link, R.J. (2012). *Handbook of International Social Work: Human Rights, Development and the Global Profession*. New York: Oxford University Press.

Heron, B. (2005). Changes and challenges: Preparing social work students for practicums in today's sub-Saharan African context. *International Social Work*, 48(6), 782–93.

Hokenstad, M.C., Khinduka, S.K. and Midgley, J. (1992). Social Work Today and Tomorrow: An international perspective. In M.C. Hokenstad, Khinduka, S.K. and Midgley, J. (eds), *Profiles in International Social Work*. Washington, DC: NASW Press, 181–93.

Ife, J. (2000). Localized needs and a globalized economy: Bridging the gap with social work practice. Social Work and Globalisation: Special Issue of *Canadian Social Work*, 2(1), 50–64.

John, L., Wehbi, S., Caputo, A., Moretti, J. and Mosticyan, S. (2003). Évaluation de l'opinion du personnel en ce qui concerne les initiatives de programmes pour faciliter l'accessibilité aux services de la santé par les clients provenant des communautés ethnoculturelles. *Intervention*, 118, 106–16.

Johnson, A.K. (2004). Increasing internationalization in social work programs: Healey's continuum as a strategic planning guide. *International Social Work*, 47(1), 7–23.

Kapoor, I. (2008). *The Post-Colonial Politics of Development*. New York: Routledge.

Kawewe, S. and Dibie, R. (2000). The impact of Economic Structural Adjustment Programs (ESAPs) on women and children: *Implications for social welfare in Zimbabwe. Journal of Sociology and Social Welfare*, 27(4), 79–107.

Lavallée, L.F. (2009). Practical application of an Indigenous research framework and two qualitative Indigenous research methods: Sharing circles and Anishnaabe symbol-based reflection. *Social Work Publications and Research*. Paper 3 [Online]. Available at: http://digitalcommons.ryerson.ca/socialwork/3.

Lough, B.J. (2009). Principles of effective practice in international social work field placements. *Journal of Social Work Education*, 45(3), 467–79.

Lyons, K., Manion, L.K. and Carlsen, M. (2006) *International Perspectives on Social Work: Global Conditions and Local Practice*. New York: Palgrave Macmillan.

MacDonald, N. and Attaran, A. (2007). The Jordan Principle, governments' paralysis. *Canadian Medical Association Journal*, 177(4), 321.

Magnus, P. (2009). Preparation for social work students to do cross-cultural clinical practice. *International Social Work*, 52(3), 375–85.

Manion, K. (2005). A global perspective on intellectual property rights: A social work view. *International Social Work*, 48(1), 77–87.

Markowitz, L. and Tice, K.W. (2002). Paradoxes of professionalization: Parallel dilemmas in women's organizations in the Americas. *Gender & Society*, 16(6), 941–58.

Marmen, L. and Delisle, S. (2003). Les soins de santé en français à l'extérieur du Québec. *Tendances Sociales Canadiennes*, 71, 27–31.

Midgley, J. (2000). Globalization, capitalism and social welfare: A social development perspective. *Canadian Social Work*, 2(10, 13–28.

Midgley, J. (2008). Promoting Reciprocal International Social Work Exchanges: Professional imperialism revisited. In M. Gray, Coates, J. and Yellow Bird, M. (eds), *Indigenous Social Work around the World: Towards Culturally Relevant Education and Practice*. Aldershot: Ashgate, 31–45.

Mohan, B. (2008). Rethinking international social work. *International Social Work*, 51(1), 11–24.

Moldovan, V. and Moyo, O. (2007). Contradictions in the ideologies of helping: Examples from Zimbabwe and Moldova. *International Social Work*, 50(4), 461–72.

Nagy, G. and Falk, D.S. (2000). Dilemmas in international and cross-cultural social work education. *International Social Work*, 43(1), 49–60.

Narayan, U. (1997). *Dislocating Cultures: Identities, Traditions, and Third World Feminism*. New York: Routledge.

Panos, P.T. (2005). A model for using videoconferencing technology to support international social work field practicum students. *International Social Work*, 48(6), 834–41.

Panos, P.T., Pettys, G.L., Cox, S.E. and Jones-Hart, E. (2004). Survey of international field education placements of accredited social work education programs. *Journal of Social Work Education*, 40(3), 467–78.

Park, H. (2005). Culture as deficit: A critical discourse analysis of the concept of culture in contemporary social work discourse. *Journal of Sociology and Social Welfare*, 32(3), 11–33.

Pawar, M., Hanna, G. and Sheridan, R. (2004). International social work practicum in India. *Australian Social Work*, 57(3), 223–36.

Pettys, G.L., Panos, P.T., Cox, S.E. and Ooshthuysen, K. (2005). Four models of international field placement. *International Social Work*, 48(3), 277–88.

Polack, R.J. (2004). Social justice and the global economy: New challenges for social work in the twenty-first century. *Social Work*, 49(2), 281–90.

Pon, G. (2009). Cultural competency as new racism: An ontology of forgetting. *Journal of Progressive Human Services*, 20(1), 59–71.

Puig, M.E. and Glynn, J.B. (2003). Disaster responders: A cross-cultural approach to recovery and relief work. *Journal of Social Service Research*, 30(2), 55–66.

Rai, G.S. (2004). International fieldwork experience: A survey of US schools. *International Social Work*, 47(2), 213–26.

Razack, N. (2000). North/South collaborations: Affecting transnational perspectives for social work. *Journal of Progressive Human Services*, 11(1), 71–91.

Razack, N. (2002a). Critical race discourse and tenets for social work. *Canadian Social Work Review*, 19(2), 257–71.

Razack, N. (2002b). A critical examination of international student exchanges. *International Social Work*, 45(2), 251–65.

Razack, N. (2009). Decolonizing the pedagogy and practice of international work. *International Social Work*, 52(1), 7–19.

Razack, N. (2012). Racism and Anti-Racist Strategies. In L.M. Healy and Link, R.J. (eds), *Handbook of International Social Work: Human Rights, Development and the Global Profession*. New York: Oxford University Press, 237–42.

Rebolloso Pacheco, E., Hernandez Plaza, S., Fernandez-Ramirez, B. and Canton Andrés, P. (2003). The implications of immigration for the training of social work professionals in Spain. *British Journal of Social Work*, 33(1), 49–65.

Ross-Sheriff, F. (2006). Afghan women in exile and repatriation: Passive victims or social actors? *Affilia*, 21(2), 206–19.

Said, E. (1978). *Orientalism*. New York: Pantheon Books.

Said, E.W. (1993). *Culture and Imperialism*. New York: Vintage Books.

Said, E.W. (1997). *Covering Islam: How the Media and the Experts Determine how We See the Rest of the World*. New York: Vintage.

Saleebey, D. and Scanlon, E. (2005). Is a critical pedagogy for the profession of social work possible? *Journal of Teaching in Social Work*, 25(3/4), 1–18.

Sewpaul, V. (2006a). Regional perspectives ... from Africa. *International Social Work*, 49(1), 129–36.

Sewpaul, V. (2006b). The global-local dialectic: Challenges for African scholarship and social work in a post-colonial world. *British Journal of Social Work*, 36(3), 419–34.

Tice, C.J. and Long, D.D. (eds). (2009) *International Social Work: Policy and Practice – Practical Insights and Perspectives*. Hoboken, NJ: John Wiley.

Traub-Werner, B., Shera, W., Villa, B.M.R. and Peon, N.T. (2000). International partnerships: A Mexico-Canada social work education project. *Canadian Social Work*, 2(1), 184–97.

Tsang, A.K.T. and George, U. (1998). Towards an integrated framework for cross-cultural social work practice. *Canadian Social Work Review*, 15(1), 73–93.

Webb, S.A. (2003). Local orders and global chaos in social work *European Journal of Social Work*, 6(2), 191–204.

Webber, R. (2005). Integrating work-based and academic learning in international and cross-cultural settings. *Journal of Education and Work*, 18(4), 473–87.

Wehbi, S. (2008). Teaching international social work: A guiding framework. *Canadian Social Work Review*, 25(2), 117–32.

Wehbi, S. (2009). Deconstructing motivations: Challenging international social work placements. *International Social Work*, 52, 48–59.

Williams, C. (1999). Connecting anti-racist and anti-oppressive theory and practice: Retrenchment or appraisal? *British Journal of Social Work*, 29(2), 211–30.

Williams, C.C. (2006). The epistemology of cultural competence. *Families in Society: The Journal of Contemporary Social Services*, 87(2), 209–20.

Wong, Y.R., Cheng, S., Choi, S., Ky, K., Leba, S., Tsang, K. and Yoo, L. (2003). Deconstructing culture in cultural competence: Dissenting voices from Asian-Canadian practitioners. *Canadian Social Work Review*, 20(2), 149–67.

Chapter 12

Building Bridges with Indigenous Communities through Social Work Education

Nicole G. Ives and Michael Thaweiakenrat Loft

During a trip north to the Inuit territory of Nunavik in 2008 to promote social work education to a secondary school, students were asked what they thought of when they heard the words 'social work'. The first response was 'run for your life!' What lies behind this response? Why is social work and, subsequently, social work education, reviled in Indigenous communities in Canada? And how might we support the development and implementation of culturally relevant social work practice with Indigenous Peoples? This chapter seeks to address this question by exploring ways in which schools of social work can facilitate relationship building with Indigenous communities in an educational context.

Social workers have engaged in destructive practices in the past, for example, in the 1960s when they were involved in removing Indigenous children from their homes against their will (referred to in Canada as the Sixties Scoop and similar to the Stolen Generations in Australia). In some communities, social work is still synonymous with the forcible removal of Indigenous children from their families. The delivery of child and family services in Canada is under provincial authority. Beginning in Ontario in 1990 with the Child and Family Services Act (Government of Ontario, 1990 and subsequent amendments in 1999 and 2006, explicit attempts were made to:

> recognize that Indian and native [*sic*] people should be entitled to provide, wherever possible, their own child and family services, and that all services to Indian and native [*sic*] children and families should be provided in a manner that recognizes their culture, heritage and traditions and the concept of the extended family 1999, c. 2, s. 1; 2006, c. 5, s. 1. (Government of Ontario, 1990, c. C. 11)

Similar changes followed in other provinces, such as in British Columbia with the Child, Family and Community Service Act in 1996 where provisions included that 'the cultural identity of Aboriginal children should be preserved' (Section 2(f)), 'Aboriginal people should be involved in the planning and delivery of services to Aboriginal families and their children' (Section 3(b)) and 'if the child is an Aboriginal child, the importance of preserving the child's cultural identity must be considered in determining the child's best interests' (Child and Family Services Information, Section 4(2), 2002). However, although provincial and territorial child welfare guidelines seek to honour cultural and family connections, if an Indigenous child must be removed from his or her home, these guidelines are not practised consistently across jurisdictions (Sinha and Kozlowski, 2013). Indigenous children continue to be overrepresented in the child welfare system in Canada (Trocmé, Knoke and Blackstock, 2004) and elsewhere (Tilbury, 2009). The gap in socioeconomic and health status between Indigenous and non-Indigenous Peoples is wide. While Canada ranked eighth on the United Nations Human Development Index in 2001, the Canadian Aboriginal population ranked thirty-second (Cooke et al., 2007). These realities continue the challenges facing social workers who practice in and with Indigenous communities. This chapter discusses a strategy for building bridges between Indigenous and non-Indigenous communities through social work education. It argues a lack of genuine, positive engagement between Indigenous and non-Indigenous Peoples has contributed to a deficiency in understanding contemporary issues facing Indigenous communities by those outside these communities, and to difficulties in moving forward in finding relevant, equitable solutions to these issues.

Importance of Context

Indigenous and non-Indigenous social work practitioners working with Indigenous individuals, families and communities need a comprehensive, grounded understanding of Indigenous Peoples in context: their histories and cultures and the political, economic, social, legal and health issues. There is multidimensionality in every community. Even if one were a member of a particular community, it would still be beneficial to have a contextual understanding of that community, acknowledging and working with multiple perspectives. The lack of this contextual knowledge could be ascribed to colonization, contemporary institutional structures and policies, and media, all creating barriers and nurturing cultural misconceptions and stereotyping for both Indigenous and non-Indigenous Peoples (Fenelon and Hall, 2008; Gray, Yellow Bird and Coates, 2008).

Social work programmes have been criticized for providing primarily a Eurocentric perspective that does not reflect political, social or cultural realities of Indigenous Peoples and does not prepare social work students adequately for working with Indigenous communities (Ives, Aitken, Loft and Phillips, 2007). Using what social workers think they 'know' about an individual, group or community as the basis for practice can be as harmful as having no contextual knowledge of that individual, group or community. It is not that Indigenous and non-Indigenous Peoples are unfamiliar with one another. In a historical sense, there is familiarity, but the 'knowledge' is overwhelmingly negative. Thus, more than bridge-building is required and in many, if not most cases, bridge-mending is needed. Mutual, genuine engagement is only possible with the recognition that historically, those bridges or connections with Indigenous Peoples were used to access Indigenous populations for the purpose of removing them from their lands, and thus from their traditional ways of living, which had the effect of decimating them (Paul, 2006; Richardson, 1993). Providing social work students with access to a curriculum which reflects Indigenous cultural and social realities, uses a range of pedagogical approaches, including the traditional ways of learning and knowing, involves guidance and teaching from community Elders, and is delivered in a community setting; such a curriculum will contribute to the decolonizing project of combating the structural oppression of Indigenous Peoples (Ives et al., 2007; Lee, 1992).

Before building bridges, self-reflection is important as it allows for a clearer understanding regarding the social worker's motivation in working with Indigenous Peoples. What is the social worker's role? What brought the social worker to this place? In what ways does the social worker's past and present shape his or her desire to work with Indigenous Peoples? Students enter social work education with enthusiasm, as well as idealism (Wehbi, 2009), altruism (Rotabi, Gammonley and Gamble, 2006), and naïveté. Students should process their own motivations for wanting to work with Indigenous Peoples to address possible attitudes of 'cultural imperialism and voyeurism' (Wehbi, 2009: 52, see Chapter 11).

Social work students wrestle with notions of how they can practise effectively while working with an individual, group or community with a different background from their own. It is difficult to work collaboratively with Indigenous people while simultaneously discovering one's own complicity in the oppression of Indigenous Peoples. This process of self-reflection can be transformative. Gkisedtanamoogk (2010) challenges all who work with Indigenous Peoples:

> if this work does not transform you then you are not paying attention. If you are immune, complacent, indifferent, and untouched by the horror of human avarice and aggression, then you are not paying attention. It is not possible to be engaged in this work and not behave differently. It is not possible if we are really doing what we are supposed to be doing with this work. (53)

In heeding Gkisedtanamoogk's (2010) words, part of the social work educator's task is to support students in the development of their professional identity as part of a larger whole that reaches beyond social location and is not isolated from histories, contemporary practices and policies that, on the surface, only appear to affect others (Bishop, 1994).

For social work students who want to work with Indigenous Peoples, a contextual understanding is required, with relationships with Indigenous people at the centre. While it is necessary to examine federal – national government – funding structures affecting Indigenous Peoples, local social issues require local solutions and a debunking of the myth of appropriateness: generic social work practice is not necessarily relevant or appropriate across diverse contexts (Gray et al., 2008). As Gray et al. (2008) note, most mainstream universities have a long way to go in attempting to address the history of colonization and oppression in order to promote cultural understanding, as well as combat 'outside' negative stereotypes of Indigenous Peoples.

One way to facilitate learning to address the history of colonization and oppression and challenge stereotypes directly is to create space where students can reflect on their own cultural identity, assumptions and ways of knowing, being and practising through meaningful engagement with Indigenous communities. The authors designed a social work course to facilitate these connections, help students foster self-reflection to integrate cultural knowledge and experiences into future practice and introduce a holistic approach to addressing the multifaceted challenges facing Indigenous Peoples. Facilitating relationship building among Indigenous communities, students, schools of social work and their wider universities can help students gain experience of and insight into the cultural, social, economic, legal and health contexts of Indigenous Peoples from the local community's perspective. McGill's School of Social Work embarked on its first three-week intensive cultural immersion course with the collaboration of the Kahnawá:ke Mohawk community in 2010. The following case study describes how social work instructors planned a course built around *Haudenosaunee* (*Iroquoian*) epistemologies, both perceived and enacted. This was done by engaging the Kahnawá:ke community, students and the broader university.

Social Work Cultural Immersion

Across Canada and the USA, universities are taking steps to bridge students' knowledge and gaps in experience by developing intensive cultural field courses within the social work curriculum (Canfield, Low and Hovestadt, 2009; Cordero and Rodriguez, 2009; Reid and Ives, 2009). These courses immerse students in communities where people live, and enable them to learn first-hand from community members through presentations, interactive workshops, cultural activities and ceremonies. It is recognized, however, that a short-term course or field experience provides only an introduction and, in the context of working with Indigenous Peoples, must actively address issues of essentialism by discussing 'the diversity of cultures, traditions, and differing, yet related, ways of seeing, knowing and doing of Indigenous people worldwide' (Ormiston, 2010: 50).

The creation of the course was a long-term process, requiring sustained engagement and commitment. Interest in such a course was sparked by a visit by Gord Bruyere and Michelle Reid from the Aboriginal BSW programme at Nicola Valley Institute of Technology (NVIT), who provided guidance as to how to integrate Indigenous ways of knowing and learning into the BSW curriculum at the School (see Bruyere, 2008). During their presentation, they discussed their cultural immersion course, required for all incoming BSW students. They invited members of McGill's faculty to join their cultural immersion course, which we did in September 2008. NVIT's context was very different from McGill's in that the majority of their students are Indigenous, whereas at McGill, Indigenous students are in the minority. Still, staff members returned from this experience excited to proceed with bringing this concept to McGill.

It should be noted that any type of cultural immersion course cannot simply be uprooted from one place and transplanted in another. While the goal for such a course at McGill was to design a learning experience centred around Indigenous ways of knowing, learning and being, faculty wanted to ensure each aspect of the course reflected 'Indigenous forms of practice [that enabled students] to provide professional services in a manner that is effective and consistent with local cultures and contexts – local knowledge, local traditions and local practices' (Gray et al., 2008: 6). This course would be informed from experiences from NVIT and other approaches to cultural immersion, but would be grounded in the specific, local context of the Mohawk territory of Kahnawá:ke. At the same time, it was critical to ensure the multidimensionality of the Kahnawá:ke community was highlighted, in order to facilitate discussion of Kahnawá:ke's cultural environment as not being static but 'relative to time and social context' (Parrott, 2009: 620). Colonization has sought to make people think all Indigenous Peoples are culturally similar (while dividing and categorizing Indigenous Peoples in Canada through the Indian Act for economic and political purposes).

Recognizing that outside the university faculty and students interact with people from diverse backgrounds and disciplines, faculty instructors invited students from areas of professional practice that, historically, had significant contact with Indigenous Peoples. Thus, they invited students from social work, law, anthropology and medicine to participate. The inclusion of multiple disciplines within a social work course underscored the acknowledgement of the interconnected responsibility for current issues facing Indigenous Peoples. Bringing together students from different disciplines enabled them to learn new tools for their practice with Indigenous Peoples and promoted the asking of new questions in addition to the ones generated from the knowledge base of the students' own disciplines. The course comprised three intensive weeks: week 1 at McGill with sessions led by instructors from social work, law, anthropology and medicine; Week 2, living in Kahnawá:ke; and Week 3 at McGill for debriefing sessions.

A Decolonizing Approach

Given social work's tenuous history in Indigenous communities, can social work education be used to liberate and heal the ruptures past actions and attitudes have created? The educator's pedagogical, ideological and epistemological approach will largely shape the extent to which a course might contribute to this reconciliation process. Teaching from a perspective perpetuating 'generic' social work practice would not heal these wounds and would maintain the colonial perspectives that caused the harm in the first place. In designing curricula, educators need to move away from the assumption that Eurocentric knowledge and practice approaches 'could and should be uncritically and universally applied to all peoples regardless of culture or political and historical circumstances' (Baikie, 2009: 42). An approach that seeks to liberate and heal must address colonialism directly, its past injustices and its present manifestations. One such decolonizing approach to social work necessitates a confirmation of Indigenous wisdom's place in social work curricula, requires social workers to reflect on their privilege in relation to their social location, recognizes the importance of Indigenous rights not only for Indigenous Peoples but also for non-Indigenous Peoples and addresses issues of power that come with being a social work professional (Briskman, 2008).

Engaging with Indigenous Communities

Indigenous and non-Indigenous social workers who want to work in Indigenous communities need to be aware of, and honest about, social work's past role in Indigenous communities. Social workers have participated – either directly or indirectly – in Canada's colonial legacy and continue to fulfil the colonial legacy if 'they have no political mission, which in effect supports the way things are' (Mullaly, 2010: 22). Social workers need to ask themselves and their colleagues challenging questions and be ready to 'question their role within the constrictions of the nation state and work with others to discard previously sacrosanct notions of professionalism, knowledge and power' (Briskman, 2008: 93). There should not be an assumption that social work students are more aware of their own power and positions of privilege based on their social location (including that of student of social work) than other students. They may find themselves in demanding contexts facing issues and realities that may challenge their ways of being and seeing the world (see Case Vignette 1).

Case Vignette 1

An Elder described a grade 8 teacher who taught social studies on the reservation – in effect, teaching Indian kids about Indians. He was doing the best he could but was relying heavily on some books he'd read on Indigenous Peoples, since the teacher was neither Indigenous nor a resident of the reservation. When the students didn't do well in the class, the teacher was perplexed. He was convinced he 'understood' the subject. Not for a second did the teacher realize that the discussion about 'Indian identity' has been the exclusive purview of non-Indigenous Peoples for over a century or, more importantly, that he'd been inadvertently colonizing the discussion as well by failing to seek out Indigenous Peoples to help deepen and round out his knowledge. Fortunately, the school hired an Elder, who consulted with staff. So what did the Elder have to say? He said when someone does not have in-depth knowledge of Native Peoples, about all he can rely on are stereotypes found in books. As most of the books are written by non-Native authors without a deep knowledge of their subject, non-Native teachers have difficulty conveying knowledge to the Native student. (Adapted from Roué, 2006)

The course began with the belief everyone has knowledge to contribute to learning and it is critical to create an environment respectful of diverse backgrounds and perspectives in order for sharing and meaningful discussion to take place. Secondly, it is imperative for students to have a firm understanding of how their own cultural context interacts with the cultural contexts of their client groups, as well as how their own cultural context shapes intervention approaches and their own development as social work professionals. Thus, throughout the course, while students were learning about *Haudenosaunee* perspectives, their educators wanted to ensure there was space for them to engage in self-reflection to examine their own attitudes, beliefs, traditions, faith perspectives, and so forth.

When it was first decided to move ahead with an exploration of the field course in Kahnawá:ke, the teaching team approached the Chiefs and Elders for their views and guidance, and approval was received from one of the traditional Longhouses as well as the Mohawk Council of Kahnawá:ke. Because this course would be focused on students developing a preliminary understanding of *Haudenosaunee* worldviews, it was important for students to connect *Haudenosaunee* culture, traditions, values and beliefs to their areas of practice, and identify the key values, symbols, beliefs and protocols of particular Indigenous cultures; the teachings had to be centred around Indigenous knowledge and ways of learning. This required recruiting facilitators from the community who would be able to organize and lead the sessions relevant to their area of work. Faculty wanted to capitalize on the community's capacity and, at the same time, increase students' awareness of the capacity that already existed in Kahnawá:ke. This was critical as Indigenous knowledge has been discounted and dismissed in the past, supplanted by non-Indigenous 'experts' whose knowledge claims have held legitimacy only by virtue of an academic degree. Throughout the course, students embraced their time with the Elders and community facilitators. One Indigenous student applauded the university, noting that 'McGill's willingness to open a space for Mohawk Elders and community members to participate as equally worthy professors recognizes the equal value, importance and worth of 'the Aboriginal perspective''. Facilitators included representatives of the three Longhouses: the Courthouse of Kahnawá:ke, Kateri Memorial Hospital, Turtle's Bay Elders' Lodge and *Kanien'kehá:ka Onkwuwén:na Raotitióhkwa* (Language and Cultural Center). For the duration of the time spent in Kahnawá:ke, two Mohawk Elders provided faculty and students with guidance and oversight, including leading students in each day's sunrise ceremony with the thanksgiving recitation of the *Ohen:ton Karihwatehkwen* ('the words that come before all else'). Faculty instructors wanted to adopt a non-expert stance and asked their Mohawk community partners to take a leadership role promising they would 'take action in support of the direction that Indigenous people have determined' (Davis, 2010: 5). For the author who was from Kahnawá:ke, this was an acknowledgement of the expertise in his community. For the other author, who was not from the community and whose background included African American, German, Slovakian, Seminole, Cherokee and Hungarian, the role was as an ally who provided support but did not lead (Sinclair, 2009).

Another critical element of the course was the acknowledgement of Indigenous sovereignty. There is a paucity of Indigenous academics in mainstream universities across Canada and, moreover, 'Indigenous Peoples' knowledge has been given little, if any, legitimate academic role in higher education, and foundational aspects to Indigenous knowledge, such as spirituality intertwined with the land, are ignored,' (Hart, 2009: 27). While some courses invite Indigenous people into their classrooms to tell their stories, faculty wanted to go beyond the classroom setting to have students interact with and learn from Indigenous Peoples *on their own land*. One Indigenous student reflected upon the importance to a future law practice of being in Kahnawá:ke personally as well as professionally:

> Now when I think about the Sunrise Ceremony, and other moments of personal reflection such as the Pipe Ceremony, the Sweat Lodge, and conversations I had with Kahnawa'kehró:non, I realize it was the personal connection I felt with other people, with the Earth, and with things I cannot understand which give the activities such great value, rather than an academic tidbit (sic) of knowledge, a ratio decidendi, that will provide me with a specific tool to solve problems I may encounter in my future work as a lawyer.

Providing the central content of the course on Mohawk territory contributed to constructing the space where the marginalization of Indigenous teachings in the colonized past was dismantled, and Indigenous 'cultural sovereignty' of the Mohawk Nation in this case was demonstrated (Coffey and Tsosie, 2001).

Engaging with Students

Connections with Indigenous communities can facilitate students' developing a deeper understanding of the cultural, social, economic, legal and health contexts of Indigenous communities from the local community's perspective. Moreover, changing the learning setting from the classroom to the community can foster students' integration of cultural knowledge and experience into future practice and can 'experientially increase[e] the [student's] empathy and awareness' (Miley, O'Melia and DuBois, 2009: 392) regarding practice with Indigenous Peoples.

Following the decolonizing approach described above, faculty instructors incorporated opportunities for students to reflect on their privilege in relation to their social location within the class schedule. In order for Indigenous and non-Indigenous people to work together, they have to know one another, but not only from the stereotypes and biases they may hold.

How do Indigenous and non-Indigenous Peoples come to know each other? Weaver (2008) described cultural competence as arising from the knowledge about a specific cultural group as well as self-reflection and sensitivity to one's personal biases. One non-Indigenous student highlighted her ignorance of Indigenous Peoples even after taking a number of courses offered at McGill in the departments of anthropology, education and social work, despite their focus on

Indigenous issues. She noted that, 'most importantly, participating in this course has shown me how little I know about the Aboriginal Peoples of this country'. Thus, faculty instructors started with self-reflection, which included critical self-examination, but also needed to address 'the othering' of Indigenous Peoples and create space, both in small groups and individually, for these discussions.

Using writing assignments, such as journaling or reflection papers, can allow instructors to monitor students' engagement with the material and provide a vehicle for instructor feedback. These types of assignments can also be a significant source of student learning and self-reflection (Furman, Coyne and Negi, 2008; Miller, 2001). Instructor-facilitated small group discussions can also act as a 'reflexive echo' for students and contextualize their reactions to the material (Connolly and Reilly, 2007). Thus, faculty included these elements within the course to provide an opportunity for students to respond to readings and or presentations to facilitate their understanding of their experiences and allow them to 'periodically review earlier writings and trace their evolving perceptions and progress' (Miller, 2001: 164).

Taking a holistic approach, faculty purposefully designed the course to be an integrated learning environment where they hoped to *create* a sense of community among students in the process of *learning about* a community. Adapting an idea from NVIT, faculty divided the students into the main clans present in Kahnawá:ke. Each clan comprised students from different disciplines. Within these clans, students performed tasks necessary for the field week (for example, cooking and cleaning) as well as produced their final presentation assignment. Thus, the students within each clan not only had to learn to collaborate with one another for the good of the whole group, but also needed to learn how to communicate meaningfully and effectively with one another, moving outside the familiar vocabulary of their discipline. One of the course goals was to create connections with one another, not only intellectually but experientially, as well as with the people from whom they were learning and what they were learning, again, addressing their lack of familiarity with people different from themselves.

Instructors as well as students were included in the community of the course. For students from each discipline to participate, their respective departments had to organize and lead a session at McGill in the first week, as well as 'send' their instructor to Kahnawá:ke for the field week, which was no small investment on the part of each department. Thus, the instructors were also engaged in learning – learning from other instructors who focused on Indigenous issues as related to their discipline, from students enrolled in the course, and, most importantly, from instructors from the community who led all sessions in Kahnawá:ke. This approach required departments to devote considerable resources to the course if they wanted their students to be able to participate, and highlighted the instructors' commitment to their own learning and continued development as teachers, practitioners and allies.

Engaging the University

The establishment of this interdisciplinary course within the Faculty of Arts was a first of its kind at McGill. This course addressed a critical gap in students' knowledge about Indigenous cultures and worldviews (with a particular emphasis on *Haudenosaunee* teachings) while creating linkages to students' areas of practice in a community context. Previously, there was no course providing an opportunity for students to increase their understanding of Indigenous Peoples and their contexts (histories, cultures and the political, economic, social, legal and health issues they face) using an interdisciplinary, local community-focused framework.

In order to move beyond 'indigenizing' courses in the School of Social Work and to avoid 'tokenist inclusions of Indigenous material' (Gair, 2008: 223) in a heavily Eurocentric curriculum, the instructors sought to design a course centring Indigenous knowledge. Reasons included wanting to: (i) create a course to showcase the expertise in Kahnawá:ke in the various disciplines represented by the students, and (ii) provide a course to validate and celebrate Indigenous students' heritage and discredit the assumption that 'expert' knowledge and skills were obtained solely via academic training at mainstream, nationally accredited universities (Haug, 2005). Members of the Kahnawá:ke community were the only appropriate teachers to share their perspectives on their 'rights to practice traditional ways of life, including language, religious beliefs, property values, and social systems toward relatives and family' (Fenelon and Hall, 2008: 1872). Contextual reading assignments from the first week at McGill were written by Indigenous and non-Indigenous authors. The equivalent weight given by the students to the oral presentations in Kahnawá:ke and the assigned readings from Week 1 was evidenced in the way they referenced this knowledge in their final oral presentations and written reflection papers.

A significant challenge arises in generating support for collaboration with Indigenous Peoples within a university. There may be a historical relationship with Indigenous Peoples, but often it is related to the production of research. Thus, it was critical for the creation of the course that there was an emerging infrastructure to support collaboration with Indigenous communities from a partnership perspective. Faculty instructors worked with members of McGill's First People's House as well as senior-level faculty and administrators who saw the potential in this course to provide students with a unique opportunity to apply what they had learned in the classroom to a real-life setting, thereby learning in ways that are not possible in the classroom. Though there was precedent for taking students to different cultural contexts (for example, anthropology journeys to Northern Quebec, biology and geography travel to Panama), this was not the case in social work, and never to a place as geographically close as Kahnawá:ke. Field courses already established at the university took students far away, in some cases, to different countries. Initial discussions with other disciplines regarding the McGill course included suggestions of going to distant communities. However, instructors were firm about the need to start the refamiliarizing process between Indigenous and non-Indigenous Peoples in the community next door. They were already cautious given a history of the 'exotification' of Indigenous Peoples, and wanted to emphasize the importance of getting to know a community which was geographically close to Montreal and yet culturally different.

Working across Disciplines

Social work is in unique place to bring together practitioners from multiple disciplines to address issues from a holistic, interdisciplinary perspective. Even within the field, social work is inherently diverse: offering counselling, researching issues affecting clients or client groups, analysing policies affecting clients and educating students in social work programmes. Whether working from a generic person-in-environment or an Indigenous approach seeking 'wholeness, balance, relationships, harmony, growth, healing, and *mino-pimátisiwin* [the good life]' (Hart, 2009: 35), a holistic approach is designed to work with individuals and communities on the psychological, emotional, social, spiritual, economic, political and physical level simultaneously. Integrating students from other disciplines in the university highlighted the social work commitment to broader engagement with the range of issues shaping the lives of those with whom social workers work.

'Multidisciplinary' has been defined as each individual discipline bringing its profession to a group while maintaining its own identity within interactions with other disciplines (Hinshaw and DeLeon, 1995; Korazim-Kõrösy et al., 2007). Key components to multidisciplinary collaboration include understanding multiple perspectives involved, willingness to share knowledge, flexibility and knowing one's role within the group as well as understanding the roles of other members (Hinshaw and DeLeon 1995; Lifshitz, 1996). Working collaboratively with other disciplines challenges the long tradition of specialization and fragmentation of services, particularly within the social and health services field (Bronstein, 2003).

One of the clans of students, in their final presentation for the course, called for a 'post-disciplinary' perspective, hoping their work together would take them out of their discipline's traditional silo, embrace new perspectives and questions and create something new together. This could also be described as an 'interdisciplinary' approach where individuals actively and collectively interact across the disciplines, combining knowledge to create a new path. The students' call underscored their desire to integrate the strengths of their disciplines and move past the territoriality inherent within disciplines, often to the detriment of clients. It also highlighted their internalization of the necessity of integrating 'Indigenous knowledge and methods into professional social work [and other disciplines'] education and practice ... as an imperative for all of us' (Faith, 2008: 255). The social work discipline's social justice framework embodies what Dr Martin Luther King wrote in his famous letter from the Birmingham jail on April 16, 1963: 'injustice anywhere is a threat to justice everywhere'. Decades later, Bruyere (1999) contended that Indigenous and non-Indigenous Peoples should work in solidarity with non-Indigenous Peoples 'focus[ing] upon the nature of the relationship Aboriginal communities have with mainstream Canadian social service agencies and political bodies' (178). Western reality is of Indigenous and settler societies' cohabitation. Thus, it is imperative to find ways of moving forward together.

Conclusion

Eons of Indigenous history have been reduced to figurative paragraphs in relation to the telling of Canadian history, leaving a majority of Canadian students ignorant of the histories, teachings, customs, traditions and values of Indigenous Peoples. This 'not telling' strengthens Canada's assimilationist policies by marginalizing Indigenous Peoples' histories and contemporary contexts and devaluing Indigenous knowledge as a legitimate source for practice. It furthers the chasms of misunderstanding among Indigenous and non-Indigenous Peoples (see Case Vignette 2).

Case Vignette 2

During the early years of her marriage Mrs K did not know what ailed her partner, a residential school survivor. He was violent, moody, and uncommunicative. What kept her in the marriage was her belief that he was a good man beneath it all. From time to time, he would mutter things about residential school but she couldn't connect it to anything she knew. In response, she tuned him out, having to attend to pressures of work and raising children. Mr K worked sporadically and rarely discussed his feelings let alone his experiences in the residential school with his spouse. Only much later in their marriage did the couple begin to realize they should have discussed these issues earlier. For him, this necessitated sharing about his abuse at the hands of school staff and for her, empathizing and truly listening to him. The couple was eventually able to reconcile and transform their relationship based on mutual respect and love.

This sketch of a distressed couple provides a glimpse into the wider dynamics underway toward healing and reconciliation. Recognition of the importance of dialogue and public education is critical to healing and recovery. For example, residential school survivors must feel understood and others must work toward comprehending the totality of the residential school experience and what it has brought to Indigenous Peoples and their communities. Social work education can bridge this gap between Indigenous and non-Indigenous groups. This process can be accelerated when Indigenous and non-Indigenous people are brought together, particularly on Indigenous territory. Being on the land provides a unique space for non-Indigenous people to empathize and listen to what Indigenous people are saying and vice versa.

The task of social work educators is to challenge social work – and other – students to reconceptualize how they perceive their disciplines – past, present and future. Whether this reconceptualization happens depends to a large extent on the perceptions and actions of the students who complete the course. For one Indigenous student, the course fulfilled the final requirements of her undergraduate degree. She was used to spending time on the land with her family, which was something she missed strongly during her years in Montreal. Nevertheless, for her, the course became an 'example of [teaching] cultural relevance, and it brought my soul back to where I came from. When I return home, I will have both academic experience and cultural renewal to apply to my work'.

A non-Indigenous student not only sought to rethink how he perceived law but also challenged his faculty 'to reshape its ... understanding of the law and to recognize, respect and integrate Indigenous teachings as part of the core legal curriculum' (Douglas, 2011: 47). Following the course, other non-Indigenous students began to see their roles more clearly as allies and thought the teachings from the community facilitators deepened their understandings of the way in which culture and traditions, family and community systems might promote individual and group health, well-being and resilience. One student recognized the impact of personal perspectives and context on the practice relationship by 'being immersed in another worldview, [thus being] forced to encounter my own'. Another student characterized participation in the course as transformative, noting:

> This was not a total immersion in Mohawk culture (one week is short after all), but we managed to touch the essential: the theoretical, practical, spiritual and human. My idea about the Mohawks, Indigenous Peoples and myself underwent a transformation during the week. I link this to the fact that I had an experience rooted in the academic that touched me on a personal level ... I will continue to reflect on the relevance of a white person (me) working with Indigenous communities.

This kind of reimagining of one's personal and professional self and practice approach is a small step in re(shaping) the reconciliation that must take place in order to heal relationships between Indigenous and non-Indigenous Peoples.

References

Baikie, G. (2009). Indigenous-Centred Social Work: Theorizing a social work way-of-being. In R. Sinclair, Hart, M.A. and Bruyere, G. (eds), *Wicihitowin: Aboriginal Social Work in Canada*. Halifax, NS: Fernwood, 42–61.

Bishop, A. (1994). *Becoming an Ally: Breaking the Cycle of Oppression*. Halifax, NS: Fernwood.

Briskman, L. (2008). Decolonizing Social Work in Australia: Prospect or illusion? In M. Gray, Coates, J. and Yellow Bird, M. (eds), *Indigenous Social Work around the World: Towards Culturally Relevant Education and Practice*. Aldershot: Ashgate, 83–93.

Bronstein, L.R. (2003). A model for interdisciplinary collaboration. *Social Work*, 48(3), 297–306.

Bruyere, G. (1999). The decolonization wheel: An Aboriginal perspective on social work practice with Aboriginal Peoples. In R. Delaney, Sellick, M. and Brownlee, K. (eds), *Social Work with Rural and Northern Communities*. Thunder Bay, Canada: Lakehead University Centre for Northern Studies, 170–81.

Bruyere, G. (2008). Picking up what is left on the trail: The emerging spirit of Aboriginal education in Canada. In M. Gray, Coates, J. and Yellow Bird, M. (eds), *Indigenous Social Work around the World: Towards Culturally Relevant Education and Practice*. Aldershot: Ashgate, 231–44.

Canfield, B.S., Low, L. and Hovestadt, A. (2009). Cultural immersion as a learning method for expanding intercultural competences. *The Family Journal: Counseling and Therapy for Couples and Families*, 17(4), 318–22.

Child and Family Services Information. (2002). *Child welfare in Canada 2000: The role of provincial and territorial authorities in the provision of child protection services*. Ottawa, ON: Health Canada Healthy Communities Division [Online]. Available at: http://www.hrdc-drhc.gc.ca/socpol/cfs/cfs. shtml [accessed: 25 July 2011].

Coffey, W. and Tsosie, R. (2001). Rethinking the tribal sovereignty doctrine: Cultural sovereignty and the collective future of Indian nations. *Stanford Law & Policy Review*, 12, 191–202.

Connolly, K. and Reilly R.C. (2007). Emergent issues when researching trauma: A confessional tale. *Qualitative Inquiry*, 13, 522–40.

Cooke, M., Mitrou, F., Lawrence, D., Guimod, E. and Beavon, D. (2007). Indigenous well-being in four countries: An application of the UNDP's Human Development Index to Indigenous Peoples in Australia, Canada, New Zealand and the United States. *BMC International Health and Human Rights*, 7(9), 1–40.

Cordero, A. and Rodriguez, L.N. (2009). Fostering cross-cultural learning and advocacy for social justice through an immersion experience in Puerto Rico. *Journal of Teaching in Social Work*, 29(2), 134–52.

Davis, L. (2010). Introduction. In L. Davis (ed.), *Alliances: Re/Envisioning Indigenous-Non-Indigenous Relationships*. Toronto, ON: University of Toronto Press, 1–12.

Douglas, J. (2011). The next incarnation of 'trans-systemic' legal education at McGill Law. *Kanata*, 4, 46–55.

Faith, E. (2008). Indigenous Social Work Education: A project for all of us? In M. Gray, Coates, J. and Yellow Bird, M. (eds), *Indigenous Social Work around the World: Towards Culturally Relevant Education and Practice*. Aldershot: Ashgate, 245–55.

Fenelon, J.V. and Hall, T.D. (2008). Revitalization and Indigenous resistance to globalization and neo-liberalism. *American Behavioral Scientist*, 51(12), 1867–1901.

Furman, R., Coyne, A. and Negi, N.J. (2008). An international experience for social work students: Self-reflection through poetry and journal writing exercises. *Journal of Teaching in Social Work*, 28, 71–85.

Gair, S. (2008). Missing the 'Flight from Responsibility': Tales from a non-Indigenous educator pursuing spaces for social work education relevant to Indigenous Australians. In Gray, M., Coates, J. and Yellow Bird, M. (eds), *Indigenous Social Work around the World: Towards Culturally Relevant Education and Practice*. Aldershot: Ashgate, 219–30.

Gkisedtanamoogk. (2010). Finding our Way despite Modernity. In L. Davis (ed.), *Alliances: Re/Envisioning Indigenous-Non-Indigenous Relationships*. Toronto, ON: University of Toronto Press, 42–53.

Government of Ontario (1990). Child and Family Services Act; Revised Statute of Ontario (RSO), 1990, c. C. 11 [Online]. Available at: http://www.e-laws.gov. on.ca/html/statutes/english/elaws_statutes_90c11_e.htm [accessed: 25 July 2011].

Gray, M., Yellow Bird, M. and Coates, J. (2008). Towards an Understanding of Indigenous Social Work. In M. Gray, Coates, J. and Yellow Bird, M. (eds), *Indigenous Social Work around the World: Towards Culturally Relevant Education and Practice*. Aldershot: Ashgate, 49–58.

Haug, E. (2005). Critical reflections on the emerging discourse of international social work. *International Social Work*, 48, 126–35.

Hart, M.A. (2009). Anti-Colonial Indigenous Social Work: Reflections on an Aboriginal approach. In R. Sinclair, Hart, M.A. and Bruyere, G. (eds), *Wícihitowin: Aboriginal Social Work in Canada*. Halifax, NS: Fernwood Press, 25–41.

Hinshaw, A.S. and DeLeon, P.H. (1995). Toward achieving multidisciplinary professional collaboration. *Professional Psychology: Research and Practice*, 26(2), 115–16.

Ives, N., Aitken, O., Loft, M. and Phillips, M. (2007). Rethinking social work education for Indigenous students: Creating space for multiple ways for multiple ways of knowing and learning. *First Peoples Child and Family Review*, 3(4), 13–20.

Korazim-Kőrösy, Y., Mizrahi, T., Katz, C., Karmon, A., Garcia, M. L. and Bayne Smith, M. (2007). Towards interdisciplinary community collaboration and development. *Journal of Community Practice*, 15(1–2), 13–44.

Lee, B. (1992). Colonialization and community: Implications for First Nations development. *Community Development Journal*, 27(3), 211–19.

Lifshitz, J. (1996). Developing the role of a social worker within a multidisciplinary team in an HIV/AIDS outpatient clinic. *The Social Worker*, 64(4), 34–42.

Miley, K.K., O'Melia, M. and DuBois, B. (2009). *Generalist Social Work Practice: An Empowering Approach* (6th edn). Boston, MA: Pearson.

Miller, M. (2001). Creating a safe frame for learning: Teaching about trauma and trauma treatment. *Journal of Teaching in Social Work*, 21, 159–76.

Mullaly, B. (2010). *Challenging Oppression and Confronting Privilege* (2nd edn). Oxford: Oxford University Press.

Ormiston, N.T. (2010). Re-conceptualizing research: An Indigenous perspective. *First Peoples Child & Family Review*, 5(1), 50–56.

Parrott, L. (2009). Constructive marginality: Conflicts and dilemmas in cultural competence and anti-oppressive practice. *Social Work Education*, 28(6), 617–30.

Paul, D.N. (2006). *First Nations History: We Are Not the Savages* (3rd edn). Halifax, NS: Fernwood Press.

Reid, M. and Ives, N. (2009). Lessons from the Nlakapmux cultural immersion course: NVIT's response to shaping social work identity and practice in a time of globalization. Paper presented at the 2009 Canadian Association of Social Work Education Annual Conference, Carleton University, Ottawa, Ontario, Canada.

Richardson, B. (1993). *People of Terra Nullius: Betrayal and Rebirth in Aboriginal Canada*. Vancouver, BC: Douglas & McIntyre.

Roué, M. (2006). Healing the wounds of school by returning to the land. Cree elders come to the rescue of a lost generation. *International Social Science Journal*, 58(187), 7–14.

Rotabi, K.S., Gammonley, D. and Gamble, D.N. (2006). Ethical guidelines for study abroad: Can we transform ugly Americans into engaged global citizens? *British Journal of Social Work*, 36(3), 451–65.

Sinclair, R. (2009). Bridging the Past and the Future: An introduction to Indigenous social work issues. In R. Sinclair, Hart, M.A. and Bruyere, G. *Wícihitowin: Aboriginal Social Work in Canada*. Halifax, NS: Fernwood, 19–24.

Sinha, V. and Kozlowski, A. (2013). The Structure of Aboriginal Child Welfare in Canada. *The International Indigenous Policy Journal*, 4(2).

Tilbury, C. (2009). The over-representation of Indigenous children in the Australian child welfare system. *International Journal of Social Welfare*, 18(1), 57–64.

Trocmé, N., Knoke, D. and Blackstock, C. (2004). Pathways to the overrepresentation of Aboriginal children in Canada's child welfare system. *Social Service Review*, 78(4), 577–600.

Weaver, H. (2008). Indigenous Social Work in the United States: Reflections on Indian tacos, Trojan horses and canoes filled with Indigenous revolutionaries. In M. Gray, Coates, J. and Yellow Bird, M. (eds), *Indigenous Social Work around the World: Towards Culturally Relevant Education and Practice*. Aldershot: Ashgate, 71–82.

Wehbi, S. (2009). Deconstructing motivations: Challenging international social work placements. *International Social Work*, 52(1), 48–59.

Acknowledgement

The authors wish to thank the students of Aboriginal Field Studies who gave permission to share excerpts from their final papers for this chapter: Anne Blumenthal, Joseph Paul Flowers, Hubert-François Rochon, Mary Tukkiapic and Pamela Weightman.

PART IV
Research: Decolonizing Methodologies

Chapter 13

Kaupapa Māori Social Work Research

Anaru Eketone and Shayne Walker

The current Indigenous context for social work practice and research in Aotearoa New Zealand was not created in a vacuum. It is the product of approximately 200 years of human relationships. The colonization of New Zealand began in earnest in 1840 after the Indigenous people, the Māori, gave permission for the establishment of British government within their country in exchange for recognition and protection of their property rights, the continuation of their authority over local matters and receiving the rights of British citizenship. The document that laid out these terms is called the Treaty of Waitangi, and while many of its guarantees were subsequently ignored by the British settlers who followed, the Treaty provided a framework for Māori to seek justice and argue for greater influence in the political, social and economic life of the country (Humpage and Fleras, 2001; Walker, 1990).

Since the 1970s, Māori have struggled for and achieved a great deal of progress. The Waitangi Tribunal was set up to examine breaches of the Treaty and has operated as a permanent commission of enquiry with the ability to deliver non-binding recommendations, such as return of lands and financial compensation. These 'Treaty Settlements', as they are known, have enabled some tribes to replace some of the economic base that was lost through the Crown's refusal to protect property rights (Ward, 1999). Two major tribes, Waikato-Tainui and Ngai Tahu, have, through the investment and use of these settlements, essentially quadrupled their assets in 15 years to NZ$700m each and are now major financial players in their respective districts (Gibson, 2011).

There has also been an increased Māori influence over government policy, with the funding of Māori health, education and welfare initiatives being highlights (Walker, 2004). White New Zealand was coming to grips with the oppressive and racist nature of the monocultural system their forefathers had instituted while at the same time Māori were arguing to have greater self-determination over government services that were impacting on their lives (Walker, 2004).

Many have referred to the last 40 years as the Māori renaissance (for example, Webster, 1998; Wilson, 2009). However, it could be argued that it has been the Pakeha population (British settlers and their descendants) that has gone through a process of change. Māori desires for justice, along with economic and social aspirations, have changed little in the last 100 years. One of the authors (Anaru Eketone) has a copy of a petition from 1905 found in his great grandfather's papers written to King Edward VII outlining many of the issues still raised 80 years later. What has changed could be called a 'Pakeha Transformation', where white New

Zealand moved from justifying the misdeeds of colonization as beneficial to Māori, to a position of understanding (generally of course) that technological superiority does not equate to cultural superiority. Many white New Zealanders had taken to the streets to fight against apartheid in South Africa when the Springbok rugby team had toured New Zealand in 1981 (Walker, 2004). Many Māori challenged the protestors about why they were fighting to end racism in South Africa but ignoring racism in New Zealand and the promises and guarantees made in the Treaty of Waitangi. There had already been growth in Pakeha support for Māori issues, but this interaction with the protest movement ensured more advocates for greater Māori self-determination, the resolution of historical grievances by the failure to uphold the Treaty of Waitangi, and, a focus on acknowledging Māori cultural values in government departments (Walker, 2004). Māori continued to struggle, but now had more allies among public servants, social workers, policy writers and politicians who were viewing resolving the problems around the Treaty of Waitangi as a matter of honour. The challenge to the myth that New Zealand was an egalitarian country had been made and a slow groundswell was building (Walker, 2004).

Māori, while appreciating the transformation of Pakeha, are not dependent on Pakeha patronage to advance their own development. Māori have been the recipients of Pakeha goodwill that Freire (1970: 26) termed 'false generosity' in that:

> any attempt to soften the power of the oppressor in deference to the weakness of the oppressed almost always manifests itself in the form of false generosity; indeed the attempt never goes beyond this. In order to have continued opportunity to express their generosity the oppressors must perpetuate injustice as well.

In other words, any pathways forward for Māori must come out of the heart and mind of Māori. In 1984, Whatarangi Winiata, a tribal leader from the southern part of New Zealand's North Island, adapted Abraham Lincoln's words and called for services that were 'of the Māori, by the Māori, for the Māori' (Winiata, 1984). This call was taken up by both Māori and the government of the day to deliver services that came to be known as 'by Māori for Māori' services.

As part of these movements, 1985 saw the establishment of the first of a new kind of primary school using the Māori language in a Māori cultural context that was named 'Kura Kaupapa Māori'. This then became a descriptive term for a range of social services run 'by Māori for Māori'. Kaupapa Māori-defined services sprang up all around the country delivering education, health and welfare services as government sought to devolve responsibility to the various communities and find new ways of dealing with the negative social statistics indicating the extent of the Māori suffering (Walker, 1990). Although 'by Māori for Māori' was the definition, it was incomplete because, to have validity and dare we say authenticity it needed to take place in a Māori context, that is, using Māori values and customs as the norm (Eketone, 2008). For example, one of the authors worked for a service that called itself Kaupapa Māori because it delivered health screening services to Māori using Māori cultural values in its delivery of services. This claim of being a Kaupapa Māori service was challenged by other Māori providers because the governance and management structure were part of a Western mainstream hospital and, therefore, in their opinion, could not claim to be a truly Kaupapa Māori service. As far as the clients and patients were concerned, the services were culturally appropriate and Māori specific. However, the Māori staff could not say the same as any accountability to the Māori community was voluntary whereas the Pakeha management always had the final say and could direct practice based on financial imperatives rather than Māori values. The challenge was, could an organization call itself Kaupapa Māori if it was not operating from a Kaupapa Māori perspective at all levels of the organization. The term Kaupapa Māori had become a contested term rather than a grand narrative.

Alignment of Kaupapa Māori and Critical Theory

One of the early developments of the discussion of Kaupapa Māori approaches was Graham Smith's (1997) promotion of Kaupapa Māori as a theory of change, that is, as more than a philosophical approach to research, practice and service delivery, but where these services emerged as sites of resistance to Western hegemony. To achieve this objective, Kaupapa Māori needed to be described in cultural as well as theoretical terms. In his PhD thesis on 'The Development of Kaupapa *Māori: Theory and Praxis*', Smith (1997: 38) described the alignment of Kaupapa Māori with critical theory. He saw Kaupapa Māori theory as having three significant components: (i) a 'conscientization' that critiqued and deconstructed the hegemony of the dominant culture of the Pakeha and the associated privilege that came with that dominance; (ii) a focus on resistance to the dominant Western structures that created and maintained 'oppression, exploitation, manipulation and containment'; and (iii) praxis or the need to reflect on the world in order to change it.

In terms of critical theory, conflict arises because of tensions between those with power and those without (Munford and Walsh-Tapiata, 2001). Critical theory is part of the wider Socialist/Marxist theoretical tradition that focuses on power differentials caused by class distinction (Crotty, 1998). For change to occur, the layers of power need to be identified, deconstructed and challenged. Māori and other Indigenous Peoples were in marginalized positions because of colonization which undermined land and property rights, instituted discriminatory policies and ignored or considered Māori values inferior. Smith (1997: 98) acknowledged that 'Kaupapa Māori Theory [had] developed out of a description of the alignment of Critical Theory and Kaupapa Māori praxis in [his] writings of the late-1980s'. Thus it became a critique of New Zealand power structures and the imposition of power over Māori by the dominant settler culture. Because of its close association to a critical theory analysis – resistance to the imposition of power was one of the hallmarks of writers and researchers of Kaupapa Māori theory in the 1990s (Bishop, 1996; Kiro, 2000; Pihama, 1993; Smith, 1999). Critical Kaupapa Māori analysis was seen as an answer to the oppression of Māori people and its consequent relegation of Māori knowledge as exotic but inferior to Western knowledge.

While Smith (1999), Pihama (1993) and Kiro (2000) highlighted the emancipatory aims of Kaupapa Māori theory, others, including Linda Smith (1999), described Kaupapa Māori using Māori cultural terms that could not be translated directly into English. These terms contained a number of layers of meaning where someone outside the culture would not immediately recognize the significance of what was being described. They included:

1. *Aroha ki te tangata* (a respect for people)
2. *Kanohi kitea* (the seen face)
3. *Titiro, whakarongo ... korero* (look, listen ... speak)
4. *Manaaki ki te tangata* (share and host people, be generous)
5. *Kia tupato* (be cautious)
6. *Kaua e takahia te mana o te tangata* (do not trample over the *mana* of people)
7. *Kaua e mahaki* (do not flaunt your knowledge) (Smith, 1999: 120).

At face value they may seem generic but *kanohi kitea,* term (2) above, refers to the reciprocal nature of Māori society where 'the seen face' infers that you are someone who supports what is happening in the Māori community to the extent that you are seen as a trusted or, at least, a recognized part of that community. Also *kaua e takahia te mana o te tangata.* term (6), refers to not trampling on the *mana* – intrinsic and extrinsic prestige – of people. To comply with this, one would need to know the nature and meaning of *mana* and how it could be diminished or enhanced by another's actions. Also, within that is the requirement to have some form of elder support so that if you make a mistake you know how to repair the damage. In a way, many of these early writings were to ensure that Pakeha people would not have the arrogance to think that they could jump on the Kaupapa Māori band-wagon without a lifetime of experience of living in the Māori community and knowledge of the language, customs and values. In its resistance to Western domination, Kaupapa Māori created a space where Māori approaches were validated and its link to critical theory gave it legitimacy in the academic world where it embraced the emancipatory rhetoric of Paulo Freire (1970) and was transferable to other Indigenous situations.

Alignment of Kaupapa Māori Theory and Constructivism

Besides its links to anti-oppressive critical theory, Kaupapa Māori also aligns with critical constructivist theoretical approaches. Constructivism holds that, rather than an objective reality, society is a social construction manufactured, confirmed and validated through our interactions with the world (Crotty, 1998; Tolich and Davidson, 1999). Hence there are multiple constructions of reality – or 'truths'

– depending on one's cultural, historical, political and economic perspective. Different cultures, then, develop a shared perspective moulded by historical, cultural and social forces.

From a constructivist perspective, Māori knowledge is a cultural construction shaped by a Māori worldview which is moulded and shaped by changing social and historical events. The arrival of Europeans brought Western ideas about science and religion which challenged Māori beliefs, perceptions and values. However, many Māori still hold to the foundational beliefs of Māori society, such as the interconnection between the material and spiritual world, especially in concepts like *mana, tapu, noa, wairua, mauri, aroha, tika* and *pono* believed by many to be integral to a traditional as well as modern Māori identity (Mead, 2003). It is worth taking the time to examine these concepts to show how a constructivist shared understanding impacts on the way a group views the world and how social work practice and research need respond to these values to honour the legitimation they bring to knowledge and provide safe ways of engaging with Māori in the research process. These concepts are difficult to translate into the English language, and in fact have many different layers of meaning, hence any explanation is incomplete:

1. *Mana* is most often translated as power, authority and prestige (Williams, 1971) and refers to 'the enduring, indestructible power of the gods' (Barlow, 1991: 61) passed down from chiefly ancestors. It can be acquired through a person's deeds and can be given by the gods to perform certain rituals (Barlow, 1991).
2. *Tapu* is also linked to the 'power and influence of the gods' (Barlow, 1991: 128) and is often translated as 'sacred' though it also refers to the religious restrictions (Williams, 1971) attached to items, places, people and parts of people (Mead, 2003). It has passed into the English language through the Tahitian word 'taboo' – meaning forbidden –though, for Māori, 'under restriction' has a closer meaning. Those restrictions can often be removed and become '*noa*'.
3. *Noa* is something that is under no restriction, which can be used freely or the individual can move about freely. An example is, when entering a *marae* – traditional gathering place – for the first time, a person is considered *tapu* and so there are limitations on where he or she can go and in what he or she can participate. To remove that *tapu*, he or she goes through a welcoming process of speeches and song, where he or she declares his or her intentions. Thereafter, the hosts and the visitors greet face to face before sharing a meal. They then become *noa* and have the freedom to move about the village (Mead, 2003).
4. *Wairua* is most easily translated as a person's spirit, that part of him or her that is not the physical presence; once the body dies the spirit moves on (Barlow, 1991).
5. *Mauri* is one of the most complex concepts and refers to the 'life essence' (Barlow, 1991) or 'life principle' (Williams, 1971), a force that allows

'living things to exist within their own realm or sphere' (Barlow 1991: 83) and binds the *wairua* – spirit – and the body together. It has importance in that it is often believed that when the *mauri* is affected, the well-being of the individual is also affected.

The first five concepts described relate primarily to one's relationship to God or the gods, while the last three concepts relate to how people relate to one another:

1. *Aroha* is often translated as love, but also has meanings of charity, sympathy and compassion or having a selfless regard for others (Barlow, 1991).
2. *Tika* relates to operating in a way where processes are correct, thus honouring and protecting others (Mead, 2003).
3. *Pono* is often translated as being true, true to your culture, true to others and true to God or the gods (Mead 2003).

These concepts and the values they uphold are considered important in the delivery of Kaupapa Māori services and in conducting social work research (Ruwhiu, 1995, 2001).

In this context of shared values and processes, Kaupapa Māori is not just simply about critiquing and resisting Western hegemony but is also about an inherent acceptance of the validity of this accumulated knowledge within Māori society. While a number of the aforementioned writers talked of the alignment between Critical Theory and Kaupapa Māori theory, they also included socially constructed Māori values, cultural ethics, knowledge and languages (Bishop, 1996; Kiro, 2000; Smith, 1997, 1999).

From a constructivist perspective, the issue is not so much whether or not something is 'true' but whether it is useful in protecting and advancing the aims of the community holding these values. In many discussions outside the academy, Kaupapa Māori is not the theoretical abstraction of conscientization, resistance and praxis but a practical constructivist focus on the underpinning values of Kaupapa Māori services. To practitioners in the Māori community, Kaupapa Māori service is simply explained as an organization that operates from a Māori philosophical position, that is, it is one where these important Māori cultural values dominate the expression and practice of the organization (Eketone, 2008). Therefore, Māori concepts are over riding and from a Māori perspective, inform service provision. Māori are judged on their adherence to Māori values and processes – often referred to as *kawa* and *tikanga* (Mead, 2003).

Russell (2000: 10) took this further and identified what she referred to as 'Native Theory' as an expression of 'the right of indigenous people to make sense of their time and place in this world'. Native theory implies that Indigenous people do not need the West to validate their knowledge or values. Indigenous theory, research and practice do not need to come from Western academic traditions or be accountable to them. Rather, they come from the experience, values and customs of Indigenous Peoples through which these processes and knowledges are validated, challenged and developed.

Research as Decolonizing Practice: Example of *Maatua Whangai*

No matter what theoretical understandings underpin research, questions of mandate and integrity are important. What makes the research a safe and useful process for Indigenous Peoples such as Māori? What can guarantee outcomes that improve Māori lived experience? Walker's (2002) study and Russell Bishop's (1996) principles of initiation, benefits, representation, legitimation and accountability are useful in Māori and other Indigenous research settings.

In Walker's (2002) study of *Maatua Whangai O Otepoti*, generally translated as a Māori – Indigenous – form of fostercare in Dunedin, New Zealand, it was important to ask the right questions to guarantee the emergence of *Kaupapa* Māori research practice principles and the participation of Māori in the process (Smith, 1999). The nature of Māori familial structures was implicit within the research process, the participants were *tuakana* – elder brother or sister – to the researcher who was *teina* – younger brother or sister – as some of the participants had 30 years (plus) experience in fostercare with Māori children. The researcher's personal commitment of fostering approximately 200 children with his wife also added to the mutual respect between the parties and the development of a 'working research *whanau* (extended family)' (Bishop, 1996). The methodology used needed continually to place the locus of control over the research with Māori participants, and Bishop's (1996) principles of initiation, benefits, representation, legitimation and accountability were used to achieve this (Walker, 2002). These principles are consistent with Russell's (2000) 'Native Theory' and a number of 'other' emancipatory approaches, for example, participatory action research. The subsequent questions generated provided a framework for competent research within a Māori – Indigenous – context.

Walker (2002) conducted in-depth *kanohi ki te kanohi* – face-to-face – interviews with individual caregivers in which he explored: (i) their induction into the *Maatua Whangai* programme; (ii) the meaning of *Maatua Whangai* for the participants; (iii) the manipulation and use of the programme by the Department of Social Welfare, the statutory agency responsible for overseeing *Maatua Whangai*; (iv) the effects of *Maatua Whangai*; and (v) future implications. Following the interviews, data was categorized, analysed and presented back to participants at *hui* (gatherings). Key findings were:

1. Caring for Māori young people was the most important part of the *mahi* (work).
2. This *mahi* (work) had its costs in terms of their own families, children and finances.
3. Generally support from the Department of Social Welfare was negligible.

4. However, individual DSW *Maatua Whangai* workers were supportive.
5. The participants – *whanau* – were their own support and their personal networks kept *Maatua Whangai* alive.
6. The young people who were placed in their care were often really disturbed.
7. Some of the relationships that developed became long-term (Walker, 2002).

This study led to possible solutions based upon *tino rangatiratanga* – self-determination – principles. In regards to practice, *iwi* (literally, bone; Māori word for a set of people bound together by descent from a common ancestor or ancestors or, in its modern meaning, tribe), *hapu* (clan or subtribe comprising a number of *whanau*) and *whanau* (extended family) control was critical, as was returning fostercare to a pre-colonial concept of *Maatua Whangai* through the development of *iwi* social service provision (Walker, Eketone and Gibbs, 2006).

Bishop's (1996) Principles for Decolonizing Research

Initiation

Technically, the research was *initiated* by the researcher as a result of his personal involvement in *Maatua Whangai* in Dunedin (Walker, 2002). Before the process started, the researcher sought guidance from the *Upoko o Te Runanga o Otakou* (the head of the local tribal council). Once *whakawhanaungatanga* (roughly translated 'establishing family linkages and reciprocal obligations') had been established the process could begin. His guidance was integral in terms of the necessary pathways the research would take and the *tikanga* or *kawa* – culturally correct processes – needed to ensure enthusiastic and safe Māori involvement. The researcher undertook the work of formulating aims and objectives, writing the research proposal, designing the research, setting-up supervision, gaining ethical approval, drafting interview questions and initial reporting. However, these tasks were reviewed and revised by the 'working research *whanau*' – participants – at the initial interviews, and subsequent *hui* – gatherings – held to discuss the major findings emerging from the data (Walker, 2002).

Benefits

A number of groups and individuals *benefited* in a variety of ways from this research, including the researcher, the participants, *Otakou Runanga* (local tribal council) and *Te Runanga o Nga Tahu* (*iwi* tribal council). This study supported the cultural and language aspirations of Māori by providing evidence that gave voice to and validated Māori lived experience. The use of *whakawhanaungatanga* (establishing linkages) extended and supported *whakapapa* (genealogical links), *tikanga* (Māori values) and *te reo* (the Māori language). Finally, the university was given a unique piece of research to use as a resource. The *Otakou Runanga* and

Te Runanga O Ngai Tahu (tribal councils) were provided with empirical data that would strengthen their social service research base, especially in terms of social service partnerships with the Crown (Aotearoa New Zealand government). Also, one of the participants used the research in her teaching on a polytechnic course and the researcher gained personal satisfaction, extended his research base and skills, and gained a master's degree (Walker, 2002).

Representation

In terms of *representation*, the participants and researcher, together, decided what constituted an adequate depiction of participants' social reality concerning the *Maatua Whangai programme*. The written text represented their interests, needs and concerns. Though much of the work of the thesis was done by the researcher, it would not have been possible without the foundation of hard work by the participants. Regarding agency, though the participants were able to operate independently of the determining constraints of the social structure of the university this, of necessity, brought some limits to their role in the research. For example, the transcribing and coding of interview transcripts raised issues of representation and control since, as noted by Te Henepe (cited in Bishop, 1995: 218), 'only collaborative coding would be legitimately representational'. Hence, while the researcher began the process of data interpretation, mindful of the importance of participant agency, he also involved them so their voice came through in the narrative and shared meanings of the research report (Walker, 2002).

Legitimacy

Though, ultimately, the researcher processed the data, the participants, local *runanga* and University of Otago exercized authority over and gave *legitimacy* to proceedings. For example, the initial results were considered by the participants at two *hui* to decide what was accurate and complete. Thereafter the researcher processed the data and theorized the findings mindful of this participant feedback (Walker, 2002).

Accountability

The researcher was *accountable* to the participants, the *Upoko* of the local *runanga* and his supervisors through a variety of processes. The research findings were made accessible through the university library and the researcher also distributed them to the participants, *Otakou Runanaga*, *Te Runanga o Nga Tahu*, University of Otago, and, through publications, to the general Māori population. This process was decided by the participants, the researcher and the University of Otago. This *accountability* was so important to the researcher that he refused to graduate until he had presented the finished copy of the thesis to and celebrated with the participants (Walker, 2002).

In providing a mandate for the research, Bishop's five principles ensured the integrity of the researcher, participants, academy and research process. Though not an exclusive list, its beauty lies in its simplicity as a set of questions researchers might ask themselves. The 'how to' can vary in terms of underpinning theories, settings, contexts and people though by themselves the principles do not guarantee a favourable outcome. The overall issue is one of 'power' and how we treat people as 'fully human' in the research process.

Conclusion

Our experience has taught us that research and the academy are no longer the exclusive bastion of the non-Indigenous. We Indigenous Peoples have our own ways of thinking and doing (praxis) all of which should and can be researched in ways that inform and enhance our futures. The theoretical underpinnings of research – and social work processes generally – are important but it is the researcher's conduct and the way he implements the research that enhances the prestige – *mana* – of the participants. Bishop's (1996) principles work well within Kaupapa Māori and its critical constructivist perspective. They suggest processes to share power in a way that is useful to all stakeholders concerned and provide a platform for both Māori and Pakeha to evaluate programmes, research methods, policy and institutional arrangements. Whether we like it or not, the Aotearoa New Zealand experience has shown that we can only get so far using our own processes and values because it is the dominant culture that holds the power. There are many ways to try and create spaces for Indigenous development. Critical Kaupapa Māori approaches fight for that space by exposing, deconstructing and challenging layers of power and advocating for structures and processes that allow for authorship and control 'by Māori for Māori'. While Māori in Aotearoa New Zealand have fought and struggled for Kaupapa Māori approaches to be accepted and implemented, we have also benefited from what could be called a 'Pakeha awakening' or a 'Pakeha transformation' that encourages whites to put to death the colonizer within them (Memmi, 1965) (see also Coates, Chapter 3).

In December 2009 one of the authors attended the Aboriginal Strengths Conference in Newcastle Australia. On the second day of the conference, a fellow Māori community worker commented that the Australian Aboriginals were 20 years behind Māori. Anaru considered this and decided no, while Australian Aboriginals may have similar aspirations and dreams for the economic and political development of their people, in his view it was the Australian whites who were 20 years behind Aotearoa New Zealand whites. Whether we like it or not, it is often politicians influenced by public opinion that determine the speed of progress. Māori have never had much problem in making societal gains. Holding onto those gains has been the problem. As soon as Māori initiatives become too successful, the authorities throw on the brakes, remove the funding or change the policy. Māori and Australian Aboriginals have been told that they are too different to learn from one another's experiences and in a sense that is true. However, while Māori are very different with different processes, histories and values, both were colonized at the same time, by the same people, the British, and it is these people that have identical processes, history, values and approaches even to social work practice and research. The nineteenth century was the height of British colonial expansion in Africa, Asia, Canada and the Pacific and there is much to learn from one another by comparing our experiences of colonization and seeing where we are each able to make breakthroughs in public opinion. For example, the British that colonized us are very strong on justice, equality and fair play. These are the concepts we in Aotearoa New Zealand have focused on. Some of the tribal settlements that have been achieved would be unsellable to the Aotearoa New Zealand public without a caveat saying that the resolution was about settling an injustice. Social work practice and research in both Aotearoa New Zealand and Australia would benefit from a continued and strengthened dialogue of these experiences. While some of the space has been created by Māori and Pakeha together, Kaupapa Māori processes have enabled us to take many of the opportunities open to us. As a 'native theory', Kaupapa Māori has allowed us to justify that space and argue for equality. As an action, Kaupapa Māori research and practice has allowed us to provide decolonizing services to our people in culturally appropriate ways that validate our knowledge, our values and our processes.

References

Barlow, C. (1991). *Tikanga Whakaaro: Key Concepts in Maori Culture*. Melbourne: Oxford University Press.

Bishop, R. (1995). Collaborative research stories: Whakawhanaungatanga. PhD thesis, University of Otago, New Zealand.

Bishop, R. (1996). *Collaborative Research Stories: Whakawhanaungatanga*. Palmerston North, NZ: The Dunmore Press.

Crotty, M. (1998). *The Foundations of Social Research: Meaning and Perspective in the Research Process*. Sydney: Allen & Unwin.

Eketone, A.D. (2008). Theoretical underpinnings of Kaupapa Maori directed practice. *MAI Review, 1* [Online]. Available at: http://www.review.mai.ac.nz [accessed: 11 November 2011].

Freire, P. (1970). *Pedagogy of the Oppressed*. London: Penguin.

Gibson, A. (2011). Ngai Tahu upbeat despite big hit from quakes. *New Zealand Herald*, 19 October 2011 [Online]. Available at: http://www.nzherald.co.nz/property/news/article.cfm?c_id=8&objectid=10760067 [accessed: 21 November 2011].

Humpage, L.V. and Fleras, A. (2001). Intersecting discourses: Closing the gaps – 'Social justice' and the Treaty of Waitangi. *Social Policy Journal of New Zealand*, 16, 37–53.

Kiro, C. (2000). Māori research and the social services: Te Puawaitanga o Te Tohu. *Te Komako. Social Work Review*, 12(4), 26–32.

Mead, S.M. (2003). *Tikanga* Māori: Living by Māori Values. Wellington, NZ: Huia Publishers.

Memmi, A. (1965). *The Coloniser and the Colonised*. Boston, MA: Benson Press.

Munford, R. and Walsh-Tapiata, W. (2001). *Strategies for Change: Community Development in Aotearoa / New Zealand* (3rd edn). Massey University, Palmerston North, NZ: School of Social Policy and Social Work.

Pihama, L. (1993). *Tungia te Ururua, kia tupu whakaritorito te tupu o te harakeke: A Critical Awareness of Parents as First Teachers*. Unpublished MA thesis, University of Auckland.

Russell, K.J. (2000). *Landscape: Perceptions of Kai Tahu*. Dunedin: Thesis submitted for the degree of Doctor of Philosophy in Anthropology at the University of Otago.Ruwhiu, L. (1995). Home fires burn so brightly with theoretical flames. *Te Komako Social Work Review*, 7(1), 21–5.

Ruwhiu, L. (2001). Bicultural Issues in Aotearoa New Zealand Social Work. In M. Connolly (ed.), *New Zealand Social Work Contexts and Practices*. Auckland, NZ: Oxford University Press, 54–72.

Smith, G.H. (1997). *The Development of Kaupapa* Māori: Theory and Praxis. IRI PhD thesis series number 3. Auckland, NZ: University of Auckland.

Smith, L.T. (1999). *Decolonizing Methodologies: Research and Indigenous Peoples*. Dunedin, NZ: University of Otago Press.

Tolich, M. and Davidson, C. (1999). *Starting Fieldwork: An Introduction to Qualitative Research in New Zealand*. Auckland, NZ: Oxford University Press.

Walker, R. (1990). *Ka Whawhai Tonu Matou*. Auckland, NZ: Penguin.Walker, S. (2002). *Maatua Whangai: The Perspective of Caregivers*. Dunedin, NZ: Unpublished Master's thesis, University of Otago.

Walker, R. (2004). *Ka Whawhai Tonu Matou* (2nd edn). Auckland, NZ: Penguin.

Walker, S., Eketone, A. and Gibbs, A. (2006). An exploration of Kaupapa Maori research, its principles, processes and applications. *International Journal of Social Research Methodology*, 9(4), 331–4.

Ward, A. (1999). *An Unsettled History: Treaty Claims in New Zealand Today*. Wellington, NZ: Bridget William Books.

Webster, S. (1998). *Patrons of Maori Culture: Power, Theory and Ideology in the Maori Renaissance*. Dunedin, NZ: University of Otago Press.

Williams, H. (1971). *Dictionary of the Maori Language* (7th edn). Wellington, NZ: Legislation Direct.

Wilson, J. (2009). Literature as resistance in the Maori renaissance: Patricia Grace, Witi Ihimaera, Alan Duff. *Anglistik: Journal of International English Studies*, 173–86. 0947-0034 [Online]. Available at: http://nectar.northampton. ac.uk/2218/ [accessed: 6 December 2011].

Winiata, W. (1984). Speech. Proceedings of the Maori Economic Development Summit Conference, Wellington, Ministry of Maori Affairs. G.3–H.1.

Chapter 14

Indigenizing Research for Culturally Relevant Social Work Practice

Jon K. Matsuoka, Paula T. Morelli and Hamilton McCubbin

This chapter examines the unique features of Indigenous populations. As shown in Chapter 4, cultural relevance is an issue of great importance for Indigenous and other minority groups, such as migrant populations who choose to use their own cultural approaches to social work in their host country (see also Gray, Coates and Yellow Bird, 2008; see also Chapter 6). Transnational identities have relevance in many first world countries where immigrants (including work migrants and refugees) with strong cultural and national identities might be excluded from their home country for economic or political reasons. In many countries migrant and Indigenous populations face similar issues of misrecognition. This leads to discrimination based on cultural stereotypes that create a dichotomous insider/outsider divide. Most apposite then is the concept of culturally relevant Indigenous research, given the attention given to the historical trauma of Indigenous Peoples in the social work literature (Brave Heart, 2000; Campbell and Evans-Campbell, 2011; Evans-Campbell, 2008; Gray et al., 2008; see Chapter 7). Indigenous and migrant communities present important challenges for social work and ways have to be found to minimize the profession's historic dependence on stereotypes by proactively seeking to better understand the historical and cultural roots of Indigenous and migrant populations, their belief systems and values, cultural traditions and practices, and assimilation and adaptation to the host or majority culture. The social work profession is challenged to develop theories, research methodologies and intervention strategies based upon knowledge of the unique histories and cultures of Indigenous and migrant populations, and their vulnerabilities, strengths and resilience. The profession has a responsibility to serve these populations guided by competencies based on culturally relevant research and evidence-based practice and policies.

Unique Features of Indigenous and Immigrant Populations

Indigenous Contexts: Culture and Ancestry

As a society becomes increasingly culturally diverse, competing forces ultimately determine the form and ideology underlying institutional arrangements (Freire,

2002). Under a dominant design, all subsequent cultural entries are subjugated and modified. For example, in US society, whose cultural formation is driven by economics, the cultural base is primarily Euro-American. As new cultures enter US society, the base of imported cultures eventually erodes and is replaced by Euro-American beliefs and values. While Indigenous populations preceded colonization, migrants are self-selected cohorts who leave their homelands in search of more promising economic or political opportunities and a better future for themselves and their families. After generations of acculturation and miscegenation, ancestral traits become lost.

This social process stands in stark contrast to Indigenous Peoples and groups who were involuntarily marginalized and subordinated in their ancestral homelands. In the United States, American Indians, Alaskan Natives, Native Hawaiians and other Pacific Islanders have qualitatively different cultural experiences than migrants from other countries. First Nation Peoples of North America, Native Hawaiians and other Pacific Islanders had thriving and sovereign societies when Europeans arrived on the scene and the subsequent subjugation and genocide of these Indigenous populations is well documented (Benham and Heck, 1998; Stannard, 1992). Resistance to the imposing forces of the West, especially when protecting their valued resources, accelerated the decline of the Indigenous people.

Indigenous experiences of imposition and genocide, and their resulting experiences and behaviours, diverge from those of migrants. This is not to minimize the overt racism and struggles faced by migrant groups, especially the first generations that came from abroad. Their experience reflects a 'push-pull' dynamic – the pull of a better place with new opportunities, where acculturation is a means of improving their socioeconomic standing (see Chapter 4). This experience is in sharp contrast with that of Indigenous Peoples whose identities, strengths, resources, beliefs and values were trivialized or eliminated, leaving them with a loss of self-governance accompanied by diminished hopes and aspirations.

Thus, the experiences and social outcomes of migrant and Indigenous populations depend in large part on where they find themselves on the continuum of assimilation and acculturation. Those that wilfully migrate are predisposed to acculturate to North American cultural norms. Those who were invaded or relocated under duress may be less motivated if not outright resistant to adopt what they perceive to be an invasive, foreign and hostile culture. Ethnic minorities who resist US culture are chastised for being unpatriotic or ungrateful. These notions turn into a collective sentiment of 'blaming the victim'. Perhaps this sentiment is most prominently directed toward migrants who came to this country seeking a better life and entered into open competition with the majority stakeholders for resources and status.

Disparities in educational achievement and socioeconomic mobility are reflected in differential group histories. Asian Americans have been deemed the 'model minority' and are often compared to other minority groups who have struggled to 'make it' in US society. Attributions for differential success include higher intelligence, strong work ethic and cultural affinity. Pervasive notions exist that Asians are predisposed to success because they possess inherent qualities of discipline and motivation. In contrast, Indigenous populations, such as Native Hawaiians, are characterized as unmotivated with minimal aspirations. Thus, they are overrepresented in vocational and special education programmes (Benham and Heck, 1998; Kamehameha Schools/Bishop Estate, 1983). Contrasting depictions of migrant and Indigenous populations should not detract from the salience of their strengths and capabilities that are often masked by stereotypes and overgeneralizations. Equally important is the emergent voices of these minority groups that render clarity as to how they see themselves, their cultures and their futures.

Unique Intelligence

Indigenous and migrant populations in the USA are often confined to living within segregated communities removed from society's socioeconomic mainstream. Within these enclaves, people are socialized according to unique behavioural and cognitive norms. Insular and often materially deprived environs can serve to repress healthy human development but such circumstances can also breed creativity and innovation. A unique intelligence emerges that reflects a blend of cultural elements and oppressive circumstances. Innovations in music and the arts, fashion and idiomatic language have emerged from ethnic subcultures and crossed over into mainstream popular culture. Trends emerging from Native Hawaiian and American Indian youth culture have become the cultural standard in US society.

Intelligence is very much determined by situation and context. In resource-deprived environments, intelligence is measured by a person's ability to survive by developing life skills that enable him/her to function while tending to constant and immediate threats from their surroundings. Those living in privileged environments are at an advantage in that they can focus more directly on personal educational and career goals as well as family needs. In other words, attending to personal safety issues and basic survival needs are not primary issues of concern for privileged sectors of society; however, these issues can limit the achievements of people from less advantaged environments.

Despite the great variations in social environs and associated intelligences, in society's effort to promote homogeneity, notions of intelligence are narrowly defined by standardized psychological measures developed on the majority population. They often also exhibit a gender bias. These measures are used to assess individual intellectual capacity and affect opportunities for education and career development. Hence people raised in insulated environs, who choose to venture out to pursue new opportunities, are required to adopt broader behavioural, cognitive and linguistic patterns in order to function effectively in mainstream society. Except in rare circumstances, Euro-Americans are not required to venture out in the same way and acquire new cultural skill sets. 'Making it' requires familiarity with a cultural context. Members of minority groups who succeed in the larger society are required to be multicultural by the very nature of such success. That is, they must possess a repertoire of behaviours that allows them to move readily between sociocultural spheres and manage parallel and sometimes contradictory realities. Thus, in the process of becoming multicultural, minority populations must develop a high level of social intelligence, which includes the ability to:

- Acquire dual and sometimes conflicting behavioural and cognitive sets.
- Develop highly refined observational and sensory skills in order to read accurately and respond effectively to cues across sociocultural spheres.
- Master the sociopolitics of culture and race while pursuing educational and career interests.
- Negotiate value conflicts shaped by ancestry and cultural differences.
- Balance demands and social expectations and priorities of different cultural groups and recalibrate competing priorities to fulfil cultural and achievement goals (Wardle and Cruz-Janzen, 2004).

Historical Trauma and Ancestral Memory

Notions of post-traumatic stress disorder as defined in the DSM-IV-TR (American Psychological Association, 2000) suggest that symptoms associated with this disorder occur as a direct result of discrete and relatively recent life events. It is surmised that exposure to violent events, such as military combat or rape, predisposes individuals to exhibit uncontrolled rage, nightmares and isolationism. Aetiological conceptions generally do not consider the cumulative effects of historical trauma and a long-term process of reconciling pain that extends across generations. Trauma alters human behaviour and associated thinking such that populations subjected to collective trauma have modified their strategies of socialization and survival as a way to protect themselves from external threats. Native people in all of North America experienced holocausts that culminated in their near extermination.

The first Western voyagers to Hawai`i estimated a native population of approximately 400,000. Subsequent estimates based on more scientific data place the number of Hawaiians at the point of Western contact closer to 800,000 to 1 million. Hawai`i is one of the most isolated landmasses in the world. It lies in the middle of the world's largest body of water. Because of its remoteness, anthropologists theorize that Hawai`i was one of the last places on earth to be inhabited by humans, and that occurred about 1,000 AD. The first Europeans, led by British sea captain James Cook, arrived in Hawai`i in 1778. Missionaries arrived from New England in 1820. By 1831, through a mixture of choice by the Hawaiian people and the pressing influence of missionaries, the Indigenous spiritual and cultural system was abolished and a thousand Christian schools were built. The second generation of missionaries abandoned their religious pursuits and embraced self-serving opportunities for wealth once they realized the vast economic opportunities in Hawai`i.

In 1848, businessmen were the major force behind changing the traditional system of land ownership. The *Mahele*, as it is referred to in the Hawaiian language, allowed non-native people to own Hawaiian land for the first time. From that point on, US Americans hoarded lands through purchase, quit title and adverse possession. By the turn of the century, a mere 50 years later, whites owned four acres of land for every one acre owned by Indigenous Hawaiians. They used their vast land holdings to cultivate sugar and pineapples. Once firmly situated in the Hawaiian economic and political system, a group of US American sugar barons, whose lineage could be tied directly to the original missionaries, staged an overthrow, with the backing of the US Marines that ousted the last reigning monarch of Hawai`i, Queen Lili'uokalani in 1893.

By this time, the native Hawaiian population was decimated. Captain Cook's maiden voyage to Hawai`i brought sexually transmitted diseases and missionaries, whalers and other foreigners brought a host of other diseases to which Native Hawaiians had no immunity. By some estimates, the Indigenous Hawaiian population diminished by 90 per cent of its pre-Western contact level and Indigenous Hawaiians continue to suffer severe health and social problems. Native Hawaiians have some of the highest per capita rates of heart disease and cancer, diabetes, severe problems related to drug and alcohol abuse and consequent domestic violence problems, disproportionately high levels of mental health problems and suicide, the lowest educational achievement and employment levels, the highest number of teen pregnancies and the highest rates of criminal convictions and incarceration (Office of Hawaiian Affairs, 2002).

In Hawai`i, Native Hawaiians constitute the highest number of residents in public housing and the highest percentage of homeless people in the United States. Demographers predict that the population of pure Native Hawaiians will be extinct by the year 2040. The contemporary status of Hawaiians is obviously the result of their history of marginalization and dispossession. This storyline of overthrow and colonization has been played out multiple times throughout North America and the Pacific region and the social consequences are strikingly similar. Trauma is incurred from the loss of culture, traditional lands and resources, family members and leaders; violent encounters and witnessing the physical and emotional suffering of your people; being rendered a minority in one's homeland; being required to live by the strictures of an alien society; and a deep inner sense of social injustice.

On a collective scale, symptoms of post-traumatic stress disorder are manifested in various ways, including anger turned outward into violence or inward in the form of substance abuse and helplessness, refusal to conform to Western strictures or an obsessive adherence to tradition, high rates of fertility and teenage pregnancies, and political radicalism. Not all of these manifestations are negative if placed in a certain context. Being steadfast in protecting traditions is critical in perpetuating cultures. High fertility can be viewed as a form of sociobiological compensation for decimated populations, and political activism is a healthy expression of social discontent.

The attitudes and dispositions of oppressed and traumatized populations do not necessarily follow a predictable schema but are a part of a larger and highly complex intaglio. As mentioned, strategies to avoid conflict and violence served to alter settlement and socialization patterns. Interpretations of direct experience and oral knowledge handed down by predecessors are mixed into a cognitive brew that influences political orientation and behavioural expression.

In cases where traditions and associated behaviours have been severed, efforts to restore culture have been met with competing notions of originality and authenticity. While such efforts are noble in the sense that entities are committed to cultural revival, they also serve to fracture cultural and political movements. In short, attitudes and behaviours that are borne out of collective trauma are not always decipherable and the unaccountability is especially perplexing to those not living the experience. Historical legacies can be used to understand post-traumatic reactions that extend well beyond current conceptions. Two hundred years of oppression and trauma are not remedied through job opportunities and new economies. Ancestral memory leads Indigenous people to distrust other people and rebel against the system, especially when conformity means buying into a system that eradicated their stabilizing foundation through colonization (see also Chapter 7).

Collectivity and Culture

Collective cultures, or those oriented toward group behaviours, exist because group members rely heavily on each other for their livelihood and survival. Many cultures that originated from agricultural and subsistence-based economies continue to espouse collective values emphasizing social cohesiveness. Through their socialization, collective people are inherently sensitive to their social ecology, its dynamic forces and the ramifications of change within their social milieu. A critical objective is to maintain balance and harmony in the social economy in their milieu. Collective peoples have developed highly sophisticated social economies that are essentially safety nets for families and communities. Extended family and communal networks are relied on for support in raising children and caring for the aged, assisting in times of crisis, organizing special events and engaging in work projects that benefit the community at large. With the exception of the aged and infirmed, participation in providing support is a prerequisite. Prescriptive and proscriptive norms guide a stringent system of reciprocity that provides order and assigns roles to the group.

For both immigrant and Indigenous people in the United States, settlement patterns and the formation of enclaves served to further affirm cultural values related to collectivity. A collective orientation was the basis for the development of community-based practices leading to economic self-reliance. Cultural and political associations, rotating loan and banking systems, and other informal services that aided the socioeconomic mobility of fellow ethnics emanated from community-based institutions that offered greater reliability and trust to the communities they served. Resistance to change could be attributed to self-protective mechanisms. Cultural conservatism is reinforced by undesirable changes individuals observe in other domains. Through this orientation, they have created novel ways to protect their self-esteem and mental health.

Early research indicated that culturally divergent childrearing practices resulted in differential personality traits in people (Jared, 2012). In some cultures, attachment and emotional bonding with parent and child, especially mothers, was observed through continuous physical attachment and tactile stimulation. The outcome of these behaviours, along with brevity of speech and verbal exchange, was developing children who were less verbally expressive. Children were also observed to be more attentive to other people and to their environment.

What emerges from differential childrearing practices is an intelligence that is influenced by cultural values (Pagel, 2012; Poston, 1990; Powell, 1988). In the West, intelligence is often equated to the ability to express ideas in words and through articulation of thought. In the Eastern and Pacific regions, intelligence is often equated to an ability to read social situations and to act in accordance with socially prescribed roles and protocols. A heightened sensitivity to social situations, as well as a self-consciousness regarding how people engage others socially, has also been explained as a basis for highly developed appraisal skills and social intelligence. This heightened sensitivity is also an explanation for the development of neurotic behaviour when it goes awry. A strong collective sense is inversely related to individualism. Those who possess a collective identity generally consider the sentiment of the group before taking action.

Diverse Cultural and Ethnic Identities

Indigenous and immigrant populations change as a result of assimilation, adaptation and preservation. The evidence is clear that these populations are called upon to make some degree of accommodation by engaging in the process of assimilation and adaptation in order that they may establish themselves in foreign and sometimes resistant host populations. To achieve a sense of 'fit' these special populations have to find meaning, purpose and a way of life in the dominant culture. Even in the face of colonization or oppression, they are called upon to subordinate their identity, culture, language and traditions in order to survive (Dubos, 1974). On the other hand, it is equally true that families do preserve their cultures inclusive of language, beliefs and values while adapting to a new and demanding social context (see Wright et al., 2011). Work with Indigenous and immigrant communities reveals the diversity in adaptation which is of particular importance to the social work profession in search of understanding and finding the best ways to serve these populations.

Science has treated culture, ethnicity and cultural and ethnic identity as categorical variables used to classify Indigenous and immigrant groups in terms of their genealogical origins. Hawaiian, Japanese, Chinese, Korean, Vietnamese, Italian or Jewish families, to name a few, spring to mind. Simply put, culture or ethnicity may be viewed as a social classification grounded in our knowledge of the cultural and ethnic origins of the family unit. From this classification may flow a list of ethnically related factors or processes which best describe and predict family adjustment and adaptation, resilience and well-being (Jones and Jungmiwha, 2013; McCubbin, McCubbin, Samuels, Zhang and Sievers, 2013; Schlabach, 2013).

Unfortunately, this simple but useful system for Indigenous and immigrant classification has prominent limitations which deserve consideration in our efforts to understand Indigenous and immigrant people and their communities. Clearly, ethnic origins and cultural identity emerge by virtue of assumptions made about people's cultural legacy which is taught and transferred from parents and kin and is transferred across generations from their ancestors. When viewed from this perspective, descent may be genetic and or social (Keyes, 1981) and one comes to realize that family systems may have multiple ethnic ancestries. This family condition may emerge as a result different processes, inclusive of inter-ethnic marriages, local adoptions and international adoptions, blended family systems and a family system created by artificial insemination. This complexity is exacerbated by the fact that there is no invariable pattern to which cultural differences will be used as emblematic of their ethnic difference. Language is often identified as a universal distinguishing feature, but not all ethnic groups and families have a distinctive language. Even cultural characteristics used as emblematic of ethnic identity depend upon the interpretation of the experience and actions of ancestors or forebears. Such interpretations are often presented in the form of myths or legends in which historical events are accorded symbolic significance (Trask, 1998). Ethnic origins and identity may be founding cultural traditions related to life cycle transitions, such as coming of age, marriage, illness and death (Braun, Pietsch and Blanchette, 2000). It is particularly in rites of passage that one finds highly emotional symbolic reinforcement of ethnic patterns. Ethnic identity and classification may involve choices, among alternatives, by the individual, family, community and the professional:

- The adoption of an Indigenous Hawaiian-American genealogy might be reinforced by stressing the successes of historical leaders who have gained the respect and admiration of the people. In Hawai`i, King Kamehameha I and Bernice Pauahi Bishop come to mind as ethnic leaders worthy of emulation (see Chapter 7).
- The vulnerability and historically traumatized past of colonization might be underscored by a focus on the loss of land, culture and sovereignty. Conversely, the adoption of a social activist identity might result in a commitment to reclaim land, independence and sovereignty.
- The embrace of a Western Hawaiian-American lifestyle might emphasize achievement, materials goods and individual success.
- Adoption of citizen status could enforce an identity outside of national geographical boundaries. In these terms, the Indigenous community is not a

state of the United States, but an independent nation under US occupation.
- Identification with the Pan-Ethnic identity movement (Pan-Indian, Pan Polynesian and Pan-Asian) would result in members of an ethnic group, who perceive themselves to be too small in number, developing clout by forming a collective identity better able to engage the dominant population, find common ground and access power and influence. Once mobilized, ethnic groups cooperate to form and create an encompassing identity with the purpose of confronting the agencies of State and Federal government so as to establish autonomy and control over their lives.
- Adoption of an 'All-American' identity might mean dismissing ethnic origins and descent (Keyes, 1981).

Clearly, then, there is enormous diversity in Indigenous and immigrant people's cultural and ethnic allegiance. With this in mind, we are now in a position to clarify two myths:

- First, assimilation does not mean Indigenous or immigrant minority groups will disappear into the dominant society, as some demographers predict, and lose their ethnic distinctiveness (Dubos, 1965). This 'total assimilation' does not occur. Assimilation, as part of resilience, is best viewed as the 'reduction of cultural distance between specific groups with respect to particular aspects of behavior' (Banton, 1981: 37). Adaptation depends on a minority group retaining the distinctive identity or what Light (1981) called ethnic consciousness.
- Secondly, social workers need to recognize that Indigenous and immigrant people are engaged in a transformation process, the outcome of which is shaped, among other influences, by self, family, group and professional identification. Where the individual, family, community or the profession exercises its choice among the options noted above, has significant bearing upon our understanding and prediction of the behaviour and the professional strategy for intervention.

Developing Theories: Resilience and Relational Well-Being

Witkin and Iverson (2008) address the profession's struggles and emerging issues in US social work. Of importance to Indigenous and immigrant people, they point to the role of science and the development of theory to advance research and guide evidence-based practice. The study of Indigenous and immigrant populations reveals the underlying theories of culture-based behaviour worthy of consideration as a basis for the advancement of the social work profession. While beyond the scope of this chapter to present the various frameworks that have viability for the profession and particularly its work with Indigenous and immigrant people, it is instructive to introduce one such framework to demonstrate the potential of social work's contribution to theory development, practice and policy.

A relational worldview and measure of well-being (McCubbin et al., 2011) emerged from the community-based studies of McGregor, Morelli and Matsuoka (2003) and the therapy-oriented transactional systems theory of Papajohn and Spiegel (1975). McGregor et al.'s (2003) investigation of rural Indigenous communities revealed a worldview of relational well-being, a conceptualization based on cultural history and transactional systems theory. Central to their conceptualization are the interdependence among Indigenous people and nature, the beliefs in the sacredness of the animate and inanimate world, the collective gathering and sharing, and the organic family system. To focus their central thesis, McGregor et al. (2003: 109) claimed 'Well-being is synonymous with people-environment kinship and the organic relationship that bonds humans to the land.' When this relationship is enhanced or disrupted, the well-being of the people is impacted.

McGregor et al. (2003) point to a core Indigenous belief that the land lives as do the spirits of family ancestors who care for the ancestral land. The land, a living entity, has and will continue to provide for generations. Drawing from the ecological conceptualizations of Bronfenbrenner and Ceci (1994), McGregor et al. (2003) also created a relational-ecological model which reflects this interdependence but adds land as a sense of place and source of nurturance and energy, well-being and the health of the nation, community, family and individual. Stewardship of the land is central to the creation of Indigenous well-being which itself is rooted in spirituality and all that the ancestors have passed on to future generations. In return, the future generations gain knowledge of the life of the land, understand the fundamentals of cultural resource management and land use, and embrace the natural elements of land, air, water and ocean as interconnected and interdependent parts of their family and individual lives. In this worldview, water is wealth and ultimately the use of cultural resources for conservation is seen as an investment and giving back to future generations.

Community well-being, an integral dimension of relational well-being, is viewed as part and parcel of residing in a location thus resulting in a sense of place. From this perspective, longevity in partnership with a sense of place ensures continuity and allows for the sharing of beliefs and values across generations. It is this context in which community leadership is cultivated, economic development is nurtured, and cultural and spiritual practices give roots to their sense of security, predictability and the meaning of life. The community cultivates spiritual energy and an environment for learning and practising values and beliefs as well as the transmission of knowledge. Of importance, the community is defined by a system of rules, expectations and norms related to roles, responsibilities and behaviours.

Ancestors and ancestral history are fundamental elements of an Indigenous worldview and thus multigenerational relationships are integral to fabric of the Indigenous theory. McGregor et al. (2003: 121) state, 'The deep sense of relatedness is at the core of Indigenous values, beliefs, interactions, processes and traditions that form the foundation of harmonious family life'. In this framework, the family is connected to the past, present and future and the family system's identity or schema (McCubbin and McCubbin, 2005) is defined by its ethnic origins, values, beliefs, expectations and traditions. It thus reinforces a connection to one's Indigenous origins as key to an Indigenous identity.

Western systems theory and ecological conceptualizations cohere with a relational Indigenous worldview, where well-being depends crucially on the relationship between local – land and community – national, familial and individual well-being (Cross, 1998; McGregor et al., 2003; McCubbin and McCubbin, 2005). Well-being then results from a holistic interconnectedness (relational worldview) between humans, nature, earth, universe and the social processes of nations, communities, families and individuals and must be measured in terms of the interaction between these diverse systems or levels.

Research with Indigenous and Immigrant Populations

Current theoretical formats and paradigms are remiss when it comes to understanding the phenomenology of Indigenous and immigrant populations (Kahuakalau, 2004). Traditional research approaches relying on inferential statistics can only remotely capture the everyday social realms of these societies. Unfortunately, alternative methods, including grounded theoretical approaches that serve to provide holistic impressions of phenomena, are deemed 'soft' and lacking in credibility (Denzin and Lincoln, 1998). The tension generated from conflicting perspectives have stretched the boundaries of traditional research and led to new sensibilities that emphasize multi-method research approaches. For example, Bolland and Atherton (2000) described a heuristic paradigm that accepts all research methodologies, not privileging any ontology, epistemology or methodology. They propose a relativistic approach that suggests there are no universal standards of right or wrong and that all knowledge is dependent on the subjective knower. The acceptance of broader conceptualizations of scientific inquiry lead to the evolution of paradigms and techniques that enable social scientists and policy makers to hold a clearer and deeper understanding of alternative ways of life and associated issues.

The tradition of positivism and associated methods and paradigms has done much to damage the reputation of social science in Indigenous communities. This period has also challenged subsequent generations of researchers, both non-Indigenous and Indigenous, to erase the perceptions of anthropologists, sociologists and others who exploited their trust and goodwill. Moreover, it has been difficult to convince Indigenous leaders of the utility of empirical data in protecting their rights, resources and traditional and customary practices. As Smith (1999) stated, Indigenous people are on an important quest to recover their languages and epistemological foundations. Decolonizing research is a critical means to reclaim their histories and rests on several core principles, including the need to gain trust, employ culturally appropriate access and research protocols, strive for authenticity and use culturally appropriate research methods.

Gaining Trust

Many communities, especially Indigenous ones, have an inherent mistrust of government and university researchers. Overcoming the barrier of mistrust is the first major challenge in conducting community-based research. The mistrust is drawn from a history of exploitation from outsiders and a general community impression that study results unilaterally benefit the academic careers of researchers. Communities have acquired a political sensitivity and savvy that requires researchers to explain how the study will benefit residents. A researcher may possess an immense amount of technical and methodological knowledge and have the right motives for engaging in community-based research, yet still be denied entry into an Indigenous community. Those bent on preserving their cultures and communities are not impressed by credentials and technical know-how.

In locales where communities are tightly linked through cultural or political affiliation, there is a high level of exchange among civic leaders. Researchers acquire reputations based on who they typically are contracted by (state, private developer or community), the rigour of their work, quality of the product, applications of the study results, sensitivity to community protocols, and the extent to which they make long-term commitments to a community's well-being. In many situations, the reputation of researchers precedes them, and this influences their level of acceptance (Battiste, 2008; Kim, Yang and Hwang, 2006). For example, research consultants in Hawai`i who are frequently contracted by developers for environmental impact assessments have at times been systematically locked-out of communities opposed to development projects. However, research consultants who traditionally work in communities and have applied participatory action approaches leading to tangible benefits are often sought after and embraced by Indigenous communities. Levels of compensation can be considered a determining motivation. Some residents might question the motivations and commitment to community well-being by high-paid research consultants, while those consultants working on a *pro bono* basis would not be accused of having ulterior motives.

Trust and social bonding are contingent on the extent to which people share common features. Behaviourally disparate parties must overcome huge obstacles in order to know enough about others to trust them. Establishing trust is facilitated by behavioural and semantic concurrence. Fluency in the native language, when it is the first language of residents, removes major logistical problems related to translation and conceptual equivalence and breeds trust.

Access and Protocols

There is an array of culturally-based protocols that must be applied when initiating a research project. Contacting and gaining endorsements from the 'right' persons, who are often respected elders or *kupuna* will determine the degree to which a researcher is able to access other critical informants. Indigenous communities are fraught with dynamics related to family affiliation and length of stay, history of personal contact, political orientation, socioeconomic status and race or ethnic relations. It is requisite for researchers, through a reconnaissance, to explore and gain an awareness of these dynamics. Negotiating ties with one sector, however, may inadvertently close the door with competing sectors in the community and obviate a cross-sectional analysis.

Engaging a community in research requires many of the same strategies as community organizing, including exhibiting culturally appropriate mannerisms and a non-intrusive style. In communities, maintaining objectivity through social distance is counterintuitive to gaining the trust of residents through a process of social immersion. Social distancing does not permit a researcher to embrace the culture and its intricacies and subtleties, let alone gain access to residents who are inherently suspicious of strangers. Abiding by cultural protocols, such as asking permission rather than imposing oneself, sensitivity to non-verbal situations, sharing family background and genealogies, especially if they are tied to the geographic area, speaking the dialect and using idiomatic language, and generally building a base of commonality are all essential means of establishing rapport and trust.

Thrusting uninvited researchers onto the community scene with a research agenda is a form of 'carpet-bagging.' This seemingly standard approach in earlier years has generated widespread scepticism in communities and subsequently created barriers for well-intentioned researchers who are committed to gathering critically needed data. Under such conditions, researchers must lay the groundwork for research by convincing community leaders that qualitative and quantitative data can be vital ammunition for promoting policies and planning decisions aimed at community preservation and social development.

In Pacific cultures, social reciprocity is a critical aspect of interpersonal relations. From an Indigenous perspective, the economy of speech between negotiating parties is a good predictor of balance and parity in a working relationship. The role of the researcher is to listen, acknowledge residents' intelligence and wisdom, incorporate Indigenous perspectives into the research methodology and involve a working team of residents at every phase of the research process. 'Politically enlightened' communities strive to develop true partnerships with researchers by providing critical information that guides the research process.

In many Pacific societies, strangers greet each other by reciting their family genealogy. This protocol is significant in that it serves to inform each party of the other's lineage and pays homage to each person's ancestors (Marsella, Olivera, Plummer and Crabbe, 1998; Walker, 2004). Though there are varying degrees of this practice, from the highly ritualized to a less formal and indirect inquiry into one's family background, the practice remains strong. In Hawai`i, for example, the typical first questions of a stranger are 'what high school did you attend' and 'are you related to so and so' (with the same surname). These questions tie a person to a community or island and gather important information on their family background. Such contextualization is a means to appraise the person and researchers are not immune to this practice. Despite having credentials that reflect academic qualification, Indigenous residents are keen to learn more about the researcher's values and motives that are often linked to place and family of origin. For many Indigenous people, credibility is derived from the integrity of the individual and less so from academic degrees.

Striving for Authenticity

Researchers working in Indigenous communities must recognize that society is indoctrinated with a colonial version of historicity whose rendition serves to justify colonial mastery. Much of the accepted narratives on Indigenous Peoples are really the narratives of colonialists and cultural hegemons (Touraine, 2001). In the Pacific, Indigenous claimants have emerged to assert contending visions of the cultural past. There is a revitalized struggle occurring globally among Indigenous people to manage, define and promulgate their own histories and cultural realities.

This legacy, and subsequent movements to alter previous conceptions, has politicized the research process. Indigenous communities are becoming aware of the power of research and its utility and are assuming greater control over who is involved, how research is conducted, and how data are interpreted and used. Past attempts to document the ways of life of Indigenous Peoples were fraught with cultural biases, misinterpretations and even deliberate efforts to deceive foreign observers as a form of mockery. Communities are taking corrective action by supporting research that promotes authenticity and sets an important standard for future investigations.

Authenticity has many attributes. It is about peoples' interpretations of and reactions to phenomena that are drawn from deeply imbedded cultural values and culturally constructed notions of reality. Researchers bent on finding the 'truth' must reconsider mythology, lore and superstition as terms used to describe and denigrate Indigenous beliefs. That is, a phenomenon that is not easily demystified and apprehended through measurement is often deemed to be imaginary. In many Pacific cultures, spirituality and metaphysics are essential elements in an ecology that supports human well-being. Western social science does not have available methodologies capable of apprehending Indigenous spirituality and other empirically elusive phenomena. Authenticity is brought to bear through methods that are adapted to capturing the inherent qualities of spirituality and other cultural phenomena.

While objectivity may be viewed as critical in any research venture, maintaining personal distance impedes the comprehension of authentic culture. Even researchers who manifest excellent rapport and behavioural sensitivity must spend time with the subjects of their inquiry in order to observe a spectrum of situational and multidimensional behaviours. Immersion in a context provides researchers with an opportunity to understand social interaction. Relying on multiple data sources enable researchers to combine empirical themes and draw whole and more complete impressions.

Appropriate Research Methods

The positivism that emerged during the modern era is gradually being replaced with heuristic paradigms promoting notions of data discovery and triangulation (Bolland and Atherton, 2000). This multi-method approach is well suited for securing rich descriptions of Indigenous life conditions. Statistics drawn from multivariate analysis are useful in determining broad relational patterns between factors. Statistical results, however, may only represent the tip of the iceberg and should be placed amid other forms of data as a way to cross-validate impressions.

Some researchers who subscribe to a multi-method research approach use survey results as the central force that drives the acquisition and interpretation of qualitative data. This is problematic if measures are unreliable across cultures, data processing is prone to systematic error, samples are unrepresentative of Indigenous populations, and so on. Methods used in data gathering should not be staged as an incremental process with one method taking precedence over another. Rather, they should be 'stand-alone' activities contributing to a broad, multidimensional dataset that is triangulated or woven together into mosaic-like community profiles. After all, communities are nested, layered and multidimensional systems, and single data source profiling is reductionistic.

Other than the typical quantitative survey and qualitative key informant methods, highly viable research methods are used with Indigenous communities (Turner, Beeghley and Powers, 2002), one of which is geographic information systems (GIS) mapping that Minerbi, McGregor and Matsuoka (2003) used to chart behavioural patterns related to traditional and customary practices, subsistence patterns and resource areas, sacred sites and population changes. In other studies, GIS has been used to demarcate land ownership boundaries and jurisdictions, zone designations, service locations and catchment areas. Data acquired in this manner is transformed into GIS maps and used to assist social planners and decision-makers in determining the location and extent of cultural impacts related to proposed development projects. The technique resonates with Indigenous informants because it is used to collect 'place-based' data.

A major challenge in Indigenous research is settling on a time frame that satisfies the expectations of funders and contractors and addresses community issues related to the time-consuming process of building trust and rapport (Morrow, 1994). Researchers must find a pace that moves the study process forward to meet contractual agreements and is sensitive to participant involvement. For Indigenous participants not used to being subjects of scientific inquiry, it may require more time and persuading to garner a sample large enough to validate results. Westernized cohorts who understand the utility and power of empirical data are generally less resistant, and thus time requirements are easier to meet. Although research plans are posed at the outset of a study, it is critical to maintain a degree of flexibility. If a methodological approach is not resonating well with participants, then alternatives must be considered. In some cases, even pretesting instruments do not always provide investigators with enough predictive information regarding their applicability.

Larger communal research processes are frequently most effective when they involve civic and Indigenous leaders, heads of government agencies and business leaders from the geographic areas of interest. The study or task group serves to develop a conceptual framework, reviews questionnaires for language and content, publicizes the study, organizes community involvement, assists in interpreting study results, and helps develop an empirically based action plan. From beginning to end Indigenous leadership can be enmeshed in the research process. The depth of their involvement encourages communities to assume ownership of the data and to realize the significance of research in terms of policy development and social planning. The joint involvement of multiple stakeholders ensures objectivity and a government-facilitated planning and action process. Constituents sitting at the table create a context for multi-perspectivism, mutuality and buy-in, and ultimately, the validation of Indigenous issues and practices.

Emergent Decolonizing Methodologies

The transformation of communities, particularly the people of Indigenous communities, to achieve a stronger alignment with their cultures, beliefs and values is a formidable challenge. Of Smith's (1999) 25 identified processes to advance this transformation, 6 are mentioned below as central to the theme of generating knowledge and research to improve the well-being and health of Indigenous and immigrant populations.

Storytelling and Testimonies

Scholarly work must capture the essence and identity of cultures that have depended on oral histories and life experience as the basis for the transformation and transfer of knowledge across generations. Testimonies provide the basis for claims by articulating the truth and offer a process and means by which a research respondent is afforded protection and space for expression.

Storytelling is a process for gaining the perspectives of native people, particularly the elders and women whose voices were silenced in the colonizing process. For many Indigenous writers, storytelling is the means of passing down belief and values of a culture with the expectation future generations might find meaning and a sense of place and identity. The storyteller is able to connect the past with the future. Storytelling is also a fundamental process of facilitating dialogue and conversations among Indigenous people as people of the culture and the land. As suggested, research on storytelling indicates that it is a culturally appropriate tool 'of representing the "diversities of truth" within which the story teller rather than the researcher maintains control' (Bishop, 1996: 24). Storytelling is a process through which 'the indigenous community becomes a story that is a collection of individual stories ever unfolding through the lives of the people who share the life of that community' (Bishop, 1996: 169).

Celebrating Survival

Scientific inquiry into Indigenous communities has emphasized the demise and cultural assimilation of native peoples. Often these individuals' life experiences have been characterized as fragile in the wake of the historical trauma resulting from the colonizing process. This trauma includes aspects of genocide, loss of identity, culture, language and land. Survival is key process of Indigenous nations, characterized by 'the degree to which indigenous peoples have retained cultural and spiritual values and authenticity' (Smith, 1999: 145). Celebration may take the form of dancing, music, athletic events, a collective experience intended to create a sense of life of shared history, meaning and identity. Critical to this process is the contemporary concept of resilience. This requires research with Indigenous people, both as individuals and collectively, to acknowledge their strengths, capabilities and commitment to the preservation and meaning of their history and past.

Intervening

Under the rubric of action research, intervening is a process of becoming involved and proactive in an effort to improve on current conditions, rectify wrongs and shape policies and conditions for the benefit of Indigenous people. Of greatest importance, intervening is characterized as a community process that invites an intervention process into the community and sets the parameters for the intervention. Intervening from this perspective is directed at changing institutions, policies, programmes, educational experiences and training of staff. This programme is not about changing Indigenous people, but rather transforming the institutions that serve the people. All decolonizing Indigenous research ultimately has this purpose.

Revitalizing

Crisis-oriented and problem-focused professions and related programmes set their parameters and targets directed at the immediate issues that lead to resolution, reconciliation and improved well-being. Revitalizing research focuses the essential elements that have ensured Indigenous Peoples' survival, foremost among them is the historically embraced element of cultural revival and maintenance. Revitalizing calls on professional researchers to expanded their worldview when approaching Indigenous people to be inclusive of cultural preservation and revitalization as critical elements to the well-being and development of Indigenous and immigrant populations. Language and its revitalization have been, and will continue to be, critical elements in the preservation of many Indigenous and minority cultures. Strategies to support or cultivate policies directed at language revival, of promoting exchanges among native speakers, and promoting the publication of information in native languages are a critical part of the revitalization process.

Discovering

This is a process of central importance to Western and Indigenous populations. Science has been an integral part of Indigenous ways of knowing. Western science, however, has been neither sensitive to nor respectful of these alternative ways of knowing. Indigenous knowledges remain an untapped and underdeveloped resource of scientific information since they have been relegated to being inconsequential and the antithesis to the advancement of knowledge particularly in the social, behavioural, biological and medical sciences. Yet, discovering remains a priority in both worlds. The bridging concepts of ethno-science are among many ideas that can serve to foster the advancement of knowledge to better serve Indigenous and immigrant communities.

Sharing

The dissemination of knowledge among Indigenous and immigrant communities emanating from research in which they have been directly involved is vital to their well-being and continuous social improvement. Professional disciplines have emphasized the dissemination of knowledge among professionals and specialized audiences, thus leaving the populations being served outside the loop of information sharing. The current emphasis on community-based research, provided researchers conform to cultural protocols, will shape the future of decolonizing research if the preparation of professions to involve the community, before, during and after the conduct of inquiries, is given a higher priority in the training process. Dissemination, in the Indigenous community, is more than the transmission of knowledge gained. It is also a process of 'demystifying knowledge and information' and the presentation in plain terms: 'Oral presentations must confirm to community protocols and expectations' (Smith, 1999: 161).

Conclusion

For Indigenous and immigrant populations, the future is today. The metaphor of a dormant volcano erupting depicts the once silent or muted voices of colonized people throughout the Pacific, in the continental United States inclusive of Alaska – seething, seeking an outlet and expression, and claiming what was once theirs. Western stereotypes and analytical categories to explain the behaviour of immigrant and Indigenous people are being challenged. Western – Euro-American grounded theories used to guide, predict and explain human behaviour and social processes are being confronted and questioned, and tried-and-true research methodologies are being reframed in the context of culture, beliefs, respect and values.

Colonization and exploitation have marginalized and nearly destroyed communities of Indigenous and minority people enriched by a past, language, traditions, values, beliefs and expectations. Their demands are reasonable and serve as reference points to guide the social work profession in its efforts to search for deeper understanding of immigrant and Indigenous people. If the profession expects to develop relevant theories, research and practice interventions, it must be prepared to conduct research based on protocols of respect and partnership with Indigenous and migrant communities. In this sea of change, the profession has aligned itself with best practices and committed itself to cultural relevance.

Elements of Indigenous strategies for understanding, explaining, predicting and studying Indigenous and immigrant people and communities in a culturally sensitive and respectful manner were discussed. While provocative in its confrontation of current practices, the Indigenous strategy is inviting and calling for the profession to engage the population in its own quest for understanding and to search for ways to improve Indigenous People's spiritual, social, emotional and economic well-being.

References

American Psychological Association (APA). (2000). *Diagnostic and Statistical Manual of Mental Disorders: Fourth Edition (DSM-IV-TR)*. Washington, DC: APA.

Banton, M. (1981).The Direction and Speed of Ethnic Change. In C. Keyes (ed.), *Ethnic Change*. Seattle: University of Washington Press, 32–52.

Battiste, M. (2008). Research ethnics for protecting indigenous knowledge and heritage: Institution and researcher responsibilities. In N. Denzin, Lincoln, Y. and Smith, L. (eds), *Handbook of Critical and Indigenous Methodologies*. Thousand Oaks, CA: Sage, 497–510.

Benham, K.P.M. and Heck, R.H. (1998). *Culture and Educational Policy in Hawaii: Silencing of Native Voices*. Hillsdale, NJ: Erlbaum.

Bishop, R. (1996). *Collaborative Research Stories: Whatawhanaungatanga*. Palmerston North, New Zealand: Dunmore Press.

Bolland, K. and Atherton, C. (2000). Heuristics versus logical positivism: Solving the wrong problem. *Families in Society*, 83(1), 7–13.

Braun, K., Pietsch, J. and Blanchette, P. (eds). (2000). *Cultural Issues in End-of-Life Decision-Making*. Thousand Oaks, CA: Sage.

Brave Heart, M.Y.H. (2000). Wakiksuyapi: Carrying the historical trauma of the Lakota. *Tulane Studies in Social Welfare*, 21–2, 245–66.

Bronfenbrenner, U. and Ceci, S. (1994) Nature-nurture reconceptualized in developmental perspective: A biological model. *Psychological Review*, 101(4), 568–86.

Campbell, C. and Evans-Campbell, T. (2011). Historical Trauma and Native Child Development. In P. Farrell, Spicer, P. Fitzgerald, H. and Sarche, M. (eds), *American Indian and Alaska Native Children's Mental Health: Development and Context*. Santa Barbara, CA: Praeger Publishers.

Cross, T. (1998). Understanding Family Resilience from a Relational World View. In H.I. McCubbin, Thompson, E.A., Thompson, A.I. and Fromer J.E. (eds), *Resiliency in Ethnic Minority Families: Native and Immigrant American Minority Families*, vol. 1. Thousand Oaks, CA: Sage, 143–57.

Denzin, N.K. and Lincoln, Y.S. (eds). (1998). *The Landscape of Qualitative Research: Theories and Issues*. Thousand Oaks, CA: Sage.

Dubos, R. (1965). *Man Adapting*. New Haven, CT: Yale University Press.

Dubos, R. (1974). *Of Human Diversity*. New York: Clark University Press.

Evans-Campbell, T. (2008). Historical trauma in American Indian/Native American communities: A multi-level framework for exploring impacts on individuals, families, and communities. *Journal of Interpersonal Violence*, 23(2), 316–38.

Freire, P. (2002). *Pedagogy of the Oppressed*. New York: Continuum.

Gray, M., Coates, J. and Yellow Bird, M. (eds). (2008). *Indigenous Social Work around the World: Towards Culturally Relevant Education and Practice*. Aldershot: Ashgate.

Jared, D. (2012). *The world until yesterday: What we can learn from traditional societies*. New York: Viking.

Jones, N. and Jungmiwha, J. (2013). Understanding who reported multiple races in the U.S. Decennial Census: Results from Census 2000 and the 2010 census. *Journal of Family Relations*, 62(1), 5–16.

Kahakalau, K. (2004). Indigenous heuristic action research: Bridging western and indigenous research methodologies. *Hulili: Multidisplinary Research on Hawaiian Well-Being*, 1(1), 19–33.

Kamehameha Schools/Bishop Estate. (1983). *Native Hawaiian Educational Assessment*. Honolulu, HI: Kamehameha Press.

Keyes, C. (1981). The Dialectics of Ethnic Change. In C. Keyes (ed.), *Ethnic Change*. Seattle: University of Washington Press, 3–30.

Kim, U., Yang, K. and Hwang, K. (2006). Contributions to indigenous and cultural psychology: Understanding people in context. In U. Kim, Yang, K. and Hwang, K. (eds*), Indigenous and Cultural Psychology: Understanding People in Context*. New York: Springer, 3–26.

Light, I. (1981). Ethnic Succession. In C. Keyes (ed.), *Ethnic Change*. Seattle: University of Washington Press, 54–86.

Marsella, A., Oliveira, J., Plummer, C. and Crabbe, K. (1998). Native Hawaiian (Kanaka Maoli) culture, mind and well-being. In H. McCubbin, Thompson, E., Thompson, A. and Fromer, J. (eds), *Resiliency in Native American and Immigrant Families*. Thousand Oaks, CA: Sage, 93–114.

McCubbin, L. and McCubbin, H. (2005). Culture and Ethnic Identity in Family Resilience: Dynamic processes in trauma and transformation of indigenous people. In M. Unger (ed.), *Handbook for Working with Children and Youth:*

Pathways to Resilience across Cultures and Contexts. Thousand Oaks, CA: Sage, 27–44.

McCubbin, L., McCubbin, H., Kehl, L., Strom, I. and Zhang, W. (2011). *Relational Well-Being and Resilience: An Indigenous Family Perspective and Measure*. Honolulu: Le'a and Xlibre Publications.

McCubbin, H., McCubbin, L., Samuels, G., Zhang, W. and Sievers, J. (2013). Multiethnic children, youth and families: Emerging challenges to the behavioral sciences and public policy. *Journal of Family Relations,* 62(1), 1–4.

McGregor, D., Morelli, P.T. and Matsuoka, J.K. (2003). An Ecological Model of Well-Being. In H. A. Becker and Vanclay, F. (eds), *The International Handbook of Social Impact Assessment*. Camberley, England: Elgar.

Minerbi, L., McGregor, D. and Matsuoka, J. (2003). Using Geographic Information Systems for Cultural Impact Assessment. In H.A. Becker and Vanclay, F. (eds), *The International Handbook of Social Impact Assessment*. Camberley, England: Elgar.

Morrow, R.A. (1994). *Foundations of Metatheory: Between Subjectivism and Objectivism, Critical Theory and Methodology*. Thousand Oaks, CA: Sage.

Office of Hawaiian Affairs. (2002). *Native Hawaiian Data Book* 2002. Honolulu, HI: Office of Hawaiian Affairs.

Pagel, M (2012). *Wired for Culture: Origins of the human social mind.* New York: Norton

Papajohn, J. and Spiegel, J. (1975). *Transactions: The Interplay between Individual, Family and Society*. New York: Science House.

Poston, W. (1990). The biracial identity development model: A needed addition. *Journal of Counseling and Development*, 69, 152–5.

Powell, A. (1988). Raise your child with ethnic pride. *Ours*, 21(6), 26–9.

Smith, L.T. (1999). *Decolonizing Methodologies*. London: Zed Books.

Schlabach, S. (2013). The importance of family, race and gender for multiracial adolescent well-being. *Journal of Family Relations*, 62(1), 154–74.

Stannard, D. (1992) *American Holocaust*. London: Oxford University Press.

Touraine, A. (2001). *Beyond Neo-Liberalism*. Cambridge: Polity Press.

Trask, H.K. (1998). Native Sovereignty: A strategy for Hawaiian family survival. In H.I. McCubbin, Thompson, E.A., Thompson, A.I. and Fromer, J.E. (eds), *Resiliency in Ethnic Minority Families: Native and Immigrant American Minority Families*, vol. 1. Thousand Oaks, CA: Sage, 133–9.

Turner, J.H., Beeghley, L. and Powers, C.H. (2002). *The Early Masters and the Prospects for Scientific Theory: The Emergence of Sociological Theory* (5th edn). Belmont, CA: Wadsworth.

Walker, R. (2004). *Ka Whawhai Tonu Matou: Struggle without End.* New Zealand: Penguin.

Wardle, F. and Cruz-Janzen, M.I. (2004). *Meeting the Needs of Multiethnic and Multiracial Children in Schools*. New York: Pearson Press.

Witkin, S. and Iversen, R. (2008). Issues in Social Work. In B. White, Sowers, K. and Dulmus, C. (eds), *Comprehensive Handbook of Social Work and Social Welfare*, vol. 1. New Jersey: John Wiley and Sons, 467–96.

Wright, R., Mindel, C., Thanh, V. and Habenstein, R. (2011). *Ethnic Families in America: Patterns and Variations* (5th edn). New York: Elsevier North-Holland.

Chapter 15

Neurodecolonization: Applying Mindfulness Research to Decolonizing Social Work

Michael Yellow Bird

In order for decolonization to be successful it must begin in our minds (Wilson and Yellow Bird, 2005). Creative, healthy, decolonized thinking, actions and feelings positively shape and empower important neural circuits in our brain, which, in turn, provide us with the personal resources, strengths, talents and abilities we need to overcome and transform the oppressions of colonialism (Yellow Bird, 2012). On the one hand, a healthy, well-balanced mind and brain are essential to helping one to engage in proactive, creative and successful decolonization activities and, on the other, unconstructive, negative thinking, feelings and behaviours dampen and short-circuit our brain's creativity and optimism networks and increase our susceptibility to the many stresses that arise in everyday life. The customary stressors, especially for Indigenous Peoples, are exacerbated by the additional trauma of colonialism (Yellow Bird, 2012; see Chapter 7).

This chapter shows how neuroscientific research can be applied to decolonizing social work interventions to enhance human well-being. It focuses on *neurodecolonization*, a conceptual framework which uses mindfulness research to facilitate an examination of ways in which the human brain is affected by the colonial situation and an exploration of mind-brain activities that change neural networks and enable individuals to overcome the myriad effects of trauma and oppression inherent in colonialism. Understanding how the mind and brain are affected by colonialism is an important paradigm in decolonizing social work. While many Indigenous Peoples experience the direct, unrelenting, negative effects of colonialism, social workers, who choose to confront it directly and vigorously, eschew its false privileges and promises, and face secondary trauma as they encounter the tsunami of devastation it creates and realize they can do little about it. Neurodecolonization benefits both Indigenous Peoples and social workers and is critical to the overall enterprise of decolonization.

In this chapter, the *mind* can be thought of as encompassing perceptions, higher order thinking, consciousness and the 'relational and embodied process that regulates the flow of energy and information' (Siegel, 2001: 52). The *brain* is the physical organ that changes its structure and function according to the needs of the mind. It is regarded as having 'great computational capability, while constructing our sensory experiences, regulating our thoughts and emotions, and controlling our actions' (Kandel, 2007: 69).

This chapter addresses four issues:

1. A definition of mindfulness is presented and its connection to negative emotions is discussed. Negativity is seen as important since the colonial experience is saturated with oppressions and stressors that exacerbate negative emotions, illness and trauma.
2. Neurodecolonization and its connection to mindfulness – grounded in Buddhist as well as many Indigenous Peoples' traditions – is explored in the belief that mindfulness practice can minimize the negative sequelae of trauma related to colonization and enhance psychological and community well-being in Indigenous communities. While mindfulness is becoming more commonplace, neurodecolonization to enable Indigenous Peoples and social workers to decolonize through the engagement of particular mind-brain strategies is a new idea.
3. The neurobiology of mindfulness, that is, what happens to the brain during meditation and its implications for overcoming colonialism is then discussed.
4. A case study of the processes and outcomes of neurodecolonization is shared.

The chapter ends with a discussion of the policy implications of mindfulness-based neurodecolonization.

Mindfulness

Mindfulness is an important activity of decolonizing social work since it is a powerful tool for liberating the mind and brain from oppressive thoughts, emotions and actions. Boyce (2011: xi)) says that mindfulness means 'the mind is fully attending to what is at hand, what you're working on, the person you're talking to, the surrounding you're moving through. It is a basic human capacity. It's not a talent. We all have it. We all need it'. However, a great deal of our daily activities is fairly routine and of a non-deliberative nature (Varela, Thompson and Roach, 1991) to the extent that Langer (1989: 26) maintains that 'we don't realize how mindless our interactions with the world and each other can become. It's common for us not to question even absurd information when it presents itself, because it fits some established belief or ingrained form of behavior'. Mindlessness then does not refer to expertise or the activities most of us do without thinking like riding a bike or driving a car. It refers to non-reflective, unthinking behaviour when more thought is required, especially in our relationships with one another. In this respect we might see mindlessness as a principle reason why Western social work has not engaged in decolonizing approaches to overturn the oppressive features of the colonial enterprise on behalf of Indigenous Peoples.

The ancient practice of mindfulness serves as an antidote to mindlessness since it enables the mind and brain to enter into states of deep, sustained wakefulness for the purpose of gaining greater awareness and insight into one's life and reality.

Siegel (Mindsightinstitute, 2009) maintains that all cultures have incorporated practices for deep reflection, be they meditation, contemplation or prayer, and these practices are necessary for community health and well-being. Adaptation of Buddhist mindfulness practice, however, presents a particular approach to meditation in which meditators are taught to be present in the moment and experience thoughts, emotions or memories as they arise freely, without judging or reflecting on them. They are taught not to try to hold onto them or push them away but to be with them just as they are. Non-judgemental observation of one's internal experience activates the prefrontal cortex – the brain's executive circuit used for planning, making choices and governing social control – and facilitates learning about routine tendencies (Davidson et al., 2003). Thus mindfulness strives for deep awareness of what is happening from moment to moment, outside and inside us, without judging or forming attachment to our thoughts, feelings and emotions – no craving and no aversion (Kabat-Zinn, 1994a). It is about living deeply and richly in the present moment rather than being distracted and preoccupied. For instance, when we listen to our clients mindfully and pay attention to what they are telling us without judging them, they are more likely to be heard and feel valued. So much of what social workers are required to do in managerial environments involves the mindless processing of clients, and to listen mindfully has become harder than we tend to realize (Langer, 1989). When we listen mindfully to Indigenous Peoples, we are more likely to develop an understanding of their struggles against colonial oppression, their resilience and our responsibilities to aid in their liberation.

Hick (2009: 2) says that, because mindfulness incorporates meditation and includes personal introspection, it is often thought of as a self-centred activity when 'it actually has more to do with how we live in society. Self-awareness is central, but within a context of understanding yourself before you can effectively help others'. Self-awareness and self-reflection has been a central focus of the social worker's 'use of self' in Western social work (England, 1986) with many social work texts listing self-awareness as a core social work skill (Egan, 2010). However, mindfulness has a broader focus with attention to the context and lifestyle issues that facilitate a larger, nobler, more just worldview. Its aim is self-awareness so we might better serve others, consistent with Indigenous Peoples' collective values and deep connection to the natural environment.

An Indigenous worldview recognizes the complete and indivisible interdependence and connection of all things and is consistent with Buddhist philosophy. The fourteenth Dalai Lama (2011: 248) stresses that, while mindfulness training on an individual basis 'to endure suffering and attain a more lasting state of happiness [is important], it is necessary to develop a sense of "universal responsibility", a deep concern for all, irrespective of creed, color, sex, or nationality'. These universal values have been embraced by Western social work in its anti-discriminatory and anti-oppressive practice models but cultural awareness requires a deep awareness of Indigenous People's history and culture as well as ongoing oppression. This type of awareness can be developed through mindfulness, which involves systematic training and practice over a period of time. Mindfulness is then a particular practice which involves meditation inter alia through mindful sitting, walking, doing specific exercises, such as the *body scan*, or almost any other activity involving focused attention (LeShan, 1974).

Negative Emotions

The theory of mindfulness recognizes the destructive emotions clouding human judgement, a connection long understood by Eastern philosophers and Indigenous Peoples. Mindfulness is seen as a powerful antidote for the regulation of negative emotions (Brown and Cordon, 2009). This is important since neuroscientific research has repeatedly demonstrated that the human brain is wired for negativity (Goleman, 2003; Hanson and Mendius, 2009) and negative information more strongly influences people's evaluations and attention than comparable neutral or positive information (Peeters and Czapinski, 1990; Skowronski and Carlston, 1989; Tartar et al. 2010). Overall, bad events trump good ones in nearly every instance. In a review of the literature, Baumeister et al. (2001: 223) highlighted:

> the greater power of bad events over good ones is found in everyday events, major life events (e.g., trauma), close relationship outcomes, social network patterns, interpersonal interactions, and learning processes. Bad emotions, bad parents, and bad feedback have more impact than good ones, and bad information is processed more thoroughly than good.

Many Indigenous social work scholars highlight the ongoing negativity, illness and trauma of Indigenous Peoples resulting from colonization (Gray, Coates and Yellow Bird, 2008).

Cognitive scientists have shown that the human brain is hardwired for rapid decision-making (Picchetti, n.d; Varela, 1999) which they refer to as *cognitive heuristics*. They work on the basis of pattern recognition arising from experience and, while they can lead to good decisions and judgements, they can also lead to systematic errors and cognitive biases. Mindlessness is one way in which ingrained negative and obstructive beliefs – our cognitive heuristics – arising from colonialism can be changed.

Still, there are some advantages in negativity. According to Hanson and Mendius (2009), the human species would not be able to survive without negative emotions since they provide a warning signal when danger is at hand. To briefly illustrate, imagine one of our ancient ancestors hiking home along a riverbank after a visit with relatives downstream. After many miles and hours of not eating, he suddenly comes upon a bush loaded with bright, beautiful, plump berries, which he has never seen before. Two alarms in the brain go off. The first is 'Wow!' 'Food!' The second is more measured, thoughtful and pessimistic: 'Hmmmm. They look tasty but what if they're poison? Better to wait and eat when I get home.' In the second scenario, negativity certainly becomes an attribute if, in fact, the berries are poison

– disaster averted. One might think of the negative brain bias as an on/off switch that is mostly turned off but all too easily flipped to the on position.

Negativity is embedded in the brain. Evolutionary neurobiologists refer to the oldest part of the brain as the *hind brain* or *reptilian brain* which humans share with other vertebrates – or species with a backbone. The reptilian brain is on duty 24/7 and is in charge of our survival. It controls our body functions, such as breathing, heart rate, balance and body temperature, which are essential to life. This part of the brain is regarded as reliable but rigid and compulsive. Defending territory, ideas, beliefs and your girl or boyfriend, husband or wife from other suitors is a key function of this part of the brain. Sexual behaviour is instinctive, responses are automatic, emotions are stimulated, and negativity and anxiety flow easily. When this part of the brain is in charge, it is much harder to access the neural networks of the *anterior cingulate cortex* that regulate sympathetic activity, such as compassion, self-awareness and emotional intelligence (Goleman, 2003; Luu and Posner, 2003; Newberg and Waldman, 2009). This region of the brain is associated with the ability to decrease the propensity to express and react with anger and fear. It is where our deepest feelings of love reside. The neurons in this area of the brain are highly vulnerable to being overridden by our reptilian brain, which has been around much longer (Newberg and Waldman, 2009).

The neurons in the *anterior cingulate cortex* have only been around for about 15 million years while the *amygdala* responsible for generating fear and aggression in the reptilian part of the brain has been around for 450 million years. In terms of strength of influence on human behaviour and attitudes, the reptilian brain is 30 times older – and stronger – than the compassionate, empathetic, socially aware *anterior cingulate cortex*. Hence, Newberg and Waldman (2009) maintain that humans are much more likely to engage in fighting, aggression, anger and fear than in acts of love, compassion, generosity, and acceptance.

It is estimated that humans have 12,000 to 50,000 thoughts a day and up to 80 per cent of those thoughts are negative (Dvorsky, 2007). While most are little irritants like our petty likes and dislikes, negative thoughts can be horrifying beyond belief. Sustained, intense trauma can result from the belief that one has contracted a terminal illness, or the world is going to end in a fireball in the year 2012, or the afterlife is one of extreme heat, pain and suffering. In such cases, negativity becomes a liability. Emotions originally designed to protect the human organism become toxic. This flawed thinking, which predisposes us to make faulty judgements based on negative thoughts, is referred to as *cognitive bias*. Because of our tendency toward negative thinking, imagined threats are typically far more disturbing than actual ones – one reason that anxiety and depression are so excruciatingly painful. As neuroscientist Robert Sapolsky (2009) put it in a lecture delivered at Stanford University, 'Imagine being chased by a lion 24/7. That's what depression is – without the lion.'

There are many ways out of this negativity bias. Some of the ways are as old as Indigenous cultures themselves, for example, acknowledging the power of thoughts, emotions and words (Waller et al., 1998). Many Indigenous traditions advocate watching what we think, say and do. The 'power of positive thinking' and the actions that generally follow were practised long before the publication of Norman Vincent Peale's (1952) famous book of that title. In Dine (Navajo) tradition this way of conscious living is called, 'walking the Beauty Way'. One Taos Pueblo elder terms it 'being a straight arrow'. So many of us have been advised by our elders to 'pay attention, be careful, and watch what you are doing'. Neurodecolonization through the practice of mindfulness provides a next step that allows us to move beyond the pain and anger of colonialism.

In short, it does not take colonialism to create deep feelings of negativity. While oppressions from colonialism exacerbate negativity, traditional trickster stories, that long predated European and American colonialism, remind us that humans can be egotistical and negative. Recognition of the risks of overinflated ego and negativity likely led the wiser of our ancestors to teach the practice of deep introspection and humility during transition rituals, and in daily life.

Defining Neurodecolonization

The first part of the term *neuro* – in neurodecolonization – refers to neurons which are specialized cells in the nervous system – brain and spinal cord – that send and receive electric signals throughout the body. *Decolonization* refers to activities that weaken the effects of colonialism, facilitate resistance and create opportunities to promote traditional practices in present-day settings. *Neurodecolonization* involves combining mindfulness meditation, with traditional and contemporary secular and sacred contemplative practices to replace negative patterns of thought, emotion and behaviour with healthy, productive ones. Drawing on recent neuroscientific research, neurodecolonization builds on the idea that healthy, constructive thoughts, emotions and behaviours can change our brains (and our lives) for the better. Many Indigenous contemplative practices incorporate the same principles and processes as mindfulness, and are important components of physical, emotional, behavioural and spiritual well-being and healing.

Neurodecolonization seeks an understanding of how mind and brain function are shaped by the stresses of colonialism and compromise the well-being of Indigenous Peoples. Some stressors include, but are certainly not limited to, racism and hate crimes; loss of territories, culture and pride; high levels of mortality, poverty and poor health; and disregard of Indigenous Peoples' sovereignty and rights. Along with building new empowered neural networks, neurodecolonization activities are aimed at deactivating old, ineffective brain networks that support destructive thoughts, emotions, memories and behaviours, particularly, past and contemporary oppressions associated with colonialism. For example, past colonialism that might have created negativity, sadness and anger – and activated our brains' networks of feelings of helplessness – might be our memories of our parents' or grandparents' horrific treatment in residential schools or dealing with contemporary racism and discrimination.

Novel perspectives about how one might overcome colonialism rather than be a victim can help facilitate the growth of new beneficial brain networks that enable us to engage in a level of optimistic thinking that promotes optimism and resilience (Waller, 2001). Thus, neurodecolonization makes it possible to overcome oppression, develop the courage to confront it, and cultivate the creativity to strategically challenge it. However, neurodecolonization does not mean that we should suppress or deny negative thoughts and emotions related to colonialism. Through the mindfulness theory and practice that is embedded in neurodecolonization we are informed that when we spend time thinking, feeling and reacting to the events in unproductive ways, we inadvertently strengthen the unproductive neural networks and become even more prone to anger, depression and frustration. (This is known as the plasticity paradox discussed in the next section). Our grandmothers, meditation masters and modern researchers are in accord when they say, 'Be careful how you think, what you say, and what you do ... or you will become that'. A healthy functioning mind and brain are the greatest assets we have to promote healthy, intelligent and mindful decolonization processes.

Fortunately, modern neuroscience also reveals that we humans are capable of *compassion* and *self-awareness*. These positive emotions originate in a younger part of the brain – the *anterior cingulate cortex*. However, as the *plasticity paradox* demonstrates, these positive emotions can be easily overridden by negative ones, such as and *aggression* situated in the oldest part of the brain – the *amygdala*. In order to transform harmful, obstructive emotions, thoughts and behaviours into compassion and self-awareness, it is necessary to understand our tendency toward negativity and have the courage to confront it (Goleman, 2003).

Neurobiology of Mindfulness

Extensive neuroscientific research shows that the human brain has the capacity to change throughout life, based on relationships and experience. This adaptive capacity is referred to as the *neuroplasticity* of the brain (Begley, 2007; Goleman, 2006; Schwartz and Begley, 2002). Many sophisticated brain imaging studies show that neural circuits associated with human well-being and other positive attributes become activated and strengthened when individuals purposefully engage positive thoughts, emotions and behaviours (Davidson et al., 2003). For instance, functional magnetic resonance imaging uses powerful magnets to record blood flow to functioning areas of the brain that become activated during different experiences, while electroencephalograms allow us to see electrical changes in the brain – as brain band waves – when it is engaged or at rest. Brain plasticity is an important idea in neurodecolonization and decolonizing social work since it establishes that Indigenous Peoples and social workers can use mind-brain strategies to empower themselves more creatively to change their understanding, actions and relationship to colonialism.

Understanding the role that neurons and their networks play is important. The neurons in the brain are responsible for organizing and processing the five senses, thoughts, moods and emotions. Neurons assemble themselves into neural networks in the brain which enable them to communicate and work together on a particular task. For instance, if we want to learn something new (creating a neurodecolonization iPhone meditation application to listen to through the day) or remembering something old (empowering words from our Indigenous language that our grandmothers taught us), we call upon our neurons to help us do so. There are about 100 billion neurons in the brain and 100 billion in the rest of the body constantly communicating and taking action or remaining in a state of readiness.

In 1949 Canadian psychologist Donald Hebb proposed that learning experiences and memory are based upon the firing of neurons in a precise order which affect the synaptic connections in the brain (in Schwartz and Begley, 2002). Each experience we encounter, whether a feeling, emotion, thought or sensation is embedded in our neurons and forms a network: 'If two neurons tend to be active together their connection is strengthened' (Varela et al., 1991: 87). For instance, in the case of decolonizing social work, the longer, more frequently and intensely social workers engage their neural networks to creatively overcome the effects of colonialism, the stronger and more capable these neural networks become. Repeating these activities and experiences become embedded in the network making it easier for neurons to fire to support and respond to the activity and experience.

However, the reverse is also true. When one approaches colonialism feeling overwhelmed, full of negative and fearful feelings, and believing that it cannot be resolved, neurons to support these feelings and thoughts fire and wire together and become embedded into our networks compromising any efforts put forth to overcome colonialism. As these states of negativity persist, the brain's neural circuits of despair, fear, anger and helplessness get increasingly stronger and it is not long before we develop pessimistic attitudes, blaming and bad thinking behaviours. Doidge (2007) refers to the brain's ability to stubbornly retain and display such bad habits and thought disorders as the 'plasticity paradox'.

The theory and practice of mindfulness connects Western neuroscientific research with Eastern Buddhist religion, which has long extolled the value of meditation for human well-being (Dalai Lama, 1999; Nhat Hanh, 1976, 1991). Most non-Indigenous, Western, mindfulness researchers and practitioners that write about mindfulness refer to these traditions beginning with the enlightened being known as Buddha who lived more than 2,500 years ago. It is important to note that The Buddha was Indigenous. He was member of the Shakya tribe, his clan name was Gautama and his given name was Siddhartha. While there were many buddhas, yogis and other enlightened beings over the centuries, Gautama is distinguished by having developed a technique of meditation that he then taught widely. Western scientists and scholars in the mindfulness movement, which began in the 1990s, have engaged in dialogues with the Dalai Lama and conducted research on experienced meditation practitioners to produce extensive neuroscientific evidence demonstrating the benefits of meditation for human well-being (Goleman, 2003, 2006, 2007; Kabat-Zinn, 1994a, 1994b; Varela et al., 1991). Data indicate that mindfulness practices have profound positive neurobiological impacts and improve health and well-being in relation to a range of disorders, including depression, anxiety, eating disorders, chronic mental illness, cancer, chronic pain and violence (Baer, 2006). Davidson et al. (2003) showed the positive effects of mindfulness on the brain and immune system in helping to deal with difficult emotions under stress. Kabat-Zinn et al. (1998) showed that the skin of people with *psoriasis* (a skin disease) who were receiving ultraviolet light treatments cleared four times faster when they practised mindfulness compared to a group that only received the ultraviolet light treatment.

Politics of Mindfulness

While Western psychologists, social workers, psychiatrists, medical doctors, counsellors, school teachers, probation officers, clergy, nurses, life coaches and others have incorporated mindfulness theory and principles into their professional practice and research, there is a part of mindfulness that most fail to mention or understand: the 'politics of mindfulness'. Mindfulness is flooding the Western world and many are engaged in practising its principles of awareness, compassion, understanding and empathy. Within the eye of Western mindfulness there is rarely, if ever, a discussion of the power and control that colonizers exerted over Indigenous Peoples' spiritual mindfulness practices, nor is there a mention of the ways colonization activities were instrumental in destroying Indigenous Peoples' mindfulness traditions. For instance, a major aim of white education in the United States, beginning in the 1800s, was Christianizing Indigenous Peoples (Adams, 1995). Whites looked upon 'native religious practices as primitive and barbaric remnants of a precivilized society' (Adams, 1995: 23). One Indian educator noted that 'A really civilized people cannot be found in the world except where the Bible has been sent and the gospel taught: hence, we believe that the Indians must have, as an essential part of their education, Christian training' (ibid.: 23).

In the current context of Western mindfulness there is still resistance to discussing how colonizers have benefited from the losses experienced by Indigenous Peoples. For example, a colleague of mine went to a mindfulness retreat a few years ago to centre herself and seek insights about her work on Indigenous Peoples' rights. At one point there was a discussion among some attendees of how China had invaded Tibet and caused great suffering. After a few moments she spoke up and reminded folks that that is exactly what European and North American colonizers did to Indigenous Peoples in the USA. Being at a mindfulness conference she believed she would find 'enlightened' and 'sympathetic' responses. Instead, she soon found herself isolated from the group, with someone even commenting that her attachment to anger about how Indigenous Peoples lost their land to colonizers was causing her suffering

Neurodecolonization now enables us to understand the effect that colonizers had on the minds and brains of Indigenous Peoples as it concerns Indigenous mindfulness and spirituality. When colonizers outlawed or ridiculed important ceremonial songs, dances and other ceremonies, many Indigenous Peoples' neural networks of hope, happiness and purpose associated with these practices were undoubtedly negatively affected. As these brain networks became deactivated, people's awareness of the importance of ceremonial activities faded, and these mindfulness-engendering activities lost their importance and appeal.

Neurodecolonization also informs us of how mindlessness is deeply embedded in the neural networks of those that disregard Indigenous Peoples' rights and concerns. For instance, instead of honouring the diversity and uniqueness of Indigenous spirituality, European colonizers imposed Christian religious beliefs, claiming that they were received directly from the Creator and were indispensable because they would 'save' Indigenous Peoples from their primitive beliefs, forestall certain descent into a fiery Christian Hell and open the way to Christian Heaven or Paradise (Adams, 1995). Indigenous people then suffered being saved from their languages, traditional practices, family and community structures, worldviews and everything else that gave life meaning. In the United States, it was not until passage of the American Indian Religious Freedom Act in 1978 that the traditional religious rights and cultural practices of American Indians, Eskimos, Aleuts and Native Hawaiians were preserved and received federal government protection.

Case Study One

Background

In the fall of 2009, after I joined the social work faculty at Humboldt State University, I was invited to do a workshop for social work field instructors on the benefits of mindfulness and how it might be used as a social work practice intervention. Part of my presentation involved discussing how I believed it was an important intervention for Indigenous Peoples since mindfulness principles are incorporated into many aspects of tribal, ceremonial life. I also mentioned how I believed mindfulness is important for Indigenous communities in their decolonizing processes in order to recover traditional practices that can heal minds and brains from the oppressions of colonialism; thus neurodecolonization was born.

Following my presentation, I was contacted by a non-Indigenous graduate student in our programme that had attended my workshop and was doing her practicum at a tribal high school in a nearby reservation community. She expressed concern for several of the students since they had been struggling academically and socially and thought that teaching them mindfulness practices and discussing neurodecolonization might be helpful, especially since some of the students often blamed themselves for what was happening to them and had no idea of how structural oppressions, such as colonialism, may be at the root of their struggles. Most of the students in the school were Indigenous although some were non-Indigenous.

I thought that teaching mindfulness to tribal youth was appropriate since a review of the literature revealed that a growing number of K-12 schools in the USA, with students from many different ethnicities and socioeconomic backgrounds, are using mindfulness practices to improve academic performance and deal with student stress and troublesome behaviour (Brown, 2007; Elias, 2008; Jan, 2008). Many schools report that students who learn mindfulness practices improve their concentration, focus, awareness, relaxation, self-management, memory, self-esteem, vitality, positive affectivity, optimism and self-actualization (Brown and Ryan, 2003). In addition, formal mindfulness practices are credited with decreasing student school dropout rates, depression, stress and anxiety, conflict and fighting, and improving attendance and interest in learning (Brady, 2004; Brown, 2007; Chen, 2008; Hooker and Fodor, 2008; Jan, 2008; Kassabian, 2009; Suttie, 2007).

Assessment

My first neurodecolonization project was launched when I was invited to the school by the social work intern who introduced me to teachers and administrators. I discussed with them the benefits of mindfulness and, in turn, they shared with me that a number of students were experiencing interpersonal and social situations that made them more vulnerable to stress and challenged their well-being. The situations that school officials believed put the students at risk included living on the reservation, a history of fostercare, homelessness, court-ordered probation, school truancy and having been identified as having special learning needs requiring an Individualized Educational Plan (IEP), that is, a remediation plan for children who have learning disabilities, emotional disturbances or other impairments.

The demographic profile of this group of young people was alarming. Nearly two-thirds of the 40 students attending the school lived on the reservation. Living on the reservation has benefits and costs. Reservation life is often teeming with healthy, vibrant cultural relationships, language, practices and identities. However, for some, reservation life is associated with disproportionate rates of family and community breakdown, family violence, child welfare troubles, poverty, substance abuse and compromised mental and physical health.

One-fifth of the students had a history of fostercare. Fostercare is indicative of the breakdown of the family and community network. In the case of Native Americans, it signifies deep-rooted historical trauma related to disrupted natural systems of caring, parenting and support within tribal communities (Yellow Bird, 1999). Homelessness is, perhaps, an even greater marker of structural disruption than fostercare. Disturbingly, nearly one-third of all students had a history of homelessness, while close to one-fifth were defined as currently homeless. Native American homelessness is associated with deprivation, poverty, inequality and high mortality (Westerfelt and Yellow Bird, 1999). Close to one-fifth of the students had a past and current history of probation and more than one-fifth a history of school truancy.

Although supported by structured, academic arrangements, a number of students had distinct learning difficulties that challenged their academic success. Over one-fifth had an IEP with about half of this group participating in a 504 plan, which refers to section 504 of the Rehabilitation Act and Americans with Disabilities Act. A 504 Plan helps a special needs student to participate fully in school.

Intervention

A small grant made it possible for me, with four social work graduate students, to examine the experiences of the tribal youth participating in the mindfulness programme. The project was scheduled to last for one academic semester; however, when the semester ended it continued into the next year and was eventually incorporated into the school's health and social wellness curriculum.

Through a series of short presentations over the course of three morning meetings (normally reserved for guest speakers or other 'non-academic' activities), I shared with classroom teachers and students what mindfulness is, how it works and some basic mindfulness practices (Bien and Didonna, 2009; Didonna, 2008). I also discussed its connections to neurodecolonization, explaining how colonialism has created intense stressors and negative outcomes for many Indigenous Peoples, and that mindfulness practices could help one heal from the effects of colonialism and discover new ways to overcome it.

The project was open to all students, and participation was voluntary. Participants were male and female, Native and non-Native students. Approximately 30 students participated, but the count fluctuated according to student interest and availability, for example, when students dropped out or transferred to another school. Since the project involved data collection and analysis, it went through the Institutional Review Board (IRB) process at Humboldt State University. During the three-month data collection phase, ten students agreed to participate in qualitative interviews.

The intervention included the students learning appropriate mindfulness posture, open attitude toward the practices and exercises and techniques that they applied during practice sessions. Students learned strategies for recognizing and changing their relationship to distracting, wandering thoughts, memories, body sensations and emotional states that interfered with their practice. They learned 'mindfulness of breathing', 'sitting meditation', 'mindfulness of the body' and 'mindfulness of sight and sound' exercises (Bien and Diadonna, 2009: 477–83). They were encouraged, but not required, to practice mindful eating and mindful walking (Bien and Didonna, 2009).

During the first month of the project I drove to the school once or twice a week and spent from one to two hours giving instruction to the teachers who had volunteered to help facilitate mindfulness practices with the students. During this time, the teachers practised mindfulness, learned more about the hows and whys of practice, discussed their experiences and anticipated questions that students might ask them. I provided them with printed materials and Internet resources that would reinforce their learning and answered many of their questions. After the first month, I travelled to the school every two to three weeks and spent about an hour coaching students in mindfulness practices. I listened to their experiences and responded to their concerns. The project grant enabled students from the tribal school to make three trips to our university to participate in mindfulness practices with graduate students in my mindfulness and social work class. They were able to listen to my students discuss the connections between mindfulness and well-being and its value and relationship to decolonizing social work practice.

Results

Midway through the project, during informal discussions, a number of students began to identify how the awareness and concentration aspects of mindfulness paralleled mindfulness skills practised in tribal activities, such as fishing, basket-making, prayer, storytelling and the singing of tribal songs. Several students related that elders had urged them and others to concentrate and be aware of what they were doing, thinking and feeling. Many reported having been told by their elders that tribal practices were sacred and that it was necessary to put good thoughts and feelings into them in order to achieve a good result.

Some of the students began to see the connections between these practices and decolonization. For instance, one student said that a colonized mind would not allow him to be aware of sacredness in what he was doing when he was fishing or listening to a traditional story. Another said she felt that mindfulness helped her become more peaceful and aware of what she was doing when she listened to her elders pray in her Indigenous language. She said that if she had followed her colonized mind she would probably be out with friends messing around.

One of the research questions asked students what they thought about mindfulness practice. One student said it was similar to traditional prayer practices that emphasized being thankful for what you have, 'from the trees outside to the toes on my foot'. Another student remarked that he gradually became 'more aware of connections among all things as well as the human place in the universe'. When asked if the tribal school should continue mindfulness practices after the project was over, all ten students interviewed said they would. One said that he loves it and it 'should be required for all schools' for it is 'part of what makes their school unique'. One student said that many of the students in the school felt connected to the practices. When asked whether they would continue to practice mindfulness when they graduated from school, seven of the ten said they would. One student remarked, he would continue to practice mindfulness, combining it with traditional tribal practices because 'it helps to focus me, plus it's helpful to use formal mindfulness practices when I am away from home and traditional practices are not available'.

Indigenous Peoples' Neurodecolonization Policy

The first perceptions of the oppressive aspects of colonialism happen in our minds, which send signals to the brain as to how we should respond. A brain that is healthy and well-balanced can respond to colonialism in an optimistic, courageous, intelligent, creative and resilient manner. On the other hand, an unhealthy brain is more likely to respond with fear, frustration, anger, helplessness and negativity. Considerable evidence demonstrates that the brain that has been shaped by mindfulness and other positive contemplative practices will respond in a much more optimistic and effective manner to these and other stressors (Amen, 2005).

Neurodecolonization is an emerging field of study that examines how the human brain functions in a colonial situation and how the use of specific mind-brain activities and projects can change important neural networks to enable one to overcome the myriad effects of colonialism. It recognizes that the brain's plasticity enables neural networks to rewire and change throughout the life course in response to diverse experiences. This chapter has argued that social workers and Indigenous individuals, communities, leaders, teachers and parents can benefit from mindfulness practices and should engage in neurodecolonization projects as a function of decolonizing social work.

In closing, I propose the following suggestions for further inquiry and practice. First, social workers work with Indigenous communities and Indigenous scholars to conduct research on the effects that mindfulness education has on communities, particularly with regard to reducing stress and negativity and increasing well-being. Secondly, social workers work with Indigenous Peoples to develop and implement curricula that teach children and adults mindfulness, to promote optimistic thinking, creative imagery and visualization, memory exercises and critical thinking. The curricula should include ways to incorporate traditional mindfulness practices in helping and healing approaches. Thirdly, social workers participate with Indigenous Peoples in neurodecolonization projects to formulate a more 'enlightened' view of the oppressions inherent in colonialism and how they might be overcome.

Our minds and brains have incredible healing powers. However, they can also exacerbate our suffering. Contemporary neuroscience provides ample evidence that mindfulness practices offer powerful antidotes to negative sequelae of colonialism. Imagine Indigenous communities full of people with balanced, healthy, creative, intelligent and courageous minds and brains (just like our ancestors who were able to cope effectively with forces even more potent than colonialism). Imagine social workers becoming empowered through decolonization projects and practising decolonized social work. In so doing, bear in mind the wisdom of our grandmothers: 'Be careful how you think, what you say, and what you do … or you will become that'.

References

Adams, D.W. (1995). *Education for Extinction*. Lawrence, KS: University Press of Kansas.

Amen, D. (2005). *Making a Good Brain Great*. New York: Three Rivers Press.

Baer, R.A. (ed.). (2006). *Mindfulness-Based Treatment Approaches: Clinicians Guide to Evidence Base and Application (Practice Resources for the Mental Health Professional)*. Burlington, MA: Elsevier.

Baumeister, R.F., Bratslavansky, E., Finkenauer, C. and Vohs, K.D. (2001). Bad is stronger than good. *Review of General Psychology*, 5(4), 323–70.

Begley, S. (2007). *Train Your Mind, Change Your Brain: How a New Science Reveals an Extraordinary Potential to Transform Ourselves*. New York: Ballantine Books.

Bien, T. and Didonna, F. (2009). Appendix A: Mindfulness practice. In F. Didonna (ed.), *Clinical Handbook of Mindfulness*, New York: Springer, 477–88.

Boyce, B. (2011). Introduction: Anyone Can Do It, and It Changes Everything. In B. Boyce (ed.), *The Mindfulness Revolution: Leading Psychologists, Scientists, Artists, and Meditation Teachers on the Power of Mindfulness in Daily Life*. Boston, MA: Shambhala, 248–51.

Brady, R. (2004). Schooled in the moment: Introducing mindfulness to students and teachers. *Independent School*, 64, 82–7.

Brown, K.B. and Ryan, R.M. (2003). The benefits of being present: Mindfulness and its role in psychological well-being. *Journal of Personality and Social Psychology* 84, 822–48.

Brown, K.W. and Cordon, S. (2009). Phenomenology and Emotional Correlates of Mindfulness. In F. Didonna (ed.),*Clinical Handbook of Mindfulness*. New York: Springer, 59–81.

Brown, P.L. (2007). *In the classroom, a new focus on quieting the mind* [Online]. Available at: http://www.nytimes.com/2007/06/16/us/16mindful.html?_r=1. [accessed: 30 November 2009].

Chen, A.C. (2008). *Students of stillness: By teaching school kids to be 'in the moment,' an Oakland educator helps them focus* [Online]. Available at: http://www.diablomag.com/Diablo-Magazine/August-2008/Students-Of-Stillness/ [accessed: 30 November 2009].

Dalai Lama. (1999). *Ancient Wisdom, Modern World: Ethics for a New Millennium*. London: Little, Brown and Company.

Dalai Lama. (2011). Taking Responsibility for the World's Well-Being. In B. Boyce (ed.), *Psychologists, Scientists, and Meditation Teachers on Mindfulness in Daily Life*. Boston, MA: Shambhala, 248–51.Davidson, R., Kabat-Zinn, J., et al. (2003). Alterations in brain and immune function produced by mindfulness meditation. *Psychosomatic Medicine*, 65(4), 564–70 [Online]. Available at: http://dunntastic.com/sources/Davidson%202003%20-%20Alterations%20 in%20brain%20and%20immune%20function%20produced%20by%20 mindfulness%20meditation.pdf [accessed: 10 February 2012].

Didonna, F. (ed.). (2008). *Clinical Handbook of Mindfulness*. New York: Springer.

Doidge, N. (2007). *The Brain That Changes Itself: Stories of Personal Triumph from the fRontiers of Brain Science*. New York: Penguin Books.

Dvorsky. G. (2007). Managing your 50,000 daily thoughts. *Sentient Developments* [Online]. Available at: http://ieet.org/index.php/IEET/print/1448/ [accessed: 19 February 2012].

Egan, G. (2010). *The Skilled Helper: A Problem-Management and Opportunity-Development Approach to Helping* (9th edn). Pacific Grove, CA: Brooks Cole.

Elias, M (2008). *Stressed-out teens get lessons in relaxing* [Online]. Available at: http://www.boston.com/news/local/articles/2008/03/05/stressed out teens get lessons in relaxing/ [accessed: 30 November 2009].

England, H. (1986). *Social Work as Art: Making Sense for Good Practice*. London: Allen and Unwin.

Goleman, D. (2003). *Destructive Emotions and How We Can Overcome Them: A Dialogue with the Dalai Lama*. London: Bloomsbury.

Goleman, D. (2006). *Social Intelligence: The New Science of Human Relationships*. London: Hutchinson.

Goleman, D. (2007). Forward. In Y.M. Rinpoche, *The Joy of Living: Unlocking the Secret and Science of Happiness*. New York: Three Rivers Press, xii–ix.

Gray, M., Coates, J. and Yellow Bird, M. (eds). (2008). *Indigenous Social Work around the World: Towards Culturally Relevant Education and Practice*. Aldershot: Ashgate.

Hanson, R. and Mendius, R. (2009). *Buddha's Brain: The Practical Neuroscience of Happiness, Love, and Wisdom*. Oakland, CA: New Harbinger Publications.

Hick, S.F. (2009). Mindfulness and Social Work: Paying attention to ourselves, our clients, and society. In S.F. Hick (ed.), *Mindfulness and Social Work*. Chicago, IL: Lyceum.

Hooker, K.E. and Fodor, I.E. (2008). Teaching mindfulness to children. *Gestalt Review*, 12(1), 75–91.

Jan, T. (2008). *Stressed-out teens get lessons in relaxing* [Online]. Available at:http://www.boston.com/news/local/articles/2008/03/05/stressed_out_teens_get_lessons_in_relaxing/ [accessed: 30 November 2009].

Kabat-Zinn, J. (1994a). *Wherever You Go, There You Are: Mindfulness Meditation in Everyday Life*. New York: Hyperion.

Kabat-Zinn, J. (1994b). *Mindfulness Meditation for Everyday Life*. London: Judy Piatkus Publishers.

Kabat-Zinn, J., Wheeler, E. et al. (1998). Influence of a mindfulness meditation-based stress reduction intervention on rates of skin clearing in patients with moderate to severe psoriasis undergoing phototherapy (VB) and photochemotherapy (PUVA). *Psychosomatic Medicine*, 65, 625–32.

Kassabian, A. (2009). *ADHD and mindfulness activism* [Online]. Available at:http://www.tikkun.org/article.php?story=sept_oct_09_Kassabian [accessed: 30 November 2009].

Kandel, E.R. (2007). The New Science of the Mind. In F.E. Bloom (ed.), *Best of the Brain from Scientific American*. New York: Dana Press, 68–75.

Langer, E. (1989). *Mindfulness*. Cambridge, MA: Da Capo Press.

LeShan, L. (1974). *How to Meditate: A Guide to Self-Discovery*. New York: Bantam Books.

Luu, P. and Posner, M.I. (2003). Editorial: Anterior cingulate cortex regulation of sympathetic activity. *Brain,* 126, 1219–1220 [Online]. Available at: http://brain.oxfordjournals.org/content/126/10/2119.full.pdf+html [accessed: 10 February 2012].

Mindsightinstitute. (2009). Hawn Foundation Video with Dr Dan Siegel [Video file]. Video posted to http://www.youtube.com/watch?v=5dFrOTgAIzY.

Newberg, A. and Waldman, M.R. (2009). *How God Changes Your Brain: Breakthrough Findings from a Leading Neuroscientist*. New York: Ballantine Books.

Nhat Hanh, T. (1976). *The Miracle of Mindfulness: An Introduction to the Practice of Meditation*. Translayed by Mobi Ho. Boston: Beacon Press.

Nhat Hanh, T. (1991). *Peace Is Every Step: The Path of Mindfulness in Everyday Life*. New York: Bantam Books.

Peale, N.V. (1952). *The Power of Positive Thinking*. New York: Prentice-Hall.

Peeters, G. and Czapinski, J. (1990). Positive-Negative Asymmetry in Evaluations: The distinction between affective and informational negativity effects. In W. Stroebe and Hewstone, M. (eds), *European Review of Social Psychology*, vol. 1. Chichester, England: Wiley, 33–60.

Picchetti, N. (n.d.). Cognitive heuristic [Online]. Available at: http://www.cognitiveatlas.org/term/id/trm_4a3fd79d09d58 [accessed: 19 February 2012].

Sapolsky, R. (2009). *On depression in U.S.* (Full Lecture) [Online]. Available at: http://www.youtube.com/watch?v=NOAgplgTxfc [accessed: 19 February 2012].

Siegel, D. (2001). *Mindsight: The New Science of Personal Transformation*. New York: Bantam Books.

Skowronski, J.J. and Carlston, D.E. (1989). Negativity and extremity biases in impression formation: A review of explanations. *Psychological Bulletin*, 105, 131–42.

Suttie, J (2007). Mindful kids, peaceful schools. *Greater Good Magazine* [Online]. Available at:http://www.mindfuleducation.org/documents/JS.pdf [accessed: 30 November 2009].

Schwartz, J.M. and Begley, S. (2002). *The Mind and the Brain: Neuroplasticity and the Power of Mental Force*. New York: HarperCollins.

Tartar, J.L., de Almeida, K., McIntosh, R.C., Rosselli, M. and Nash, A.J. (2010). Emotionally negative pictures increase attention to a subsequent auditory stimulus. *International Journal of Psychophysiology*, 83(1), 36–44.

Varela, F.J. (1999). *Ethical Know-How: Action, Wisdom and Cognition*. Stanford, CA: Stanford University Press.

Varela, F.J., Thompson, E. and Rosch, E. (1991). *The Embodied Mind: Cognitive Science and Human Experience*. Cambridge, MA: Cambridge University Press.

Waller, M. (2001). Resilience in ecosystemic context: Evolution of the concept. *American Journal of Orthopsychiatry*, 71(3), 290–97.

Waller, M., Risley-Curtiss, C., Murphy, S., Medill, A. and Moore, G. (1998). Harnessing the positive power of language: American Indian women, a case example. *Journal of Poverty*, 2(4), 63–81.

Westerfelt, A. and Yellow Bird, M.J. (1999). Homeless and Indigenous in Minneapolis. *Journal of Human Behavior in the Social Environment*, 2(1/2), 145–62.

Wilson, W.A. and Yellow Bird, M. (2005). *For Indigenous Eyes Only: A Decolonization Handbook*. Santa Fe, NM: School of American Research.

Yellow Bird, M. (1999). Indigenous Peoples' Parent Roles. In C.A. Smith (ed.), *The Encyclopedia of Parenting Theory and Research*. Westport, CT: Greenwood Press, 231–3.

Yellow Bird, M. (2012). Neurodecolonization: Using mindfulness practices to delete the neural networks of colonialism. In Waziyatawin and Yellow Bird, M. (eds), *For Indigenous Minds Only: A Decolonization Handbook* (2nd edn). Sante Fe, NM: School of American Research.

Chapter 16

Using Indigenist Research to Shape Our Future

Shawn Wilson

This chapter demonstrates the necessity of developing and utilizing an Indigenist research paradigm to create an Indigenous vision for the future. If Indigenous social services are to progress beyond their constant reactionary crisis mode of functioning, Indigenist research is needed to shift the focus away from how communities want *not* to be and instead create a vision for how communities and families want to be. Armed with this vision, Indigenist research might guide social work education and practice towards this desired future. Indigenist research works from a worldview that understands knowledge is relational: Indigenous People are not *in* relationships; they *are* relationships. This is Indigenous truth and reality. Implementing this philosophy or research paradigm requires Indigenist researchers to build theoretical frameworks and research methods congruent with Indigenous belief systems. Indigenist research views knowledge production through the lens of researchers being accountable to and for maintaining healthy relationships. In other words, data is formed through the building of relationships via the research process, and relational accountability is required to analyse and interpret this research data and turn it into Indigenous knowledge. Action based upon this knowledge may then lead to the gaining of wisdom. Only when wisdom flows from Indigenist knowledge-building processes can it meaningfully create the vision to guide social policy and service provision, thus completing the cycle of building social work interventions that are truly accountable to Indigenous communities.

Tansi (Greetings)

I am Shawn Wilson, an *Opaskwayak* Cree from northern Manitoba in Canada. *Opaskwayak* is a *Naynowak* (Cree) community situated along the Saskatchewan River, upstream from Lake Winnipeg that *Inninniwuk* (the people) have inhabited for a long time. From analysing stories and legends as well as the meaning of Cree words, it is evident that we returned to this location after briefly (a few thousand years) being forced south by the last ice age. *Opaskwayak* can be translated into English in a couple ways: the version that my father heard from the old men is that it means 'wooded like a narrows'. The first part of the word *Opa* should be *wapak* meaning narrows and the second part *skwayak* is the woods part. They said it is called that because when you are in the *Saskram* (part of the Saskatchewan River delta) and look east what you see is the high ridge of land running north and south with the tall black spruce on each side of the river (used to be anyway) and where the river runs through the ridge there is a gap and hence it looks like a narrows. Others say that it means a rise in the landscape like a ridge – this version is what younger people translate it to mean.

My parents are Stan and Peggy Wilson. My grandparents on my father's side are Charlie and Beatrice Wilson (Jebb) and my ancestors are Wassenas and Kanacheech. On my mother's side my grandparents are Alexander and Marie Robertson (McLean/Anderson). I am father to three beautiful sons, husband to Helen, ceremony leader, community psychologist, uncle, nephew, teacher and Indigenist researcher. Though I can't see you, I hope that you are well as you read this. I am feeling good as I write it – a bit worn out but also enthusiastic and always full of hope.

When I was asked to write this chapter on Indigenist research I must admit my first thought was to be concerned with the title of the book *Decolonizing Social Work*, since to me decolonization is like taking antibiotics: at times, antibiotics are necessary to treat infection, but much more is required for healthy living than recovery from disease (Hodge, Limb and Cross, 2009) and much more is required for healthy Indigenous communities than recovery from colonization (Crichlow, 2003). The dilemma or paradox of healthy living and healthy families is inherent in social work practice: it would be great if social workers did their jobs so well we were no longer required. If all children lived in healthy and supportive environments then no child, family or community would need protection, parenting classes or sexual abuse response teams. There would be no 'vulnerable' or 'at risk' people in Indigenous communities if all were cared for with compassion and allowed to grow to their fullest potential.

If this dream for Indigenous communities is to become reality, Indigenist researchers have to develop and use an Indigenist research approach. Indigenist researchers have a responsibility to help clarify an Indigenous vision for the future of our communities, even though it is extremely difficult to do so when simultaneously engaged in frontline clinical practice and faced with ongoing crises. Researchers are needed to study how to develop more effective antibiotics to respond to people still bearing the brunt of colonization, and also to engage in action research to rebuild Indigenous communities. But it is not possible to decolonize Western ideas or research concepts. As my father says, 'If you delouse a dog, it's still a dog'. Time spent discussing decolonization detracts from creating a vision of how Indigenous people might reach their full potential in the modern world. For this visioning to happen, Indigenist research is necessary: research that reflects an Indigenous view of reality, knowledge and the gaining of wisdom to shape the future of our communities and social work education and practice.

Let me pause here to clarify my usage of the word *Indigenist*. Indigenist describes a shared philosophy and its resultant ontology or way of being in the world without claiming ownership or exclusivity. While *Indigenous* describes some peoples' ethnicity and claims to distinct identities, it is a marker of race-based difference. However, Indigenist is also a descriptive label for a way of thinking I know and have been taught by my Elders. Others are welcome to share in and benefit from this knowledge and use it in their own way. This inevitably leads to the question of whether non-Indigenous people can do Indigenist research and my answer is an emphatic yes. Just as you do not have to be a woman to be a feminist, you do not need to be Indigenous to do Indigenist research. You are doing Indigenist research if you share its beliefs and philosophical underpinnings and put them into action in the knowledge-building process.

However, understanding the nature of this belief system or philosophical base is a much trickier problem as there is a conundrum to be faced: To understand the answer to the question 'what is Indigenist research?' you need to understand the philosophy to begin with. This is due to the fact that it is a context-based understanding of knowledge, based on a non-linear oral tradition, not best described in *content*-based written text as in a book chapter. Thus it is best learned from experience and discussion with your Elders. However, being the ambitious and perhaps arrogant academic I am, this chapter is an attempt to provide you a written answer to help guide social work theory to a deeper level of understanding. This also explains why I am addressing 'you' specifically as the reader, rather than a gender-neutral third person 'one', in an attempt to recreate some of the protocols of oral tradition.

Just as many academics start by describing the limitations of their studies, even though they seldom describe the limitations of their view of 'science', I start by claiming these are my own understandings and might not be those of all Indigenous people, or even all Cree people (Kovach, 2009, 2010; Michell, 2005; Steinhauer, 2001). However, though we are diverse peoples, my experience resonates with the understanding of many other Indigenous people with whom I have talked.

Being in relationship with other Indigenist philosophers, talking about relationships with and between abstractions, ideas, family and environment, I have come to understand that I'm not just *in* these relationships, but rather that I *am* these relationships (Wilson, 2008). Stated another way, the nature of Indigenist philosophy, my understanding of knowledge itself, is relational. Relationships are reality, and reality is relationships (Baskin, 2006; Crofoot Graham, 2002; Sinclair, 2004). As Indigenous people, we 'are' our relationships with other people. We do not claim a singular identity but are Auntie, Uncle, grandfather, great-grandson, mother, friend, teacher and nemesis – sometimes all at once! These are probably the easiest relationships to understand as everyone knows and can recognize that my mother is also someone else's aunt, someone's grandchild and so on.

We 'are' also our relationships with environment and everything within it. For some, this is the special relationship that sets Indigenous Peoples apart from many others: we recognize we are a product of the land, that is, we are our relationship with the land, which extends to the whole surrounding cosmos and makes us who we are (Zapf, 2005, 2009). This understanding is a bit more difficult for some people to comprehend as we are not owners of the land, nor do we seek to control it or shape it to our will. We are formed by our relationship with the land, as much as it is formed by us.

Indigenist philosophy is built upon understanding as we 'are' our relationships, with thoughts and concepts of science and spirituality, ideas and abstractions. We do not discover or claim ideas or concepts, rather we learn by making relations with the ideas shaping our being just as much as we shape the ideas in return. Certainly the relationships I have developed with the concept of 'Indigenist research' are a large part of who I am as I have taken on the role of Indigenist researcher. This is a really important point, so I'm going to say it again: Indigenist reality is relationships. We are not just in relationships, we are relationships. And so is everything else in the cosmos. In Indigenist research the unit of analysis is the relationship, not the individual. As Burkhart (2004: 25) says, 'We are, therefore I am'. This is the philosophy underlying the nature of Indigenist knowledge.

Complex relationships and interrelationships exist between and create or shape all things and the implications of this extend into how knowledge itself is understood (Barnhardt and Kawagley, 2005; Milne, 2011). Indigenist knowledge, ideas or even thoughts are not the product of the individual researcher, but are shared by the collective relationships making them (Aikenhead and Ogawa, 2007). While individuals may describe knowledge in different ways using numbers, words, pictures, songs, metaphors or stories, communicating or describing knowledge does not mean it belongs to the communicator. When describing knowledge, we are attempting to communicate a spiritual sense of connection, to bring others into our understanding of a set of relationships. Just as my mother might be your cousin and either role or relationship does not make the other right or wrong, so is one way of describing no more important than another. Each description of a relationship produces its own perspective and shapes its own reality.

Further, since our actions or roles in relationships determine the truth, it is important for these actions and their descriptions to be based upon relational accountability. Hence each role or relationship comes with a set of responsibilities. Parents have responsibilities towards their children while, in turn, having simultaneous responsibilities with their own parents, the rest of their family, community, nation and so on. Some responsibilities we are born into. Some we create for ourselves through our actions. Creating a child also conceives a set of responsibilities in our role as parent. Creating and growing a child is a process and product of creating relationships, just as shaping and growing an idea is a process and product of forming relationships with the concepts surrounding the idea. This is how Indigenist knowledge is conceived and grown. Children, ideas, knowledge and our reality are all relationships, and as each of these relationships come into our individual consciousness, we become accountable to them. I am accountable to more than just my children or my family. I am accountable to 'all my relations' (Wilson, 1999). This is the process or protocol of Indigenist research; a process of systematically bringing relationships into consciousness and becoming accountable with, for and to them. Thus our research methodology –

and our systems of ethics and ways of judging the 'worthiness' of research – is based upon relational accountability. So if you understand that philosophy, now I can talk about how to put it into action.

Philosophy to Action Guided by an Indigenist Paradigm

> Coyote also shows us that the questions we choose to ask are more important than any truths we might hope to discover in asking such questions, since how we act impacts the way the world is, the way in which a question will get answered. The way in which we ask questions (the way in which we act toward our relations) guides us, then, to the right answers, rather than the other way around wherein what is true directs the method of questioning and the question itself (i.e., we can ask any question we desire and in any way we desire, and the answer will remain the same). (Burkhart, 2004: 16)

To start by stating some limitations, I am not going to give you step-by-step instructions on how to 'do' Indigenist research. Indigenist research is relational and, therefore, also contextual. To give you step-by-step instructions on how to raise your child, I would need to know your context, how old your child is, what his or her interests are and what 'makes them tick'. You are the one who has taken on primary responsibility and accountability for that relationship. What I hope I can do is to provide some principles to help guide you as you find your own way of raising your child – or research topic, to help you figure out what questions to ask.

When I talk (and write), I often slip back and forth between metaphor or abstract and concrete or direct descriptions. The metaphor I want to use here is an island. So go ahead and picture an island in your mind. You are probably imagining tropical palms and coconuts on a white sandy beach surrounded by the ocean, or a pine tree covered rocky outcrop in a lake, depending upon where you grew up. Now shift your point of view so you are seeing both the island above the water as well as the much greater bulk of island underwater. Keeping that image in mind, attach more ideas to it and create more relationships. This island is a model of your culture: the visible part of the island is the visible part of your culture – your style of dress, what you eat, your home, how you dance, music you like and so on. Below the waterline, holding the visible part out of the water is your philosophy, your beliefs and values. This philosophy explains *why* you eat certain foods or dress the way you do. Indigenist philosophy makes us collectively who we are, giving us a distinctive group identity over and above our individual identities. The clothes I wear do not make me Cree: my beliefs and philosophy do. Go back to your picture of the island, but now imagine it is winter instead of summer and you can have a different view of the island, but it is still the same island. I can be Cree and still listen to rap music or eat Chinese takeaway. We can live in Western cities, or drive a bus instead of a dog-team, and still remain Indigenous. We can show a different aspect of our visible culture, or actively change our visible culture, but by maintaining the underlying philosophy, we can maintain who we are as a people and maintain our cultural identities: our culture can adapt to a modern context (Paradies, 2006).

Taking this analogy further and extending this island to include research methodology, theoretical frameworks, theory and practice, imagine the island is still floating in the water (even though you know islands cannot float – the underlying philosophy is not visible but is there under the water). To make this a more complex model, imagine the island is layered with different kinds of soil or rocks and types of vegetation. Only the outer layer of the island is visible and can change depending upon the context or circumstances, for example, like being hit by tsunami or an extended period of drought. So the outer layer is like our visible culture and underneath is our philosophy, but again let us apply this to research or the culture of our science.

Philosophy

At the core of the island, under the layers is our *philosophy* or belief system which is not open to debate, to be proven or disproven, but only needs to be articulated or described. People can make a conscious choice whether or not this belief system accords with theirs. A main distinction between philosophy and theory is theories can be proven or disproven, whereas a philosophy or paradigm cannot (see, for example, Coates, 1991). The philosophy is the starting point from which everything else grows and, again, relationships and relational accountability are the core philosophy of an Indigenist research paradigm (Wilson, 2008). The philosophy is a matter of belief and is taken as a matter of faith just as belief in God or Eurocentric science offers the basis for Western belief systems. For most people, they are their underlying assumptions about the nature of reality and how it is known and understood.

Theoretical Framework

The next layer of the research island metaphor may be your theoretical framework. This is the interface where you make your beliefs into an actionable model of how you are going to conduct research for a particular topic. Groups of theories work together to try to make sense of the bigger picture and can be tied into theoretical frameworks. When people talk of a paradigm shift in certain aspects of science or technology (Milne, 2011), often what is meant is a change in theoretical framework, or the structure underlying the theories built upon the frame. Very seldom has a paradigm shift taken place. For example, the emergence of modern Western science may have been a paradigm shift from what is now referred to as the 'dark ages' but it has since held universalist beliefs about the nature of reality (Milne, 2011), even though theoretical frameworks have gone through major changes, for example, from Newtonian to relativity theory to quantum physics, or shifts in understanding geology to incorporate plate tectonics. The underlying philosophy has not changed though the theoretical framework has.

Strategy of Inquiry

The 'working model' of a theoretical framework has been described as a *strategy of inquiry* – and is how your relationship building becomes scientific research. Your strategy of inquiry can change or grow as your research project evolves, as this is where your philosophy and theoretical framework interact with the 'real world' context where your research is taking place. Indigenist research needs to be just as scientific as Western research, for any science is a structured body of knowledge and scientific research must yield 'systematic knowledge' (Milne, 2011). In describing your strategy of inquiry, you are describing what your 'system' for doing research is, and providing a rationale for why you are choosing this system.

The underlying Indigenist philosophy gives Indigenist knowledge its structure or epistemology so 'scientific' means being systematic in your research approach. Indigenist or Western, the concepts of epistemology and methodology, are still there. The difference is in how these concepts are understood and applied. Here I am grateful to some of the great Indigenist academic Elders I have worked with and learned from, like Bea Medicine, Eber and Mary Hampton, Lionel and Germaine Kinunwa, Fyre Jean Graveline and my parents Stan and Peggy Wilson. Because most people who were publishing scientific research when I attended university had the same – Western – philosophy, they were not required to articulate their philosophy. Even today, when doing quantitative research, one can begin describing one's methodology at the level of strategy of inquiry, assuming one's underlying philosophy and, therefore, keeping it invisible to mainstream researchers themselves. Early Indigenist scholars helped to expose the invisible culture underlying mainstream Western academia and unbolted the lock for the current generation of Indigenist researchers to get a foot in the door (for a more thorough description, see Wilson, 2003 or Hart, 2010).

Methods

Following a strategy of inquiry provides a rationale for one's chosen *methods*, which is the next layer of this research island we are creating. Research methods need to be above the waterline so they are visible for others to see and thus replicate. Methods differ for different topics just as the beach is different when the tide changes. In the modern text-based world, this layer needs to be described very clearly so others understand our topic and can follow a similar journey of discovery. This also interacts with Indigenist pedagogy where ideally, others would be exposed to the same experiences and environment – the same context – and develop their own relationships and understanding of the research topic. To express ourselves and share these relationships with others through text, researchers need to be very clear in describing – in text – the experiences that shaped the research relationships through specific, step-by-step instructions of how the research ideas and relationships were formed. Again, without knowing your context, even as an experienced researcher I cannot give you a set of instructions, so it is up to you to describe them yourself. In your context did you ask which Elders do I need to talk to? What sort of training did I need to receive? How many people were consulted, and from which communities? How many subjects were in your randomized control trial, and how were they randomized? In which ceremonies did you participate? What is your ancestral line? Which parameters did the biostatistician apply to your regression analysis? If using dreams and visions was part of your strategy, how did you keep track of your dreams? Obviously this is not an exhaustive list of questions because each context, each research island, will have its own unique methods.

Data to Knowledge

The methods of data collection have a direct impact on the data or pieces of information seen as important enough to collect and analyse so the outermost layer is the *data*, the flora and fauna inhabiting the visible part of the research island. While data are the easiest seen, an understanding is needed as to the kinds of trees able to grow in the particular climate and soil nutrients on the island. While it is likely someone has transplanted some of these, it is highly unlikely for coconut palms to grow so well on an island in northern Manitoba.

Each layer impacts upon the one above. Though progressing through the layers leads to data collection, simply having lots of bits of information does not make knowledge; 6, 9, 12, almost always, never, $p=0.05$: these bits of data are easy to describe but are absolutely meaningless without understanding what they are attached to. Hence something more must be done to work the data back into the core of the island and thus incorporate information back into Indigenist knowledge systems. This process involves moving through analysis and interpretation to knowledge formation, incorporating this into our growing or evolving philosophy or wisdom and making it available to inform policy and practice.

This is where many Indigenist students stumble. They are usually very good at describing their methods of data collection and the data, but often not at articulating their analysis of the data. The problem may be that, for many Indigenous people, daily conversation does not involve an explicit or overt analysis process. Relational and contextual knowledge means no two people will hold the exact same relationships with the phenomena under study so when describing concepts, conclusions are not formed for people. Rather personal relationships with the concept are described to let them form their own conclusions based upon their personal relationships and experience with the phenomenon. The conclusions do not need to be the same to be 'right'. Rather they go through a shared process of analysis. Good conclusions ensue when all the relationships are accounted for; that is, when relational accountability is achieved. While agreement or the same conclusions might not be reached, each understands where the other is coming from. This accountability is easier to confirm in an oral or face-to-face situation as it is possible to judge whether the others involved in the discussion 'get' what we are talking about from verbal or non-verbal clues. This where an Indigenist research culture must be adapted to a modern context, that requires the written communication of ideas. In Indigenist research, the use of metaphor and the first-person voice to describe the research process and its outcomes allows knowledge to grow. With written text, it is more difficult to ascertain whether the reader 'gets' what is being discussed. In a sense, then, a good outline of the research methods and process is, in itself, the beginning of the description of the analysis but it is, perhaps, the shift from describing what went into *forming* the relationships to describing the relationships themselves. This distinction is best understood by returning to the island metaphor: it is going beyond saying this soil and this amount of rainfall went into shaping these trees, but taking it further to describe how the trees fed back into the soil and the vegetation, in turn, affected the rainfall and vice versa. Often researchers use their own stories and reflections on personal growth to make sense of the data and relate it to their context. Their analysis involves describing how the data has changed them personally (Kovach, 2010; McIvor, 2010).

Analysis or 'making sense of the data' includes using theory to explain the findings and building theory from them. Theories attempt to explain 'why'. Data goes through analysis to theory formation and theories tie together to form a theoretical framework while, at the same time, one's philosophy and theoretical framework guides data collection and analysis – depending upon whether one is working from an inductive or deductive approach. Since Indigenist knowledge is relational, researchers are less concerned with justifying or proving the truth of a phenomenon – comparing it against universal ideas – as they are about contextualizing the knowledge. Burkhart's (2004) Coyote lesson teaches that *right actions result in truth* which, in modern Western philosophy, is a profoundly Aristotelian idea. Making meaning out of research data thus involves not only contextualizing the data but translating it into action and incorporating it into one's daily life experience. In Western Enlightenment thinking, with right action comes conscious – or mindful in Buddhist philosophy – choice about where the research might lead, and how one might get there. Indigenist researchers choose to act from an Indigenist paradigm and, by so doing, choose to act in an Indigenist way. Rather than reacting to others, they are setting their own agenda which might involve randomized controlled trials even though they follow their relational, context-based Indigenist philosophy.

There is a tendency for dogmatism when one is learning something for the first time so care must be taken when learning from Elders, spiritual advisors or doctoral supervisors, all of whom teach a particular view of the world or Aboriginal culture which is not necessarily the right way or the only way to understand or behave – merely their way. There is sometimes even a greater tendency among new researchers or new 'converts' to think their way is best because it might have saved them or changed their lives. One example is the religion that has sprung up around Native American spirituality which often reflects a need for certainty or dogmatic adherence to a particular discipline. However, within an Indigenist worldview, real spirituality is not a discipline. It is a belief system with relationality and relational accountability at its core (Wilson, 2008).

Relational Accountability: From Research to Clinical Practice

In a practice sense, research is meant to lead to evidence-based practice, that is, practice with proven effectiveness. Though primarily a research methodology, relational accountability is also a philosophy that can shape practice since it is an indispensable part of the Indigenist research island. As with research, practice is informed by and, in turn, informs theory but more is needed if knowledge is to be transferred into workable – context-based – policies and interventions. Having an overarching vision allows for and encourages change or growth and adaptation. A research paradigm also is an overarching vision or philosophy that allows researchers to use their strategies of inquiry or methods of data collection and analysis flexibly to suit the context and set of relationships within it, whatever the research topic. Within an Indigenist paradigm, conducting good research follows the same rules and procedures as good clinical practice. Relational accountability is as important for practitioners as it is for researchers for whom it includes the responsibility to publish to help future generations of Indigenous scholars, and guide clinicians and policy makers in Indigenist evidence-based practice to improve Indigenous health and well-being. Relationship building is as important in practice (MacKinnon and Stephens, 2008; Melin, 2008) as it is in Indigenist research. Interpersonal collaborations are a necessary part of good research and practice (Evans et al., 2009; Bennett, Zubrzycki and Bacon, 2011). It is not necessary – nor is it possible – to know everything about every issue or topic to be a good researcher or practitioner though there is room for specialized skills in enlisting and working with our Indigenist allies. However, in Indigenist research and practice, full participation in community affairs and embeddedness in an Indigenist philosophy or worldview is also needed.

Researching and Creating a Healthy System for the Future

Decolonization and rediscovery within a foreign system of 'governance' are *reactions* rather than *positive actions* which can be achieved only via engagement, self-determination and true participation following our own Indigenist philosophies, theoretical frameworks and research approaches. The dilemma or paradox of healthy living and healthy families is inherent in social work practice: it would be great if social workers did their jobs so well we were no longer required. If all children lived in healthy and supportive environments then no child, family or community would need protection, parenting classes or sexual abuse response teams. There would be no 'vulnerable' or 'at risk' people in Indigenous communities if all were cared for with compassion and allowed to grow to their fullest potential. In order to guide our actions towards this dream for Indigenous communities to become reality, we must *create our own vision for the future* by developing and using Indigenist research methods and approaches as researchers. We do not need to fight *against* the system for we cannot win. Instead, we should use our fighting energy to think, dream, envision and create an image of how we want to be. We need to use that vision as a guiding light to work towards, a vision that is worth fighting *for*. We need to be researching and creating social work systems that function for us in our modern context, not in reaction to a system working against us or in deference of historical romanticism, but in proactively pursuing relational accountability. That is, being accountable to and for our relations. To 'all my relations'.

References

Aikenhead, G. and Ogawa, M. (2007). Indigenous knowledge and science revisited. *Cultural Studies of Science Education*, 2, 539–620.

Barnhardt, R. and Kawagley, O. (2005). Indigenous knowledge systems and Alaska Native ways of knowing. *Anthropology and Education Quarterly*, 36, 8–23.

Baskin, C. (2006). Aboriginal worldviews as challenges and possibilities in social work education. *Critical Social Work*, 7(2) [Online]. Available at: http://www.uwindsor.ca/criticalsocialwork/ [accessed: 29 November 2011].

Bennett, B., Zubrzycki, J. and Bacon, V. (2011). What do we know: The experiences of social workers working alongside Aboriginal people. *Australian Social Work*, 64(1), 20–37.

Burkhart, B.Y. (2004). What Coyote and Thales Can Teach Us: An outline of American Indian epistemology. In A. Walters (ed.), *American Indian Thought: Philosophical Essays*. Malden, MA: Blackwell Publishing, 15–26.

Coates, J. (1991). Putting knowledge for practice into perspective. *Canadian Social Work Review*, 8(1), 82–96.

Crichlow, W. (2003). Western colonization a disease: Native adoption and cultural genocide. *Canadian Social Work*, 5(1), 88–107.

Crofoot-Graham, T.L. (2002). Using reasons for living to connect to American Indian healing traditions. *Journal of Sociology and Social Welfare*, 29(1), 55–75.

Evans, M., Hole, R., Berg, L., Hutchinson, P. and Sookraj, D. (2009). Common insights, differing methodologies. *Qualitative Inquiry*, 15(5), 893–910.

Hart, M. (2010). Indigenous worldviews, knowledge and research: The development of an Indigenous research paradigm. *Journal of Indigenous Voices in Social Work*, 1(1), 1–16.

Hodge, D., Limb, G. and Cross, T. (2009). Moving from colonization toward balance and harmony: A Native American perspective on wellness. *Social Work*, 54(3), 211–19.

Kovach, M. (2009). *Indigenous Methodologies: Characteristics, Conversations and Contexts*. Toronto, ON: University of Toronto Press.

Kovach, M. (2010). Conversational method in indigenous research. *First Peoples Child & Family Review*, 5(1), 40–48.

MacKinnon, S. and Stephens, S. (2008). *Is Participation Having an Impact? Measuring Progress in Winnipeg's Inner City through the Voices of Community-Based Program Participants*. Winnipeg, MB: Canadian Centre for Policy Alternatives – Manitoba.

McIvor, O. (2010). I am my subject: Blending Indigenous research methodology and autoethnography through integrity-based, spirit-based research. *Canadian Journal of Native Education*, 33(1), 137–51.

Melin, C. (2008). Exploring relationship building between social science researchers and Indigenous communities. Unpublished Masters thesis, University of Toronto.

Michell, H. (2005). Nehithawak of Reindeer Lake, Canada: Worldview, epistemology and relationships with the natural world. *Australian Journal of Indigenous Education*, 34, 33–43.

Milne, C. (2011). *The Invention of Science: Why History of Science Matters for the Classroom*. Rotterdam: Sense Publishers.

Paradies, Y.C. (2006). Beyond black and white: Essentialism, hybridity and Indigeneity. *Journal of Sociology*, 42(4), 355–67.

Sinclair, R. (2004). Aboriginal social work education in Canada: Decolonizing pedagogy for the seventh generation. *First Peoples Child & Family Review*, 1(1), 49–61.

Steinhauer, P. (2001). Kihkapiw: Sitting within the sacred circle of the Cree way. Unpublished Doctoral thesis, University of Alberta, Edmonton.

Wilson, S. (1999). Native viewpoints: Honouring our relations: Aboriginal spirituality as comprehensive relational accountability. *Canadian Social Studies*, 33(3), 76–86.

Wilson, S. (2003). Progressing toward an Indigenous research paradigm in Canada and Australia. *Canadian Journal of Native Education*, 27(2), 161–80.

Wilson, S. (2008). *Research is Ceremony: Indigenous Research Methods*. Halifax, NS: Fernwood Publishing.

Zapf, M.K. (2005). The spiritual dimension of person and environment: Perspectives from social work and traditional knowledge. *International Social Work*, 48(5), 633–42.

Zapf, M.K. (2009). *Social Work and the Environment: Understanding People and Place*. Toronto, ON: Canadian Scholars' Press.

Conclusion: Continuing the Decolonization Agenda

Mel Gray, John Coates, Michael Yellow Bird and Tiani Hetherington

> Columbus was a wétiko. He was mentally ill or insane, the carrier of a terribly contagious psychological disease, the wétiko psychosis. The Native people he described were sane people with a healthy state of mind. Sanity or healthy normality among humans and other living creatures involves a respect for other forms of life and other individuals. I believe that is the way people have lived (and should live). The wétiko psychosis, and the problems it creates, have inspired many resistance movements and efforts at reform or revolution. Unfortunately, most of these efforts have failed because they have never diagnosed the wétiko as an insane person whose disease is extremely contagious. (Forbes, 2008: 22)

In this book, we have attempted to address the role of social work in colonization and, more importantly, the process of decolonization: in theory, practice, education and research. While we have drawn attention primarily to Indigenous Peoples, the physical and mental aspects of decolonization apply equally to Indigenous and non-Indigenous communities. We need to recognize that there are other radically different ways to live in this world, learn how to break through our identification with the colonizer, and recognize the detrimental impacts of colonization in our own lives and communities (see for example the Unsettling Minnesota Collective, 2009; Wilson and Yellow Bird, 2005; Zig-Zag, 2006). This process of decolonization requires 'truth telling' – both personal and public. It requires that we acknowledge the history and genocide of colonization (see Stannard, 1992 of Indigenous Peoples). It requires that we recognize the numerous manifestations of colonialism that continue to exploit people and their environments. Finally, it requires a willingness to stand up for the rights of Indigenous Peoples. There are many opportunities for social workers of all backgrounds, not only to work in solidarity and as allies with Indigenous people, but also to engage in active decolonization in their thinking and in their own communities.

Decolonizing the 99 per cent

Recently, some very important and critical events have happened across the world, such as the 'Occupy Wall Street' movement in the United States and the 'Facebook revolution' in the Middle East. In many respects, these represent major decolonizing events for non-Indigenous Peoples as the occupy movement has brought the oppression of the majority by the economic and political elite into public discourse. Perhaps this is especially the case for white middle-class Americans, who due to economic marginalization, social rejection and political isolation by capitalist elites and economic structures, have, in a sense, become the 'new natives' and the 'other'. The term 'occupy', however, is problematic in the sense that the USA and Wall Street are situated on Indigenous Peoples' lands, as some Indigenous activists have pointedly protested (see for example Harris, 2012). Thus we suggest that the term 'Decolonize Wall Street' is a far more appropriate term. Instead of the slogan 'we are the 99 per cent' (see The 99 per cent Declaration Working Group, 2011), which addresses the growing income inequality between the wealthiest 1 per cent in the USA and the rest of the population, perhaps a far more apposite shibboleth would be 'decolonize the 99 per cent' (see Unsettling America, 2011). In an open letter to Occupy Wall Street activists, John Paul Montano (2011) writes:

> *I* am not one of the 99 percent that you refer to. And, that saddens me. Please don't misunderstand me. I would *like* to be one of the 99 percent … but you've chosen to exclude me. Perhaps it was *unintentional*, but, I've been excluded by you. In fact, there are millions of us indigenous people who have been excluded from the Occupy Wall Street protest. Please know that I suspect that it was an unintentional exclusion on your part. That is why I'm writing to you. I believe that you can make this right …
>
> It seems that ever since we indigenous people have discovered Europeans and invited them to visit with us here on our land, we've had to endure countless '-isms' and religions and programs and social engineering that would 'fix' us. Protestantism, Socialism, Communism, American Democracy, Christianity, Boarding Schools, Residential Schools … well, you get the idea. And, it seems that these so-called enlightened strategies were nearly always enacted and implemented and pushed upon us *without our consent*. And, I'll assume that you're aware of how it turned out for us. Yes. Terribly.
>
> Which brings me back to your mostly-inspiring Occupy Wall Street activities. On 22 September, with great excitement, I eagerly read your 'One Demand' statement. Hoping and believing that you enlightened folks fighting for justice and equality and an end to imperialism, etc., etc., would make mention of the fact that the very land upon which you are protesting does not belong to you – that you are guests upon that stolen indigenous land. I had hoped mention would be made of the indigenous nation whose land that is. I had hoped that you would address the centuries-long history that we indigenous peoples of this continent have endured being subject to the countless '-isms' of do-gooders claiming to be building a 'more just society,' a 'better world,' a 'land of freedom' *on top of our indigenous societies, on our indigenous lands, while destroying and/or ignoring*

our ways of life. I had hoped that you would acknowledge that, since you are settlers on indigenous land, you need and want our indigenous consent to your building *anything* on our land – never mind an entire society. See where I'm going with this? … We're still friends, so don't sweat it. I believe your hearts are in the right place. I know that this whole genocide and colonization thing causes all of us lots of confusion sometimes. It just seems to me that you're *unknowingly* doing the same thing to us that all the colonizers before you have done: you want to do stuff on our land without asking our permission.

But, fear not my friends. We indigenous people have a sense of humor. So, I thought I might make a few friendly suggestions which may help to 'fix' the pro-colonialism position in which you now (hopefully, unintentionally) find yourselves …

By the way, I'm just one indigenous person. I represent no one except myself. I'm acting alone in writing this letter. Perhaps none of my own Nishnaabe people will support me in having written this. Perhaps some will. I respect their opinions either way. I love my Nishnaabe people *always*. I am simply trying to do something good …

So, here goes …

1. Acknowledge that the United States of America is a colonial country, a country of settlers, built upon the land of indigenous nations; and/or …
2. Demand immediate freedom for indigenous political prisoner Leonard Peltier; and/or …
3. Demand that the colonial government of the United States of America honor all treaties signed with all indigenous nations whose lands are now collectively referred to as the 'United States of America'; and/or …
4. Make some kind of mention that you are indeed aware that you are settlers and that you are not intending to repeat the mistakes of all of the settler do-gooders that have come before you. In other words, that you are willing to obtain the consent of indigenous people before you do *anything* on indigenous land.

Indeed, Indigenous Peoples may be more accurately portrayed as the 'other 1 per cent'. They have no connection to the elite upper 1 per cent, except that this group gained much of its wealth from the exploitation and illegal taking of Indigenous Peoples' lands and resources. And, as Montano (2011) states, they are not aligned with the 98 per cent that continue to occupy their territories with little regard for, or knowledge of, the rights of Indigenous Peoples – instead focusing their protests against income inequality and wealth distribution.

In examining the occupations of Wall Street in New York City and in many other cities of the world, we see that middle-class folk are raging in organized, non-violent ways against their economic system due to its greed, and its negative effects on people who are poor and middle class, and the environment. It is highly important to point out that decolonization must also include occupying the colonial educational system that has prevaricated on critical aspects of history; the judicial system that has disproportionately and unjustly sentenced and incarcerated the colonized and, the neoconservative political system that has served the interests of the colonial elite and corporations. Occupy Wall Street has spread and is now a global phenomenon (Occupy Wall Street, 2012). One might say that global decolonization is 'picking up steam'. In other words, this is a beginning for decolonization or, as Frantz Fanon (1965) might say, 'a dying colonialism'. However, without consideration and honouring of the rights of Indigenous Peoples, this global decolonization movement may be just another colonial sheep in wolf's clothing.

The Social Work Profession and Decolonizing the 98 per cent

Obviously there are differences of opinions about the best way to seek change; however, there can be little doubt that many social workers across the world share the concerns of the Occupy Wall Street protesters about the impact of the economy on marginalized individuals and families, the prospect for any constructive change in the near future, and the complete lack of political as well as financial liability for the crisis (see Schachter, 2011). For social workers, worsening economic conditions, including the impact of the 2008 Global Financial Crisis, have only added to the significant challenges faced by the communities they serve, while the need for services increases. Whether explicitly articulated by Occupy Wall Street or not, what is clearly needed is decolonization. We must openly recognize that colonization continues today under several guises including globalization, corporate greed and capitalist expansion. We need to make connections between the histories and trajectories of inter alia capitalism, globalization, imperialism, genocide and ecocide (Gray, Coates and Yellow Bird, 2008; Smith, 1999; Wilson and Yellow Bird, 2005).

The crux of the matter for social workers is that the real needs of people, both Indigenous and non-Indigenous, are not being addressed in this age of service and tax cuts, punitive social policies and corporate dominance. Decolonization can be seen as an extension of the critical tradition in social work (such as structural, feminist, and anti-oppressive perspectives, and environmental social work) that draws attention to the oppressive and exploitative elements inherent in societies. In addition, the reality is much more complex than what has been mentioned thus far. For instance, examples of ongoing colonization are seen in unabated reliance on fossil fuels, which advances corporate profit while harming the environment and long-term health of people everywhere; Western governments being elected by increasingly fewer voters as voter futility and alienation is bolstered by corporate political spending; and the refusal of governments to work with First Nations people in Canada and the USA to ensure that proper housing, sanitation and drinking water are available in their communities. Protest plays a critical role when political institutions are not up to the task of promoting social justice, or actively working against it, as evidenced by the reaction of governments to the G8 protests in Quebec and Seattle, and what has been called the 'Arab Spring' spreading across the Middle East (see for example Dalacoura, 2012; Zhuo, Wellman and Yu, 2011). If Occupy Wall Street is to have lasting impact, perhaps it can be an impetus for the social work profession to engage proactively in working towards a decolonized future to remove the many ways that colonization is perpetuated.

Decolonizing Language

The first step in the decolonization process, as we have seen in the chapters of this book, is awareness and a big part of this awareness involves cognizance of the language we use. The language of colonialism is deeply embedded in Western culture and awareness involves understanding the history attached to important symbols linked to our national identity. Hence, in order to decolonize, we must understand as much as we can about colonialism. In the United States, for example, colonialism has and continues to take many forms. One of the most prevalent is the names of colonialism. While we have paid attention to how colonialism operates in Western social work approaches, we have also taken note of how it has appeared by way of words, images, symbols, policies, ideas and names. In this volume, the name 'Columbia' appeared in one of the chapters, which to most would not appear to be an issue. However, many Indigenous Peoples in the Western hemisphere consider it to be a name of colonialism.

Columbia is considered to be an historical name for the United States and the female counterpart to Christopher Columbus. She was invented by US Americans to denote their patriotism and is associated with their idea of being a world power. After WWII she was replaced by 'Lady Liberty', a goddess-like female personification of the US. Perhaps the most famous image of Columbia was created by US American painter John Gast. You can find his painting of Columbia on the Internet, along with a description of what she represented in terms of US American progress. Many people have, and continue to, associate her with US American 'Manifest Destiny' (again, some refer to it as US American progress from the period 1820 to 1860) which was the idea, believed by many, that US Americans were divinely inspired (by God) to settle the entire United States from east to west. Manifest destiny meant that US Americans must bring their ideas of commerce, education, religion, democracy and civilization to all areas unsettled by white people. This of course meant dispossessing Indigenous Peoples of their lands, resources and rights (often using war, murder, deliberately spreading diseases, such as smallpox, or hunting out all of the game so Indigenous Peoples would starve, or making and breaking treaties with Indigenous Peoples to get the job done). To the land and resource hungry Americans, Indigenous Peoples were not civilized. They were savages who knew nothing of God, had no laws, morality or industry. Their communal ways of sharing the land, loyalty to the community and respect for nature were considered to be primitive, backward and barely, if at all, human attributes. Of course, the US Americans – and colonizers everywhere, considered themselves God's chosen people, endowed with the responsibility to civilize Indigenous Peoples. Some scholars believe that manifest destiny is still a major objective of the United States. For instance, Gronquist (2005) writes:

> Although the shameful concept of Manifest Destiny should be confined to history books, it has reared its ugly head, as reflected in our government's 21st century mission to reshape the Middle East. Of course, the psychology of Manifest Destiny – the projection of Anglo-Saxon supremacy – never really went away, it has always been used to justify America's expansionist adventures. Losing the Vietnam War drove it toward covert action, i.e., U.S. attempts in the 1980's to undo the Nicaraguan revolution and support for death squads in El Salvador and Guatemala. But U.S. foreign policy has consistently been based on an arrogant and racist view that 'America knows best'. (para.4)

The name Columbia did not come about by accident. She is the female counterpart of the same Christopher Columbus that ushered in the colonization of the Western Hemisphere by European nations and later on the United States of America. Columbus and his men were personally responsible for numerous, brutal acts of murder, rape, pillaging, slave trading, spreading disease and the annihilation and genocide of many Indigenous Peoples (De Las Casas, 1992). Catholic priest Bartolome De Las Casas (1992: 15), who accompanied Columbus on one of his voyages, wrote, as an eyewitness to the invasion of the Christian Europeans and what they did to the Indigenous Peoples of Hispaniola:

> They forced their way into native settlements, slaughtering everyone they found there, including small children, old men, pregnant women, and even women who had just given birth. They hacked them to pieces, slicing open their bellies with their swords as though they were so many sheep herded into a pen. They even laid wagers on whether they could manage to slice a man in two at a stroke, or cut an individual's head from his body, or disembowel him with a single blow of their axes. They grabbed suckling infants by the feet and, ripping them from their mother's breasts, dashed them headlong against the rocks.

Many Americans, and often a good part of the world's population, overlooks, ignores and trivializes the impact that Columbus had on Indigenous Peoples and continue to celebrate Columbus' 'discovery' as a hallmark of human progress and civilization. However, numerous Indigenous Peoples in the Western hemisphere continue to oppose and protest the celebration of 'Columbus Day'. Change is slowly coming about and now some cities, towns, institutions and groups do not celebrate Columbus and instead have begun to regard 12 October as Indigenous Peoples' Day.

In our efforts to decolonize, we urge vigilance about the many forms that colonialism takes. That said decolonizing social work requires that we either discard colonial names or point out them out for what they are. Challenging the names of colonialism is not an attempt at political correctness. It is an act of intellectual liberation that corrects a distorting narrative of imperialist notions of 'discovery' and 'progress' in the Western hemisphere that has been maintained far too long by Europeans and European Americans (Yellow Bird, 1999).

In another chapter, the sixteenth US American president Abraham Lincoln was cited for his democratic ideas and the inclusion of the voices of all the people in the American republic. In the United States, Lincoln is regarded as the great emancipator of black slaves and is pictured on the US five-dollar bill. US President Barack Obama has often quoted Lincoln and been compared to him by some political observers. However, Lincoln's image as a great humanitarian and unifier of a great nation has been challenged by many others, including Indigenous Peoples. For instance, Michael Gaddy (2003: para. 2) observes:

> The false sainthood and adulation afforded Lincoln has its basis in the incorrect assumption he fought the war to free an enslaved people. To believe this propaganda one must ignore most everything Lincoln said about the Black race and his continued efforts at colonization.

Lincoln's treatment of, and lack of regard for, Indigenous Peoples in the United States has generally been ignored or covered up by American politicians and educators. Henry Clay was a political idol of Abraham Lincoln and, when he was elected president, Lincoln implemented Clay's political ideas (Gaddy, 2003). As Secretary of State, Clay declared, 'The Indians' disappearance from the human family will be no great loss to the world. I do not think them, as a race, worth preserving' (Gaddy, 2003, para. 4).

Among many Indigenous Peoples in the United States, Abraham Lincoln is nothing more than a representative of American invasion and colonialism. He is more infamously associated with giving orders to hang 38 Dakotas (Indigenous Peoples) following the so-called Dakota Uprising in Minnesota, which Brookeman (1984) described as the greatest mass execution in US history. According to the *Guinness Book of Records*, lynching these Dakotas made 'Old Honest Abe' the record holder for the largest hanging of people from one gallows (*Guinness Book of Records*, 1991). Brown (1991: 40) notes:

> During Lincoln's presidency, the Dakota were mistreated, cheated, and abused by white settlers, Indian agents, and traders who had pushed them off their lands, leaving them only one-tenth of their original territory. They were starving because the wild game was gone from their hunting grounds, which were claimed by white settlers. They were also deceived in the treaties that they made with

the United States and did not get annuities and food promised to them. When Dakota chief Little Crow requested food from Indian agent Thomas Galbraith for his starving people, he was condescendingly told by trader Andrew Myrick that they should 'eat grass or their own dung.'

Gaddy (2003: para. 7) writes that Lincoln assigned General John Pope to put down the uprising and the General announced at the beginning of his campaign: 'It is my purpose to utterly exterminate the Sioux. They are to be treated as maniacs or wild beasts, and by no means as people with whom treaties or compromise can be made'. At no point did Lincoln challenge this statement.

Moving towards a Decolonized World

A truly decolonized world is very difficult to envisage, given that even the physical landscape of Earth is so very different now than it was prior to colonization. We need to first openly recognize colonization as the informal and formal methods that have maintained the subjugation of Indigenous Peoples lands and resources (see Wilson and Yellow Bird, 2005). This includes the legacies of internal and intergenerational layers of psychological colonization (Zig-Zag, 2006, see Chapter 16). Secondly, we must free ourselves from complacency (Unsettling Minnesota, 2009). This requires an awakening of how harmful colonization has been to us and to all populations. Open dialogue and collaboration between Indigenous and non-Indigenous people is vital for this process to occur (McKenzie and Morrissette, 2002; Verniest, 2006; Watson, 1988). Decolonizing requires re-imagining a liberated future and then taking the necessary steps to realize this in practice: 'We have been forced into dependence on the very capitalist system that is killing us and the planet, and [our better future] … is the escape from and destruction of this conundrum' (Healing the Earth, 2007, [Audio podcast]). The process of decolonization can help us move forward in continuing the story of Indigenous Peoples' survival and working towards 'decolonizing the 98 per cent'.

References

Brookeman, C. (1984). *American Culture and Society since the 1930s*. Basingstoke, Macmillan.

Brown, D. (1991). *Bury My Heart at Wounded Knee: An Indian History of the American West*. New York: Henry Holt.

Dalacoura, K. (2012). The 2011 uprisings in the Arab Middle East: Political change and geopolitical implications. *International Affairs*, 88(1), 63–79.

De Las Casas, B. (1992). *A Short Account of the Destruction of the Indies*. Edited and translated by N. Griffen. New York: Penguin Books.

Fanon, F. (1965). *A Dying Colonialism*. New York: Grove Press.

Forbes, J.D. (2008). *Columbus and Other Cannibals: The Wetiko Disease of Exploitation, Imperialism, and Terrorism*. New York: Seven Stories Press.

Gaddy, M. (2003). *United Native America. The American Indian and the 'Great Emancipator'* [Online]. Available at: http://www.unitednativeamerica.com/issues/lincoln_print.html [accessed: 2 March 2012].

Gray, M., Coates, J. and Yellow Bird, M. (eds). (2008). *Indigenous Social Work around the World: Towards Culturally Relevant Education and Practice*. Aldershot: Ashgate.

Gronquist, K.M. (2005). *The myth of U.S. cultural, religious, political, and social superiority: Manifest destiny – twenty-first century style* [Online]. Available at: http://www.informationclearinghouse.info/article8657.htm [accessed: 2 March 2012].

Guinness Book of Records. (1991). New York: Bantam Books.

Harris, W.E. (ed.). (2012). *The Un(occupy) Movement*. New York: Allbooks.

Healing the Earth. (2007). *Talking decolonization with Waziyatawin* [Audio podcast] [Online]. Available at: http://rabble.ca/podcasts/shows/healing-earth/talking-decolonization-waziyatawin-part-1 [accessed: 29 February 2012].

Occupy Wall Street. (2012). *The revolution continues worldwide!* [Online]. Available at: http://www.occupywallst.org [accessed: 29 February 2012].

McKenzie, B. and Morrissette, V. (2002). Social Work Practice with Canadians of Aboriginal Background: Guidelines for respectful social work. In J.R. Graham and Al-Krenawi, A. (eds), *Multicultural Social Work in Canada: Working with Diverse Ethno-Racial Communities*. Oxford: Oxford University Press, 251–79.

Montano, J.P. (2011). An Open Letter to the Occupy Wall Street Activists. *The Zashnain Daily*, 24 September 2011 [Online]. Available at: http://mzzainal-straten.blogspot.com.au/2011/09/open-letter-to-occupy-wall-street.html [accessed: 29 February 2012].

Schachter, R. (2011). 10 *things social workers have in common with the Occupy Wall Street Movement* [Online]. Available at: http://naswnyc.wordpress.com/2011/10/11/10-things-social-workers-have-in-common-with-the-occupy-wall-street-protests/ [accessed: 29 February 2012].

Smith, L.T. (1999). *Decolonizing Methodologies: Research and Indigenous Peoples*. New York: St. Martin's Press.

Stannard, D.E. (1992). *American Holocaust: The Conquest of the New World*. New York: Oxford University Press.

The 99 per cent Declaration Working Group. (2011). *The 99 per cent Declaration: There is a solution! By the people, for the people* [Online]. Available at: http://www.the99declaration.org/ [accessed: 29 February 2012].

Unsettling America: Decolonization in Theory and Practice. (2011). *Decolonize Wall Street!* 3 October 2011 [Online]. Available at: http://unsettlingamerica.wordpress.com/2011/10/03/decolonize-wall-street/ [accessed: 29 February 2012].

Unsettling Minnesota Collective. (2009). *Reflections and resources for deconstructing colonial mentality* [Online]. Available at: http://unsettlingminnesota.org/ [accessed: 29 February 2012].

Verniest, L. (2006). Allying with the medicine wheel: Social work practice with Aboriginal Peoples. *Critical Social work*, 7(1) [Online]. Available at: http://www.uwindsor.ca/criticalsocialwork/allying-with-the-medicine-wheel-social-work-practice-with-aboriginal-peoples [accessed: 29 February 2012].

Watson, L. (1988). An Aboriginal Perspective: Developing an Indigenous social work. In E. Chamberlain (ed.), *Change and Continuity in Australian Social Work*. Melbourne: Longman Cheshire, 177–84.

Wilson, A. and Yellow Bird, M. (2005). *For Indigenous Eyes Only: A Decolonization Handbook*. Santa Fe: School for Advanced Research.

Yellow Bird, M. (1999). Indian, American Indian, and Native American: Counterfeit identities. Last word. *Winds of Change: A Magazine for American Indian Education and Opportunity*, I(1), 86.

Zhuo, X., Wellman, B. and Yu, J. (2011). Egypt: The first Internet revolt? *Peace Magazine*, 27(3), 6–10.

Zig-Zag. (2006). *Colonization and decolonization: A manual for Indigenous liberation in the twenty-first century* [Online]. Available at: http://www.anti-politics.net/distro/ [accessed: 29 February 2012].

Glossary

Aboriginal: The term aboriginal means First Peoples. In Australia, it is used to refer to the Indigenous Peoples often referred to as Aboriginal and Torres Strait Islander Peoples, sometimes abbreviated as ATSI.

Agent of community transformation: Refers to the Cuban social worker's role in mobilizing community members to address their problems and in assessing the service needs of vulnerable populations.

Americanization: Term used to refer to the military and economic power of the US in shaping economic structures and systems, and cultures and lifestyles. It is a misleading term since it implies that there is only one America when in fact there are several, including North America that includes Canada, South America, often referred to as Latin America, and Central America.

Assistentialist social work: Refers to a tradition of social work practice in Cuba and other Latin countries, where the process of responding to a person's needs is limited to providing them with economic and other types of resources rather than mobilizing the particular needs of the community and its members.

Colonization: In recent times the process by which European imperial powers gained military control of, and subjugated the peoples of 'colonies' in Africa and Asia. It also refers to the historically earlier, but ongoing, process of gaining control in the Americas and Australia.

Community-oriented Cuban social work: Refers to a multisectoral (see below) method of social work practice on the island in which the social worker establishes links with municipal and regional organizations to support interventions in the community.

Contextualized social work: Social work that is context focused and born out of the relationships people develop, while interacting to learn and exchange their histories, cultures and values. It is a model of practice that is locally developed and thus void of transferable recipes or rigid formulae.

Cuban community: In Cuba, a 'community' is typically composed of 250 houses and 750 inhabitants. The community constitutes an electoral district.

Cultural imperialism: Refers to the practices of colonial powers to subvert local cultures and supplant them with European cultural practices, including conversion to Christianity and use of the language of the colonizer.

Culture: Refers to shared beliefs, practices, lifestyles and worldviews among groups of various sizes. However, it is increasingly recognized that cultures and groups are not fixed and stable entities or attributes, but dynamic and shifting depending on the influences of changing historical, sociocultural and political trends.

Decolonization (British spelling decolonisation): Refers to the undoing of the more pernicious aspects of colonialism that resulted in unequal power relations between people and nations whereby one people or nation established and maintained dominance over another. It also refers to the processes by which the neo-imperial empires – established prior to the 1914–1918 war – were dismantled throughout Africa and Asia in the years after World War II (1939–1945). After this time, many countries in Africa and Asia gained their independence from the imperial powers and established their own sovereign states. Decolonization is not a term favoured by international development agencies that prefer the language of democratization, institution and nation building, and human rights rather than the return of political control to conquered peoples.

Decolonization refers to the actions by, or in support of, subjugated people to regain their political independence and sovereignty or to reclaim their cultures and languages. In addition to reclaiming political rights, it also refers to the long-term process of overcoming the ideologies and mechanisms of control that continue to oppress and control how people understand themselves and their world. Decolonization is, as Smith (1999: 98) points out, 'a long-term process involving the bureaucratic, cultural, linguistic and psychological divesting of colonial power'.

In the contemporary context decolonization is both an event and process. Yellow Bird (2012) maintains that as an event decolonization concerns reaching a level of understanding that one had been colonized and is responding to life circumstances in ways that are limited, destructive and externally controlled. As process decolonization means engaging in activities that create, restore and consciously use strategies to liberate oneself from, or successfully adapt, to oppressive conditions inherent in colonialism. It means restoring cultural practices, beliefs and values that continue to be relevant for well-being. It means generating new ideas, thinking, technologies and lifestyles that contribute to the advancement of Indigenous Peoples (Yellow Bird, 2012).

Dialogue: A mutual learning practice whereby people listen to each other with intent to understand and learn from each other's cultural, sociopolitical, economic and historical contexts and communicate with each other with the intent of re-examining their assumptions about one another.

Ecology: Most commonly understood as the relationship of organisms to their environments; in social work it has come to refer to the relationship of humans to their social and physical environments, and involves concern and responsibility for the short and long-term impacts of human behaviour on other people and on the physical environments of which we are a part.

Ecospiritual: An approach to social work that develops from the assumption that the Earth, and all on it, is sacred. Based on this, both social justice and ecological justice are primary values, and there is an inherent responsibility for humans to manage their activities (economic and social) with regard to the well-being of all things. Ecospirituality is holistic, and recognizes the interdependence and connectedness of all things, and that evolutionary processes are in place.

Elder: The roles that elders play in Indigenous societies are similar but can vary according to the norms of the people. Nonetheless, when their actions are aimed at restoring cultural practices, traditions and rights, they are engaged in decolonization. The following definition was taken from a statement by the Innu delegation from Sheshatshiu Native Canadian Centre of Toronto (in Stiegelbauer, 1996). While the focus is on Innu Elders, the definition reflects how Mohawk Elders are described in *Kahnawá:ke*:

> Elders should be role models for everyone else. Elders should be teachers to the grandchildren and all young people because of their wisdom. Elders should be advisors, law-givers, dispensers of justice. Elders should be open to everyone. Elders should be knowledgeable in all aspects of Innu culture. Elders should be teachers for everyone of the past history of Innu people ... Elders should be teachers of values important to Innu to be passed on from generation to generation. Elders should be teachers of language and oral history. Elders should be teachers of Innu medicine. We place great importance in our Elders. Their directions for us will guide our lives. (Stiegelbauer, 1996: 39)

Emergente: A social work school graduate of a paraprofessional training programme in Cuba, *emergentes* typically work in their own communities after they finish their studies. They are named *emergentes* because they address emergent social problems, such as child malnutrition, school absenteeism and the needs of the elderly for economic and social assistance.

Empirical social worker: A uniquely Cuban term for a member of the community who provides guidance and support on an informal and voluntary basis to delinquent youth, older persons living alone, and other at-risk individuals. Empirical social workers lack formal training in social work and interact with mass organizations and popular councils to help at-risk persons get assistance (see 'mass organization' and 'popular council' below).

Ethic of care: In the context of decolonization, a moral and political frame of reference that can help social workers decolonize their actions. It helps them to think of relationships as key, and reciprocity and mutuality as crucial to how people coexist. It acts as a focal point for unveiling Whiteness and rethinking practice as a means of assuring each person can 'care for' and 'be cared for' by another.

Globalization: In its original meaning, globalization refers to an economic process that began with trade (economic globalization) and expanded from there to include processes of cultural transfer facilitated by communication technology. Increased economic interdependencies are a product of trade agreements and the frequently imposed Structural Adjustment Programs (SAPs). The anti-free trade movement and protests in Seattle, Quebec City and elsewhere took advantage of the increase in global communications and aligned with fair-trade and other movements to create a resistance to the tsunami of globalization of trade. There are different types of globalization and the globalization of communication and culture, lifestyles and so on, are concurrent outcomes of the globalization of trade that have served to increase communication and awareness that has contributed to greater consciousness of the world as a whole. Globalization, in general, refers to the increasing linking of economic, cultural, technological and social institutions of countries around the globe. It is revealed in the development of a global economy and of a social life informed by a global awareness.

Group for the Integral Development of the Capital (GDIC): An entity in Cuba which implements 'transformation workshops' in socioeconomically marginal neighbourhoods. These workshops gather together professionals to identify the main problem areas in the neighbourhood and mobilize community and outside resources to address them.

Haudenosaunee: 'People of the longhouse'. Today, the *Haudenosaunee* Confederacy is composed of six Nations – Mohawk, Oneida, Onondaga, Cayuga, Seneca and Tuscarora. Historically, residing around the Great Lakes and St Lawrence River in the USA and Canada, the Confederacy was called the Iroquois Confederacy by the French and the League of Five Nations by the English (prior to Tuscarora joining the Confederacy) (Haudenosaunee Development Institute, n.d.) (Chapter 12).

Heterogenization: Refers to diversification such that most modern, multicultural societies comprise a diversity of cultures.

Holomua: In the Hawaiian language means *improvement, progress* the same as *holo i mua* (Pukui, 1986). Faculty at the University of Hawai'i determined *holomua* a more appropriate description, rather than 'retreat', of the special work meetings.

Homogenization: Is used in a number of ways: (i) can refer to tendencies towards 'sameness' as when Indigenous Peoples claim a common unique identity; (ii) processes of standard setting and regulation or the search for a shared universal identity in social work might be seen as homogenizing; (iii) also used in relation to assimilation processes whereby foreigners are expected to adopt the host culture; and (iv) in colonial history, homogenization processes aimed to force Indigenous people to adopt the ways of the colonizer.

Hybridity: Usually used to highlight the fact that there is no 'pure culture' but that all cultures in modern, multicultural societies have been influenced by and, in turn, influence one another such that various degrees of hybridity or cultural mixing exists.

Indigeneity: Refers to a unique cultural identity which Indigenous people claim the right to assert based on their Indigenous ancestry and heritage.

Indigenization: In social work, a narrow understanding of indigenization refers to a process by which Western knowledge is made to fit local non-Western contexts. There is also a broader understanding where indigenization represents a departure from Western multiculturalism as it involves defining an identity and mission relative to the local community to which the social work profession is accountable. (See localization).

Indigenist: Describes a shared philosophy and its resultant ontology or way of being in the world without claiming ownership or exclusivity. While Indigenous describes some peoples' ethnicity and claims to distinct identities, it is a marker of race-based difference. However, Indigenist is a descriptive label for a way of thinking that is based upon an epistemology of relationships and methodology of relational accountability (see Chapter 16).

Indigenous: There are many definitions but in social work there is general agreement that Indigenous refers to the 'original inhabitants' of a particular region. Currently, it most often refers to groups that resided in a region prior to colonization.

Indigenous Peoples (Aboriginal, First Nations, or First Peoples): Indigenous Peoples refers to Aboriginal and First Nations Peoples who lived in lands prior to, and sometimes for thousands of years prior to, colonization. Indigenous people also call themselves First Peoples or First Nations – a term used in relation to the Indigenous Peoples of North America just as Aboriginal is used to refer to the Indigenous Peoples of Australia, that is, Aboriginal and Torres Strait Islander Peoples, sometimes abbreviated as ATSI.

Internationalization: In a positive sense, internationalization refers to increased interaction among people and cultures that focuses on mutual understanding and respect (Yang, 2005) but in a negative sense it might mean the imposition of international standards or practices on national or local contexts. It could also refer to a process by which educational curricula become infused with course content on international issues and perspectives, that is, with information on foreign contexts. Many universities have internationalized their curricula to attract foreign students as this is a lucrative form of income and local markets are not big enough to ensure the financial sustainability of university programmes.

Kahnawa'kehró:non: 'People who come from the place of rapids' (Chapter 12).

Kupuna: Hawaiian for grandparent, ancestor, relative or close friend of the grandparent's generation, grandaunt, or granduncle (Pukui and Elbert, 1986).

Kūpuna plural of kupuna: Used in Hawai`i to refer to an honoured elder who has acquired enough life experience to become a family and community leader, hence the Kūpuna Council was a group of elders who had achieved this status.

Localization: Refers to the adaptation of Western knowledge, theories and practices to make them relevant to local contexts and cultures (see Indigenization).

Longhouse: A traditional lodging structure of northern *Haudenosaunee* peoples. A longhouse would provide housing for several matrilineally related families. Today, the longhouse serves as the political and spiritual body of the *Haudenosaunee* Confederacy.

Māori words (Chapter 9)
  Hui: purposeful gatherings
  Kaitiaki: guardians, protectors
  Kapa Haka: cultural performance
  Karakia: prayer
  Matauranga: Māori – Māori knowledge that derives from ancient wisdom
  Noa: state of normalcy, commonplace
  Reo: language
  Taonga: gift including children, land, knowledge, language
  Tapu: sacredness, state of higher order, conscientiousness
  Te Atua: Creator, God
  Tuku iho: to descend, come from
  Waka: canoe, voyaging vessel
  Whakatauāki: proverb
  Whakapapa: genealogy
  Whanau: family

Mass organizations: In Cuba entities, such as the Federation of Cuban Women (FMC), were created after the revolution and entrusted with a variety of public health, educational and security functions, and serve different levels of society from the neighbourhood to the national level.

Modernization: Refers to the process by which countries industrialized and formed social institutions modelled on the Enlightened Western world, including capitalism and a political system of liberal, democratic governance.

Mohawk Council of *Kahnawá:ke*: Administrative body that provides governmental and operational services to the community of Kahnawá:ke (Mohawk territory). The Council is composed of an elected Grand Chief and 11 Council members. It is also referred to as a Band Council, one of the 614 bands of First Nations Peoples across Canada.

Multisectoral social work: In Cuba, social work is multisectoral; that is, the activities of social workers are closely coordinated and integrated with community members and their leaders, family doctors and health care centres, with municipal and regional authorities, and with professionals from different ministries.

Mutuality: Refers to a process facilitated by dialogue, intended to encourage reciprocal relationships among those interacting. The exchanges that result invite a sharing of power and privilege and a common ground of genuine mutual respect and curiosity.

National Social Work Program: A programme of the Cuban government created in the year 2000 to coordinate social work activities throughout the country. Created in 2000, the National Social Work Program was an initiative of Cuba's top political leadership. The programme's directorate helps to define the aims and goals of the programme.

Native Hawaiian words (Chapter 9)

> *`Aikapu*: to observe historical eating taboos that separated males and females
> *Hula*: dance form accompanied by chant (oli) or song (mele)
> *Lua*: hand-to-hand fighting that included bone-breaking, quick turns and twists of the spear, noosing; and leaping
> *Māhele:* land division of 1848
> *Mālama* `āina: caring as stewards for the land
> *Nī`aupi`o*: offspring of the marriage of a brother and sister; chiefly mating by incest
> *Oli*: chant

Neighbourhood movement: New type of community development programme started in Havana in the late-1980s to assist at-risk groups in poor neighbourhoods. These programmes mobilize community members to find their own way of addressing economic, environmental and social problems with the help of professionals from both within and outside the community.

Neocolonialism: This term came into use, particularly in relation to Africa, as African nations began to obtain independence from the colonial powers after 1945, when some national leaders and opposition groups argued that their countries were being subjected to a new form of colonialism, waged by the former colonial powers and other developed nations. One of the most notable figures to use this term was Kwame Nkrumah, who became leader of newly independent Ghana in 1957. In the introduction to his *Neocolonialism: The Last Stage of Imperialism*, Nkrumah (1965) argues that:

> The result of neo-colonialism is that foreign capital is used for the exploitation rather than for the development of the less developed parts of the world. Investment under neo-colonialism increases rather than decreases the gap between the rich and the poor countries of the world. The struggle against neo-colonialism is not aimed at excluding the capital of the developed world from operating in less developed countries. It is aimed at preventing the financial power of the developed countries being used in such a way as to impoverish the less developed. (n.p.)

Neoliberalism: Refers to a political economic process that aspires to foster globalization, marketization and entrepreneurship. It has been associated with government reduction of public expenditure for social services and with the transfer of resources from the public to the private sector in Western democracies.

New racism: Racism that moves away from overt acts of discrimination based on biology, such as violent physical attacks on black people, to discrimination based on cultural difference, such as the stereotyping of Aboriginal culture as non-contemporary and thus deficient in some way.

Ohen:ton Karihwatehkwen: 'The Words That Come Before All Else', also referred to as 'The Thanksgiving Address', 'Giving Greetings to the Natural World', or 'The Opening Address'. Traditional *Haudenosaunee* speak these words at the opening and closing of each day as well as at important meetings, ceremonies and social gatherings. The *Ohen:ton Karihwatehkwen* expresses the 'acknowledgement, greetings, love, and appreciation for every part of the Natural World and helps to bring the thoughts of the people together'. The words serve to acknowledge that as human beings, we 'are only one strand in the Web of Life and that we are all connected to each other and to the rest of Creation' (Iroquois Indian Museum, n.d.).

People of refugee background (*instead of refugees*): Using the words 'people of refugee background' instead of 'refugees' to refer to people who experienced forced dislocation from their country of origin and thus sought and were granted refuge in countries like Australia, is an effort to acknowledge that the refugee experience need not totalize a person's identity. Two messages are attempted by this effort: first, that being a refugee ought to end once refuge is found and, secondly, the refugee experience may or may not be part of a person's historical context. Ultimately, it is the individual person who defines what forms part of their context. He or she determines the extent to which certain experiences in life warrant acknowledgement and, if so, to what extent these should be acknowledged by others.

People's Council: Regional bodies in Cuba that bridge the gap between municipalities and local communities, people's councils are composed of community delegates or representatives, mass organizations and administrative entities. The people's council addresses the economic, social and medical needs of community members under their jurisdiction and they administer the resources to address these needs.

Resettlement (*instead of settlement*): The term 'settlement' is often associated with what 'people of refugee background' and Indigenous Peoples experience when forced to adjust to a Western way of life. It is often presented as a 'new process', requiring the development of 'new skills' and the ability to transition smoothly to a 'new and more desirable lifestyle'. Using the word 'resettlement' is an attempt to signal that 'people of refugee background' and Indigenous Peoples are not 'new' to 'settling' into a Western lifestyle and possess the skills, capacity and resilience to make all kinds of readjustments in life should they so choose. However, what they lack, because of colonialism, is choice to determine whether or not they will make a transition to a Western lifestyle.

Special Period in Time of Peace: The period of worsening economic and social conditions in Cuba, including rising unemployment, which occurred after the break-up of the Former Soviet Union in 1989. It lasted through the mid-1990s.

Spirituality: Canda and Furman (2010: 5) provide the widely accepted understanding of spirituality in social work – 'spirituality refers to a universal quality of human beings and their cultures related to the quest for meaning, purpose, morality, transcendence, well-being, and profound relationships with ourselves, others, and ultimate reality'. Individuals may define ultimate reality in their own way, and involves a view of the interdependence of all things as people explore and seek to understand their life and experience beyond simply materialist views.

Westernization: Used to refer to the process by which Western knowledge, ideas, perspectives and practices are transferred to non-Western contexts, often as part of the modernization process. Nowadays it also refers to the spread of global capitalism.

Whiteness: An ideology that blinds people to what is essentially silent and mainstream; an invisible benchmark against which everyone is measured, and which dictates how people live. It advantages one way of being, one way of thinking, and one way of doing above all others. It is at the heart of contemporary colonialism.

Workshops for Systematizing Social Work Practice: These are in place in all Cuban municipalities where social workers meet to discuss and exchange experiences about how to analyse and address community problems.

References

Canda, E.R. and Furman, L.D. (2010). *Spiritual Diversity in Social Work Practice* (2nd edn). New York: Oxford University Press.

Haudenosaunee Development Institute. (n.d.). *What is the Confederacy?* [Online]. Available at: http://www.haudenosauneeconfederacy.ca/whatisconfederacy. html. [accessed: 3 March 2012].

Iroquois Indian Museum. (n.d). *The Words that Come Before All Else* [Online]. Available at: http://www.iroquoismuseum.org/thanksgiving2.htm [accessed: 5 March 2012].

Nkrumah, K. (1965). Introduction. *Neocolonialism: The Last Stage of Imperialism*. London: Thomas Nelson & Sons [Online]. Available at: http://www.Marxists. org/subject/africa/nkrumah/neocolonialism/introduction.htm [accessed: 18 October 2010].

Puku`i, M.K. and Elbert, S.H. (1986). *Hawaiian Dictionary*. Honolulu: University of Hawai`i Press.

Smith, L.T. (1999). *Decolonizing Methodologies: Research and Indigenous Peoples*. New York: Zed Books.

Stiegelbauer, S.M. (1996). What is an elder? What do elders do? First Nation Elders as teachers in culture-based urban organizations. *Canadian Journal of Native Studies,* 16(1), 37–66.

Yang, R. (2005). Internationalisation, indigenisation and educational research in China. *Australian Journal of Education*, 49(1), 66–88.

Yellow Bird, M. (2012). Neurodecolonization: Using mindfulness practices to delete the neural networks of colonialism. In Waziyatawin and Yellow Bird, M. (eds), *For Indigenous Minds Only: A Decolonization Handbook* (2nd ed.). Sante Fe, NM: School of American Research.

Index

Page numbers in *italics* refer to figures and tables